W9-AHA-005

WATCH IT MADE
IN THE U.S.A.

WATCH IT MADE IN THE U.S.A.

**A Visitor's Guide to the Companies
That Make Your Favorite Products**

Bruce Brumberg and Karen Axelrod

Foreword by Mo Siegel
President, Celestial Seasonings

John Muir Publications
Santa Fe, New Mexico

The information in this book is subject to change without notice. We strongly recommend that you call ahead to verify the information presented here before making final plans or reservations. All companies are included without charge to them. The companies whose photographs appear here have paid a modest fee to help defray publication costs.

John Muir Publications, P.O. Box 613, Santa Fe, New Mexico 87504

© 1994 by Bruce Brumberg and Karen Axelrod
Cover © 1994 by John Muir Publications
All rights reserved. Published in 1994.
Printed in the United States of America.

First edition. Second printing January 1995.

Library of Congress Cataloging-in-Publication Data
Brumberg, Bruce.
Watch it made in the U.S.A. : a visitor's guide to the companies that make your favorite products / by Bruce Brumberg and Karen Axelrod.
    p.   cm.
    Includes index.
    ISBN 1-56261-157-7 : $16.95
1. United States—Industries—Directories. 2. United States—Manufacturers—Directories.
3. United States—Tours—Handbooks, manuals, etc. 4. Tour guides (Manuals)
I. Axelrod, Karen. II. Title.
HF5035.B64 1994
338.7'4'02573—dc20   94-5999
                                                        CIP

Typesetter: Richard Harris
Typeface: Garamond
Printer: Publishers Press
Cover Photo: Hershey's Visitors Center in Oakdale, CA; featured on page 16.
Back Cover Photo: Martin Guitar in Nazareth, PA; featured on page 206.

Distributed to the book trade by
Publishers Group West
Emeryville, California

Dedications

To the American workers, engineers, and managers who have regained their pride by making the best quality products in the world.

To our marriage and the love and times we share together.

Contents

Foreword

When Celestial Seasonings (see feature, page 26) opened its doors to public tours in 1991, we viewed the program as a way to show a few devoted customers our home. Little did we realize what the response would be! Eight thousand guests visited our plant that year, and now, several years later, over 50,000 visitors annually will travel here from around the world.

Factory tours have become increasingly popular as low-cost vacation attractions for family and business travelers, day outings for local residents, and educational trips for schools. At Celestial Seasonings, we have expanded our vision of the tour program as a tool for teaching the art of tea and asking customers their opinions of our products, as well as an educational and entertainment venue. One visit to the "Mint Room," where we store 1,400 crates of mint shipped directly from the Northwest United States and Egypt, will live in a child's memory for a lifetime.

When our customers visit our home, that's a perfect opportunity to give to them in a caring, responsible, and innovative way. As guests walk through our facility and see our talented employees, colorful graphics, and displays and photographs, they feel our commitment to quality. One visit has more value than one hundred commercials, when guests relate their positive experiences to friends and family.

The authors of *Watch It Made In The U.S.A.*, Bruce and Karen, have done an outstanding job of creating a book that illustrates America's commitment to quality manufacturing practices. As we see more items imported into this country, we need a reminder that "Made in the U.S.A." means high quality. This book shows Americans that we can and do make many of the finest products in the world.

As you read the descriptions of tours at the companies that make Ben & Jerry's ice cream, Tabasco brand pepper sauce, and Maker's Mark bourbon, you will get the flavor of the regional products made by Americans who devotedly care for their customers. By touring "state of the art" facilities like Boeing, John Deere, and General Motors, you will get a glimpse of cutting-edge manufacturing plants. Many business travelers enhance their trips by visiting companies they can learn from and compare themselves to, thus "benchmarking" with other businesses.

And last, it's just simply fun to take tours and visit company museums. You'll get a kick out of seeing how tea gets into tea bags, how fortunes get into fortune cookies, and how robots weld together car bodies.

So take some time to visit the companies featured in this book, even if it's just through your mind's eye. And if you find yourself in Boulder, Colorado, stop by, take our tour, learn how to make your tea, meet the Sleepytime Bear, and taste some teas. We'd love to meet you!

Mo Siegel
President, Celestial Seasonings
Boulder, Colorado

Preface

When you were younger, you probably read *Charlie and the Chocolate Factory*, later made into the movie *Willie Wonka and the Chocolate Factory*. As you may remember, Charlie won the opportunity to visit a chocolate factory by finding a special golden ticket in his Wonka Bar. His luck led to a fascinating journey.

This book is like that golden ticket in Charlie's chocolate bar. With this guide you can visit factory tours and company museums throughout the U.S.A. Whether you're with your family, traveling alone, or on a business trip, you'll have fun, discover how well-known products are made, and learn what these companies did to grow and prosper. Along the way, you will receive plenty of free samples and tastes.

Ours is a harried society that just wants to plug it in, mix it with milk, turn the ignition, or open the box. We want you to experience the excitement of watching people and machines make the food we eat, the cars we drive, the musical instruments we play, and the sporting goods we use.

After visiting the nearly 250 companies featured in this book, you'll marvel at the behind-the-scenes processes involved in producing the products we take for granted. You'll be proud of the hardworking American people and companies that make it all possible. We like to say that this book gives you the opportunity to go out and "kick the tires" of the American economy. Watch how American companies have proudly regained their competitive edge and are again perceived as the world leader in many industries.

To compile the list of companies that offer tours, museums, and visitor centers we followed many paths and traveled thousands of miles. The book focuses on recognized national or regional companies that make familiar products, whether they be chocolates, cars, clothes, toys, or beers. Each tour or museum either has regular hours or is open to the general public by reservation.

Enjoy the tours. But don't stuff yourself with the free samples like the guests did on the tour of Willie Wonka's chocolate factory!

Acknowledgments

First and foremost we want to thank the companies that provide tours and museums, and also the people at those businesses who met with us, answered our numerous questions, verified the accuracy of our information, and gave us encouragement. Twenty years ago this book wouldn't have been needed, as just about all companies gave public tours. Now many forces, including budget cuts, insurance rates, trade-secret protection, and government regulations, have caused companies to end them. The firms that open their doors to the public have a story to tell about their place in America's heritage and in its economic future.

We would also like to specially thank those companies with photographs in the book. While no company paid for its inclusion in *Watch It Made in the U.S.A.* or for our publishing its logo, companies did pay a modest fee to include black-and-white or color photos. This was a very expensive book to research, write, and produce. Without this small amount of funding the book either would not have been published or its purchase price would have been far beyond what the average person spends for a travel book.

Convention and visitors bureaus, state tourism boards, and chambers of commerce gave us information and materials, which we appreciated. Susan Koffman, a friend and colleague, provided writing, editing, computer assistance, and emotional support throughout the two-year marathon to produce this book. When the going got tough, Susan was there with her advice and time. Valerie Dumova, Laura Hayes, and Matthew Regen helped with the research, writing, editing, word processing, and chocolate and potato-chip sampling. Other friends, relatives, and freelance writers who assisted us with a few features are (in alphabetical order): Perry Apelbaum, Harriet Brumberg, Scott Dimetrosky, Sam Donisi, Katrinna Huggs, John Landretti, Mark Lichterman, Elliott Puretz, and Owen Taylor. Also, Pam Kubbins, who doubles as a flight attendant at Delta Airlines, wrote the most features of any freelance writer and gave us constant encouragement.

Other folks who tangibly helped us out include Greg Adams and Leah Weintraub, Vladimir Edelman, Ilyse Kramer, Dan and Katherine Kurtzman, Gregg and Sheryl Nathanson, Richard Nowitz, Amy and Mark Seiden, and Howard Zaharoff. We enjoyed the support from our parents, Elaine and Norman Brumberg (actually, Bruce's parents became supportive once we gave his dad a Harley-Davidson T-shirt and his mom T-shirts from Ben & Jerry's and Wild Turkey), and Harriet and David Axelrod (my mother's love of travel inspired me to do this book; I wish she were alive to see it in print), strength from our grandmother Franziska Hirschhorn, and the guidance from our aunt and uncle, Erika and Larry Casler. Elaine Brumberg and Larry Casler set good examples for us, as they authored books of their own. Unfortunately, limited space prevents listing all those friends and relatives who provided general advice, support, and ideas–but we do express our heartfelt appreciation to all of them. Finally, we thank the staff at John Muir Publications for sharing our vision for this book.

Safety Guidelines

Lawsuits are a product we make too many of in the U.S.A. During our research we discovered many companies that have discontinued their tours because of fears of lawsuits from injured guests and increases in liability insurance rates for allowing public visitors. Follow basic safety rules and your common sense to avoid injury.

The authors and publisher of *Watch It Made in the U.S.A.* make no warranty, express or implied, regarding the safety of any of the tours in this book and assume no liability with respect to the consequences of using the information contained herein. If you have any special safety concerns, contact the companies directly before you decide to visit.

The factories in this book are all working facilities, not full-time tourist attractions. While many of them contain the kind of space-age excitement you only see in the movies, they are the "real thing" with potentially dangerous machines.

If you are injured, it is likely that the company will completely discontinue its public tours. Please listen to your tour guide and read any safety warnings. Remember the following rules:

1. Do not wander away from your tour guide or away from any specified tour path. Many factory tours have lines painted on the floor. You must stay between them.

2. Parents and adult group leaders should keep a close watch on children. Kids will be very curious about the sights, sounds, and smells, and may be tempted to wander off and touch things that could be dangerous.

3. Wear any protective equipment that you are provided with on your tour. These may include eyeglasses, earplugs, hard hats, or hair nets. If you have trouble wearing any of these items, tell your tour guide immediately.

4. Do not touch anything, including machines, products, parts, or boxes, unless your tour guide specifically hands something to you.

5. Wear closed-toe shoes with rubber soles that have good traction. Do not wear sandals or high heels (many companies will not allow you to go on tour). Wear shoes that will provide protection against sharp objects and that are comfortable for walking. Floors can be slippery. For safety reasons, it is best not to wear shorts.

How Companies Were Selected

Our search for companies to include in *Watch It Made in the U.S.A.* began in stores where their products are sold. We went through supermarkets, department stores, car dealerships, and sporting goods stores, searching for the names of companies that make popular products in the U.S.A. Sometimes store owners thought we were competitors, as we would pick up a box, turn it over to see who made the product, and scribble down information about the company's address and phone number.

We also searched through directories and magazine ads hunting down more manufacturers of U.S.A.-made products. We contacted state travel offices, local convention and visitor bureaus, and chambers of commerce looking for names of companies in their area that may give tours. These lists, which we continued making and updating throughout our writing and traveling, were only the start of our research.

Then we called . . . and called . . . and called. We spoke with companies and factories throughout the U.S.A. asking whether they gave tours or had a museum (often called a "visitors center"). We didn't hide the fact that we were writing a book. We wanted to include only those companies that regularly accept public visitors and would talk with us about their history, tours, and products.

No company paid for its written feature in *Watch It Made in the U.S.A.* The companies had to meet the following criteria:

1. **Tours open to the general public.** Throughout our research we found companies that give tours only to buyers, to technical organizations, or upon special request. We did not include these companies or any others that had too many requirements for visitors.

2. **Tours available to individuals and families.** Some companies will give tours only to local school groups, senior citizen clubs, boy and girl scout troops, or bus tour companies. To be included in *Watch It Made,* a company had to at least allow individuals and families not affiliated with a group tour to visit. You may need to join a scheduled group tour (or the company may combine individual requests to form a group) and make reservations far in advance, but every facility in this book should be open to you.

3. **Products of general interest that are worth traveling to see made.** Unless you have a technical background or are in a specific industry, we thought that seeing how your favorite everyday products are made would hold the most fascination. In addition to tours of the icons of American business, we sought out small companies that have good products and interesting tours. Most of the companies in the book make consumer-related or widely recognized products. We also selected companies where you could watch the completion of the final product and therefore excluded parts manufacturers.

4. **Company did not object to being featured in book.** Companies generally do not make money from their tours. They give tours as a public and community service, often pulling employees from their regular jobs to conduct the tours. We excluded companies that did not want the calls and tour requests that this widely distributed book would generate, if the tour was not already mentioned in other public sources. A small number of companies asked not to be included after we

had visited them and written our extensive features. In most cases, we were able to retain their features after adjusting the tour information to meet the companies' concerns. In a few instances, we had to drop tours of well-known companies.

We strove to select companies from diverse industries and all areas of the country. We wanted to capture the industries for which different regions are known, such as cheese in Wisconsin and Vermont, glass in West Virginia, movies in Southern California, bourbon in Kentucky, RVs in Northern Indiana, Cajun hot sauces in Louisiana, and wood products in the Pacific Northwest. Certain high-tech industries, such as computer manufacturing and biotechnology, do not give regular public tours for proprietary reasons, so they are excluded by their choice. In other industries, such as beer brewing and newspaper publishing, tours are a standard practice; from this group we selected the most high-profile companies or those with interesting processes or histories.

We were surprised that companies in certain states, even though very industrial, do not seem interested in giving public tours. For example, while manufacturing-intensive states such as Pennsylvania, Wisconsin, and Ohio offer a variety of captivating tours, most New Jersey and Connecticut companies remain closed to the public. In contrast, companies in less-industrial states such as Kentucky and Vermont have exhibited great pride in opening themselves to the public.

In addition to factory tours, we also included company museums or visitor centers devoted to one company's products and history. Some companies have replaced the public factory tours with educational and entertaining museums that explain how they started, succeeded, and make their products. More companies are now establishing museums to preserve their heritage, instill corporate culture, and tell their story to the public, new employees, and customers. We did not include company museums that are like art exhibits. The museums we selected, like the tours, had to give you a sense of what the company is all about.

Going Beyond This Book

We excluded wineries, power plants, chemical factories, most service industries, and tobacco manufacturers, for reasons that we will explain upon request. The company tours in this book are the easiest ones to join—you either just show up or call in advance to reserve a space. If you are interested in visiting a company not featured here, contact the public affairs or human resources department at the corporate headquarters or local plant. With persistence, you can tour many firms if you're not a direct competitor. Explain your individual request and also ask if the company offers tours for specialized business and technical groups (often for a fee).

No book like this has ever been published before. Although we tried hard to find the public factory tours and company museums currently available, we do not claim that this guide contains all of them. Since we will update this book, we would like your comments on the sites you visit from this guide and on tours we should consider for the next edition. Please write us at John Muir Publications (P. O. Box 613, Santa Fe, NM 87504). We hope this book's success will lead more companies to open their doors to the general public.

How to Use This Book

We wanted *Watch It Made in the U.S.A.* to be much more than a directory. Therefore, we *did not* write it by sending surveys out to companies and then publishing a compilation of the responses. We visited most of the companies included here. For almost two years we took periodic breaks from our regular jobs to travel the U.S.A. in search of its economic soul. For those companies that time did not permit us to visit, we either hired writers to do so or conducted in-depth phone interviews that required companies to send us videos, articles, and tour scripts. After we wrote each feature we verified its accuracy with the company.

Each company tour or museum feature includes a narrative description and a practical information section. This book is organized alphabetically by state. The features appear in alphabetical order unless positioning of photographs necessitated slight alteration.

Narrative Description

Some of us are awed by fast-moving bottling machines and fascinated by robotic welders or giant presses, while others enjoy the artisanship of a glassblower, woodworker, or potter. The narrative description will help you determine which tours you and your family will enjoy.

Each feature has a three- to-five paragraph write-up that captures the highlights of the tour and some background on the company. The write-ups also provide a basic understanding of how different products are made. We try to give you a sense of being there—what you might see, hear, smell, taste, or even touch; if a company is big or small; and whether you actually visit the factory floor or watch production through glass windows. We wrote this part in a conversational tone so that even the armchair traveler will be able to vicariously experience the tour or museum.

Practical Information Section

The second part of the feature provides basic practical information on location, hours, admission charge, freebies, age and group requirements, disabled access, gift shop and outlet stores, and nearby attractions. The category titles in this section are self-explanatory. The following are some special notes on the different categories in this section:

Cost: Many company tours and visits are free or have a nominal charge, which makes them a great vacation value. Remember that any charges we list may change after this book's printing.

Freebies: Many tours give samples, ranging from beer and ice cream to miniature baseball bats. Remember—you're a guest, so be appreciative.

Video Shown: These are often interesting, informative, and even humorous. They provide a close-up view inside machines and show production steps not seen on the tour. If videos are optional, we suggest you view them before going on the tour. They help you understand what you will see.

Reservations Needed: If a company requires reservations, please respect them. *Do not just show up*—you will not get a tour. Make reservations as far in advance as possible. Some companies require individuals and families to join a scheduled group tour that has not reached its maximum size, which this section will note. For these companies, you need to be more flexible in scheduling your visit. Many companies produce a range of products; if you have certain favorites, call ahead to find out what will be in production on the day of your visit.

Days and Hours: These are the hours for the tour or museum, not for the gift shop or outlet store. Hours are subject to change and factories may shut down (hopefully for expansion construction), so call before your visit to avoid disappointment. Automobile plants, for example, often temporarily discontinue their tours so assembly lines can be reconfigured for major model changes. Many of the companies with regular tour schedules have voice-mail telephone numbers that answer common questions on schedule changes and directions. The hours listed here are the range during which tours are given, unless a frequency is specified. Holiday schedules vary by company.

Plan to Stay: We included the amount of time needed for the basic visit, plus additional time for optionals such as the gift shop. The length of time spent on self-guided tours depends on the level of your interest.

Minimum Age: Tours have minimum age limits because of safety and insurance requirements. Companies strictly enforce these limits.

Disabled Access: Almost all of the tours in this book are working factories first and not full-featured visitor attractions. They try to accommodate people with disabilities while focusing on the safety concerns of both visitors and workers. Few companies told us absolutely "no" for disabled access. Almost all plants, however, have some limited-access areas, which we tried to note, and some may require advance notice. We are not commenting on the restrooms or compliance with the Americans with Disabilities Act standards, only the ease with which people with disabilities can visit these companies.

Group Requirements: Advance reservations are almost always required for groups, and some companies have maximum group sizes. This section is useful for group tour planners.

Special Information: Re-read the safety rules at the beginning of the book, as we do not repeat them in this section. For worker safety and proprietary reasons, many tours do not allow photography (which includes snapshot and video cameras). "No photography" refers to factory production areas, not gift shops, museums and display areas. If you or a family member are sensitive to noise, smells, or temperature changes, be aware of these conditions when selecting a tour. However, these shocks to the senses are part of the exciting realism of factory tours.

Gift Shop/Outlet Store: Most gift shops sell logoed items and company products. The real factory outlet stores offer great bargains. Hours are often different and longer than the tour hours.

Directions: Many companies have maps that they can mail or fax you. While we have made our best efforts to give you accurate narrative directions (doubled-checked with the companies and given from two possible directions), a map is always helpful. At the top of each write-up is the physical street address of the factory or museum.

Nearby Attractions: To round out your day, we list some of the nearby parks, museums, and other activities. We also draw your attention to other nearby factory tours and company museums. These factory tours and museums, which are listed first, are within a larger radius from the plant than the other nearby attractions. In addition to the nearly 250 full-page company features in the book, we list about 140 additional factory tours in this section of the write-ups. For reasons of variety, quality, tour restrictions, or time we decided not to write full features on these other tours for the first edition.

Trademarks
We have used the commonly known company name rather than the longer corporate name. To the best of our knowledge, all of the product names in this book are trademarks. Throughout the text, we capitalized the first letter of all words that are trademarks. When companies provided us with their logos, we included them at no charge. The logos in no way imply that a company is a sponsor of the book. These logos are also trademarks that cannot be reproduced without a company's express consent.

Advice for the Business Traveler

You shouldn't view these tours merely as a new way to grab a free beer during a business trip to Milwaukee or St. Louis. At its core *Watch It Made in the U.S.A.* is a travel guide to American business. Our business backgrounds led us to write it. When we went on a factory tour or visited a company museum we discovered how that company makes and markets its products and how it started and grew. We developed ideas that we wouldn't get out of any newspaper, magazine, or business book. Sure, you can read a book about Ted Turner, Lee Iacocca, or Mary Kay Ash—but *Watch It Made in the U.S.A.* tells you how to visit CNN, Chrysler, or Mary Kay Cosmetics to see the companies in action. Visiting the sites in this book will spice up a business trip with new experiences that may help you with your own job.

Improve Your Understanding of Business News and Trends

The tours offer a new perspective on our economy, workplace productivity, and job creation. After visiting a few of the companies profiled, you'll have a better filter for understanding business and economic news. The concepts of total quality management, re-engineering, just-in-time inventory, or *kaizen* (constant improvement), for example, which just about every company in this book uses in some form, have new meaning when you see how they are adapted to the production of baseball bats, cars, and chocolate. You'll also notice production and product trends before they are reported in the media and appear on store shelves.

Sources of New Ideas You Can Use

By visiting these companies you will not only experience first-hand how they operate, but also expose yourself to new business techniques. Don't think that these tours appeal only to people in manufacturing-related jobs. Many of the tours and museums show you much more than how the company makes its products; they also reveal its marketing, management, and new product development approach. To get the most from your visit, make it a point to look for and ask about innovative approaches and solutions that the company has developed, then think about how your business could adopt them. Try to discover what really makes the company successful and admired, then ponder how your firm can emulate it.

The company's public relations department may at times shape the tour script, but what you see, hear, sense, and ask cannot be totally controlled. The tour guides, especially the ones who are company retirees or volunteer line employees, can provide some great insights and amusing anecdotes. However, while you want to be inquisitive, be careful not to sound like an industrial spy. Companies are very concerned about protecting what they view as proprietary technology, processes, or information. Kellogg's, for example, ended its cereal factory tours because of suspected spying by competitors. Because of this anxiety, some businesses have limited their tours or asked us not to include them in the book.

Don't confine yourself to visiting firms that make products similar to your company's. Trips outside of your own industry can provide stimulus and new techniques. The cross-fertilization of ideas from other industries helps develop business creativity. To have a "Learning Organization," one of the current training buzzwords popularized by Peter Senge in *The Fifth Discipline*, you need to seek out new experiences. In *A Whack on the Side of the Head,* author Roger von Oech explains that "many good ideas have been discovered because someone poked around in an outside industry or discipline, and applied what he found to his own field." Follow von Oech's advice—be a business "explorer" and search for insights from companies outside your own industry.

In two of Tom Peters' best selling business books, *In Search of Excellence* and *A Passion for Excellence,* he explains how the best managers practice a form of "management by walking around." Go out and walk around someone else's company—you'll be surprised at what you learn.

You never know who or what you may see on a factory tour! "Job Switching" *episode of*
I Love Lucy, *first aired September 15, 1952* (Photo © CBS Inc.)

WATCH IT MADE IN THE U.S.A.

Disc Manufacturing ⟨⟩ *music CDs and CD-ROMs*

4905 Moores Mill Road
Huntsville, AL 35811
(205) 859-9042

If you're reading this book while listening to music from a CD sold by a major or independent recording label such as BMG, Polygram, or Capitol/EMI, the CD was probably manufactured by Disc Manufacturing, Inc. (DMI). The CD-ROM you may have used today in your computer from Apple, Hewlett-Packard, or Microsoft may also have come from DMI's factories in Anaheim, California or this one in Alabama. DMI is the largest independent manufacturer of compact discs, CD-ROMs, and CD-Interactives in the U.S.A. LaserVideo, the company's predecessor, made the first CD produced in the U.S.A. in 1983 and was the first company to master, replicate, and supply discs to the music-label industry.

The guided tour shows you the steps in creating a master, duplicating the compact discs, and packaging. The music or computer company supplies a premastered digital audiotape. The tape is reformatted to create a data master. A laser beam recorder cuts a glass master by edging the data codes into glass. A metal stamper is then "grown" from this glass by an electroforming, photographic-like process to create a mold to mass produce the compact discs.

You can peek through windows at the manufacturing part of the process, which occurs in a sterile environment with workers dressed like surgeons. The stamper is inserted into an injection molding press. Small beads of polycarbonate resin, a clear plastic-like material, flow through the press and out pops a CD. A thin layer of aluminum reflective film is coated onto the disc, followed by a lacquer protection to shelter the digital codes on the plastic disc.

A five-color screen printing press applies the multicolored label directly onto the disc in the final production step. After an intricate visual and automated inspection, the disc and its paper parts are packaged in a jewel case, shrink-wrapped, and shipped to distribution centers. This process continues to the tune of approximately 225,000 compact discs per day, with the production of CD-ROMs the fasting growing part of the business. The next time you hold one of these silver platters in your hand, you'll think about the neat machines and the complex process used to make something that looks so uncomplicated.

Cost: Free
Freebies: No
Video Shown: No
Reservations Needed: Yes. Individuals and families need to join a scheduled group tour.
Days and Hours: Mon-Fri 10:00 AM-3:00 PM. Closed holidays and week between Christmas and New Year's.
Plan to Stay: 1 hour
Minimum Age: 12
Disabled Access: Yes
Group Requirements: 2 weeks' advance notice for reservations. Minimum group size needed for a tour is 10 people, with a maximum of 15.
Special Information: No photography. For an interesting comparison to the production of player piano music rolls, an early form of recorded music, see the feature on QRS Music Rolls, Buffalo, New York, on page 171.
Gift Shop: No
Directions: Take Hwy. 231 (Memorial Pkwy.) and turn right at Hwy. 72 (Lee Hwy.). Turn left at Moores Mill Rd. and the plant is ahead on the left. From Chattanooga take Hwy. 72 and turn right on Moores Mill Rd.
Nearby Attractions: U.S. Space and Rocket Center/NASA tour; Alabama Constitution Village; Historic Huntsville Depot; 1879 Harrison Brothers Hardware; Huntsville Museum of Art.

Robinson Iron   ~   *architectural ironworks*

Robinson Road
Alexander City, AL 35010
(205) 329-8486

Have you ever taken the New York City subway from Astor Place and admired the cast-iron kiosk entrance? If so, you've already seen Robinson Iron's handiwork. Perhaps you've sat on their benches, which line Pennsylvania Avenue in Washington, D.C., or daydreamed while watching water flow through the 12,000-pound Court Square Fountain in Montgomery. Robinson restored the fountain, as well as the intricate ironwork at Singapore's renowned Raffles Hotel. Although you cannot tour the foundry, where 2500° molten iron flows like melted butter, you can watch skilled ironworkers turn the raw castings into ornate fountains, urns, lampposts, garden statuary, or perhaps customized railings for subway stations.

As you enter the shop, welding arcs hiss, grinding wheels squeal, and drills buzz, leaving no doubt that you're surrounded by heavy ironworking. Masked welders in the fabrication area wield plasma arc cutters, which produce a light as bright as a laser. A metallic, flinty odor fills your nose. When the sparks clear, you'll find the raw castings have become a 16-foot multi-tiered fountain for a municipal park, or a 400-pound deer, complete with antlers, for someone's backyard.

In the finishing area, workers spray-paint Charleston Green, Gloss White or Black in a painting booth. Some pieces receive an antiqued hand-finish of Verde Gris. An overhead crane lifts the mammoth ornaments into place, so workers can construct shipping crates around them. Before you end the tour, head outside down the path to the Pattern Shop, to see how the whole process starts. Pattern-makers follow blueprints from Robinson's designers to custom-carve, detail, and create a wooden master, which is then used to produce a plastic or metal working pattern. The foundry uses the pattern to produce a hollow sand mold into which molten iron is poured. The raw casting it produces will go to the workers in the Fabrication Area, where you began. In the Atrium Showroom, finished pieces stand ready for your close inspection, admiration, and purchase.

Cost: Free

Freebies: No

Video Shown: Optional 15-minute video on company's history, by request only.

Reservations Needed: No, except for groups of 8 or more people.

Days and Hours: Mon-Fri 8:00 AM-4:00 PM. Closed holidays.

Plan to Stay: 45 minutes, plus time in showroom.

Minimum Age: None, although some areas are restricted for children under 5, who might stay in the Atrium Showroom to watch the fountain.

Disabled Access: Yes

Group Requirements: Groups of 8 or more people should call 1 day in advance.

Special Information: Production decreases during 4th of July week and Christmas week. Plant can be quite noisy at times.

Showroom: The Atrium Showroom features a representative collection of ironworks from the company's catalog and its Architectural Handbook (both available for purchase in showroom or from above phone number), including small garden statuary, ornamental urns, and animal sculptures. Open same hours as tour.

Directions: From Birmingham, take Hwy. 280 East to Kelleton. Turn left on Business 280 (*not* Bypass 280). In 2 miles, where the road widens, watch on the right for Robinson Foundry. Take the first right after the foundry. Cross the railroad tracks. Robinson Iron is the brown metal building on your right. From Montgomery, take Hwy. 231 North to Wetumka. Turn right on Hwy. 9 North. Turn right on Hwy. 22 East. Turn left onto Hwy. 280 West. In a little over 1 mile, turn right on Robinson Rd. Bear right at the fork, and watch for Robinson Iron on your left.

Nearby Attractions: Russell Corp. clothing manufacturer tour (call 205-329-4000); Martin Lake; Kowaliga Marina; Horsebend National Military Park.

Alaskan Brewing Co. ~ *beer*

5429 Shaune Drive
Juneau, AK 99801
(907) 780-5866

Small, family-like Alaskan Brewing Company brews Alaskan Amber Beer (based on a Gold Rush-era recipe from the local extinct Douglas City Brewing Co.), Alaskan Pale Ale, and seasonal beers. Since its start in 1986, Alaskan Brewing Company's beers have won awards at annual beer festivals and, along with its logoed clothing, have appeared on the popular television show "Northern Exposure." To expand its production space, the brewery took over a golf driving range in the other half of this wooden building (to this day, some golf balls linger in the roof's insulation) and built a new addition.

The tour starts off right—with a glass of Pale Ale (their lighter, fruitier beer). Now that you're in the spirit, look through glass walls into the brewhouse at three 310-gallon kettles known as the mash tun, lauter tun, and brew kettle. If you're lucky, you'll see activity here—a worker transferring mixtures from kettle to kettle or shoveling "spent" (already used) barley. In show-and-tell, the tour guide hands out malted barley (tastes like Grape Nuts) and hops (a bittering spice). Notice "Alaska's biggest six-pack," six 10-foot-high stainless steel fermentation tanks stacked in a row.

Walk outdoors and upstairs to a landing. Through windows, peer inside at the kegging and bottling operation (usually on Thursdays and Fridays). As oxygen escapes, foam flows out. The worker hammers in the "bung" (wooden cork) and beer flies everywhere.

In the serving room and gift shop, admire the national/international bottle collections on display. Find your home state's beer. If your local brewery is not represented, be sure to mail them one when you get home for their extensive collection.

Cost: Free
Freebies: 6-oz. glasses of beer
Video Shown: No
Reservations Needed: No, but preferred for groups larger than 10 people.
Days and Hours: May through September Tue-Sat 11:00 AM-4:30 PM every 30 minutes;

October through April Thur-Sat same time schedule. Closed Thanksgiving, July 4th, Christmas, and New Year's.
Plan to Stay: 30 minutes, plus time in gift shop.
Minimum Age: None. However, you must be 21 years old to sample beer.
Disabled Access: Yes
Group Requirements: Prefers 1 day's advance notice for groups larger than 10 people. Maximum group size is 15 for more personalized tour. Groups larger than 15 people will be divided into smaller groups.
Special Information: Best days to see bottling and kegging are Thursday and Friday. If your timing is right, you can sample their seasonal beers (usually made in the spring and fall).
Gift Shop: Sells T-shirts, sweatshirts, baseball caps, and aprons (also featured on "Northern Exposure") with beer label designs, and embroidered logoed Wek shirts. Offers fishing lures with the "Made In Alaska" bear design on a beer cap, and Ulu knives, originally used by Eskimos to skin whales. Open same hours as tour. Catalog available. Gift shop displays historical photographs and artifacts of Alaskan breweries from the 1800s to today.
Directions: From Juneau, take Egan Dr. to stoplight at the base of Vanderbilt Hill. Turn only way possible onto Vanderbilt Hill Rd. Turn right onto Anka Dr. Take second right onto Shaune Dr. The brewery is 1½ blocks ahead on the left. You'll smell the strong scent of malt and hops as you approach.
Nearby Attractions: Alaska Seafood Co. tour (call 907-780-5111); Mendenhall Glacier; DIPAC (salmon hatchery); Historic Downtown Juneau's attractions include the Capitol building and the Alaskan Bar & Hotel (features their beer on tap); sport fishing.

Cerreta's Candy Co.   *chocolates, candy, caramel popcorn*

5345 West Glendale Avenue
Glendale, AZ 85301
(602) 930-9000

Since 1968, this family-owned company has been producing chocolate candy that's sold at their retail store and in supermarkets throughout the western U.S.A. From the moment you set foot in their factory, you will be overpowered by the sensory experience of candy-making. Since the entire factory is open, your nostrils fill with the sweet smell of cocoa and your ears hear the loud noises of mixers, enrobers, and conveyors turning chocolate into candy. Cerreta's makes four different types of chocolate candy in this factory: mints, creams, caramels, and clusters. Throughout the factory, you will notice workers hand-pouring and hand-mixing ingredients into oversized copper kettles. A huge box holds 1,500 pounds of chocolate waiting to be melted and then pumped through long pipes.

Since this is a self-guided tour, overhead monitors along the walkway help explain the candy-making process. Lean against the waist-high railing to see the action. The long, yellow, automatic molding machine makes French mints. A pale green, minty liquid fills one plastic tray, containing 32 molds, every six seconds. The trays are flipped over to allow the excess to flow out. Once the mint cools, chocolate centers are injected and cooled again before dollops of mint are added, sealing the chocolate inside. Notice the mile-long spiral conveyor in the glass-enclosed chilling room. After the mints travel around-and-around up the spiral, workers release the candies from their molds, much like removing ice cubes from plastic trays. The released candies travel down twin-lane conveyor belts to the specially designed wrapping machine, which swallows them up and spits them out wrapped at a rate of 1,000 candies per minute.

In the background, watch as a worker pours liquid caramel from a copper cauldron onto a long, refrigerated stainless-steel table. Once solidified, the caramel is cut into long ribbons. The ribbons are fed into an automatic wrapping machine which individually twist-wraps each caramel in clear cellophane.

The caramel and other centers, such as butter creams and peanut brittle, travel to the enrobing machine. There, centers move along a wire conveyor belt and are drenched in chocolate. If they're making caramel popcorn, workers dig into the bowl to scoop and mix the coated popcorn to prevent sticking. It looks like so much fun you'll want to put on a pair of rubber gloves and help them.

Cost: Free

Freebies: Sample of Cerreta's candy

Video Shown: Videos on overhead monitors along walkway provide up-close view of the entire chocolate-making process.

Reservations Needed: No, except for groups of 10 or more people who want a guided tour.

Days and Hours: Mon-Sat 10:00 AM-6:00 PM self-guided viewing; Mon-Thur 10:00 AM guided tour. Closed holidays. Even though there is limited production on Saturdays, you can view video monitors and see equipment.

Plan to Stay: 20 minutes for self-guided tour, including videos, plus time for retail store.

Minimum Age: None

Disabled Access: Yes

Group Requirements: Groups of 10 or more people should call 1 month in advance to arrange guided tours for Mon-Fri 10:00 AM.

Special Information: The tour is offered year-round; do call ahead, however, since limited production on Saturday and in summer. Hot in summer.

Retail Store: Sells entire selection of Cerreta's chocolates, caramels, and French mints. Open Mon–Sat 10:00 AM–6:00 PM.

Directions: From I-10, take 59th Ave. North to Glendale Ave. Turn right, and Cerreta's will be on the right. You'll recognize the building by its upside-down copper cauldron-like awning.

Nearby Attractions: Karsten Manufacturing (Ping golf club) tour (see page 5); Saguaro Ranch Park; Phoenix attractions include Breck Girl Hall of Fame at Dial Corp. headquarters (call 602-207-5338).

Karsten Manufacturing ⟿ *Ping golf clubs*

2201 West Desert Cove
Phoenix, AZ 85029
(602) 870-5385

Long before Karsten Solheim began playing golf at the age of 43, he had an interest in golf clubs. Solheim, one of the golf industry's most recognizable figures, started perfecting golf clubs with the goal of making a fiendishly fickle game easier to play. The first putter he developed made a loud, shrill "ping" sound; hence, the eventual name for his clubs. When Julius Boros won the Phoenix Open in 1967 with a Ping putter, the popularity of Ping golf clubs increased. That same year Solheim left General Electric as a project engineer to start Karsten Manufacturing Corporation in a small 20-foot-by-40-foot building. Today the company employs over 1,500 workers, the site covers most of a city block, and there is a six-week wait for its golf clubs.

Your tour begins after you view the displays of the company's golf clubs, woods, irons, apparel, and bags in the visitor center. The guide, usually a former golf professional, leads you past the original 1967 building. Currently the repair department, it initially served as Karsten's production area, machine shop, reception area, order desk, and shipping department.

Due to the size of the "campus," you walk in and out of buildings based on proximity rather than order of production. In the wood prep/wood finish building, smell the laminated maple and watch workers use routers and sanders to shape and smooth raw wooden heads. Workers painstakingly scrape off excess varnish with Exacto knives, careful not to gouge the club. Since the iron and putter grinding area is so noisy, the guide explains the process before you enter the building. The irons, cast by the company's off-site foundry, require grinding and tumbling for further shaping.

In the iron, putter, and wood assembly areas, shafts are cut to the correct length and installed into club heads, while clubs wait on shelves for grips. To attach a grip, two-way adhesive tape is wrapped around the shaft. A solvent poured onto the tape turns it into glue and the grip is slid onto the shaft. The club's lie angle is adjusted for the height and swing habits of its future owner. In the stamping area, the clubs are stamped with individual serial numbers. In a process called "whipping," a thick, black, fishing-type line is used to secure wooden heads to shafts. After the tour, you'll want to play golf at one of the many golf courses in the Phoenix area.

Cost: Free

Freebies: Information sheets, brochures, key chain, personalized fitting recommendations.

Video Shown: 12-minute video on the history of Karsten and its subsidiaries.

Reservations Needed: Yes

Days and Hours: Call for availability and reservations 1-2 months in advance.

Plan to Stay: 45 minutes-1¼ hours for tour, video, and questions.

Minimum Age: Yes, inquire when making reservations.

Disabled Access: Yes

Group Requirements: Cannot handle group tours larger than 10 people.

Special Information: No photography. Wear comfortable shoes for the half-mile of walking. Parts of tour are loud. Ping golf club owners and people interested in golf will enjoy the tour the most.

Gift Shop: No. Products sold through dealers and area golf courses.

Directions: From I-17, go east on Peoria Ave. Turn left onto 21st Ave. Visitor center is the redwood building on the right with the #120.

Nearby Attractions: Cerreta Candy Co. tour (see page 4); Metro Center Shopping Mall; Phoenix attractions include over 100 golf courses and Breck Girl Hall of Fame at Dial Corp. headquarters (call 602-207-5338).

Peanut Patch <small>――</small> *peanuts*
4322 East County 13th Street
Yuma, AZ 85365
(602) 726-6292 / (800) USA-PNUT

Peanut farming conjures images of Georgia's Jimmy Carter and other southeastern farmers. The Southeast, mainly Georgia and Alabama, produces 51 percent of all the peanuts in the U.S.A. However, Peanut Patch is the largest of the six Arizona growers that together produce two million pounds per year.

Led by one of the young family-member owners, tours begin with a peanut-growing lesson. You may be amazed to learn that peanuts do not grow on the farm's eucalyptus trees. Rather, as legumes, they grow underground, planted in March and harvested in August.

During the peanut processing period, tours go through the shelling plant. In one warehouse, five screens "size" peanuts for different uses. For example, large sizes may be sold as "jumbo" in-shell ballpark peanuts, small peanuts will be used for peanut oil, and medium sizes will be planted for next year. Watch a quick-fingered picking crew hand-cull undesirable peanuts by their appearance. On a good day, the plant produces 200 100-pound bags, or 20,000 pounds.

In another Peanut Patch warehouse, which is government-bonded, you may see huge mountains of peanuts stored for the company and the federal government. The government will auction off its peanuts. Come mid-November, it seems like not one more peanut will fit into the warehouse.

Your nose and ears will lead you to the shelling building, where noisy machines remove the hulls (shells) and skins. In the roasting area, 600 pounds of peanuts are dry-roasted at one time. Savor the taste of a warm, freshly-roasted peanut.

The Farm Store kitchen will further tempt your senses as dry- or oil-roasted peanuts are ground into natural peanut butter. Butter, peanuts, and sugar simmer together in copper kettles. The mixture is poured onto old-fashioned marble slabs for cooling, and later it's broken into pieces of peanut brittle. Warm chocolate nut clusters are individually spooned onto trays and hand-packed in the pack room. You will leave with a well-rounded introduction to farming, the peanut industry, and candy-making.

Cost: Free
Freebies: Fudge, peanuts, and candy samples.
Video Shown: No
Reservations Needed: No, except for groups larger than 10 people. In addition to scheduled tour times, individuals can join pre-scheduled group tours at other times.
Days and Hours: Open for peanut processing tours October through May only. Wed 10:00 AM. Call for other days and times. Closed Thanksgiving, Christmas, and Easter.
Plan to Stay: 1 hour for peanut processing, plus time in gift shop to see fudge- and candy-making.
Minimum Age: None
Disabled Access: Yes
Group Requirements: Call at least 2 weeks in advance for reservations. Minimum group is 10 people. No maximum group size.
Special Information: Tours vary based on the harvesting/processing cycle. Special company outing near Thanksgiving open to public. Shellers are noisy and dusty. On children's tours, kids get to make their own peanut butter.
Gift Shop: Country Store sells peanuts, other nuts, trail mixes, dried fruits, and candies displayed in family-collected antiques. Offers unique Arizona specialties (cactus jellies and other products directly from local farmers). Buy freshly made fudge, just cut from the big slab, peanut brittle, and nut clusters. Mon-Sun 9:00 AM-6:00 PM. Closed June 1-September 30, Thanksgiving, Christmas, and Easter. Catalog available at above number.
Directions: Take I-8 to Yuma. Take Ave. 3E exit. Go south to County 13th St. Turn left for 1¼ miles and Peanut Patch will be on your left.
Nearby Attractions: Saihati Camel Farm tour (call 602-627-2553); Territorial Prison; Yuma Crossing.

Wal-Mart Visitors Center *retail stores*

Visitors Center
105 North Main Street
Bentonville, AR 72712
(501) 273-1329

The Wal-Mart retail empire, with over 500,000 employees (called "associates") and billions of dollars in yearly revenues, began in the building that now houses the Visitors Center. From the outside, it's an exact replica of the first Walton's 5 & 10 opened by Sam and Helen Walton in 1950. The folksy center brings together the history, growth, philosophy, and present-day scope of the company. As you walk on the original checkerboard red and green tile floor, examining the displays and watching the videos, you're surrounded by a true American business success.

Merchandise from the 1950s and '60s sits in the front window. In the lobby is a cut-out figure of Sam Walton (the store's first manager) next to a huge mural showing a typical 5 & 10 of the early '50s. Family portraits and other murals of the company's operations also hang throughout the center, along with early newspaper ads. The center has over 40 separate displays. The most popular are the laser video programs on the history of the company and on the Walton family. One large exhibit is a timeline that traces the Wal-Mart story from its variety-store roots to the present day. Mementos, photos, and products such as old Barbie dolls fill the display. At the push of a button is a narrated, illuminated photomap tracking the nationwide spread of Wal-Mart stores.

The Visitors Center holds many of Sam's prized possessions. The Presidential Medal of Freedom, the nation's highest civilian award, which Sam Walton received in 1992, is proudly displayed. So are his old red pickup truck and original office, complete with the apple crate used as a chair for guests. Other exhibits include Wal-Mart and Wall Street, Community Involvement, Satellite Communications, and Saving the Environment.

The "Buy American" exhibit features a changing display of the American-made products that Wal-Mart sells and the jobs created by this partnership of retailers and domestic manufacturers. The long-range goal of the Buy American program is to re-establish the competitive position of U.S.-made goods. You leave understanding more about the people and heritage behind what has been called "the retailing phenomenon of the century."

Cost: Free
Freebies: No
Video Shown: Four 8-minute laser video programs on the company, the Walton family, the Medal of Freedom, and conversations between Sam and his brother.
Reservations Needed: No, however recommended for groups of 10 or more people.
Days and Hours: Mon-Sat 9:00 AM-5:00 PM. Closed Mondays November-February, and Thanksgiving, Christmas, and New Year's.
Plan to Stay: 30 minutes, plus time for videos.
Minimum Age: None, but recommends children be at least 10 to appreciate and enjoy the exhibits.
Disabled Access: Yes
Group Requirements: Groups of 10 or more people should call 2 days in advance.
Special Information: Exhibits change to reflect Wal-Mart developments. You may want to schedule your visit around Wal-Mart Stores, Inc.'s annual meeting (usually first week in June) in nearby Fayetteville. About 15,000 people attend the largest annual meeting in the U.S.A., which features live entertainment, enthused employees, and a real sense of the corporate culture.
Gift Counter: Sells Wal-Mart and Visitors Center logoed items, including mugs, key chains, and T-shirts. Open same hours as Visitors Center.
Directions: Take Hwy. 71 or Hwy. 71B to Hwy. 72. The Visitors Center is on the west side of the square in downtown Bentonville. Look for the big American flag and the building that says "Walton's 5 & 10."
Nearby Attractions: University of Arkansas; Beaver Lake; Eureka Springs.

Basic Brown Bear ~~~ *teddy bears*

444 DeHaro Street
San Francisco, CA 94107
(415) 626-0781

You'll enjoy playing teddy bear obstetrician on this tour. At this small factory, discover how teddy bears are born and participate in their delivery. One of the few U.S. manufacturers of stuffed bears, Basic Brown Bear (BBB) lets you watch them handmake the cuddly creatures from start to finish.

Upstairs in the workshop, the owner proudly explains her process. First, she draws each pattern on paper and makes a sample animal from the pattern. In the cutting area, a worker uses a bandsaw to slice 24 layers of plush fabric. Seamstresses sew together individual bear parts and outfits, stitching the sections inside-out, then reaching inside to push out the bear legs, ears, and noses. They can make about 35 baby bears or 10 grandparent bears a day plus their clothes.

Downstairs, on the first floor, you learn that the first stuffed bears had shoe-buttons for eyes. Now, grommets snap mushroom-shaped plastic eyes into place. A tour highlight is stuffing bears with polyester from a bright yellow machine used to fill life jackets during WWII. Now you can bring a bear to life by inflating it like a balloon. Wait on a line of yellow paw-prints to push the filler's foot pedal. Out shoots a mixture of air and polyester. Once a bear is cuddly enough, its back is hand-sewn shut.

At the beauty parlor, workers smooth out bear-seams with an electric wire brush. A pressurized-air "bear bath" or "bear shower" (depending on the critter's size) removes fur "fuzzies." Children (and adults) giggle when they too receive a "bear shower" or give a bear a "bath." Bears are dressed in their outfits, including company-made wire-rim glasses. Visitors leave with a special affection for the bears they brought to life.

Cost: Free tour. Prices for stuffing your own animal run from $8.50 to $300.
Freebies: No
Video Shown: No
Reservations Needed: No, except for groups of 8 or more people.

Days and Hours: Mon-Fri 1:00 PM, Sat 11:00 AM and 2:00 PM, Sun 3:00 PM. Closed holidays. Possible additional weekday tours.
Plan to Stay: 30 minutes, plus time for stuffing and showering your own bear, and the gift shop.
Minimum Age: 3
Disabled Access: First floor only. Stairs lead to second-floor cutting and sewing area.
Group Requirements: Groups of 8 or more people should call 2 weeks in advance. Maximum group size is 25.
Special Information: Can also partially stuff your own animals at BBB's other store in The Cannery, near Fisherman's Wharf.
Gift Shop: Over 30 styles of stuffed bears (and other animals) and bear clothes, all handmade by BBB, are sold exclusively at this location. Mon-Sat 10:00 AM-5:00 PM and Sun 1:00 PM-5:00 PM. Price list available from (800) 554-1910.
Directions: From the East Bay Bridge, take 9th St./Civic Center Exit and get into the immediate left-hand lane, which puts you onto 8th St. Stay on 8th St. until it ends at the traffic circle. Turn right onto Kansas St. Turn left onto Mariposa St. BBB is on the left-hand corner of Mariposa and DeHaro Sts. From the South Bay, take Hwy. 101 North. Take the Vermont St. Exit and cross over Vermont St. onto Mariposa St. Stay on Mariposa St. until you reach DeHaro St. (about 4 blocks). BBB is on the left-hand corner.
Nearby Attractions: Anchor Brewery Co. tour (across the street, call 415-863-8350); San Francisco attractions are 10–20 minutes away, including Levi Strauss factory tour (see page 17), Wells Fargo Bank Museum (call 415-396-2619), Chevron U.S.A. Museum (call 415-894-6697), and Fisherman's Wharf.

See color photos, page 157

Bradbury & Bradbury   ~ *Victorian wallpaper*

940 Tyler, Studio 12
Benicia, CA 94510
(707) 746-1900

The beautiful Victorian wallpaper from the movie *Hook*, featuring Robin Williams and Julia Roberts, came from this Victorian wallpaper factory. That movie set joined Disney World and EuroDisney, as well as countless bed-and-breakfasts and restored Victorian homes, in using Bradbury & Bradbury's handprinted wall and ceiling papers.

The smell of oil-based paint permeates the printing area, where long sheets of paper lay across six tables, each about 30 yards long and one yard wide. You'll watch as workers repeatedly bend over a table, place the patterned screen onto the specially coated paper, stroke the squeegee through the ink to create the printed design, and then switch on a small overhead fan to quicken the drying. To avoid smudges, the screen is put down only every other pattern length. After doing this for all six tables, the printer scampers back to fill in the missing patterns.

In the art department, you'll learn the strategy behind redesigning ornate 19th-century wall and ceiling papers. In a process analogous to the design of Lego blocks, the artists meticulously draw the patterns by hand on graph paper and also on a computer design system, striving to create modular patterns that can fit together in any size room. Since B&B is a small company, you can stand next to the printers and artists as they work to reproduce the past.

Cost: Free for individuals as well as school and non-profit groups. $1 per person for bus tours.
Freebies: No
Video Shown: No
Reservations Needed: Yes
Days and Hours: Mon-Fri 9:00 AM-5:00 PM. Closed holidays.
Plan to Stay: 30 minutes
Minimum Age: None
Disabled Access: The studio is all on one floor, but you must climb a few flights of stairs to reach it.

Group Requirements: Groups should call a day in advance. Maximum group is 44 people. Fee for bus tours.
Special Information: Be sure to ask if they will be in production when you plan to visit. The paint smell may bother some visitors. To make an appointment to see their San Francisco design studio, call (707) 746-6262.
Gift Area: Nothing formal, but you can look through the samples, purchase a catalog, and place orders. Catalog and design service kit available in San Francisco.
Directions: The company recommends you call for specific directions since there are many forks in the road. From I-80, take I-780 to the exit for Fifth St. (the last Benicia exit coming from the Bay area). From Fifth St., turn left onto Military East. Follow this road down, around, and under a bridge until it ends on Tyler. Make a right on Tyler. The company is located on the second floor of an old military building occupied by several arts-related companies.
Nearby Attractions: Zellique, Nourot, and Smyers glassblowers studio tours (call 707-745-5710); Old State Capitol Building.

Dreyer's and Edy's Grand Ice Cream

1250 Whipple Road ⟨⟩ *ice cream and frozen yogurt*
Union City, CA 94587
(510) 471-6622

In 1928, William Dreyer and Joseph Edy started Dreyer's and Edy's Grand Ice Cream on Grand Avenue in Oakland, California. Just one year later, they became famous by creating the world's first batch of Rocky Road ice cream. Now the company is the number-one premium ice-cream maker in the U.S. and the top exporter of premium ice cream to Japan. While your friendly guide sprinkles the tour with company trivia and industry facts, you'll learn, see, and taste how ice cream is made, from the cow to the cone.

After watching a video in the Double Scoop Depot, walk up marble-fudge-colored stairs and take a walk down the Rocky Road to peer through glass windows overlooking the production floor. The assembly lines look like a maze of steel pipes and rapidly moving ice-cream containers. The base mix travels through the flavor vats, continuous flow freezer, and fruit feeders. Workers lift plastic bags of whatever ingredients are required for the flavor in production (perhaps strawberries for strawberry ice cream), pouring their contents into the feeder.

You first see the ice cream as it drops from the container-filler machines into round cartons. The windowed lids then twist down to cover the containers. At this point, the ice cream has the consistency of soft-serve. It moves through the inspection and shrink-wrap stations before resting in the hardening freezer for about seven hours at 40° below zero. This routine continues until workers produce up to 60,000 gallons per day, in some 20 different flavors.

You'll shiver as you quickly pass through the gigantic warehouse and loading dock area, with wind chill temperatures 20-30° below freezing. It's worth being cold for a few brisk moments to see the one million gallons of ice cream and frozen yogurt piled everywhere you look. At the end of the tour, you might run into John D. Harrison, the "Official Taster." The company insured his well-publicized taste buds for $1 million.

Cost: $2 per person

Freebies: Scoops of ice cream and frozen yogurt in your favorite flavors, a bag of souvenir items that includes coupons, a factory poster, and a paper hat.

Video Shown: 11-minute video entitled "The Cool Facts" provides a close-up view of the ice-cream production process.

Reservations Needed: Yes. Prefers to consolidate individuals and families into a group tour.

Days and Hours: Mon-Fri 9:15 AM and 11:15 AM, and also Tue-Thur 2:00 PM. Closed holidays and week between Christmas and New Year's.

Plan to Stay: 1½ hours including video, tour, and ice-cream tasting.

Minimum Age: 6 (first grade)

Disabled Access: Yes, except for 5 stairs into the freezer area.

Group Requirements: Maximum group size is 40 people, with reservations recommended approximately 2 months in advance.

Special Information: No photography. Freezer area can be refreshingly chilly, so warm-weather natives should bring a sweater. Wear flat-heeled shoes.

Gift Cabinet: The Double Scoop Depot has a gift cabinet with a small selection of logoed items, including T-shirts and bookcovers. John D. Harrison's 10-minute video on ice-cream making and tasting, entitled "All In Good Taste," is available for purchase. Open after tours.

Directions: Take I-880 to the Whipple Rd. Exit. Make a right on Whipple Rd. The factory is about .7 mile ahead on the right.

Nearby Attractions: NUMMI auto plant tour (see page 21); C.F. Kennedy Community Center & Park; Town Estates Park; Oakland and San Francisco attractions about 30 minutes away.

Creamy ice cream filling cartons at Dreyer's Grand Ice Cream, Union City, California

California Cooperative Creamery

711 Western Avenue   ⟡ *cheese*
Petaluma, CA 94952
(707) 778-1234

The California Cooperative Creamery, which now represents over 520 dairies, has been making dairy products since 1913. In 1982 the Creamery actively entered the cheese-making business. They now package over one million pounds a month, including private-label cheese and their own California Gold label. At this ultra-modern plant you not only see how they do it, but also learn interesting cheese trivia, such as the historical origins of coloring Cheddar cheese. (Colonists colored their cheese to distinguish it from cheese imported from England.)

As with almost all cheese-factory tours, you watch the process through glass windows. The cheese plant is so automated that only five people are needed to run it. The cheese-making process begins as the milk is pasteurized. Starter culture, contained in 600-gallon starter tanks, is added. Only the two master cheese-makers know the makeup of this culture. A mixture of starter culture, pasteurized milk, and enzymes are pumped into the 5,000-gallon autovats. Here the curds and whey are cooked under highly controlled conditions. Curd knives, built into the autovats, continuously stir and cut the curds.

The combination of curds and whey is pumped onto finishing tables, where the whey is withdrawn. The big churns going around in the shallow mixture look like a whisk beating scrambled eggs. The cheese curds then go through a forming tower that uses gravity and vacuum pressure to press them into 40-pound blocks. Their next step is the aging room, where over 3.5 million pounds of cheese age like fine wine.

Cost: Free
Freebies: Samples of cheese in the Creamery Store.
Video Shown: A 10-minute video on the history of the Cooperative and on the cheese- and butter-making processes.
Reservations Needed: No, except for groups of more than 10.
Days and Hours: Mon-Sat 11:00 AM–3:00 PM on the hour. Closed Christmas, New Year's,

Thanksgiving, and for inspections.
Plan to Stay: 45 minutes for tour and video, plus time for gift shop.
Minimum Age: None
Disabled Access: Yes for video and gift shop only.
Group Requirements: Groups of 10 or more are requested to call 10 days ahead. Can handle groups up to 45 people.
Special Information: No photography in the plant. The Cooperative may, at some future time, open the cheese-wrapping and butter-making areas to the public for tours.
Gift Shop: The Creamery Store sells award-winning California Gold cheeses, butter, and many other dairy-related products and gift items. The store features a unique collection of over 600 "cow" gifts. Open Mon-Sat 10:00 AM–5:00 PM. Closed holidays. A catalog is available at above number. Look in front of the store for the replica of the 1913 milk wagon, complete with brass-plated milk cans, that was used to deliver milk to the original creamery.
Directions: From Santa Rosa, take Rt. 101 South. Take the E. Washington St. exit west. Turn left on Petaluma Blvd. North and right onto Western Ave.
Nearby Attractions: Marin French Cheese Factory tour (call 707-762-6001); Bodega Bay; Petaluma Adobe State Historic Park; Petaluma Historical Library; The Great Petaluma Mill.

Fortune Cookie Factory 〰 *fortune cookies*

261 12th Street
Oakland, CA 94607
(510) 832-5552

Did you ever wonder how the fortune got inside a fortune cookie? Ever want to write your own fortune? What you may think of as great Oriental secrets are revealed at the Fortune Cookie Factory, an over-30-year-old family business. Don't be disappointed, however, when the owner, a UC Berkeley-educated mechanical engineer, tells you that fortune cookies were *not* created in the Orient. An ingenious Chinese restaurant owner invented them in the 1920s as an inexpensive and unique dessert.

Fortune cookies start as a mixture similar to pancake batter, made of whole-wheat flour, cane or beet sugar, water, and powdered whole eggs. Margarine, flavoring, and artificial coloring give the fortune cookies their golden color. A young Chinese worker concocts 100 pounds of batter in a vertical electric mixer, then scurries across the floor to pour it into one of the seven custom-made fortune-cookie machines. You will be mesmerized by the circular, methodical motion of this groaning machine. Batter flows through a spigot into individual 3-inch-diameter waffle irons. The individual plates clamp shut for their 4-minute circular journey through the 225° piano-shaped oven. Small, wafer-thin pancakes emerge, cooked on both sides and pressed to squeeze out all air pockets.

With great dexterity the worker seated in front of each oven removes each pancake, randomly grabs a fortune from her lap, places it on the pancake, folds the pancake in half like a taco and bends it around a metal rod. For cooling, the cookies are placed points-down in a holding tray. Listen to the women chatter in Chinese while they hand-fold 15 to 16 fortune cookies per minute, or 50,000 per day.

Cost: $1 per person
Freebies: Sample bag of fortune cookies.
Video Shown: No
Reservations Needed: No for self-guided viewing of the production process from the entrance of the production area. Yes for guided explanation. Individuals need to latch onto guided group tours.

Days and Hours: Mon-Fri 8:00 AM-4:30 PM, but may want to call to check if English-speaking person available. Closed major Chinese and some U.S. holidays.

Plan to Stay: 15 minutes for viewing, plus time for gift counter.

Minimum Age: 7, unless with family

Disabled Access: Yes

Group Requirements: Maximum group size is 25 people, which requires reservations 1 week in advance for guided tour.

Special Information: When the owner is there he will gladly answer questions and tell you about his appearance on "What's My Line," a popular classic TV show; otherwise, look for a one-page handout on the business and fortune-cookie-making process.

Gift Counter: Small retail shop at front of factory sells bags of regular and flavored (i.e., strawberry, lime) fortune cookies, along with sassy and X-rated versions. You can also order customized fortune cookies (various sizes and messages, even with an engagement ring, if desired) and purchase bags of "misfortunes," which are broken fortune cookies. Price information available at above number. Open Mon-Fri 9:00 AM-4:30 PM.

Directions: From north of Oakland, take I-980 South and get off at the 11th/12th St. exit. Make a left onto 11th St. Turn left onto Alice and left onto 12th. Look for the factory store-front on the left side of 12th St. From south of Oakland, take I-880 North to Oak St. exit. Turn right at first intersection. Turn left on 12th. Store-front on left side.

Nearby Attractions: Lotus Fortune Cookies, in San Francisco's Chinatown, is a smaller business that has a viewing area near the retail counter (call 415-552-0759); Oakland's Chinatown; Madison Park; Lake Merritt; Oakland Museum; San Francisco's attractions are across the Bay Bridge.

Graber Olive House ~ *olives*

315 East 4th St.
Ontario, CA 91761
(909) 983-1761

Companies that mass-produce California olives tell you that the black, pitted variety found on pizzas and supermarket shelves are natural and tree-ripened. After visiting the Graber Olive House, you will know what these terms really mean. The C.C. Graber Co. is the oldest olive packer (1894) in the only U.S. state that produces olives.

The cherry-red fruits are carefully removed from the tree by a picker who holds only a few olives in his hand at one time and drops them gently into a felt-bottomed bucket. Mass-produced California "ripe" black olives are green when harvested, and then oxidized a uniform black color to hide bruises. Graber olives turn a natural nut-like color in processing.

After viewing pictures of the olives and groves, you're led through the company's production area. In the grading room, smock-clad women face a conveyor belt and carefully pick "culls" (overripe, underripe, or imperfect) out of the olive procession before them. More than one million olives roll by the graders during an 8-hour shift. The perfect olives then move to the vat room where, using the Graber family recipe, they are stirred, soaked, and tended for about three weeks in round cement vats. After the careful curing process removes the olives' natural bitterness, they are ready to be canned.

The pampered olives undergo a thorough canning and sterilization process. Workers, using the "hand-pack filling machine," scoop olives into cans as they pass under a wheel. Paddles on the "panama-paddle packer" rotate and push a small amount of water out of each can, forming a head space for steam. The machine then hermetically seals each can. In the boiler room, carts filled with sealed cans of olives are rolled into a "retort." The door is closed and the olives are sterilized with 242° steam from the boiler (like that on an old train) for over an hour. Finally, the cans are labeled with the Graber name familiar to gourmets around the world.

Cost: Free

Freebies: The "hospitality bowl" is filled with free olive samples.

Video Shown: No

Reservations Needed: No, except for groups of 10 or more people.

Days and Hours: Mon-Sun 9:00 AM-4:30 PM. Lunch break from 12:00 PM-1:30 PM. Last tour at 4:00 PM. Tours are conducted all year, but grading, curing, and canning take place in October and early November. Closed Christmas, Thanksgiving, New Year's, Easter, and July 4th.

Plan to Stay: 30 minutes for tour, plus time for museum and gift shop. Museum contains an original grading machine made by C.C. Graber and other items related to the olive business. Lawn area available for picnics.

Minimum Age: None

Disabled Access: Yes

Group Requirements: Groups larger than 10 people should call 1 week in advance. Large groups will be split into groups of 20.

Special Information: When the factory is not in production, tour goes through canning plant with a colorful explanation and photographs of the process.

Gift Shop: The Casa del Olivo Fancy Food and Gift Shop sells Graber olives, nuts, dates, fancy foods, gift baskets, candies, toys, cookbooks, and unusual pottery. La Casita sells kitchen supplies and works by local artists. Open Mon-Sat 9:00 AM-5:30 PM and Sun 9:30 AM-6:00 PM. Catalog is available at 800-99-OLIVE (65483).

Directions: From Los Angeles and Palm Springs, take I-10 (San Bernardino Freeway) to Ontario. Take the Euclid Ave. exit, then south to 4th St. Turn left onto 4th St. Graber Olive House will be on your left.

Nearby Attractions: Fleetwood Motor Homes factory tour (call 800-326-8633); San Antonio Winery tasting room (call 909-947-3995); Claremont Colleges; Griswald Center; Mission Inn.

Herman Goelitz 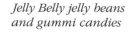 *Jelly Belly jelly beans and gummi candies*

2400 North Watney Way
Fairfield, CA 94533
(707) 428-2838

If you question whether former President Ronald Reagan's policies were good for the U.S. economy or for kids, then you should visit this factory which produces millions of jelly beans per day. The publicity surrounding President Reagan's fondness for their gourmet jelly beans ("Jelly Belly") led to increased demand, round-the-clock shifts, a new factory, and amusing tours for children and adults. The Herman Goelitz company has been making candy since 1922, but it was the introduction of the Jelly Belly jelly bean in 1976 that spurred its growth.

While you'll see how the company makes a variety of creative candies, such as its line of Pet Gummi candies, the highlight is watching how it makes the Jelly Belly beans in over 40 flavors. From an open-air walkway, you'll view the beans at different stages of their creation. Be prepared for intense aromas. Unlike standard jelly beans, Jelly Belly beans are flavored both in the center and in the shell. Machines pour the special bean-center mixture into cornstarch molds that hold 1,260 centers per tray. Guess the exotic flavors, like strawberry daiquiri or peanut butter, as the bean centers travel by in the distance.

After the centers harden overnight, mechanical arms flip the trays over and the centers pour into spinning, open copper drums. Here, workers add four layers of flavored syrup and sugars to create the outer shells. Each bean is automatically checked for correct size and color before traveling through the bagging and boxing machines. You'll look down at a hopper filled with a colorful and flavorful sea of jelly beans. The correctly weighed amount of jelly beans drops into plastic packets below. However, workers handpack the gummi candies because they are too sticky for machines. At the tour's end, you'll stare at large mosaic portraits of famous faces and figures such as Ronald Reagan and the Statue of Liberty, each made of 14,000 jelly beans.

Cost: Free

Freebies: 4-ounce bag of Jelly Belly beans with an official menu matching colors to flavors. Logoed paper hat to wear during the tour. Throughout the tour the guide periodically gives out fresh Jelly Belly beans in various stages of production.

Video Shown: 7-minute video that explains and gives a close-up view of the candy-manufacturing process.

Reservations Needed: No

Days and Hours: Mon-Fri 9:00 AM-2:00 PM. Closed holidays and the last week in June through the first 2-3 weeks of July.

Plan to Stay: 40 minutes, plus time for video and gift shop.

Minimum Age: None, with 1 adult for every 6 children.

Disabled Access: Yes

Group Requirements: None

Special Information: No photography.

Retail Store: Sells more flavors of jelly beans than you can imagine (not only exotic fruit tastes, but also unusual flavors like toasted marshmallow, buttered popcorn, and jalapeño). Look for 2-pound bags of Belly Flops, the factory rejects. Open Mon-Fri 9:00 AM-5:00 PM, Sat 10:00 AM-4:00 PM.

Directions: From the San Francisco/Oakland area, take I-80 East to Hwy. 12 East. Turn right onto Beck Ave., right onto Courage Way, and right onto North Watney Way. From Sacramento, take Abernathy exit left to Hwy. 12 East, then follow the above directions. Recording on above number provides directions.

Nearby Attractions: Anheuser-Busch (Budweiser) Brewery tour (call 707-429-7595); Marine World Africa U.S.A.; Old Town Vallejo.

Hershey's Visitors Center ~ *chocolate*

120 South Sierra
Oakdale, CA 95361-9368
(209) 848-8126

 **Hershey Foods Corporation**

"Wow, look at all those Hershey's Kisses!" will be your first words as you enter the only Hershey's chocolate factory in the U.S. that gives public tours. Watch each Hershey's Kisses chocolate, one of the most recognizable shapes in the world, receive its own silver evening gown and paper necklace. Hershey Foods Corporation, founded in 1894 by Milton S. Hershey in the small Pennsylvania town later named after him, is the country's largest candy-maker; it makes approximately 33 million Kisses per day.

At one stop on your speedy, sweet-smelling journey, peek through glass walls at rows of 10,000-pound vats called "conch machines." At all major tour stops, the guide plays a taped explanation of what's happening in front of you. You hear, for example, that the conch machines' granite rollers move back and forth on corrugated granite beds to create smooth chocolate paste from a mixture of cocoa butter, sugar, milk, and chocolate liquid.

From an overhead walkway, peer through glass windows at the high-speed computerized production lines that build well-known Hershey products like the top-selling Reese's Peanut Butter Cups. After the brown paper cups land on a moving belt, they are lined with milk chocolate and then a layer of peanut butter. The top layer of chocolate is air-blown on and vibrated to ensure a smooth surface. In the wrapping and packaging area the peanut butter cups move so quickly on a sophisticated "freeway" system that they deserve a speeding ticket. You'll leave this tour feeling like Charlie after his visit to Willy Wonka's Chocolate Factory.

Cost: Free
Freebies: Coupon for choice of free candy bar or 10% off purchase of single item valued at $5 or more.
Video Shown: Optional 13-minute video played on monitors in the visitors center building. "The Cocoa Bean Story" captures the entire production process and augments the fast-paced tour.

Reservations Needed: No, except for groups of 15 or more people.
Days and Hours: Mon-Fri 8:30 AM-3:00 PM. Closed major holidays. Shuttle buses leave the visitors center for the factory every 15-30 minutes. During peak periods (summer, Christmas and Easter weeks), 1:30 PM is recommended sign-in time for 3:00 PM tour.
Plan to Stay: 1 hour, which includes tour and shuttle bus ride (a great chocolate smell hits you when you approach the factory). Allow time for gift shop and video.
Minimum Age: None, but no strollers allowed.
Disabled Access: Yes, for the first half of the tour. If you are unable to use the stairs, tell a Hershey's Guest Relations Representative before the tour begins.
Group Requirements: Groups of 15 or more people should call at least 1 month in advance. No maximum group size.
Special Information: See the write-up on page 205 for the simulated factory tour at the Hershey's Chocolate World Visitors Center in Hershey, PA.
Gift Shop: Sells a variety of Hershey's candy, T-shirts, and gifts. Unique items include "Hershey's Chockers," the checkers game for chocolate lovers, and teddy bears holding stuffed Kisses. Exhibits include a model 1915 wrapping machine. Open Mon-Fri 8:30 AM-5:00 PM. Closed holidays.
Directions: From San Francisco, take I-580 East to I-205 East. Take Hwy. 120 East to intersection of Hwys. 108 and 120. Go through intersection, travel 1 block and turn left onto G St. Parking is on right. From Yosemite, take Hwy. 120 West. Continue on Hwy. 108/120 to Oakdale. Turn left onto Yosemite St. Turn left onto G St. Parking is on right. Recording provides additional directions.
Nearby Attractions: Western Theme Park; Knights Ferry; Oakdale Museum; St. Stans Brewing Co. tour (call 209-524-BEER); Delicato Vineyard tour (call 209-825-6212); Hershey's Visitors Center has list of nearby attractions and events.

Levi Strauss & Co. ⁓ *jeans*

250 Valencia Street
San Francisco, CA 94103
(415) 565-9153

In 1849, the discovery of gold near Sacramento ushered in California's Gold Rush, and hordes of prospectors raced west to seek their fortunes. Long hours in the mines, however, quickly wore out their pants. A young, entrepreneurial German immigrant named Levi Strauss cleverly solved their dilemma. In 1853, using leftover canvas he had hoped to use for tents and wagon covers, he designed the first pair of jeans. Exhausting his original supply of canvas, Levi switched to a sturdy fabric made in Nimes, France, called "serge de Nimes" (later shortened to "denim"). They became known as "those pants of Levi's," and quickly grew in popularity. Blue jeans have been an American icon ever since.

Entering the Levi Strauss factory will remind you more of the famous garment shops of early-1900s New York than of the Gold Rush. Smell the fresh-cut fabric and observe the ring of sewing machines. Watch the stages from the initial cutting of the denim to the final preparation for shipping. Large carts whirl past you, carrying jeans in various stages of production. In the smallest and oldest (built in 1906) Levi Strauss factory in the world, approximately 60 workers make Levi's famous 501 jeans.

The presence of the patriarchal founder and the sense of family history pervade the tour. Old looms sit in hallway displays, early advertising posters adorn the walls, and a life-size cardboard cut-out of Levi himself proudly greets visitors to the upper level. Even the shiny wooden floors are a testimonial to the kindness of the family-owned company, which employed workers to improve the factory rather than fire them during the Depression.

You will leave with the feeling that you did not merely watch pants being made, but you witnessed the making of a legendary American product by a respected U.S. company. However, you'll have to go to Asia to buy a pair of the 501s made during your tour. Almost every pair made at this factory ends up in Japan, because the Japanese insist on the high-priced San Francisco originals.

Cost: Free

Freebies: Occasionally a souvenir such as a key chain with a leather Levi Strauss trademark patch or a ballpoint pen.

Video Shown: 8-minute video, usually of classic Levi's commercials

Reservations Needed: Yes. Individuals and families must latch onto group tours. Individuals should call 1 to 2 days in advance to check for space availability, as priority is given to tour groups. Groups see below.

Days and Hours: Wed 10:30 AM and 1:00 PM. Closed holidays, 2 weeks around Christmas, and 3-4 weeks in July.

Plan to Stay: 1-1½ hours including tour, video, museum, and question-and-answer session at end of tour. Museum has pictures and displays that highlight the history of jeans and the company.

Minimum Age: None

Disabled Access: Yes

Group Requirements: Groups should make reservations as early as possible, since tours fill up months in advance. Maximum group size is 35 people.

Special Information: No video cameras. Can sometimes be difficult to reach tour director, a regular factory worker, about scheduling tour. Your persistence will be rewarded by the tour experience.

Gift Shop: No

Directions: Take Hwy. 101 to the Van Ness/Mission St. exit. Go straight onto Duboce Ave. Turn left onto Valencia.

Nearby Attractions: Basic Brown Bear Factory tour (see page 8); San Francisco's attractions include Fisherman's Wharf, Anchor Brewery Co. tour (call 415-863-8350), Wells Fargo Bank Museum (call 415-396-2619), and Chevron U.S.A. Museum (call 415-894-6697).

Intel ⟶ *computer chips*

Corporate Museum, Robert N. Noyce Building
2200 Mission College Blvd.
Santa Clara, CA 95052-8119
(408) 765-0503

Few U.S. companies embody the computer revolution like the Intel Corporation. At the company's museum, which opened in 1992, you'll learn about Intel's development, innovation, range of products, pride, and also how Intel became the world's largest computer-chip maker.

You're lured inside by shifting green, purple, aqua, and silver lights bouncing off a glass etching of an Intel computer chip. You'll quickly notice a dummy in a "bunny suit." (No, it doesn't have giant ears.) The workers who build computer chips wear this fully enclosed white suit, complete with air packs to filter their breathing. Computer-chip making requires factories thousands of times cleaner than hospital operating rooms. To illustrate this point, in the chip-making exhibit you can walk through an air shower that blows dust particles off your clothes.

The museum's exhibits appeal to all levels of technical knowledge and interest, so don't become discouraged if one display goes over your head. Visitors with technical backgrounds will enjoy exhibits of Intel's key memory products, such as EPROMs (erasable programmable read-only memory) and DRAMs (dynamic random access memory), and descriptions of memory technologies such as magnetic core and semiconductor. These products transformed computers from huge, expensive machines into affordable, powerful desktop systems available to everyone. Intel's microprocessors are displayed, from the Intel 4004 (the world's first, invented in 1971), to the newest processors. The history section includes enlarged circuit diagrams, along with the history of and the design teams behind each chip's development.

Although you cannot tour the factories where Intel actually makes its chips, the museum shows the sophisticated robotic-arm wafer transfer device and the complex steps involved in manufacturing computer chips. One of the most fascinating of the many interactive exhibits deals with "embedded controllers"—the highly integrated microcomputer chips that power everyday products, from answering machines to cars. This extensive, less-technical display, featuring a life-size plastic cow wearing a computerized collar, makes you realize how pervasive and important computers have become.

Cost: Free
Freebies: No
Video Shown: Throughout the museum are video interviews with the employees behind Intel's innovations.
Reservations Needed: No, except for scheduled group tours.
Days and Hours: Mon-Fri 8:00 AM-5:00 PM. Closed company holidays.
Plan to Stay: About 1 hour, depending on your computer and engineering background and your desire to try the hands-on displays. The museum's 3,500-square-foot open floor plan makes it easy to wander.
Minimum Age: None, but 12 is the recommended minimum. Displays have interactive components, but children should be interested in computers or science.
Disabled Access: Yes
Group Requirements: Maximum group size is 20 people. Contact Intel Museum office (408-765-0662) 1 week in advance to schedule a group tour. Special programs available for school groups.
Special Information: Dress appropriately—the museum is located in Intel's corporate headquarters. Various museum displays change quarterly to highlight recent technical developments.
Gift Shop: No
Directions: Take Rt. 101 to the Montague/San Thomas Expwy. exit. Turn onto Montague Expwy. (left at exit if going south on Rt. 101, right at exit if going north), then turn left onto Mission College Blvd. (look for Mission College sign). Company headquarters is on left; museum is in the lobby of the Robert Noyce Building.
Nearby Attractions: Ampex Museum of Magnetic Recording (call 415-367-3127); Stanford Linear Accelerator Center tour (call 415-926-2204); Tech Museum of Innovation; The Barbie Hall of Fame (call 415-326-5841); Great America Theme Park.

"The History of Microprocessors at Intel" exhibit at Intel Museum, Santa Clara, California

Close-up of "The History of Microprocessors at Intel" exhibit at Intel Museum

Los Angeles Times ⟋ *newspaper*

Times Mirror Square
202 West 1st Street
Los Angeles, CA 90053
(213) 237-5757

𝕷𝖔𝖘 𝕬𝖓𝖌𝖊𝖑𝖊𝖘 𝕿𝖎𝖒𝖊𝖘

If you ever wondered how that story in your newspaper got there, you'll enjoy touring the *Los Angeles Times*. Although the sound of clattering typewriters has given way to the relative quiet of computers, you will still be dazzled by the energy in the newsroom. This tour of one of the world's great newspapers begins with a slide show illustrating the history of the *Times* and how it has grown along with the Southern California region. After the slide show, move on to the newsroom, where a vast expanse of reporters busily work on late-breaking stories and rush to meet deadlines.

Discover that the food department even has a full working kitchen, where staff members carefully taste-test all dishes before the recipes appear in the paper. See how the news and editorial departments work together, learn about the paper's different regional sections and editions, and walk by the library and photography areas. Photography buffs will enjoy the magnificent display of old and new cameras used by *Times* photographers. Huge black cameras with giant flashbulbs recall a time before television, when newspapers were almost exclusively our eyes on the world. In the composing room, every page of the paper is carefully laid out with the news stories and ads before being printed.

The *Times* printing plant, two miles away, is also open by reservation during limited hours. You'll see the state-of-the-art pressroom, which extends nearly the length of two football fields, and the newsprint storage area, where robot-like automated guidance vehicles carry 2,500-pound rolls of newsprint. Visit plate-making, where newspaper pages are converted from photographic negatives to aluminum printing plates, and observe the distribution system that takes newspapers from the press to the delivery truck. It's exciting to watch the newspaper-printing process in this massive, super-automated plant.

Cost: Free
Freebies: Reporter's notepad, *Times* pencil.
Video Shown: 7-minute video gives a quick history of the newspaper.
Reservations Needed: Main tour: No, except for groups of 10 or more people. Printing Plant tour: Yes. However, it is best to call ahead for both tours since changes are planned.
Days and Hours: Main tour: Mon-Fri 11:15 AM and 3:00 PM. Closed holidays. Printing Plant tour: see below.
Plan to Stay: 45 minutes for video and main tour
Minimum Age: 10
Disabled Access: Yes
Group Requirements: Groups larger than 10 people need to call 1 month in advance. Scheduled group times are Mon, Wed, Fri 9:45 AM, 11:00 AM, and 1:15 PM. Tours for other hours may be arranged on an as-needed basis. Call (213) 237-5757 to schedule. Maximum group size is 35 people.
Special Information: The *Times*' Globe Lobby contains circa-1935 murals, a rotating globe of the world, and a historical display.
Information on Printing Plant Tour: Tours of the *Los Angeles Times* Olympic plant, located 2 miles away at 2000 E. 8th St., are offered by reservation only (call 213-237-5757). Tours available Tue and Thur 9:45 AM and 10:00 AM. Groups are limited to 35 people and children must be at least 10 years old or in the fifth grade. Evening and Saturday tours can be arranged.
Gift Shop: No
Directions: From 101 Frwy. North, take Broadway off-ramp. Turn right onto Spring St. Park in the *Times*' garage at 213 S. Spring. Entrance to the Globe Lobby is at the corner of 1st and Spring. From the east, take Spring St. off-ramp and follow directions above.
Nearby Attractions: Paramount Pictures, Universal Studios, and Warner Bros. Studios, tours (see pages 22, 24, and 25) are 7-15 miles away; NBC Studios tour (call 818-840-4444); Museum of Contemporary Art; the Music Center; Little Tokyo; Olvera Street.

New United Motor Manufacturing

45500 Fremont Boulevard ⌒ *Toyota and GM cars*
Fremont, CA 94538 *and pickup trucks*
(510) 498-5649 / (510) 770-4008

Automobile factory tours always offer a special excitement. Because the General Motors/Toyota joint venture (nicknamed "NUMMI") uses this refurbished GM plant, it's a showcase of Japanese manufacturing techniques within the context of U.S. union-management relations. As your electric tram motors more than one mile over the factory floor, watch workers (called "team members"), giant machines, and robots build the Geo Prizm, Toyota Corolla, and Toyota pickup truck.

Because of the plant's layout, your narrated trip does not follow the exact sequence of building cars and trucks. However, you will see most of the steps in the manufacturing process. Each of the plant's work areas—whether for stamping, body and welding, assembling, or inspecting—manufactures cars and trucks at a measured pace along the plant's 1.2 miles of conveyer belt. For example, as an engine is hydraulically lifted into the overhead car engine compartment, team members scramble to bolt the engine into place within 62 seconds, the scheduled time each unit spends at each work station in the car assembly area.

A cacophony fills the air: drilling, crunching, hissing, and buzzing. Since the plant has the largest metal-parts-stamping facility on the West Coast, a constant thumping reverberates through part of the plant. Suddenly you may hear music playing. A team member on the assembly line has spotted a quality problem and pulled the Andon Cord. If the problem can't be resolved quickly, production stops on that section of the line and the music keeps playing until the problem is fixed. (Each area has its own tune.) The ability to pull this cord empowers all team members to guarantee quality in the manufacturing process, what the Japanese call *Jidoka*. Even if you're not interested in the details of the Toyota production system, you'll marvel at the movements and flying sparks generated by over 350 computerized welding robots.

Cost: Free
Freebies: Currently no souvenirs.
Video Shown: No, but captioned pictures in the tour waiting room explain the different manufacturing steps. Video is planned.
Reservations Needed: Yes. Individuals and families must join a scheduled group tour.
Days and Hours: Tue, Wed, Thur 9:30 AM and 11:30 AM. Closed holidays and week between Christmas and New Year's.
Plan to Stay: Approximately 2 hours, including introductory talk, tour, and wrap-up Q&A session.
Minimum Age: 8. Tours for children aged 8 to 18 require one adult for every 10 children.
Disabled Access: Yes
Group Requirements: Maximum group size is 46 people. Tours need to be scheduled 3-4 months in advance.
Special Information: No photography. Because tour is by electric tram and you wear a headset, there is not much walking or excessive noise.
Gift Shop: No
Directions: From I-880 North, use the Fremont Blvd. exit just past Mission Blvd. Take right at first light. Take immediate right. Visitor parking on left after three stop signs. If traveling south on I-880, use the second Fremont Blvd. exit, just past Auto Mall Pkwy. (Do not take the earlier Alvarado Niles/ Fremont Blvd. exit). The plant is visible from the freeway. Upon exiting, stay right to loop back over freeway. Turn right at first light. Follow above directions. Ask for map when making reservations.
Nearby Attractions: Dreyer's and Edy's Ice Cream Factory tour (see page 10); Intel Museum (see page 18); Great American Theme Park; Mission Peak Regional Park.

Paramount Pictures *movies and television shows*

860 North Gower Street
Hollywood, CA 90038
(213) 956-5575

Paramount Pictures, founded in 1912, shows the true TV and movie fan current moviemaking techniques while retaining its nostalgic charm. The only major studio still located in Hollywood, Paramount provides an exciting behind-the-scenes look at movie and television production. Tours of this original, classic studio are never exactly alike, since old sets are taken down and new projects begin every day.

Your tour guide will point out a number of famous Paramount landmarks along this two-hour walking tour. You will see sets not only for such television shows as "Bonanza," "I Love Lucy," "Happy Days," "Cheers," and "Entertainment Tonight," but also for some of Paramount's best-known movies, like *The Godfather*, *Star Trek*, and *The Hunt For Red October*. Watch as sets are built and props assembled for future TV shows and movies even as you journey through the studios. Stroll by the famous Wardrobe Department, as well as a display of all of Paramount's Oscars.

As you peer through the old Bronson Gate, the arched gateway entrance synonymous with Paramount Pictures, and gaze upon the famous "Hollywood" sign in the hills, you will hear the story about this passage being the magic gateway to the Silver Screen for aspiring stars. Carefully study the roof architecture of some of the soundstages to identify the three film production companies located on the site before Paramount took over the site in 1928. Even the manhole covers distinguish the early studios.

Notice the B tank, a body of water used for shooting miniatures and special effects, such as the parting of the Red Sea in the 1956 filming of *The Ten Commandments*. The 100,000 gallon-capacity Water Tower still marks the actual borderline dividing Paramount and RKO Studios, which was acquired by Paramount. Stroll through Production Park—does it look familiar? It's not only the company's business hub, but also one of the most photographed areas in Hollywood. On screen, its buildings double as college campuses, foreign embassies,

police precincts, hospitals, and more. At any point on the tour, you may suddenly see your favorite performer.

Cost: $15 per person
Freebies: Complimentary tickets to any of the TV shows filmed daily at Paramount and "Time Frame: A Studio Tour," a brochure giving Paramount's history and setting.
Video Shown: No
Reservations Needed: No, except for groups larger than 15 people.
Days and Hours: Mon-Fri 9:00 AM-2:00 PM, every hour on the hour.
Plan to Stay: 2 hours; 4-6 hours if you stay to watch a TV show in production.
Minimum Age: 10. Minimum age to watch most of the TV shows is 16.
Disabled Access: Yes
Group Requirements: Admission is $10 per person for groups larger than 15 people. Groups should call at least 1 week in advance to check the shooting schedule and make reservations. Maximum group size is 50 people. Call (213) 956-1777.
Special Information: No photography. Check time schedule and ticket availability for the day's TV show filmings when you arrive at the visitor center. Wear comfortable shoes—this is a walking tour.
Gift Shop: No
Directions: From Los Angeles, take 101 Frwy. North to Melrose Ave. exit. Turn left onto Melrose Ave. Turn right onto Gower St. and Paramount is on your right. From San Fernando Valley, take 101 Frwy. South to Gower St. exit. Make a right onto Gower St. and Paramount is on your right.
Nearby Attractions: Universal Studios and Warner Bros. tours (see pages 24 and 25); NBC Studios tour (call 818-840-4444); Frederick's of Hollywood Lingerie Museum (call 213-466-8506); Mann's Chinese Theatre with famous people's footprints in the forecourt; Downtown Hollywood's famous streets including Hollywood Blvd. and the Sunset Strip, and the intersection of Sunset and Vine.

Sunset

magazines and books

80 Willow Road
Menlo Park, CA 94025
(415) 321-3600

"As the Sunsets in the West" are your tour hostess' words as the sun sets to end the introductory video. The words have another meaning here, since the company publishes seven regional editions of *Sunset* magazine for 13 Western states. Each edition focuses on that region's needs and interests, particularly in travel and gardening. A tour allows you to look into Sunset's test kitchen, peek into the editorial wing, and take an informative walk through their display gardens.

You feel quite welcome when the hostess invites you to sit in a "living room" in the light, airy main lobby. After the video, the hostess proudly points out some interesting interior architectural features of Sunset's adobe-style home, designed by renowned architect Cliff May and opened in 1952. Learn that the thick, 10-foot-tall front doors were hand carved, the lobby floor is desert tile, and the walls are adobe brick—each brick two feet in depth and weighing 30 pounds!

Walk along the tile floor to the test kitchen. Looking through the glass wall, you'll notice that the kitchen is actually four residential-size kitchens, each with its own sink, refrigerator, and gas or electric stove. Counter heights vary to resemble readers' homes. A food writer working two to three months ahead of publication (often up to a year, if seasonal fruit is required), develops, tests, and writes each recipe. A re-tester follows the recipe exactly, making sure it's foolproof. Don't be jealous of the employees who rate readers' recipes at luncheons. Throughout the day, employees watch for the chef's wooden flag—its different colors denote the availability of leftover food.

Outside, you'll pass the sand-floor volleyball court and porch swing before peeking into the editorial offices. Escorted by a horticulturist, stroll through the formal gardens created by landscape designer Thomas Church. This "Walk through the West" features native plants from Southern California to Washington, including Hawaii.

After the peaceful, perfectly manicured formal gardens, you visit the organic test garden used for editorial projects. Ever-changing, the beds may contain 30 varieties of gourmet lettuce, or hyacinth and tulips in the spring. Next time you browse through *Sunset*'s brightly colored garden photographs, you'll know where they were taken.

Cost: Free

Freebies: Sunset Publishing's book catalogs and recipe handout.

Video Shown: 8-minute video covers company history from 1898.

Reservations Needed: No, except for groups of 8 or more people.

Days and Hours: Mon-Fri 10:30 AM and 2:30 PM except holidays.

Plan to Stay: 1-1¼ hours, plus time in Sunset Shop.

Minimum Age: None, however, tour is geared towards adults. Children should be interested in horticulture.

Disabled Access: Yes

Group Requirements: Groups of 8 or more people should call 3 weeks ahead for reservations. Call further ahead for tours during the spring and around holidays. Groups over 25 people must call further in advance to arrange for extra guides.

Special Information: No professional photography allowed. Best times to tour are spring (when the gardens are in full bloom) and Christmas (when crafts projects are displayed in lobby).

Gift Shop: Sunset Shop features an eclectic mix of Sunset items, including T-shirts, mugs, and posters of early-edition *Sunset* magazine covers, entire collection of their books, and specialty garden items, all displayed on wooden armoires, tables, and bookshelves. Open Mon-Fri 9:30 AM-4:30 PM with shorter hours in summer. Closed holidays.

Directions: From San Francisco, take Hwy. 101 South to Willow Road/Menlo Park West exit. Follow Willow Road for approximately 1 mile. Sunset is on your left.

Nearby Attractions: Intel Museum (see page 18); Filoli Estate; Allied Arts Guild; Stanford Linear Accelerator Center tour (call 415-926-2204).

Universal Studios  *movies and television shows*

100 Universal City Plaza
Universal City, CA 91608
(818) 508-9600

Film pioneer Carl Laemmle established Universal in 1915 on a former chicken ranch. In the early days of silent pictures, visitors ate box lunches provided by the studio and sat in bleacher seats watching films being made. With the advent of "talking pictures," the tours stopped.

Largely as an effort to boost the lunchtime business at the Studio Commissary, Universal reopened its doors to the public in 1964. Millions of dollars and visitors later, Universal Studios Hollywood has developed its famed 420-acre studio lot into a first-rate theme park. Attractions provide a fun experience through which to learn the secrets of motion picture and television production.

The Starway Escalator that takes you to the tram provides a beautiful view of nearby mountains and valleys of Southern California. From here, you can enjoy the Backlot tour, which visits famous production sets of the world's largest movie studio. This tram ride takes you past renowned settings from *E.T.—The Extraterrestrial, Twins, City Slickers, Animal House,* and *Home Alone 2,* among many others. Television sets you'll recognize include those from "Murder, She Wrote," "Major Dad," "Leave It To Beaver," and "McHale's Navy." You'll find yourself shouting "I remember that," and you'll be surprised at the way the sets look in person.

After the tram ride you can stroll through parts of Universal's massive backlot, featuring over 500 outdoor sets and facades that depict locations as diverse as the Old West, New York City, and Europe. You might even see a well-known actor at work or watch the filming of a new movie.

Cost: Backlot tour price is included in the general admission charge for Universal Studios; 2-day tour passes are also available.
Freebies: No
Video Shown: Many attractions include videos.
Reservations Needed: No, except for groups of 20 or more people.

Days and Hours: Mon-Sun 9:00 AM-7:00 PM. Open later during peak days and in the summer. Box office opens 30 minutes prior to park opening. Closed Thanksgiving and Christmas.
Plan to Stay: All day at Universal Studios. The Backlot tour is 45 minutes.
Minimum Age: None
Disabled Access: Yes
Group Requirements: Groups of 20 or more people should call Group Sales (818-622-3771) 3-4 days in advance or write Universal Studios (at the above address) to reserve tickets. Groups receive 10% discount off box office prices.
Special Information: Sneakers or comfortable walking shoes are recommended. A booth at the studio offers free tickets to TV show productions, however some of these shows are not filmed at Universal. A new attraction is added each year.
Gift Shop: Many gift shops sell posters, videos, clothes, jewelry, mugs, and toys, with logos for Universal Studios, movies, TV shows, and actors.
Directions: Located between Hollywood and the San Fernando Valley just off the Hollywood (101) Frwy., Universal Studios is accessible from either the Universal Center Dr. or Lankershim Blvd. exits. Follow Universal Studios signs and marquee to park.
Nearby Attractions: In addition to the Backlot tour, other movie-related attractions include "Back To The Future—The Ride," "The Magic of Alfred Hitchcock," "The E. T. Adventure," "Backdraft," "Miami Vice Action Spectacular," and "The Wild, Wild, Wild West Stunt Show"; Paramount Pictures and Warner Bros. Studios tours (see pages 22 and 25); NBC Studios tour (call 818-840-4444).

Warner Bros. Studios ~ *movies and television shows*

4000 Warner Blvd.
Burbank, CA 91522
(818) 954-1744

By some estimates, entertainment is the United States' second-largest export and pumps $50 billion into the U.S. economy. Begun in 1918, when films were silent, today Warner Bros. displays the latest technological advances in filmmaking.

The Warner Bros. tour is different from any other studio tour in California. Here, you will take an exclusive VIP tour designed for small groups seriously interested in the inner workings of a major studio. Because this is a VIP tour, production schedules are checked every morning to ensure that visitors see the most action possible. You begin to feel like a part of the studio as your guide escorts your group through the various lots on an electric cart. Some of the biggest stars, both human and animated, have worked at Warner Bros.—since this is a busy studio, don't be surprised if you see one of them walk by!

The tour begins with a video showing highlights from some of the hundreds of movies Warner Bros. has made since *The Jazz Singer* in 1927. By electric cart, you will travel to a variety of television and movie sets. Since these sets change with each new film, you may find yourself under a blazing sun in the Sahara, in romantic moonlight on Paris' Left Bank, or on an exotic, narrow avenue in crowded old Shanghai, all while actual movies or TV shows are being filmed.

Your guide may take you to the extensive Prop Shop (which actually seems like a museum dedicated to movie props), the impressive Wardrobe Department (with one of the world's largest costume collections), or the Mill (where sets are created). You may explore exterior sets like Laramie Street, used in a number of Warner Bros. westerns, and French Street, where many scenes from *Casablanca* were filmed. Visit the sound stages and technical facilities used in many of Warner Bros. action and adventure films. At the Sound Facilities, you may catch a symphony orchestra recording a movie's theme song, actors redoing dialogue that couldn't be properly recorded on the set, or technicians creating sound effects.

Cost: $27 per person
Freebies: A VIP tour brochure.
Video Shown: 10-minute video showing the history of Warner Bros. films.
Reservations Needed: No, but recommended.
Days and Hours: Mon-Fri 9:00 AM-4:00 PM, every hour. Tour schedule can vary. During summer, some weekend and holiday tours can be specially arranged.
Plan to Stay: 2 hours for video and tour, plus time for gift shop.
Minimum Age: 10
Disabled Access: Yes
Group Requirements: Maximum standard group size is 12 people. Call in advance for reservations. $7 discount per person for groups larger than 20 people.
Special Information: Dress is casual, but wear comfortable walking shoes. Limited still-photography opportunities.
Gift Shop: Sells items with the famous Warner Bros. logo, such as T-shirts, pins, and hats. Open Mon-Fri 9:30 AM-4:00 PM. However, tour may not stop at gift shop.
Directions: From San Fernando Valley, take 101/134 Frwy. (Ventura Frwy.) East to Pass Ave exit. Turn right onto Pass Ave. Turn left onto Riverside Dr. Turn right onto Hollywood Way; the Hollywood Way gate (Gate 4) is 1 block down the street. From Hollywood, take 101 Frwy. (Hollywood Frwy.) North. Take the Barham Blvd. exit. Turn right onto Barham Blvd. and when you cross the Los Angeles River, Barham becomes Olive Ave. The studio is on your right. Stay on Olive Ave. as it curves around the studio until you reach Hollywood Way. Turn right into the studio.
Nearby Attractions: NBC Studios tour (call 818-840-4444); Paramount Pictures and Universal Studios tours (see pages 22 and 24).

Celestial Seasonings ⌒ *tea*

4600 Sleepytime Drive
Boulder, CO 80301-3292
(303) 581-1202

At the corner of Sleepytime Drive and Zinger Street, named after their two best-selling teas, lies the home of Celestial Seasonings. Since it began in 1969 with Mo's 36, president Mo Siegel's own herbal tea blend, Celestial Seasonings has become the largest U.S. herbal tea manufacturer—1 billion cups of tea per year. This tour offers much more than a standard factory floor tour. You also learn about the company's marketing approach and get your sinuses cleared while visiting the Peppermint Room.

After an enthusiastic introduction by your guide in the countrified welcoming area (be sure to hug the cuddly, 6-foot Sleepytime Bear), you may participate in a consumer test. Upstairs in the Art and Marketing departments, boards show colorful packaging designs and supermarket shelf displays. Photographs show the herb buyer and some exotic herb-growing locations.

The storage and production areas are a maze of palettes stacked with burlap bags of herbs. In a mini botany lesson, learn that black tea comes from the *camelia sinensis* tea plant and herbal "tea" from a variety of plants and herbs. To prevent its absorbing other flavors, the black tea is isolated in its own room in wooden crates stenciled with their country of origin. As the tour guide raises the metal door allowing you to enter the world of mint, you will be bombarded with intense peppermint and spearmint aromas.

On the main production floor, rock 'n' roll music plays over the roar of the machines. Here you'll see how tea gets into those little bags and brightly printed boxes. Package-forming machines simultaneously fold recycled cardboard and insert liners. Look for the big machines in the center of the production floor with wheels of porous, coffee-filter-like paper and a hopper on top. As the continuous stream of tea drops between the merging top and bottom paper layers, the paper is heat-sealed to form the bags. Groups of 24 bags are then inserted into boxes. When the open boxes roll past you on the conveyor belt, peek in at your freshly formed favorite flavors.

Cost: Free

Freebies: Samples of any or all flavors in the Tea Shop & Emporium.

Video Shown: No

Reservations Needed: No, except for groups of 8 or more people.

Days and Hours: Mon-Sat 10:00 AM-3:00 PM. Tours conducted hourly. Closed holidays.

Plan to Stay: 45 minutes for tour, plus time in Tea Shop & Emporium, Celestial Cafe, and herb garden.

Minimum Age: 5, for factory portion of tour.

Disabled Access: Yes

Group Requirements: Groups of 8 or more people call (303-581-1250) 1 month in advance for reservations. Groups larger than 15 will be divided into smaller groups.

Special Information: No photography. Flat shoes recommended. Breakfast and lunch available at the Celestial Cafe. Tours growing in popularity; may change some of the route and tour times. Call for latest developments.

Gift Shop: Tea Shop & Emporium sells all Celestial Seasonings teas and many logoed items, including mugs and magnets with tea-box designs, Sleepytime Teddy Bear T-shirts, hats, and aprons. Available items range from inexpensive sample tea packets to more expensive sweatshirts and tea pots. Bargain boxes of teas. Catalog available from 800-2000TEA. Open Mon-Fri 9:00 AM-6:00 PM, Sat 9:00 AM-5:00 PM. Closed holidays.

Directions: From Denver, take I-25 North to U.S. 36 West. Take Hwy. 157 (Foothills Pkwy.) North, which becomes Hwy. 119 heading northeast. Turn right onto Jay Rd. Turn left onto Spine Rd., then turn left onto Sleepytime Dr. From Boulder, travel northeast on Hwy. 119 (Longmont Diagonal) and follow directions above.

Nearby Attractions: Leanin' Tree Museum of Western Art; Boulder's attractions, including Pearl Street outdoor mall and hiking in the Rockies, are about 15 minutes away.

See color photos, page 156

Coors ⌣ *beer*
12th and Ford Street
Golden, CO 80401
(303) 277-BEER

The world's largest single-site brewery sits at the base of the Colorado Rockies between two "tabletop" mountains. In addition to the distinctly non-industrial setting, the brewery tour has other memorable sights. The brewhouse's observation area is bordered on two sides by 50 copper kettles, each the size of an above-ground swimming pool. Each kettle's sides are white ceramic tile, while the top is a dome of shiny copper with a long, narrow, copper neck.

The kettles have assigned roles in the brewing process, which your guide will gladly explain. Look across at the computer control room that monitors times, temperatures, and transfer of ingredients from one kettle to another, previously a manual process.

Founded in 1873, Coors claims it is the only brewer in the U.S. to do all its malting on-site. Before it can be used in the brewing process, the starch in barley must be converted into malt. The barley steeps in two-story-deep stainless steel tanks, which prepares it for growth. Next, the barley is spread out on long screens called "germination beds." After the seeds sprout, the barley is roasted for 14 hours in immense kilns, then aged and milled.

The stillness of the malting process contrasts with the speedy aluminum-can packaging machine area. Thousands of cans converge here every minute and then roll by in 6-, 12-, and 24-pack cartons.

Cost: Free
Freebies: 2 beer samples in hospitality lounge for visitors age 21 or older, with picture ID. Serves most Coors brands and assorted soft drinks.
Video Shown: Optional video, shows can and bottle manufacturing, filling, packaging, shipping, and distributing, shown in hospitality lounge.
Reservations Needed: No, except for groups of 20 or more people.
Days and Hours: Mon-Sat 10:00 AM-4:00 PM. Closed holidays. Call for schedule around holidays.

Plan to Stay: 30 minutes for brewery tour, plus time for beer sampling, gift shop, and shuttle-bus tour from Coors parking lot through Historic Golden. Coors grounds also have interesting features, including a 16-foot-high, 13-foot-wide original copper brew kettle used in the 1880s. (It stands at the main entrance.) A veterans memorial salutes the "Defenders of Freedom."
Minimum Age: Under 18 must be accompanied by adult.
Disabled Access: Yes, an alternative route is utilized.
Group Requirements: Groups of more than 20 people should make reservations 1 week in advance (call 303-277-2552). Groups can also rent Coors facilities for special events and meetings (call 303-277-3709).
Special Information: American sign language, foreign language, and disabled-access tours are available (call 303-277-2552). Tours also offered at Coors' Memphis, TN brewery (call 901-368-BEER).
Gift Shop: Sells wide range of logoed clothes and beer paraphernalia, including mugs, glasses, bar stools, and tap handles. Look for the popular blinking bottle-cap buttons and red Coors pins shaped like all 50 U.S. states. Open Mon-Sat 10:00 AM-5:00 PM. Closed holidays.
Directions: From Denver, take I-70 West to Hwy. 58 West to Golden. Exit at Washington Ave. and turn left on Washington, then left onto 13th St. to Ford St. for visitors parking. You're in Golden when you see the archway over the main street ("Howdy Folks! WELCOME TO GOLDEN—Where The West Lives!") and smell the malted barley. Parking-lot shuttle takes you on brief tour around Golden and then to brewery.
Nearby Attractions: Hakushika Sake tour (call 303-279-7253); Colorado Railroad Museum; Foothills Art Center; Buffalo Bill Memorial Museum and Grave; Rocky Mountain Quilt Museum.

Current ⟁ *cards, wrapping paper, and catalog*

1005 East Woodmen Road
Colorado Springs, CO 80920
(719) 594-4100

Current, much like a card shop in a catalog, started in 1950 as a way to sell Post-A-Notes to churches by mail. From those first Post-A-Note cards, Current's catalog line now includes greeting cards, stationery, gift wrap and gift items, calendars, cookbooks, and home accessories. The largest direct-mail marketer of value-priced quality "social expression" paper and gift products in the U.S., Current produces 55 percent of its 2,500 items in-house.

You'll get a thorough tour of Current's main complex, which houses the corporate offices, art department, manufacturing, and shipping and distribution center. With the Rocky Mountains in the background, you'll see keyers opening mail-order envelopes and speedily keying in as many as 30,000 orders per day. In cubicles, merchandisers plan and develop new products. Notice the interesting collections of knickknacks in the artists' cubicles. Boards in the technical design area show the steps that transform original artwork into final production samples, including original illustrations redrawn and color-separated on computer.

More movement takes place in the production area. Watch a massive roll of gift wrap, equivalent to 42,000 individual rolls, unwrap itself and roll around individual cardboard tubes. Wound with the brightly colored wrap, the tubes receive a shrink-wrapped outer layer before rolling down a conveyor belt into a shipping box. In the personalized area, workers hand-paint names on mugs, lunch boxes, Christmas ornaments, rulers, and refrigerator magnets. As you walk around the cavernous production floor, you can't help but notice the maze of conveyor belts and overhead pipes.

In the packing area, the case erector quickly folds flat cardboard into boxes, which move along the three 1-mile long "pick lines" that loop around this section of the warehouse. Workers called "pickers" reach into the bins of their three-tiered stations and pick merchandise to fill customer orders. Once orders are packed, they proceed to the center conveyor for quality control inspection. They pass under a huge royal-blue funnel from which padding fills the boxes for safe shipping.

Cost: Free

Freebies: Small gift bag and Current catalog.

Video Shown: No

Reservations Needed: Preferred for individuals, required for groups over 4 people.

Days and Hours: Tue 10:00 AM, Thur 10:00 AM and 2:00 PM. Closed holidays. Manufacturing and order fulfillment are busiest from September to February. During the slower summer season these areas may not be working, but the facilities can still be seen.

Plan to Stay: Usually 45 minutes-1 hour, plus time in catalog store.

Minimum Age: 18

Disabled Access: Yes

Group Requirements: Groups over 4 people should call 1 day in advance to make reservations. No minimum group size. Groups over 8 people will be split into smaller groups.

Special Information: No photography. You'll see more production during 10:00 AM tour. Wear comfortable shoes for the 2 to 3 miles of walking.

Catalog Store: Sells "social expression" products such as gifts, gift wrap and ribbon, and greeting and note cards. Carries all first-quality items featured in Current's most recent catalog at the lowest catalog prices. Bargain box includes discount cards. Open Mon-Sat 9:30 AM-5:00 PM. Closed holidays. Catalog available at (800) 525-7170. Factory outlet nearby.

Directions: From Denver, take I-25 South. Pass North Academy Blvd. Take Woodmen Rd. exit. Make left onto Woodmen Rd. Current is on your right.

Nearby Attractions: Van Briggle Art Pottery tour (see page 32); Simpich Doll factory tour (see page 29); Pike's Peak; Garden of the Gods; White House Ranch; The Broadmoor; Air Force Academy; Manitou Springs.

Simpich ⬳ *dolls*
2413 West Colorado Ave.
Colorado Springs, CO 80904
(719) 636-3272

Simpich Character Dolls

The Simpich Dolls story begins like a fairy-tale: Once upon a time (that's 1952), two newlyweds on a limited budget made dolls for family Christmas gifts. Today, although they no longer work out of their home, Bob and Jan Simpich still design all Simpich character dolls themselves. Bob specializes in elves, Santas, and historic figures, while Jan prefers cloud babies, angels, and children's storybook figures.

Ideas for character dolls come from everywhere—history, religion and even their children and grandchildren. Bob and Jan create the originals out of a clay-like, plastic "super-sculpy," which is oven-baked and sent to the casting department for an original, or "mother," mold. It may take several tries to create the perfect mother mold that captures all the facial feature details.

The "factory" thrives behind a Tudor facade and above its retail dollshop in the Old Colorado Historic District. The self-guided tour of this "Santa's workshop" takes you through the painting, sewing, and finishing steps. Astonishing attention to detail is required to paint the cheeks, mouths, eyes, and beards of these intricate miniature heads. Racks of dangling painted heads wait to join their bodies. Labeled racks, including Santas, angels, and elves, fill a long wall in the sewing room. Home workers handle many intermediary steps, such as base-wrapping each body's wire skeleton with raw cotton batting, piece-sewing petticoats and other outfit parts, and partial assembly.

The pieces magically come together in the sewing and finishing rooms. As many as a dozen outfit parts are hand-sewn onto each doll and some even get individually designed bouquets and hats to match their costumes. In the finishing room, dolls are attached to bases and receive final accessories. You will leave with affection for the dolls and an appreciation of the four-month process from mother mold to completed doll.

Cost: Free
Freebies: Catalog and newsletter
Video Shown: No. Future video or display on casting process planned.
Reservations Needed: No, except for guided group tour.
Days and Hours: Mon-Sat 10:00 AM-5:00 PM. You'll see the most production Mon-Fri. Closed holidays and Christmas through the week following New Year's.
Plan to Stay: 20-30 minutes for self-guided tour, plus time in retail store.
Minimum Age: None
Disabled Access: Doll shop, finishing, and originals are on street level. Workshop is upstairs.
Group Requirements: Groups larger than 20 people will be divided into smaller groups. Call 1 day in advance to arrange for a tour guide.
Special Information: Casting department is not on the tour.
Retail Store: Dollshop sells all Simpich character dolls, including storybook, historical, and Christmas dolls in creative displays. Look for the glass case showing a small selection of Simpich dolls created since 1952 and newspaper articles documenting the company's growth. Open Mon-Sat 10:00 AM-5:00 PM. Closed holidays and the week following New Year's. Simpich catalog and information about the David Simpich marionettes available at above number.
Directions: From Denver, take I-25 South to Garden of the Gods exit. Turn right onto Garden of the Gods Rd. Turn left onto 30th St. Turn left onto Colorado Ave. Simpich is on your right at 24th St.
Nearby Attractions: Old Colorado Historic District shops and restaurants; Van Briggle Art Pottery tour (see page 32); Current Catalog Company tour (see page 28); Patsy's Candies tour (call 719-633-6777); The Broadmoor; Cave of the Winds; Pike's Peak; Garden of the Gods.

Stephany's Chocolates *chocolates*

4969 Colorado Blvd.
Denver, CO 80216
(800) 888-1522

Colorado's high altitude and low humidity are important ingredients in Stephany's award-winning Colorado Almond Toffee. Of course, butter, almonds, and sugar help, too. On this candy-maker tour, you will be allured by sweet smells, warmed by the care given each chocolate, and tempted to stick your fingers into the chocolate or toffee bowls for tastes. This is truly chocolate-lovers' heaven.

A rich toffee smell permeates the toffee area. Melted with sugar and almonds, 68-pound blocks of butter swirl around a copper fire kettle. Two workers grab the fire kettle and pour the luscious mixture onto a cooling table. One worker uses a trowel to spread the toffee to the uniform thickness marked by metal strips at the edge of the table. The worker rolls a bladed metal rolling pin over the length and width of the table, cutting the slab into small sections. The toffee solidifies quickly. Workers then break it into individual bars, which await a chocolate shower and a chopped-almond bath.

You smell the peppermint long before you reach the Denver Mint room. Here, chocolate and mint layers are poured and spread onto a wooden former bowling lane, now a table, covered with brown paper. A worker pushes a bladed rolling pin to cut 1-inch squares. A roller on tracks moves beneath the brown paper to break the mints apart. From one end of the table, a worker pulls out the brown paper and the mints fall like dominoes onto a holding tray.

Walk between the two candy enrobing machines. Notice that each and every nut or filling is individually placed by hand on the conveyor belt. After each piece receives a chocolate coating, a thin chocolate stream flows through a stringer to put a design on top. Then it's off through the refrigerated tunnel for cooling. In the chilly packing room, workers grab different chocolates from the shelves and place them into brown paper-cup liners and gift boxes. A few strokes with the badger brush shines the chocolates and readies the gift box for shrink-wrapping or ribbons and holiday ornaments.

Cost: Free

Freebies: Taste of raspberry cream and small piece of toffee. Also, a paper hat to wear on the tour.

Video Shown: No

Reservations Needed: Yes. Families and individuals need to join scheduled group tours.

Days and Hours: Mon-Wed, Fri at 10:00 AM. Closed holidays.

Plan to Stay: 45 minutes for tour, plus time in retail store.

Minimum Age: 10, although exceptions made when with parents.

Disabled Access: Yes. While there are several steps at main entrance, the tour is on one level.

Group Requirements: Minimum group is 6 people. Groups larger than 15 people are split into smaller groups. Call at least 3 days in advance. Cannot handle large bus groups.

Special Information: Wear rubber-soled shoes—the floor can be slippery.

Retail Store: Sells various size boxes and gift baskets of Colorado Almond Toffee, Denver Mints, and assorted chocolates; also individual candies, discounted seconds, and solid chocolate sculptures such as dinosaurs, Ferraris, and teddy bears. Open Mon-Fri 9:00 AM-5:00 PM. Catalog available at above number. Other Stephany's retail stores throughout Colorado.

Directions: From Denver Airport, take I-70 West to Colorado Blvd. North to 48th St. Turn left and then immediate right. Stephany's Chocolates is on the left.

Nearby Attractions: U.S. Mint tour (see page 31); Mile High Stadium and other Denver attractions, including Denver Art Museum, Confluence Park, and Larimer Square, about 20 minutes away.

U.S. Mint ~ *coins*
320 West Colfax Avenue
Denver, CO 80204
(303) 844-3582

The Denver U.S. Mint produces over 5 billion coins per year. From a glass-enclosed observation area you'll see many of the production steps. The Mint starts with pre-shaped blanks for pennies and 8,000-pound metal coils for other coins. These coils first pass through presses that punch out blanks, which are slightly larger than the finished coins. Blanks are very hard, so they are softened in a 1400° annealing furnace.

In the coin press room, shiny blanks are converted into their familiar identities. The coin presses are sheltered in blue huts for noise abatement. While you watch blanks feeding into the stamp presses and hear the constant thump, the overhead video monitors will explain how the blanks are transformed. Some presses can produce over 700 coins per minute, with each die stamp lasting about one million strikes.

In the counting and bagging area, the enormity of the production process becomes clear. Overhead hoists dump gondolas filled with shimmering coins into vibrating hoppers on top of the counting machines. Workers standing in front of the machines use hand-held sewing machines to seal each bag once it is filled with the proper number of coins. As the tour ends you walk through richly decorated, marble-floored hallways to view a display of small half-pound gold bars—which doesn't seem so impressive after seeing approximately $250,000 in small change being processed.

Cost: Free
Freebies: Brochures in English and four foreign languages on the Mint's history and how coins are made.
Video Shown: Planned 5-minute pre-tour welcome video and videos throughout tour to provide close-ups of production process.
Reservations Needed: No
Days and Hours: Mon-Fri 8:00 AM-3:00 PM (last tour at 2:45 PM), except for 9:00 AM start on last Wed of month. Tours begin at 20-30 minute intervals on a first-come, first-served basis. During peak tour season (mid-May to mid-September) Mint uses a ticket system with assigned tour times. Tickets for each day's tours will be available starting at 7:45 AM. Call the above number for recorded information on current policy. Closed government holidays and 2 weeks at the end of June or beginning of July.
Plan to Stay: 40 minutes for exhibits, videos, and tour, plus time for numismatic sales room and tour waiting lines.
Minimum Age: Children under 14 must be accompanied by an adult.
Disabled Access: Yes
Group Requirements: Bus groups should make advance reservations by letter addressed to the Public Affairs Division. Summer bus tours should be booked by May.
Special Information: No photography. Expect lines to enter the building during summer, if the ticket procedure not used. Arrive early in the day during summer to ensure a tour or ticket. Tours available at Philadelphia U.S. Mint (see page 212).
Sales Room: Sells proof and commemorative sets, medals produced by U.S. Mint, lithographs, and other numismatic items. Has an authentic 1946 press for visitors to stamp their own Denver Mint Souvenir Medals. Store is on Delaware Street, just south of Colfax. Direct access Mon-Fri 8:00 AM-3:30 PM, except for 9:00 AM opening on last Wed of month. Closed government holidays. Catalog information at (303) 436-7400.
Directions: Located in downtown Denver between Delaware and Cherokee Sts. From I-25, take exit for downtown Denver and follow signs to Denver Mint. Look for the building with Gothic Renaissance architecture. Park on the street or in a downtown lot.
Nearby Attractions: Stephany's Chocolates tour (see page 30); Downtown Denver attractions, including the Denver Art Museum, Colorado History Museum, and State Capitol.

Van Briggle ⟨ pottery

600 South 21st Street
Colorado Springs, CO 80904
(719) 633-7729

The original designs for Van Briggle Art Pottery date back to 1899. Van Briggle's "Despondency," a vase with a figure of a despondent man molded around the rim, was first exhibited in Paris in 1900, where it won first place. A reproduction can be viewed in the Van Briggle masterpiece reproduction area. In addition to winning many awards, Artus Van Briggle reproduced a creamy, dull glaze known as "dead" matte glaze, which had been used by 14th-century Chinese. A tour of the company gives you a sense of the man and of his wife's continuation of his legacy, and an understanding of the process of making art pottery.

At the beginning of the guided portion of your tour, a potter demonstrates throwing pottery on an original early-1900s Van Briggle kick wheel. Next you move into the casting department, where rows of white chalky plaster molds are used to duplicate sculptured and wheel-thrown pieces. Liquid clay, or "slip," is poured into these molds. As the slip conforms to the exact design of the mold, the mold absorbs moisture from the slip. The longer the slip stays in the mold, the thicker the piece becomes. Excess slip is poured from the mold, leaving a hollow clay piece which is removed by hand.

The balance of your tour is self-guided, allowing you to spend as much time as you want viewing different processes and reviewing the explanatory displays, tape, and historical photographs. In the etching department, watch workers use damp sponges, carving instruments, and small turntables to smooth and refine the patterns of the unfired clay pieces called "greenware." Pottery stacked on shelves awaits one of the two kiln firings required to finish a piece. Between the first (or "bisque") firing and the second, glaze is applied to add color. In front of the kilns, displays show the piece's progression from a mold to the finished work.

Follow the curved shape of the building, past one of the largest wheel-thrown vases, to the historical photographs of Artus Van Briggle and early studios. Additional pho-

tographs show the transformation of the 1899 Colorado Midland Railroad roundhouse, where trains once chugged under the building's archways, to the current home of Van Briggle Art Pottery.

Cost: Free
Freebies: No
Video Shown: No
Reservations Needed: No, except for groups larger than 20 people.
Days and Hours: Mon-Sat 8:00 AM-4:30 PM (opens at 8:30 on Saturdays). Limited production on Saturday. Closed Thanksgiving, Christmas, and New Year's.
Plan to Stay: 20 minutes for partially self-guided tour, plus time in showroom.
Minimum Age: None
Disabled Access: Yes
Group Requirements: Groups larger than 20 people should call 1 day in advance.
Showroom: Sells art nouveau decorative pottery and lamps with pottery bases and shades decorated with genuine butterfly wings, grasses, and flowers. Also sells Van Briggle pottery collectors' books. Open Mon-Sat 8:00 AM-5:00 PM (8:30 AM on Saturdays) and Sun 1:00 PM-5:00 PM (summer only). Catalog available from 800-847-6341.
Directions: From Denver, take I-25 South to Exit 141. Follow U.S. 24 West to 21st St. You're there when you see the curved shape and large tan bricks of this former railroad roundhouse building, now on the National Registry of Historic Places. From Pueblo, take I-25 North to Exit 141. Follow the directions above.
Nearby Attractions: Current Catalog Company and Simpich Character Dolls tours (see pages 28 and 29); Patsy's Candies tour (call 719-633-6777); Pioneer's Museum; Ghost Town; The Broadmoor; Cave of the Winds; Pike's Peak; Garden of the Gods; Old Colorado City.

Mystic Color Lab   *film developing*

Mason's Island Road
Mystic, CT 06355-9987
(800) 367-6061

More than 90 percent of U.S. households own cameras, accounting for over 847 million rolls of film per year. Mystic Color Lab, started in 1969, first contracted out its film processing before moving into the mail-order end of the business. Mystic Color Lab processes three million rolls of film per year, making it the third largest mail-order film processor in the U.S.

Rolls of film wake up at 5:00 AM as they are delivered in big canvas pouches from the post office. Because of Mystic's guarantee to return customers' prints within 24 hours of receipt, a given day's workload depends on the weight of these canvas pouches. Each pouch holds up to 500 rolls of film. The number of rolls received each morning determines how long production will take that day. As you might expect, film developing is tied to the travel industry and holiday seasons, with peak demand coming immediately after Christmas and during the summer.

The rolls are manually sorted by film size, desired picture size, and requested finish (matte or glossy). A machine opens individual mailer bags, scans in customer information such as account number and address (a keypuncher assigns this information for new customers), and processes payment. Another machine cracks open and flattens the metal case surrounding each roll of film. The roll is assigned a computer number, which follows it through the entire process, and then is spliced together with 59 other rolls to form a large reel of film.

Once negatives are developed in the darkroom, new state-of-the-art Agfa machines develop up to 18,000 prints per hour. Each of the rapid ticking sounds represents an exposure being made onto paper. The machines record the number of photos printed per customer, for invoicing purposes. Another machine prints the customer order number and picture number on the back of the photo, to facilitate reprint ordering.

You will be amazed to see streams of photos emerge from the automatic printing room. Inspectors, with eyes that are not only trained but also fast, place stickers on flawed photos as they speed by. Negatives are mated with their prints, invoice, and reorder mailer, and manually stuffed into an envelope, which is hand-sorted by zip code and returned to the post office for a good night's rest before its journey back to the customer.

Cost: Free
Freebies: Gift packages, which may include a roll of film or a children's Frisbee.
Video Shown: No
Reservations Needed: Helpful but not necessary for individuals. Groups see below.
Days and Hours: Mon-Fri 11:00 AM-3:00 PM. Closed holidays.
Plan to Stay: 30 minutes
Minimum Age: None
Disabled Access: Yes
Group Requirements: Maximum group size is 30 people. Call at least 1 day in advance for reservations.
Special Information: Can arrange custom tours to your interest. No photography.
Factory Store: Sells film, cameras, photo albums, and frames. Offers drop-off and pick-up service. Open Mon-Fri 9:30 AM-5:30 PM. Closed holidays. Catalog available.
Directions: Take I-95 to Mystic Seaport exit. Turn right onto Rt. 27 and left onto Rt. 1. Turn right on Mason's Island Rd. and right onto Harry Austin Dr.
Nearby Attractions: Mystic Seaport; Mystic Aquarium; U.S.S. *Nautilus*; Mashantucket Pequot Indian Casino; Stonington Vineyards.

Bureau of Engraving and Printing   ⟶   *money*

14th and C Streets, S.W.
Washington, D.C. 20228
(202) 874-3188

After entering the mammoth gray federal building that houses this Bureau, you will be showered with a wealth of information in display cases and videos about our nation's paper currency and other items, such as U.S. postage stamps. From a narrow, glass-walled, overhead walkway, the guided tour allows you to watch several steps in paper currency production. In the first step, not on the tour, engravers hand-cut the currency design into soft steel. This engraving, used to create the master die and plate, begins the unique "intaglio" printing process that deters counterfeiting.

The printing itself is mesmerizing. Sheets of money, each with 32 bills in a four-by-eight pattern, rhythmically spin off the press at over 8,000 sheets per hour. Stacks of money, called "skids," are everywhere. You'll wonder how the workers appear to treat their jobs with such detached calmness. After inspections, overprinting of the serial number and Treasury seal, and cutting, the final product is a "brick" of 4,000 notes sent to the Federal Reserve Districts for local distribution.

Cost: Free

Freebies: Unfortunately, no! Brochures provide facts about paper currency and the money-making process.

Video Shown: A short video, "The Buck Starts Here," explains the history of paper currency in the U.S. While you wait in line, a 20-minute overhead video quiz challenges your trivia knowledge of currency and stamps.

Reservations Needed: No, except for groups larger than 40 people.

Days and Hours: Mon-Fri 9:00 AM-2:00 PM. Closed federal holidays and the week between Christmas and New Year's. This is a very popular tour, so expect a long line. During peak season (the weeks around Easter and from the Friday before Memorial Day to the Friday before Labor Day), tickets marked with a designated time must be obtained at the booth on Raoul Wallenberg Place (formerly 15th St.). Sometimes the day's

tickets are gone by 11:00 AM, so get yours early (ticket booth opens at 7:45 AM). Also can obtain tickets for tours later in same week. At other times of the year go to the 14th St. entrance for the tour. Your Congressman may be able to help you join guided tours that start at 8:00 AM, Mon-Fri.

Plan to Stay: 25 minutes, including displays, videos and tour, plus time for the visitors center gift shop, and waiting time.

Minimum Age: None

Disabled Access: Yes. Special recorded tours available for hearing- and sight-impaired visitors. Disabled groups should call in advance.

Group Requirements: Groups larger than 40 people should call above number 5 days in advance and follow voice-mail instructions. Maximum group size is 60 people.

Special Information: The Bureau plans to open tours of the stamp production area in late 1994, which is also the 100th year that the Bureau has been producing U.S. postage stamps. You will see the web-fed process of making U.S. postage stamps. Renovations to tour facility planned.

Gift Shop: Sells a variety of items relating to paper money, including uncut sheets of new money and shredded bags of old money. There are videos on engraving, stamp production, and the identification of mutilated currency. Open Mon-Fri 8:30 AM-3:30 PM. Located on the opposite side of the building from the tour entrance.

Directions: Located immediately southwest of the Washington Monument grounds and northwest of the Mall. Parking is nearly impossible to find in this area. Take the Metro (subway) blue line/orange line to the Smithsonian stop and walk out the Independence Ave. exit.

Nearby Attractions: Holocaust Memorial Museum; Washington Monument; Jefferson Memorial; Smithsonian Institute.

Correct Craft   *Ski Nautiques water-ski boats*

6100 South Orange Avenue
Orlando, FL 32809
(407) 855-4141

After seeing the water-ski extravaganza at nearby Sea World in Orlando, you may wonder how Ski Nautiques, their official ski towboats, are made. A tour of Ski Nautique manufacturer Correct Craft shows you in one hour the two-week process of building the premier inboard water-ski towboat. Correct Craft, started in 1925 by W. C. Meloon, is now a third-generation family business.

A short van ride from the corporate offices brings you to the open-air factory. Starting with a mold, fiberglass boats are actually built from the outside in. To create the shiny, colorful stripes of the hull's exterior, the interior surface of the mold is sprayed, in sections, with gelcoat. Then workers wearing floor-length aprons and safety gear use spray guns resembling oversized dentist-drill arms to apply the initial "skin coat" of fiberglass. A mixture of fiberglass and epoxy resin shoots out of the gun, looking like cotton candy when it hits the mold. Next, the entire inside of the mold is coated with cloth-like fiberglass sheets to form a solid unit. Workers smooth the hull's surface by rolling out air bubbles with a small hand-roller.

In another area, you can touch a smooth hull or deck just hoisted out of its mold. To reduce vibration and noise, ISODAMP CN (used by the Navy), is put on the inside of the hull's walls and the floor. In the engine area, a carousel-like crane swings around to lower an engine onto its frame. After the engine is bolted into place, workers install the dashboard, carpeting, interior trim, and seating. Each boat is tested under actual running conditions for at least 30 minutes in a nearby lake before decorative decals and graphics are applied. The water skiers who go on this tour will immediately want to take one of the boats out for a pull.

Cost: Free
Freebies: Choice of logoed water bottle, lapel pin, shade hanger, or car sunshade.

Video Shown: Upon request, a detailed 15-minute video on company history and production process is shown in the waiting area.
Reservations Needed: Preferred
Days and Hours: Mon-Fri 10:00 AM and 2:00 PM. Closed 2 weeks around Christmas and 2 weeks in July. Call for specific dates of shutdowns.
Plan to Stay: 1 hour
Minimum Age: Children must be able to wear safety glasses.
Disabled Access: Yes
Group Requirements: Groups should call ahead. Large groups will be split into groups of 10-15 people.
Special Information: You'll see more production on the morning tour. Even though it's an open-air facility, you'll get a strong resin smell in the area where the fiberglass is applied. Watch out for forklifts moving through the maze of hulls and decks in various stages of production. Look for a 1934 wooden replica of a Correct Craft displayed in the waiting area.
Gift Shop: Fashion Nautique carries a wide array of Correct Craft clothing and accessories. Open Mon-Fri 9:00 AM-4:00 PM.
Directions: From I-4 West, turn left onto Michigan, right onto Orange Ave. Company offices are on right. From I-4 East, take Kaley exit, head east, then turn right onto Orange.
Nearby Attractions: Magic of Disney Animation Studios and Nickelodeon Studios tours (see pages 39 and 40); Regal Marine (call 800-US-REGAL); Sea World; Wet 'n' Wild. In Sarasota, on Florida's west coast, Wellcraft boat manufacturer gives tours (call 813-753-7811).

E-One *fire trucks*

1601 S.W. 37th Ave.
Ocala, FL 34478
(904) 854-3524

Whether you've wanted to be a firefighter since childhood or you've just watched the trucks careen around street corners, this will give you a new appreciation for fire trucks. In less than 20 years, Emergency-One has become one of the world's leading manufacturers of emergency vehicles, building fire trucks, airport crash and fire rescue vehicles, and ambulances.

They make custom fire trucks according to the customer's specific requirements, such as community water sources and building heights. Two- to four-person teams work on the trucks in various stages of production. As you proceed through the 2½-mile factory floor tour, notice the different fire truck varieties (aerial and pumper), and the many cab, body, and chassis designs.

In the body plant, power shears resemble guillotines as they chop diamond-patterned aluminum sheets. Sparks fly as a face-shielded worker welds the body frame together. Once the body is structurally sound, sanders and grinders transform it into a bright, shiny fire engine. In the paint shop you'll notice that there is no one official "fire-engine red" color. E-One uses 1,200 different shades of fire-engine red! (Be sure to ask your tour guide why fire engines are red and for additional anecdotes.)

In the assembly area, two rows of black chassis patiently await their bodies and other accessories, such as pumps and electrical wiring. At the end of the line a crane lowers a freshly painted custom cab onto its chassis. Check the shipper ID label on the dashboard window or cab—some fire-fighting vehicles are headed for Small Town U.S.A., others to some exotic South Pacific island. In the final rigging area, you'll want to climb up into a fire-engine cab, sit in the thickly padded seats, touch the sophisticated control panel, and turn the steering wheel, pretending you're a firefighter.

Cost: Adults, $5; seniors, $3; children 12 and under, free. Firefighters and their immediate families, free.

Freebies: Logoed hat
Video Shown: No
Reservations Needed: No, except for groups larger than 10 people.
Days and Hours: Mon-Fri 8:00 AM-3:00 PM. Closed holidays and week between Christmas and New Year's.
Plan to Stay: 1¼-1½ hours, plus time for the gift shop.
Minimum Age: 6. Children under 6 receive a 20-minute abbreviated tour of the vehicle delivery center.
Disabled Access: Yes, call ahead.
Group Requirements: Group size limited to 25 people per tour guide. Call at least 1 week in advance.
Special Information: See more production before 2:00 PM. Since tours are handled on a drop-in basis, you may have to wait until the guide returns to begin your tour. If there are 5 or fewer people on the tour, you'll ride around in a golf cart. Otherwise you'll walk the tour route, so wear comfortable shoes. Occasionally, you may hear the sound of a fire-truck siren. Don't worry, it's just a test.
Gift Shop: The Fire Locker Shop sells T-shirts, clothes, hats, mugs, bags, and even ceramic Dalmatians, Christmas ornaments, and scale models of fire trucks, all with the E-One logo. Open Mon-Fri 8:00 AM-5:00 PM. Catalog available from (800) 788-3726 or (904) 237-1122.
Directions: From the Florida Tpke., take I-75 North to Exit 69 (the second Ocala exit). You can see the plant on the right from I-75. Go right at exit. Turn right at S.W. 33rd Ave., then right at S.W. 7th. Follow service road that cuts back to left. The Welcome Center is the first building on the left.
Nearby Attractions: Silver Springs Attractions; Wild Waters; Don Garlits' Drag Racing Museum.

Hoffman's ~ *chocolates*
5190 Lake Worth Road
Greenacres City, FL 33463
(407) 967-2213 / (800) 545-0094

You'll smell chocolate and roasting almonds long before you actually reach Hoffman's Chocolate Shoppe and Gardens. When you enter this Tudor-style chocolate haven, you'll be drawn to the windows overlooking the kitchen where these chocolates are created. Begun in 1975 when Paul Hoffman paid $1,400 at an auction for an existing candy shop, this family-operated company now makes 200,000 pounds of candy per year.

You may be lucky enough to watch peanut brittle or "turtles" being made. Two workers pour a 300° mixture of butter, sugar, and almonds from a copper kettle onto a marble slab. They spread the mixture with metal spatulas, cut it in half with a pizza cutter, and flip it over. Then, with a comb-like spatula, they spread out the edges to "stretch" the peanut brittle. For turtles, a worker squirts little blobs of caramel from a hand-held silver funnel onto small piles of pecans and chocolate.

Butter creams begin with a batch of Play-Doh-like butter cream being pushed through a die. A wire cuts bite-size pieces, which fall onto a wooden board for drying. The centers proceed on a wire belt to the "enrober," where an avalanche of chocolate coats them. As if waiting for luggage at an airport, a worker waits for the chocolates to emerge, then marks the type of center (for example, "R" for raspberry). After a long cooling tunnel, the chocolates are put into stock boxes ready for Hoffman's three retail stores.

Cost: Free
Freebies: Sample chocolates
Video Shown: 13-minute video in the gift shop covers chocolate-making and shows the company's gardens and Candyland railroad.
Reservations Needed: No, except for groups larger than 15 people.
Days and Hours: Mon-Fri 9:00 AM-4:00 PM. Closed Thanksgiving, Christmas, New Year's, and Easter.
Plan to Stay: 25 minutes for video and self-guided viewing through observation window, plus time for gardens, trains, and gift shop. The ¾-acre garden features 7,500 plants and trees, gazebo, goldfish pond, and waterfall. Look for the two tropical cocoa trees, warmed by heat lamps in the winter. During the holiday season, the garden comes alive with lights, animated displays, and Christmas carolers. An outdoor G-scale Candyland railroad has 500 feet of track with villages and houses, such as "coconut cream cottage."

Minimum Age: None
Disabled Access: Yes
Group Requirements: Groups larger than 15 people should call 1 week in advance to arrange a customized presentation. Groups over 40 people will be split into smaller groups. No maximum group size.
Special Information: Best time to see production is from August 15 to Easter. During summer, call ahead for production schedule; they may not be in production some days.
Retail Store: Chocolate Shoppe sells 60-70 varieties of chocolates in display cases, prepackaged gift baskets and mugs, and assorted and molded boxed chocolates. Open Mon-Sat 9:00 AM-6:00 PM; Sun 12:00 PM-6:00 PM. From the Saturday before Thanksgiving to December 31, open Mon-Sun until 10:00 PM. Closed Thanksgiving, Christmas, New Year's, and Easter. Catalog available from (800) 545-0094.
Directions: From I-95, exit at 6th Ave. South in Lake Worth. Head west approximately 2 miles to Military Trail. Turn right onto Military Trail. Turn left onto Lake Worth Rd. Hoffman's is down the road on the left. From Florida Tpke., take Exit 93 (Lake Worth Rd.). Turn left and travel about 3 miles. Hoffman's is on the right.
Nearby Attractions: Palm Beach Groves tour (see page 41); Lion Country Safari; Palm Beach Community College Museum of Art; Morikami Museum and Japanese Gardens; Lake Worth Beach.

Key West Hand Print Fabrics ⟋ *fabrics, sportswear, T-shirts*

Curry Warehouse
201 Simonton Street
Key West, FL 33040
(800) 866-0333

Key West Hand Print is located in a brick structure built circa 1880 as a tobacco holding warehouse. The building's historic charm is an appropriate setting for the art of making hand-print fabrics and clothing. The guided tour shows you how Key West Hand Print Fabrics designs and prints the bright colors, subtle hues, and subjects that invoke the relaxed atmosphere of the tropics.

Paint, screens, and fabric are the raw ingredients. The various colors are mixed from raw pigments. Original art and pattern designs are transferred onto the silk screens by a photographic-type process. Workers stretch and staple the screens around a wood frame. Fabric is then stretched out on long narrow tables, about the size of one lane of an Olympic-size swimming pool.

Two printers handle each framed screen. They meticulously place it on a section of the fabric, push a squeegee back and forth across the screen so the paint soaks through the pattern, then pick up the screen to place it on the next section of cloth. This rhythmic movement continues for the length of the fabric roll and is repeated for each different color paint. To keep the fresh pattern from smearing, the printers leapfrog every other section of the fabric with the screen and then return to the missed sections, thus requiring ten trips down the table for a pattern that requires five color screens. It's like seeing slow-motion animation as the image on the fabric, whether a colorful tropical floral pattern or a jungle scene, comes together.

After air-drying, the fabric bolt goes into gas curing ovens to lock the colors into the cloth. Workers then inspect each yard of fabric to insure pattern uniformity. In another part of the factory, watch through glass windows as seamstresses create shirts, dresses, and sportswear from the fabric. You'll appreciate the care involved in making these beautiful fabrics and clothing.

Cost: Free

Freebies: No

Video Shown: A continuously playing video in the factory store captures the production process highlights. Shows steps not always seen on the tour, such as creating the silk screen.

Reservations Needed: No, except for groups larger than 25 people who want a specially guided tour.

Days and Hours: Mon-Fri 10:30 AM; 11:30 AM; 2:00 PM; 3:30 PM. Closed holidays.

Plan to Stay: 30 minutes for the tour and video, plus time for the factory store.

Minimum Age: None. Children enjoy watching the silk-screening of T-shirts.

Disabled Access: Yes

Group Requirements: Groups larger than 25 people who want a specially guided tour should call 10 days in advance.

Special Information: Can give weekend tours upon special request, although not always in production.

Factory Store: Sells hand-screened fabrics and clothing, including men's shirts and ties, ladies' sportswear and dresses, giftware, and accessories. Outlet store sells discontinued, overruns, one-of-a-kind items at discounted prices. Open Mon-Sun 10:00 AM-6:00 PM. Open 365 days a year. Catalog available from above number.

Directions: From Rt. 1 South, turn right onto Duval St. Turn right onto Greene St. at Sloppy Joe's (a well-known landmark) and go 2 blocks. The factory and store occupy an entire block of Simonton St. in the heart of Old Town.

Nearby Attractions: Key West Aloe Factory tour (call 305-294-5592); Ernest Hemingway Home and Museum; The San Carlos Institute; Mel Fisher Maritime Society; Key West's beaches.

Magic of Disney Animation Studios ⟶ *animated features*

Disney-MGM Studios Theme Park
Walt Disney World
Lake Buena Vista, FL 32830-0040
(407) 824-4321

The Walt Disney Company, with its giant theme parks, real estate holdings, and Oscar-winning movies, started as an animation studio in 1923. Whether you wonder how cartoon characters (like the ubiquitous Mickey Mouse) are drawn or what the newest Disney animated film will be, the answer is found on the Magic of Disney Animation tour at the Disney-MGM Studios Theme Park. The lobby displays of Disney Studios' Oscars and of animation cels from current movies, the entertaining videos throughout the tour, and the busy animators all combine to bring this creative art to life.

Through glass walls surrounding the animation studio, you oversee the production of animated shorts and movies. Animators have assigned roles, much like the characters they draw. Some animators sketch the character only at its furthest points of movement, while other artists add the in-between positions, redraw the series to refine the detail, or create special effects and the "sets" on which the animated characters perform.

Although computers have crept into the process, the Disney family remains committed to the art of hand-drawn animation. The animators, whose cubicles display interesting collections of personal knickknacks and posters, sketch a few lines and flip back to other drawings on their light boards to see if the current etching follows sequence, often erasing and resketching. Other parts of the self-guided tour show you what's involved in transferring the paper drawings to plastic cels, in mixing the paints and inking the cels to create the colors needed for every character and scene, and in photographing the cels to create the illusion of life.

Cost: Included in admission charge to the Theme Park at Walt Disney World Resort.
Freebies: No
Video Shown: At the beginning of the tour you watch "Back To Neverland," featuring Robin Williams and Walter Cronkite, which explains animation basics and what it's like to be a cartoon character. During the self-

guided tour, overhead videos (also featuring Williams and Cronkite) explain each department. At the end of the tour a brief video shows what it's like to be an animator and presents clips from classic Disney animated films.
Reservations Needed: No
Days and Hours: Mon-Sun 8:00 AM-7:00 PM. Most activity during Mon-Fri 9:00 AM-5:00 PM. Hours change depending on Park hours and season. Open 365 days a year.
Plan to Stay: All day at Disney-MGM Studios Theme Park. The Magic of Disney Animation tour lasts 45 minutes, plus the wait time before the tour.
Minimum Age: None
Disabled Access: Yes
Group Requirements: Groups larger than 15 people can call (407-824-6750) in advance to order tickets to the Theme Park.
Special Information: Take this tour in the morning to avoid the longest lines and try to go during animators' standard business hours. Tour is available during weekends and holidays, and you'll sometimes see an animator hard at work on a project.
Gift Shop: The Animation Gallery (follow the Roger Rabbit footsteps at the end of the tour) sells figurines and cels of your favorite animation characters, along with books, videos, and other Disney cartoon character items. Open same hours as Theme Park.
Directions: From Orlando, take Exit 26 off I-4 and follow the signs. From Kissimmee, stay on U.S. 192 and enter at the main Disney entrance.
Nearby Attractions: All rides and shows at the Disney-MGM Studios Theme Park. The Special Effects and Production tour and the Backstage Studio tour teach you about moviemaking and television production, and provide glimpses of current Disney projects in production.

Nickelodeon Studios 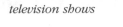 *television shows*

Universal Studios Florida
1000 Universal Studios Plaza
Orlando, FL 32819
(407) 363-8500

On this tour you'll learn about sophisticated television technology. You may also taste Gak or get slimed with edible green goo. Sound contradictory? It won't, once you visit the world's first television network designed especially for kids. Nickelodeon's production complex at the Universal Studios theme park is a combined state-of-the-art television studio and backstage tour facility. On days that shows are taped, your kids can join the live studio audience and even audition.

Look down through glass windows at the cobweb of lighting-grid hoists that hover over the ultra-modern sound stages. Each stage is big enough to park a 747 jet. See the sets for Nick shows and maybe even a taping. You'll appreciate the magic of television when you notice the difference between how sets for "Welcome Freshman" or "Clarissa Explains It All" look in person, compared to on television. Glass walls also expose the audio and video working control rooms. The 50 monitors in the video control room resemble a giant jigsaw puzzle, with the director picking the best shots for the program.

You'll also see the wardrobe room, the hair/make-up room, and the open-walled "kitchen" where they "cook" slime, Gak, and other recipes unique to Nick programs (there's actually a Gak-meister who concocts messes). After viewing the behind-the-scenes stuff, kids and their families can engage in some favorite Nick games and help create new ones. In the Nickelodeon Game Lab you feel like you're on a real game show, as you participate in "Double Dare" stunts, "Total Panic" street games, and "Outta Here" bleacher activities—with luck, you may get slimed! You leave with a new pop-culture vocabulary and an appreciation for what's involved in producing kids' TV.

Cost: Included in the general admission charge for Universal Studios Florida.
Freebies: No
Video Shown: Throughout the tour, brief videos describe the production process. The videos add to the tour, especially if shows are not in rehearsal during your visit. For example, one video shows how Nick creates sound effects for its "Ren & Stimpy" cartoons.

Reservations Needed: No
Days and Hours: Mon-Sun 9:00 AM-6:00 PM. Last tour 1 hour before Universal Studios closes. Open later during peak days and in summer. Open 365 days a year.
Plan to Stay: All day at Universal Studios. Nickelodeon tour is 40 minutes, plus any wait in line before the tour.
Minimum Age: None
Disabled Access: Yes
Group Requirements: For group ticket information call 407-363-8210.
Special Information: Tour lines are shorter in the morning. As you wait in line, kids will be entertained by Sega video games and the Green Slime Geyser, a 17-foot high green fountain made of pipes, tubes, and other odd-looking machines, that rumbles, hisses, and periodically erupts slime. It's a landmark at the Nick studio entrance. Call (407) 363-8500 2 weeks in advance to find out what shows will be in production, whether a live audience is needed, or whether kids will be picked as game-show contestants. Families need to be in the Nick line by 8:30 AM on game-show taping days when Nick is looking for contestants.
Gift Shop: Two carts on the corner sell Nick T-shirts and sweatshirts, Ren & Stimpy dolls, and other Nick paraphernalia.
Directions: Take I-4 to Exit 29 or Exit 30B. Follow the signs for Universal Studios.
Nearby Attractions: Over 40 rides, shows, and attractions at Universal Studios Florida, including the Production Tram tour, "Hitchcock's 3-D Theatre," "ET Adventure," "King Kong Kongfrontation" and "Back To The Future . . . The Ride."

Palm Beach Groves *citrus fruit*

7149 Lawrence Road
Lantana, FL 33462-4808
(407) 965-6699 / (800) 327-3208

More citrus fruit grows in Florida than almost anyplace else in the world. Unfortunately, none of the large commercial groves and processing plants offer public tours. However, at Palm Beach Groves you can tour a small working grove, visit the processing and packing area, wander through tropical gardens, and go home with plenty of fresh fruit and juice from their abundant retail store.

You'll see and learn about a wide variety of citrus fruits during your ride through the grove in a tractor-pulled covered cart. Each type of orange, such as navel, temple, and honeybell (a hybrid between grapefruit and tangerine), has a 4- to 15-week season. Surrounded by orange trees, enjoy the peaceful, fragrant journey—a real contrast to the noisy south Florida malls. After the tram ride, walk through the areas where the fruit is washed, sorted, and packed, the intermediate steps between the tree and your table.

On the washing line the oranges wiggle and roll around through a shallow water-bath and rinse, then travel to the sponge and hot-air dryers. Notice the simple, but effective, method of mechanically sorting the oranges by size. The grading machine resembles a pin-ball machine. The fruit rolls down a ramp, leaning against an opening which gradually increases in size. The smaller fruit fall through the narrowest opening at the beginning and the biggest, most expensive ones fit through the largest opening toward the end. The oranges drop into hammocks, which cushion their fall into wooden crates. You'll enjoy trying to guess which orange will fall into which size crate.

Cost: Free
Freebies: Tastes of refreshing citrus fruits; samples of juice and other foods the company makes.
Video Shown: No
Reservations Needed: No
Days and Hours: November through April only: Mon-Sun 10:00 AM-4:00 PM on the hour for tours of the orange grove. The tour of the

packing and processing area is self-guided. Call ahead to see when they will be packing and processing the fruit.
Plan to Stay: 20 minutes for tour, plus time for gift shop and gardens.
Minimum Age: None
Disabled Access: Yes, with a few steps up to tram.
Group Requirements: Can handle any size group. Suggest 1 day's advance notice.
Special Information: In addition to the tour and gift shop, a small nature walk through the grove's tropical gardens features colorful peacocks and unique sausage trees. Make sure you try some of the seasonal oranges, such as the juicy honeybells (available only in January).
Retail Store and Market: Sells a variety of tasty items, including a wide selection of fresh citrus fruit, Florida-made products such as jellies and gourmet sauces, and home-made fudge. Also sells native foliage and plants. For special deals, go to the Juice Fruit Room, where you pack your own fruit that's irregularly shaped, in assorted sizes, and slightly over-ripe. Visit or call their mail order department for shipments of fresh fruit and gift baskets. Open November through April only, Mon-Sun 9:00 AM-5:00 PM. Catalog available from 800 number above.
Directions: Take I-95 to Hypoluxo Rd. exit, then go west to Lawrence Rd. Turn left and go about ¼ mile. Look for signs on the right.
Nearby Attractions: Hoffman's Chocolate tour (see page 37); Loxahatchee Game Preserve; Lion Country Safari; and the beach.

Whetstone Chocolates ~ *chocolates*

2 Coke Road
St. Augustine, FL 32086
(904) 825-1700

The small ice-cream and candy shop founded by Henry and Esther Whetstone in 1967 is now a 45,000-square-foot chocolate candy factory that produces 500 chocolates per minute. This self-guided tour provides a view of the major steps in making Whetstone's specialty chocolates. Although much of the production is now automated, workers still make the animal and shell-shaped candies by depositing liquid chocolate into small molds.

In the molding room, the chocolate begins its 35-minute journey from liquid to finished product. Approximately 350 molds, each containing as many as 24 cavities, wait patiently to be filled with chocolate from a 10,000-pound melter. The melter, which resembles a double boiler, maintains the chocolate at a temperature of 115°. The chocolate is pumped from the melter into a tempering machine, which cools it to 85° by moving it through a series of cooling chambers, giving the chocolate a shiny appearance. The tempered chocolate is then sent through heated pipes to the depositors, which funnel it into the molds. If the product requires a filling (such as a nut, caramel, or truffle center), the molds are sent to another filling station. After filling, more chocolate is added to finish the piece.

As you walk along the factory's elevated, glass-enclosed walkway, signs above the machines give a brief description of the processes below. The chocolates move into the packing room, where stacks of boxes await filling. Here, the pieces are inspected for flaws (unacceptable chocolates are recycled) and then hand-packed. Some varieties of Whetstone chocolates are individually adorned with printed foil wrap by the wrapping machine before being packaged.

The specialty room is used to make novelty candies, often produced in smaller quantities. Depending on the demand, you might see chocolate pumped from a melter into dolphin, bunny, or alligator molds. Chocolate bars and truffles are also produced here, as well as Whetstone's famous chocolate shells. Look for the coating, or "enrober," machine where nuts, toffee crunch, or caramel squares on a conveyor pass through a chocolate stream. In this room, Whetstone also researches and tests new flavors and shapes of chocolate.

Cost: Free
Freebies: Shell-shaped chocolate sample
Video Shown: 12-minute video in theatre shows chocolate-making history and technology.
Reservations Needed: No, except for groups larger than 15 people.
Days and Hours: Mon-Sat 10:00 AM-3:00 PM. Limited production on Saturdays. Closed holidays and the week between Christmas and New Year's. Since factory production schedules frequently change, call ahead to find out when factory is in operation. Call (904) 825-1700, ext. 25, for 24-hour recorded message.
Plan to Stay: 30 minutes for self-guided tour and video, plus time for the Chocolate Shop.
Minimum Age: None
Disabled Access: Yes
Group Requirements: Groups larger than 15 people can request a special guided tour by calling a minimum of 2 weeks in advance. Maximum group size is 45 people.
Outlet Store: The Chocolate Shop sells entire selection of Whetstone chocolates and candies (such as Caramel Pecan Monkeys and Florida Sea Shells), souvenirs, and gift items. Catalog available at (800) 849-7933. Cocoa Cafe features a chocolate dessert bar and refreshment area with a West African theme. Open Mon-Sat 10:00 AM-5:30 PM.
Directions: From I-95, take SR 207 East to SR 312 East. Whetstone is located at the intersection of SR 312 and Coke Rd.
Nearby Attractions: St. Augustine's Historic District includes the Nation's Oldest House, Castillo de San Marco Spanish fort, Spanish Quarter Museum, Lighthouse Museum and Lighthouse; coastal beaches.

CNN ~ *television news*

One CNN Center
Atlanta, GA 30348-5366
(404) 827-2300

CNN Center's naturally-lit atrium greets you at the global headquarters of Turner Broadcasting System. Your tour begins as you ride one of the world's largest free-span escalators (eight stories) to an area exhibiting the TBS Collection. A CNN touch-screen computer gives you the opportunity to go behind the scenes at the network, test your knowledge with a news quiz, or see CNN's live coverage of the Gulf War. Other featured exhibits include MGM-RKO film memorabilia, such as the Oscar won by *Gone With The Wind.*

Through glass walls, you witness the reporting of news on the newsroom floor below. The tour guide explains how producers, writers, and anchors work together on the complex news-gathering process, which continues 24 hours a day, seven days a week. It takes two to three hours to put together a news segment, but late-breaking stories can be broadcast immediately. Everywhere you look on the news floor, dozens of neatly dressed people seem to be staring intently, either up at the news monitors, ahead at their computer screens, or down at their keyboards and notes while talking on phones. Satellites feed the news from around the world into hundreds of computer terminals.

News-personality-wannabees have the opportunity to play weatherperson. You may be surprised to discover that as you point out various weather conditions on the U.S. map, what you're actually pointing to is a blank blue wall. This is known as the blue chroma-key system. The map is superimposed onto the blank wall by the camera.

Cost: Adults, $6; seniors 65 and older, $4; children 12 and under, $3.50.
Freebies: CNN "Press Pass" button
Video Shown: Short video highlights the history of TBS.
Reservations Needed: No, but advance reservations are accepted.
Days and Hours: Mon-Sun 9:00 AM-5:00 PM every 15 minutes, except holidays. Tours often sell out 1 or 2 hours in advance. Each day's tour tickets go on sale at 8:30 AM.

Plan to Stay: 45 minutes including video and tour, plus time for The Turner Store.
Minimum Age: Not recommended for children under 6.
Disabled Access: 24-hour notice required for handicapped access.
Group Requirements: Groups of 35 or more people should call 2 months in advance for reservations and can receive discounts on tours Mon-Fri. VIP tours, available for groups of 10-12 people, last 1½ hours and require reservations.
Special Information: No flash photography. Many local television and radio stations give tours by reservation; contact yours for tour information.
Gift Shop: The Turner Store is on the retail level of CNN Plaza. Sells logoed merchandise from all Turner properties, including CNN, TBS, TNT, The Cartoon Network, and Sport South Network. Store also displays an original Academy Award for the movie *Ben Hur* and a replica of Dorothy's ruby slippers from *The Wizard of Oz.* Open Mon-Fri 9:30 AM-6:00 PM, Sat-Sun 9:30 AM-5:30 PM. Closed holidays. Call (404) 827-2100. CNN Plaza also has other restaurants and shops.
Directions: By train, take MARTA to Stop W1, "Omni, World Congress Center, Georgia Dome." By car, take I-75/85 North to Exit 96 (International Blvd.). Follow signs to the Georgia World Congress Center. From I-75/85 South, take Exit 99 (Williams St./Downtown). Again, follow signs to the Georgia World Congress Center. CNN Center is on the corner of Techwood Dr. and Marietta St. in downtown Atlanta, across the street from the Georgia World Congress Center and next door to the Omni.
Nearby Attractions: Downtown Atlanta's attractions including World of Coca-Cola (see page 45), World Congress Center, and Underground Atlanta.

Gulfstream Aerospace   ~   *corporate jets*

500 Gulfstream Road
Savannah, GA 31408
(912) 965-3407

In 1959, then part of Grumman Corporation, Gulfstream Aerospace built the Gulfstream I, the first small jet designed specifically for business use. Since it became an independent company in 1978, Gulfstream has become a major manufacturer of corporate-business and government jets. The highly acclaimed Gulfstream IV broke not only sales records but also two around-the-world flight records, piloted by then-president Allen Paulson. The company's newest jet under design, the Gulfstream V, has a flying range of 6,300 nautical miles, which allows it to fly nonstop from New York to Tokyo. Even if you're not a corporate executive or high-ranking government official, Gulfstream lets you tour this plant—as long as you make reservations and fax in the names of all accompanying visitors.

Gulfstream builds approximately 30 jets per year, so the production moves at a pace that is easy to grasp. It's like assembling a jigsaw puzzle: lots of small pieces come together to form the complete picture. After you walk through the Quality Hall of Fame (which recognizes employees who make substantial contributions), your guide takes you out to the main manufacturing area used for assembly, installation, and testing. Here you'll see the big pieces of the aircraft, such as the fuselage (the framework of the body that holds passengers and cargo), and how they come together. When all sections of the fuselage are joined together and spliced, the resulting unit is affectionately known as the "cigar" because that's what it looks like. It takes about four days to splice the cigar together, but workers spend 12 days stuffing the cigar with its electrical wiring.

After the electrical, hydraulic, air conditioning, controls, and avionics are installed in the cigar, an overhead crane picks it up and places it on top of a set of wings (wings are made by an outside vendor). This step is performed early in the morning, primarily for safety reasons but also because it is fairly spectacular and would draw a crowd of workers if done during the day shift. In the completion center hangar, workers install the custom interior of the aircraft, which can seat up to 20 passengers. Even if you don't know much about aerospace technology, you'll appreciate the company's care and enjoy a close-up look at what's involved in building the jets.

Cost: Free
Freebies: Photographs of all Gulfstream jets and product literature.
Video Shown: No
Reservations Needed: Yes. For security reasons, once you make reservations by phone you must fax in the names of all persons who will be taking tour. Send fax to (912) 965-3775.
Days and Hours: Tue and Thur 9:00 AM-2:30 PM. Closed holidays and week between Christmas and New Year's.
Plan to Stay: 45 minutes for tour, plus time for gift shop.
Minimum Age: 12
Disabled Access: Yes
Group Requirements: Groups larger than 12 people should call 1 week ahead. No maximum group size.
Special Information: No photography.
Gift Shop: Sells logoed items, such as cups, T-shirts, pins, and scale-model planes. Open Mon-Fri 11:00 AM-1:30 PM. Closed holidays.
Directions: Located near the Savannah International Airport. From I-95, exit at Hwy. 21. Take Hwy. 21 South and turn right onto Gulfstream Rd. Plant is on the left.
Nearby Attractions: Savannah's beaches and historic sites, including Cathedral of St. John the Baptist, Savannah Historical Museum, Ft. McAllister Historic Site, and River Street.

World of Coca-Cola ~ *soda*
55 Martin Luther King, Jr. Drive
Atlanta, GA 30303-3505
(404) 676-5151

A mammoth neon logo and colorful flags from 185 Coca-Cola-enjoying nations welcome you to this Coca-Cola museum. At this three-story, multimedia celebration of Coke, you will learn about the savvy marketing that catapulted what originally started as a headache remedy into the world's number-one soft drink. In fact, if all the Coca-Cola ever produced were placed in 6½-ounce bottles and laid end-to-end, the line would stretch to the moon and back 1,045 times. (This and other impressive facts are continuously flashed on an electronic billboard.)

View the "Bottling Fantasy," a whimsical sculpture that turns the bottling process into art. Then take a nostalgic journey through 100-plus years of history, past display cases showing early bottling equipment and advertisements, billboards, and trinkets featuring 1920s vaudeville stars. For more interactive time travel, step into giant Coca-Cola cans called "Take 5 Units" and touch the video screens inside. Five-year sips of world events and lifestyles from 1886 to the present are combined with Coca-Cola history. Sit in a replica 1930s soda fountain while a soda jerk flicks the fountain handle one way for fizz and the other way for flavored syrup.

The Coca-Cola Great Radio Hits kiosk blares with pop music stars singing Coke radio jingles from the 1960s to the present. (Even the Moody Blues sang "Things Go Better With Coke"!) Nearby you'll learn about Coke's journey into space and enjoy viewing Coke's classic television commercials.

In Club Coca-Cola, aerial liquid jets deliver your free soft drink. Once you place your cup under the fountain, an infrared sensor triggers overhead spotlights that illuminate your cup. The glass tubing and neon around you begin to pulsate and soda arches twenty feet from a hidden high-pressure nozzle, scoring a hole-in-one into your cup. After leaving this futuristic soda fountain, be sure to watch the international Coca-Cola commercials and sample exotic flavors (like Fanta Peach from Botswana).

Cost: Adults, $2.50; seniors 55+, $2; children 6-12, $1.50; under 6 (with adult), free.

Freebies: Large variety of Coca-Cola products, plus 18 exotic flavors not available in the U.S.

Video Shown: Optional 13-minute presentation called "Every Day of Your Life," shown in large-screen, high-definition cinema. Other videos shown throughout the exhibits. All videos close-captioned for the hearing impaired.

Reservations Needed: No. Recommended for groups over 25 people (otherwise wait in line).

Days and Hours: Mon-Sat 10:00 AM-9:30 PM; Sun 12:00 PM-6:00 PM. Last admission 1 hour before closing. Expect long waits during holiday periods and special Atlanta-area events. Closed some holidays.

Plan to Stay: 2-3 hours for displays, plus time for gift shop and waiting period.

Minimum Age: None

Disabled Access: Yes

Group Requirements: Groups larger than 25 people can make reservations in advance to receive a 50¢-per-person discount. Call (404) 676-6074 Mon-Fri 9:00 AM-5:00 PM.

Special Information: Foreign language overviews. Arrive earlier in day to avoid longest wait.

Retail Store: The Coca-Cola Trademart features logoed clothing, gifts, and collectibles. Open same hours as museum. Catalog available from (800) 872-6531.

Directions: From I-75/85 North, take Exit 91 (Central Ave. Exit). Follow Central Ave. as it goes over expressway to Martin Luther King, Jr. Dr. Museum is at intersection. From I-75/85 South, take Exit 93 (State Capitol/MLK Dr.). Go straight on Martin Luther King, Jr. Dr. 3 blocks to intersection with Central Ave.

Nearby Attractions: Downtown Atlanta's attractions, including CNN tour (see page 43); Underground Atlanta; State Capitol; Georgia World Congress Center; Atlanta Heritage Row (history museum).

See color photos, page 135

Maui Divers of Hawaii ～ *jewelry*

The Maui Divers Jewelry Design Center
1520 Liona Street
Honolulu, HI 96814
(808) 949-6729

MAUI DIVERS
OF HAWAII

Since its 1958 days of filling scuba tanks, Maui Divers has become the world's largest precious coral jewelry manufacturer. The company's founders experimented first with rare black coral from the deep waters off Lahaina, then with pink and gold coral, as jewelry material. The video and tour show how they make their unique jewelry, which combines coral with gold, diamonds, pearls, rubies, or other precious gems.

You watch most of the detailed process through glass walls next to the work stations. Designers make sketches for the goldsmiths, who then turn the sketches into three-dimensional jewelry carved from solid gold. Under the lost-wax casting process, wax patterns of the jewelry are assembled into what looks like a small tree. Plaster molds, formed around this tree, are heated in an oven to melt away the wax patterns, hence the name "lost wax." Depending on when you visit, workers may be pouring liquid 14-karat gold into flasks that contain these plaster molds. Once shattered, the molds reveal an exact gold replica of the wax tree. Gold rings and pendants are cut from the tree, then sanded and polished.

The tour guide leads you through other stations where skillful workers carefully cut, solder, polish, and inspect the gold pieces, or set precious gems into them. Before you go through the final setting area, notice the "Million Dollar Wall" in the coordinating area. Here, containers are filled with diamonds, pearls, emeralds, or sapphires waiting to be sorted and sized. Workers run diamonds through sieves to filter out different sizes or sort oversized South Sea pearls.

Notice the vacuum hoods behind many of the machines in the finishing areas. These help the company recover about $50,000 per month in gold removed during sanding and polishing. The hoods suck the gold mist into a central water bath, which is then refined. Observations like this will make your visit more than an educational shopping trip.

Cost: Free
Freebies: Catalog
Video Shown: 9-minute video on deep-sea coral mining and jewelry production. Available in major foreign languages.
Reservations Needed: No, except for groups larger than 50 people.
Days and Hours: Mon-Sun 8:30 AM-3:00 PM. No production Sat, Sun, and holidays, although tours show video and see manufacturing area and display cases on production steps.
Plan to Stay: 30 minutes for video and tour, plus time for gift stores.
Minimum Age: None
Disabled Access: Yes
Group Requirements: 2 hours' advance notice requested for groups larger than 50 people. No maximum group size. Light refreshments for groups on request.
Special Information: No photography.
Showroom: Sells the world's largest selection of original fine coral jewelry designs, including black and pink coral rings, earrings, cufflinks, and pendants in 14 kt. gold settings, pearl earrings and necklaces, and gold dolphins, pineapples, and whales. Open same hours as tour. Catalog available at (800) 253-6016. Second floor has stores that sell costume jewelry and gift items.
Directions: Free shuttle bus available from many hotels. Within walking distance of Ala Moana Shopping Center. If driving, take Alawai Blvd. Turn right onto Kalakaua Ave. Turn left at Beretania St., left at Keeaumoku St., and left at Liona St. Maui Divers is on your left.
Nearby Attractions: Dole Cannery Square (no cannery tour, but juice tasting, pineapple gardens, video, and "Pineapple Pete." Call 808-548-6600); Waikiki Beach; Ala Moana Shopping Center; Academy of Art Museum; Capitol Building; Iolani Palace.

See color photos, page 142

Mauna Loa *macadamia nuts and candy*

Macadamia Road
Hilo, HI 96720
(808) 966-8612

Few factory tours offer the sweet smells of roasting nuts and melting chocolate *and* a nature trail to walk off the free samples and goodies available at the gift store. Although almost all the macadamia nuts (or "mac nuts") sold worldwide are produced in Hawaii, the nut is actually native to Australia and wasn't grown in Hawaii until 1921. When C. Brewer, the oldest U.S. corporation west of the Rocky Mountains, began marketing mac nuts under the Mauna Loa brand in 1976, their popularity mushroomed. This tour of the world's largest mac nut company provides a look through gallery windows at mac nut processing and packaging and at chocolate production.

Fresh from the 40-foot high macadamia tree, the mac nut kernel sits inside a leathery, brown, extremely hard shell. After shelling (burnt shells and husks fuel the entire plant), the nuts enter the main processing factory. Electric eyes automatically grade and sort the nuts, allowing only light, uniformly colored nuts to continue along to the roaster. Blue-hatted workers stand over the conveyor belt, also searching the stream of nuts for rejects.

The nuts are oil-roasted in big square drums. When roasting ends, the drums spin like a washing machine to drain off the oil. Again the nuts are sorted and some are salted, candy glazed, or made into mac nut brittle. Watch the packaging machine shoot the nuts into fast-moving open metal tins, which then move down the line for vacuum sealing.

The smell of chocolate replaces the aroma of mac nuts in the candy factory, where chocolate waits in big steel melters. The nuts drop onto chocolate pads, then travel through the enrobing machine that covers them in a wave of chocolate. Rows of white-gloved, blue-smocked workers neatly hand-pack the chocolates in boxes after they leave the long cooling tunnels.

Cost: Free

Freebies: Samples of nuts and candy

Video Shown: 7-minute video on mac nut farming, harvesting, and production. Shows continuously on the lanai near the gift store. Available in Japanese.

Reservations Needed: No, except for groups larger than 50 people that want guided tour.

Days and Hours: Mon-Sun 8:30 AM-5:00 PM. Limited production 11:00 AM-noon. Guided tours about every 30-45 minutes starting at 9:30 AM. Self-guided tour with overhead signs all other times. Even though not in production on holidays and on weekends from late February through July, can still walk through tour route.

Plan to Stay: 30 minutes for tour, plus time for video, nature walk, and gift store.

Minimum Age: None

Disabled Access: Yes for candy factory, 20 stairs in the mac nut processing factory.

Group Requirements: Groups larger than 50 people should call 5 days ahead to schedule guided tour. No maximum group size.

Special Information: September-May is busiest production schedule. Call for production schedule during other months.

Gift Shop: Sells all Mauna Loa mac nuts and candies, mac nut ice cream, mac nut popcorn, and logoed items including shirts, hats, and key-chains. Open same hours as tour. Catalog available from (800) 832-9993.

Directions: Take Hwy. 11 to Macadamia Rd. Turn left if coming from Hilo and right if coming from Hawaii Volcanoes National Park. Drive through the Keaau Orchards to the yellow-and-blue Mauna Loa Macadamia Nut Visitor Center on the left.

Nearby Attractions: Royal Kona Coffee Mill and Museum (coffee-farm equipment, historic photos, free coffee, and coffee processing video; call 808-328-2511); Big Island Candies viewing windows (call 808-935-8890); Hawaii Volcanoes National Park.

Potlatch ⟶ *lumber, paperboard, and tissue*

805 Mill Road
Lewiston, ID 83501
(208) 799-1795

Potlatch

While most plants just have a lumber or paper mill, Potlatch's Lewiston complex is an integrated sawmill, pulp and paper mill, and tissue mill. The tour lets you see the transformation of wood into lumber, paperboard, and tissue products, all at one site. Wood waste from the lumber mill is used by the pulp mill and also converted into energy for the entire complex.

The sawmill produces approximately 120 million board feet of lumber annually, enough to build about 8,000 average-size homes. The mill's saws are computer-assisted and use laser scanners to determine the best combination of cuts. The buzz of saws and the clatter of chains and conveyors moving the logs through the process of debarking, squaring, edging, and trimming make the mill a very noisy place.

Large piles of wood chips and sawdust wait near the digesters that cook them into pulp. The digesters (not on the tour), break down the natural glue, called "lignin," that holds the wood fibers together. The pulp goes to the fiber line, which removes additional lignin and purifies and whitens the pulp. The seemingly endless paper machines produce the paperboard used in milk and juice cartons, paper cups, and other food packages. The extruders laminate polyethylene to the paperboard to make liquid-tight containers.

The tissue machines produce paper towels, toilet paper, napkins, and facial tissue (at a rate of one mile per minute), which is sold under private label by major supermarket chains. The mixture of pulp and water is formed on a screen which drains water from the sheet. Additional water is squeezed from the sheet before it circulates around a large, steam-heated "Yankee" dryer. A thin blade then peels the dried tissue sheet from the Yankee and the tissue sheet is wound onto what looks like the world's largest paper towel roll. For some products such as bathroom and facial tissue, parent rolls are combined to make multiple-ply tissues. It's no surprise that they manufacture enough single rolls of toilet paper each year to supply the equivalent of at least one roll to every American.

Your tour ends in the calm of the greenhouse. Row upon row of young pine, fir, and cedar seedlings, each under 1 foot tall, illustrate how much wood is used in the production of lumber and paper products. The greenhouse produces over 2.5 million seedlings per year for reforesting the company's lands.

Cost: Free

Freebies: Pencils and brochure about the company and its product manufacturing.

Video Shown: 12-minute video overviews the tour by kids interviewing their parents and grandparents who work at the plant.

Reservations Needed: Yes

Days and Hours: Mon, Wed, Fri 9:00 AM and 1:30 PM. Closed holidays and during weeklong maintenance shutdowns.

Plan to Stay: 3 hours

Minimum Age: 10, accompanied by adult.

Disabled Access: Stairs throughout tour route. Can do drive-through tour if prior arrangements are made.

Group Requirements: Groups larger than 15 people should make reservations at least 1 week in advance.

Special Information: No flash photography. Some areas are very noisy and can be hot during the summer. Wear comfortable shoes for at least 1 mile of walking. Certain areas may not be open due to construction.

Gift Shop: No

Directions: In Lewiston, follow Main St. East to Mill Rd. You will see signs for Potlatch. Enter complex at the main gate. Guard will direct you to parking.

Nearby Attractions: Twin City Foods tour (call 208-743-5568); Luna House Museum; Nez Perce National Historical Park; Appaloosa Horse Club Museum; Hell's Canyon Recreational Area.

Chicago Board of Trade ~ *grain and financial futures and options*
141 W. Jackson Blvd.
Chicago, IL 60604
(312) 435-3590

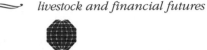

Chicago Mercantile Exchange ~ *livestock and financial futures*
30 South Wacker Drive
Chicago, IL 60606
(312) 930-8249

CHICAGO MERCANTILE EXCHANGE°

Major futures markets at work combine Super Bowl competitiveness, Rose Parade colors, and Mardi Gras pandemonium. Unless you're a serious investor or financial professional, the viewing experiences at the Chicago Mercantile Exchange (Merc) and the Chicago Board of Trade (CBOT) are basically the same. From large, glass-walled observation galleries above the trading floors, you'll see throngs of traders feverishly shouting, waving their arms, using hand signals, and throwing pieces of paper.

The trading floors themselves are bigger than the combined playing fields of the Chicago Cubs and White Sox. At the tops of the side and far walls are boards with numbers that show futures prices. Overhead monitors and computers around the trading floor don't block your view as they do at the New York Stock Exchange (see page 167).

In the various "pits," traders use a variation of the centuries-old auction system—appropriately called the "open outcry method"—for buying and selling. With all the skill of a third-base coach, they also use hand signals to cut through the noise. The sea of colors comes from ID badges and lightweight jackets worn by floor personnel. After examining the mechanics of floor trading, you'll be even more intrigued by the process.

Cost: Free
Freebies: Merc—"Merc At Work" brochure and postcard of the trading floor; CBOT—brochure entitled "From Beans To Bonds."
Video Shown: Merc—visitors gallery has interactive videos that explain the trading process and Merc history, (special version for children under 12). CBOT—included in presentation.
Reservations Needed: No, except for groups over 10 people at both the Merc and CBOT.
Days and Hours: Merc—Mon-Fri 7:15 AM-

3:15 PM (hours vary by trading floor), with presentations between 8:00 AM-3:15 PM. CBOT—Mon-Fri 9:00 AM-1:15 PM, with presentations and video at 9:15 AM, 10:00 AM, then every half-hour until 12:30 PM. Merc and CBOT closed national holidays.
Plan to Stay: 40 minutes to see action and hear presentation, plus time for videos and displays.
Minimum Age: No, except for groups.
Disabled Access: Yes
Group Requirements: Both Merc and CBOT require reservations at least 2 weeks in advance for groups of 10 or more, with customized presentations available. Minimum age for groups is 8th grade for Merc and 16 years old for CBOT.
Gift Shop: Merc and CBOT visitor galleries both have gift counters that sell logoed items, including pens, caps, T-shirts, mugs, golf tees, and teddy bears. Merc has a catalog available at (312) 930-8249.
Directions: Merc and CBOT are located within a few blocks of each other in downtown Chicago. The landmark art-deco CBOT building, topped by a 31-foot statue of Ceres (Roman goddess of grain and harvest), is at the intersection of LaSalle and Jackson. The Merc is at Wacker & Monroe, 1 block from the Sears Tower.
Nearby Attractions: Chicago Post Office tour (see page 57); *Chicago Tribune* tour (see page 50); Chicago Stock Exchange Visitors Gallery (call 312-663-2222); Chicago Board Option Exchange Observation Gallery (call 312-786-5600); Quaker Oats Lobby Exhibit (call 312-222-6887); and Chicago's many attractions, including the Sears Tower.

Chicago Tribune ⌒ *newspaper*

Freedom Center
777 West Chicago Avenue
Chicago, IL 60610
(312) 222-2116

Chicago Tribune

The *Tribune* printed 400 copies of its first issue on June 10, 1847. It now prints that many papers in less than one second on 10 massive offset presses that produce up to 70,000 newspapers per hour and more than one million every Sunday. This tour gives you a firsthand look at how the *Tribune* is printed, inserted, bundled, and delivered by one of the world's largest and most technologically advanced newspaper printing facilities.

If you look into the mammoth newsprint warehouse area, about the size of two football fields, the amount of paper used to print this popular newspaper seems overwhelming. Looking straight up you'll see newspaper rolls the size of small cows. The *Tribune* uses 5,000 one-ton paper rolls every week. Fortunately, the newsprint produced by the *Tribune*'s major supplier is made from 60 percent recycled paper. Train tracks run alongside the warehouse to accommodate the 18 railroad cars full of paper it receives five days per week.

From the observation deck you'll see the tower presses move so fast that the newspaper looks like a gray checkerboard blanket rolling up and down along the plates and cylindrical drums. Each press is a series of 10 units. The *Tribune* is proud of its increased color-printing capacity, which is the tenth unit. The color tower units contain four vertically stacked printing machines, one each for blue, red, yellow, and black ink. Each press also cuts and folds the paper into sections.

From an overhead walkway in the busy packaging area, you'll see how the advertising sections are automatically bundled for insertion into the completed paper. Machines stack the papers, bundle them together with a brown paper wrap stamped with an ink code, and send them on their way in bright yellow carts. The tour guide, taped messages from a speaker system, and display cases help explain the production process over the roar of the presses and packaging equipment.

Cost: Free

Freebies: Special section of famous *Tribune* front pages, ranging from the Bulls' first NBA title to Abraham Lincoln's election as president, and a button.

Video Shown: 9-minute video reviews the *Tribune*'s history and the process of writing, printing, and selling the newspaper.

Reservations Needed: Yes

Days and Hours: Mon-Fri 9:30 AM, 10:30 AM, 11:30 AM, 1:00 PM, 2:00 PM, and 3:00 PM.

Plan to Stay: 1 hour

Minimum Age: 10

Disabled Access: Yes. One attendant needed for each individual using a wheelchair.

Group Requirements: Maximum group size is 50 people, with 1 adult required for every 10 children. Make reservations as far ahead of tour date as possible.

Special Information: Cannot always predict whether presses will be running during your visit. Most local newspapers give tours; contact your local paper for tour information.

Gift Shop: Not in Freedom Center. Store in the Tribune Tower at 435 N. Michigan Ave. sells *Chicago Tribune* merchandise (books, clothing, etc.). Open Mon-Fri 8:00 AM-5:00 PM. Call (312) 222-3080.

Directions: From I-90/94, take the Ohio St. exit. Turn left onto Orleans St. and left onto Chicago Ave. The guard in the security booth will direct you to visitors' parking.

Nearby Attractions: Chicago Board of Trade and Chicago Mercantile Exchange tours (see page 49); U.S. Post Office tour (see page 57); *Chicago Sun Times* tour (call 312-321-3000). Chicago's attractions include Sears Tower, Shedd Aquarium, Adler Planetarium, Lincoln Park Zoo, and the Museum of Science and Industry.

Haeger Potteries *artwork pottery*

7 Maiden Lane
East Dundee, IL 60118
(708) 426-3033 / (708) 426-3441

Founded by David Haeger in 1871, Haeger Potteries today is directed by Alexandra Haeger Estes—the fourth generation of the Haeger family to be involved with the company. Started as a brickyard that helped rebuild Chicago after its Great Fire, Haeger Potteries is now one of the world's largest art pottery factories.

After an introductory talk about the production process, your tour begins downstairs in the "closet" where extra molds are stored. Watch the automatic casting machine fill plaster molds with "slip"—liquid clay. Notice the hanging "trolley" system that slowly travels its 4-mile course with dried pottery ("greenware") perched on wooden shelves that look like birdcage swings.

Workers carefully pry the molds open, then give each artwork a hand sponge bath before drying. The block-long kiln and the round kiln are located in the Great Kiln room, where you'll feel the heat. The brown brick kilns are 220° at the entrance and 2000° in the center. Workers neatly stack the greenware pieces—close to each other but not touching—onto railcars headed for a 12-hour trip through the kiln.

After its first kiln baking, the "bisque" is hand-dipped into a water-based glaze. The glaze, absorbed into the dry, porous bisque, dries almost immediately. A worker then takes the piece from a lazy-Susan table and showers it with glaze in a spray booth. These alternative glazing methods give the pottery its vibrant colors when it's fired again in the kiln.

Upstairs is a museum that includes a vase determined by the *Guinness Book of World Records* to be the world's largest. Made in 1976 by Haeger's master potter, it took three months and 650 pounds of clay to complete. Among other Haeger items, the display cases show discontinued ceramic animal designs, a Harley-Davidson hog bank, a sculptured bust of Carl Sandburg, and a large Hummel figure (Hummel and Haeger exchanged artworks on Haeger's 100th anniversary). The tour ends in the 25,000-square-foot, seven-show-room outlet store that sells most of Haeger's 800 different items.

Cost: Free
Freebies: No
Video Shown: No
Reservations Needed: No, except for groups of 10 people or more.
Days and Hours: Mon-Fri 10:00 AM and 1:00 PM. No tours during holidays, July tent sale, and two-week summer shutdown.
Plan to Stay: 30 minutes for tour, plus time for museum and outlet store.
Minimum Age: 4, when accompanied by responsible adult; 5 for school groups.
Disabled Access: No in factory; outlet store and museum are accessible.
Group Requirements: Groups of 10 people or more need to make reservations. Groups larger than 20 will be split into smaller groups. Call (708) 426-3033 for more information.
Special Information: Temperature can be very warm because of heat from kilns. Some tours begin with a demonstration by the master potter in the back of the outlet store.
Outlet Store: Sells pottery lamps, vases, bowls, sculptures, the best-selling "Rendezvous" (lovers back-to-back), dried and silk floral arrangements, housewares, factory seconds, overruns, and one-of-a-kind and discontinued pieces. Open Mon-Fri 10:00 AM-6:00 PM. Open Sat, Sun, and most holidays 10:00 AM-5:00 PM.
Directions: From Chicago, take I-90 West to Rt. 25 North. Turn left onto Rt. 72. Turn left onto Van Buren St. Haeger Potteries is on your right.
Nearby Attractions: Spring Hill Mall; Santa's Village Theme Park and Racing Rapids Action Park; Fox River Recreational Trail; The Milk Pail Village.

John Deere ~~ *harvesters*

Harvester Works
1100 13th Avenue
East Moline, IL 61244
(309) 765-4235

The harvester, or "combine" as it's called in the trade, is one of the machines that revolutionized farming and made possible America's tremendous production of grain and corn. For example, a combine with a claw-like "header" attachment can harvest as many as 12 corn rows at a time, picking and shelling the ears along the way. At John Deere, the world's largest producer of agricultural equipment, you'll see many steps involved in making its Maximizer combines.

The techniques definitely differ from those used by pioneer blacksmith John Deere when he started the company in 1837. Along with the hissing and thumping machines heard at most factories, you'll also see robots welding, lasers cutting steel, and electrical charges applying paint in this 260-acre, world-class manufacturing plant. Considering this factory's size, don't be surprised to see workers scurrying around on bicycles. Your John-Deere-retiree tour guide will hand you a piece of metal. Feel the smooth cut on it, made by the combination laser-and-punch machine. Sparks fly as hooded welders apply their skills on smaller pieces, while robotic arms on the automated welding systems seal frames and grain-tank cells.

Watch a combine body slowly emerge and then hover on its hoist after being dipped into an electrically charged bath of green paint. The electric charge bonds the paint to all exposed surfaces on the submerged combine, even in joints and hidden crevices. After seeing several subassembly stations, you'll watch combines come to life on the main production line. Assemblers carefully position completed parts, such as the power shaft, cab, feeder house, and engine. You will sense the pride of the worker who smoothly applies the finishing touch: the John Deere decal.

Cost: Free

Freebies: A colorful brochure with brief description and pictures of the manufacturing process.

Video Shown: No

Reservations Needed: Yes, ask for map.

Days and Hours: Mon-Fri 10:00 AM. Closed major holidays, the week between Christmas and New Year's, and two weeks in the summer (usually end of July and beginning of August).

Plan to Stay: 1½ hours

Minimum Age: 12

Disabled Access: Yes. You ride through the factory in a tram pulled by a small John Deere tractor.

Group Requirements: Make reservations at least 1 month in advance. Maximum size is 80 people.

Special Information: No video cameras allowed. For write-up on Waterloo, IA, tractor plant, see page 65. For information on other John Deere factory tours, call above number.

Gift Shop: Located at Anchor Do-It Center, a nearby John Deere dealer (1501 1st Avenue, Silvis, IL). Sells a variety of John Deere memorabilia, replica toys, and logoed clothing.

Directions: When you make reservations, ask the Visitor Services Department for a map, since many area highways have multiple designations—almost guaranteeing confusion. From Chicago, take I-88 to the exit for Hwy 5. Turn right at 70th St., which becomes 7th St. Turn right on 13th Ave. Look for the big green John Deere Maximizer combine parked on the factory's front lawn. From Iowa, take I-80 to I-74 East. Get off at the John Deere Rd. East exit. Turn left at 70th St. and follow the above directions.

Nearby Attractions: Deere & Co. Administration Center, with floor display of current and historical John Deere products, the Girard Mural (includes more than 2,000 farming-related historical items dated 1837 to 1918), and a video tour of this architecturally famous world headquarters at 10:30 AM and 1:30 PM. (Directions available from tour guide.) John Deere factories in Moline and Davenport, IA (call above number for information); John Deere Historic Site; Black Hawk Historic Site; Buffalo Bill Cody Homestead; Fejervary Park Zoo.

Kathryn Beich Inc.

Nestlé Fundraising Company
2501 Beich Road
Bloomington, IL 61701
(309) 829-1031

chocolates, caramels, and candies

Kathryn Beich Inc. is one of the oldest continuous candy-makers in the country, founded by Paul F. Beich in 1854. It's well-known for its flavorful Laffy Taffy caramels and its fund-raising candies such as Katydids and Golden Crumbles. With its 1984 purchase by Nestlé, it also became the home of Bit-O-Honey. This factory provides one of the few opportunities in the U.S.A. to watch a major candy manufacturer making its sweet stuff.

An elevated, glass-enclosed walkway leads you through a main part of the factory. On your left, retail products Bit-O-Honey and Laffy Taffy are made. A narrow stream of gooey mixture travels from the "kitchen" area through machines that cut, wrap, and box the bars and bite-size pieces.

It's a real treat to watch the Katydid and Golden Crumbles lines on your right. Katydids begin with thousands of pecans moving down the assembly line. Rich dollops of caramel plop on top, followed by a chocolate cascade. When candies emerge from the cooling tunnel, workers hand-pack the Katydids at such a fast rate that the workers avoided replacement by robots. The Golden Crumbles, crunchy puffs of freshly ground peanut butter, have been made almost the same way for over 70 years. See the light outer-shell mixture cooking in copper kettles, the grinding of nuts for the peanut-butter center, and the handwork that combines them into small "golden pillows."

Cost: Free
Freebies: Candy bar
Video Shown: 20-minute video entitled "The World In A Wrapper" gives the history of chocolate, the Nestlé company, and chocolate manufacturing. Shows parts of the process not seen on the tour, such as the making of chocolate bars.
Reservations Needed: Yes, but will take a limited number of walk-ins if the tour group has not reached its 60-person maximum.
Days and Hours: Mon-Fri 9:00 AM, 10:00 AM, 11:00 AM, 1:00 PM, 2:00 PM. Closed holidays,

last 2 weeks of June, and week between Christmas and New Year's.
Plan to Stay: 45 minutes for the tour and video, plus time for gift shop.
Minimum Age: Recommended (not mandatory) minimum age is 5.
Disabled Access: Limited; a flight of 20 stairs leads to the video room and glass walkway overlooking the factory floor.
Group Requirements: Advance notice required for large groups; longer notice necessary for the spring tours. Maximum group size is 60 people.
Special Information: No photography. Assembly lines for retail candies run almost year-round. Fund-raising candy lines are busiest September through February.
Gift Shop: Sells bags, boxes, and tins of all the candies made here, including Krunch Bars, Katydids, Golden Crumbles, Imps, Truffles, and chocolate-covered pretzels and cookies. Specials on factory seconds and overruns. Open Mon-Fri 9:30 AM-5:00 PM and Sat 9:30 AM-2:00 PM. Open during plant shutdown periods, but not holidays.
Directions: From the north, take I-55/I-74 to the Veteran's Pkwy. exit. Take first left off Veteran's Pkwy. at Cabintown Rd., make immediate right onto service road (Springfield Rd.) that parallels Veteran's Pkwy. Turn left onto Beich Rd. and follow the signs. (You will cross over I-55/I-74 just before turning left onto the plant service road.) From the south, either take I-74 and follow the directions above, or take I-55 to the Shirley exit (154) and turn right onto the Beich service road.
Special Information: Beer Nuts Factory Outlet (has video of how Beer Nuts are made, call 309-827-8580); Diamond-Star Motors tour (call 309-888-8203, currently on hold); Miller Park Zoo; McLean County Historical Society; Constitution Trail; Prairie Aviation Museum; ISU Planetarium.

McDonald's Museum   ~ *fast food*

400 N. Lee Street
Des Plaines, IL 60016
(708) 297-5022

If you're a hungry traveler, the sign advertising 15-cent hamburgers may beckon you like a desert mirage. But after parking next to a vintage Chevrolet Bel Air coupe and walking up to this retro-restaurant's counter you'll realize that what you've discovered is not the cheapest burger this side of 1960, but the McDonald's Museum.

This museum is an exact replica of the first McDonald's franchise on its original site. Four clean-cut mannequins tend the restaurant. The menu is simple: burgers, cheeseburgers, fries, shakes, milk, coffee, and soda. Nothing of the compact, clean operation is hidden from customers. Outside on the original sign, Speedee, a winking little logo-man with a hamburger head, advertises "speedee" service and 15-cent burgers.

It was restaurants like this that launched the McDonald's empire which now includes more than 14,000 restaurants in 69 countries. In 1955, milkshake multimixer salesman Ray Kroc, intrigued by an order for eight of his products, flew out to California to observe the restaurant operation of brothers Dick and Maurice McDonald. Kroc left California as the brothers' franchise agent. He had a vision that the future was fast food, and opened his first franchise on April 15, 1955.

The museum was built according to the original blueprints for that first franchise. In the customer service and food preparation areas, you'll see the authentic equipment used in those days. Hamburgers and cheeseburgers were grilled; fresh potatoes were sliced, blanched, and fried; while milkshakes were whipped up, of course, on multimixers. Although these techniques may not strike you as antiquated, the prices will. The most expensive item on the menu was a 20-cent milkshake. A museum host will happily answer any questions and serve up McDonald's trivia. Downstairs in the small exhibit area, you can examine memorabilia such as a training manual, old advertisements, and Ray Kroc's ledger book.

Cost: Free
Freebies: Postcard of museum
Video Shown: 3-minute video on McDonald's history.
Reservations Needed: No, except recommended for groups larger than 10 people.
Days and Hours: April and October Wed, Fri, and Sat 10:00 AM-4:00 PM; May and September Tues, Wed, Fri, and Sat 10:00 AM-4:00 PM; June-August Tue-Sat 10:00 AM-4:00 PM, Sun 1:00 PM-4:00 PM; Closed November-March.
Plan to Stay: 20 minutes
Minimum Age: None
Disabled Access: Restricted to upper floor
Group Requirements: Groups larger than 10 people call at least 15 days in advance. Maximum group size is 25 people inside at one time.
Special Information: The high-tech Ray Kroc Museum, located in McDonald's Oak Brook corporate headquarters, is open to visitors by invitation only. Multimedia presentations feature Ray Kroc from his beginnings as a salesman to his success as a business legend.
Gift Shop: No, but if you're hungry a real McDonald's is across the street.
Directions: Located in vicinity of O'Hare Airport. From the south, take I-294 (Tri-State Tollway) North to Dempster West exit. Go west on Dempster (U.S. 14) to Lee St. Turn right onto Lee and go about 2 blocks. Just before Lee converges with Rand Rd., you'll see the Museum on your left. From the north, take I-294 to Golf Rd. West exit. Go west on Golf Rd. (Rt. 58) to Mannheim Rd./River Rd. (U.S. 45). Turn left on U.S. 45 and proceed South. Just after you cross Rand Rd., you'll see the Museum on your right.
Nearby Attractions: Revell-Monogram tour (see page 56); Botanical Gardens; Des Plaines Historical Museum; Chicago's attractions, including the Sears Tower, are about 30 minutes away.

Motorola   ~ *electronics*

Museum of Electronics
1297 East Algonquin Road
Schaumburg, IL 60196
(708) 576-8620

After touring this museum, you will not doubt U.S. companies' technological prowess or their ability to innovate. From the mezzanine, look over the airy museum. Notice the 1930s Oldsmobile, the 1950s TV sets, the 35-foot radio antenna tower, and the robots used to manufacture circuit boards

After watching the introductory video, view the historical displays that frame the exhibition hall. Then explore the center section, devoted to electronics technology. Learn about Motorola's pioneering work in radio, including the first car radios, its famous WWII Handie-Talkie two-way portable radio, its television designs, and its early development of integrated circuits. Follow Motorola's advancement into microchips, its redirection toward such sophisticated commercial electronic products as pagers and portable phones, and its flexible manufacturing.

The museum is filled with hands-on exhibits. You can sit in the 1930s-style living room to hear broadcasts from the Golden Age of Radio. To learn about high-tech manufacturing and Motorola's "smart factories," use real industrial robots to make a souvenir plastic circuit board.

The exhibits appeal to all levels of knowledge. At the microelectronics display you can read about silicon wafer design, manufacturing, testing, and packaging; look at a full size cleanroom where computer chips are made; and play binary bingo. Another favorite multimedia exhibit lets you become a radio dispatcher to learn about the use and design of communication systems. You must respond to a simulated 911 emergency call by selecting the proper police, fire, and ambulance crews. You can also design the best radio communication system for cowboys or taxicab drivers. Interactive exhibits let you experience the electronics technology revolution, and learn about the intertwined evolution of Motorola and the electronics industry.

Cost: Free
Freebies: Postcard; plastic circuit board

Video Shown: "In One Lifetime" provides an overview of Motorola's history and the museum exhibits. Throughout the museum, videos explain the displays.
Reservations Needed: Yes, except family days.
Days and Hours: Mon-Fri 9:00 AM-4:30 PM. Will assign a tour guide if available; otherwise, audio-tape tours available in English and other languages. Closed holidays observed by Motorola and the first 2 weeks in January.
Plan to Stay: At least 1½ hours depending on your interests in the displays, selected videos, and interactive exhibits.
Minimum Age: None for families; 6th grade for school and camp groups.
Disabled Access: Yes
Group Requirements: Does not encourage traditional bus-group tours. Museum geared to educational groups from 6th grade up with maximum size of 60. Special tours and programs for students from schools and camps, grades 6 through 12. For information, call the Manager of Educational Programs, (708) 576-7813.
Special Information: Dress appropriately—the museum is in the corporate education complex. Displays change for new products and developments.
Gift Shop: No
Directions: From Chicago, take I-90 West to the Rt. 53 North (Rolling Meadows) exit. Remain in the right lane, and immediately exit at Rt. 53 to Rt. 62 (Algonquin Rd.). Follow the exit ramp around to the stoplight and turn right onto Algonquin Rd. Motorola Center is past the intersection of Algonquin and Meacham Rds. Enter the Motorola visitors entrance gate. Can also take I-290, exiting onto Rt. 53 as described above.
Nearby Attractions: Historic Long Grove; Cuneo Museum and Gardens; Chicago's attractions, including the Sears Tower, are approximately 25 miles away.

Revell-Monogram   ~ *plastic model kits*

8601 Waukegan Road
Morton Grove, IL 60053-2295
(708) 966-3500

This plant makes more tires than Goodyear, more cars than General Motors, and more airplanes than Boeing. The big difference is that here, the product is made of plastic and is a fraction of the original's size. This factory floor tour gives you a close-up view of the steps involved in designing, manufacturing, and packaging plastic scale-model kits.

In the design area, artists draw schematics for models. They then turn these drawings into wooden models. Notice the details on the wooden cars and airplanes—you might think you're in the studios of a skilled whittler instead of a plastic model factory.

Revell-Monogram boasts that its kits have a "healthy glow." The plastic in its models start as small pellets, no larger than confetti, which the tour guide lets you feel. In addition to using various colored pellets, the company adds clear polystyrene. This mixture of colored and clear pellets gives their models a special shine, as a clear-coat does for a real automobile.

The automatically blended combination of different-color pellets is piped to the injection molding machines that occupy most of the factory. These machines resemble cannons. At the heart of each one is a metal mold that forms all the model's pieces together on a frame. The machine electronically heats and injects the plastic pellets into the mold. The mold then closes. About 20 seconds and thousands of pounds of pressure later, the warm parts tumble out in one connected piece. Workers carefully inspect the parts as they drop out of the injection molding machine.

After the pieces cool, they are bagged almost as quickly as they are made. On the packaging lines, the plastic parts are assembled into finished kit boxes ready for shipping to stores. You leave amazed at how little time it takes to produce and package the plastic model pieces that you spend many happy hours snapping or gluing together.

Cost: Free
Freebies: Plastic model or toy depending on availability and tour group age.
Video Shown: No
Reservations Needed: Yes. Individuals and families need to join a scheduled group tour.
Days and Hours: Mon 12:00 PM-2:30 PM, Tue-Thur 9:00 AM-2:30 PM. Closed holidays.
Plan to Stay: 40 minutes
Minimum Age: 4. Children must be able to wear safety goggles, which company provides.
Disabled Access: Yes
Group Requirements: Tours should be scheduled at least 1 month ahead. Maximum group size is 25 people. Does not want standard bus-group tours; prefers children.
Special Information: No photography. This is a factory floor tour so, for safety reasons, children must be reminded not to touch anything. Tour guide is injection molding manager, so limited tour spaces available.
Gift Shop: No
Directions: Take I-294 North and exit at Dempster St. (Rt. 14 East). Stay on Dempster St. for about 3 miles. Turn right at Waukegan Rd. Revell-Monogram is on the left near traffic light.
Nearby Attractions: McDonald's Museum (see page 54); Chicago's attractions, including Sears Tower, are about 30 minutes away.

U.S. Post Office ✎ *mail*
433 West Van Buren Street
Chicago, IL 60607
(312) 765-3035

There are few things we take more for granted than the delivery of our mail. After this tour of the world's largest post office, you'll no longer wonder what happens to your letter between the time you drop it in the mail box and the time it's delivered. As you walk the two-city-block length of each floor, you'll discover the steps involved in processing the mail, from initial cancellation of postage stamps to final sorting by carrier route.

The post office uses all conceivable methods to sort the mail. Automation plays a big role, but some mail is still canceled and sorted by hand. The post office simultaneously uses different generations of technology, so the tour presents a living museum on the evolution of automation equipment. Rows of 12 operators sit in front of keyboards at the multiposition letter-sorting machines (MPLSMs), working relics from the 1970s. Single pieces of mail are picked up from the MPLSM's conveyor (one per second) by one of 12 vacuum arms and placed into position for an operator to read. The operator then keys in a few numbers from the zip code, sending the letter to the proper destination bin.

The newest equipment moves at lightning speed, using bar code technology and optical character readers (OCRs) to sort the mail. The OCR scans the address and sprays a bar code on the bottom of each letter at a rate of 11 pieces of mail per second. The OCR does a rough sort by region, with other machines reading the bar codes to sort by delivery route. The mail moves so quickly through these machines that it looks like one continuous stream of paper. The mail races through the bar code readers and parks itself in the proper zip code slot. Machines in other areas cancel the stamps, weed out oversized pieces, or handle bundles and large flat pieces. The next time you open your mail you'll appreciate what that envelope has been through.

Cost: Free
Freebies: No
Video Shown: No
Reservations Needed: Yes. Keep trying—it can sometimes be hard to get an answer at the above number.
Days and Hours: Mon-Fri 10:30 AM and 12:30 PM. Closed national holidays.
Plan to Stay: 1-2 hours depending on what areas you visit.
Minimum Age: 10
Disabled Access: Yes
Group Requirements: Can handle groups of up to 100 people with at least 1 week's advance notice. Lunch available in cafeteria with advance notice.
Special Information: Substantial walking involved. Guides can individualize tour to special interests, which is why tour length varies. Post office plans to move next door into new building in 1995. Tours will continue in new building, with even more of the newest automated mail-processing equipment. Many post offices like to give tours, so contact your local P.O. for information.
Gift Shop: Philatelic store in building lobby. Sells a large collection of commemorative stamps and books. Open Mon-Fri 8:00 AM-5:00 PM.
Directions: From I-90/94, take the exit for Congress Pkwy. East. Take the Canal St. exit. The post office sits directly in front of exit. From I-290, take the Canal St. exit.
Nearby Attractions: Chicago's attractions, including the Chicago Board of Trade and Chicago Mercantile Exchange tours (see page 49), *Chicago Tribune* tour (see page 50), Quaker Oats Lobby Exhibit (call 312-222-6887), Sears Tower, Shedd Aquarium, Adler Planetarium, Lincoln Park Zoo, Art Institute, and the Museum of Science and Industry.

Hillerich & Bradsby

Slugger Park
1525 Charlestown-New Albany Road
Jeffersonville, IN 47130-9327
(502) 585-5229

Louisville Slugger baseball bats and PowerBilt golf clubs

Louisville Slugger®

The Louisville Slugger bat, first created by Bud Hillerich in 1884, has been called "one of the greatest original American products ever made." With the ever-present smell of wood in the air, H&B uses three techniques to turn northern white ash billets into bats. A majority of the bats are made on automatic lathes which carve out the most popular models, about one every 15 seconds. Look for the card on the front of each machine that lists current and former players who use that particular model bat.

It takes about 40 seconds to make a bat on the tracer lathes. Workers use a metal pattern of the exact bat shape and guide the machine to trace this pattern, a similar process to copying a key at the hardware store. Only about 5 percent of their professional bats are hand turned, a technique used only for unusual models.

With sizzle and smoke, the famous oval trademark, model number of the bat, and the player's autograph are seared into the "flat of the grain." Behind the branders are large green cabinets holding over 8,500 professional baseball players' autograph brands. The bats go through more production steps, but it's the thrill of watching the branding that you'll remember the best.

Even more intricate craftsmanship is involved in making high-quality PowerBilt golf clubs, an H&B product since 1916. Overhead signs indicate that workers are grouped into teams with clearly defined functions. Iron Team C, for example, cuts shafts to the proper length, assembles iron heads finished by Teams A and B, applies the rubber grip, decals, and shaft bands, and tests the clubs. Woods Teams perform over 70 steps to produce the top persimmon woods in the U.S. You'll leave the tour having witnessed a true part of Americana.

Cost: Free
Freebies: 16-inch miniature wood bat
Video Shown: 10-minute video overviews the history of the company and the production of bats and clubs.

Reservations Needed: No, except for groups larger than 24 people.
Days and Hours: Mon-Fri 8:00 AM, 9:00 AM, 10:00 AM, 11:00 AM, 1:00 PM, 2:00 PM. Closed holidays, week between Christmas and New Year's, and 2 weeks starting at the end of June or the beginning of July. During the 2-week summer shut-down, the museum remains open.
Plan to Stay: 1 hour for video and tour, plus time for museum and souvenir counter. The museum area is filled with baseball artifacts, such as bats used by Babe Ruth and Ty Cobb.
Minimum Age: None, except for groups.
Disabled Access: Yes
Group Requirements: Reservations needed for groups over 24 people; maximum group size is 125. One-month advance notice suggested for summer tour. Call (502) 585-5229, ext. 227. Minimum age is 8 for larger groups.
Special Information: No photography in plant. Can be hot in the summer.
Gift Counter: Sells Louisville Slugger and PowerBilt logoed items, including T-shirts, hats, towels, gym bags, and pen bats. Catalog available. Gift counter and museum open Mon-Fri 8:00 AM-4:00 PM. Closed holidays.
Directions: From Indianapolis, take I-65 South to Exit 4 (Clarksville-New Albany exit). At end of exit ramp, turn left at traffic light. Turn right at the next light, and H&B is on your left, just over railroad tracks. From Louisville and south, follow I-65 North. Take Exit 4 (Clarksville-Cementville exit), through traffic light and over railroad tracks. H&B is on the left.
Nearby Attractions: The Kentucky Derby Museum, Churchill Downs, and other downtown Louisville attractions about 20 minutes away; Southern Indiana attractions include River Falls Mall, Buffalo Farm, Wave-Tek Water Park, and Howard Steamboat Museum.

Holiday Rambler

recreational vehicles

65906 State Road 19
Wakarusa, IN 46573
(219) 862-7211

 HOLIDAY RAMBLER

Holiday Rambler began in 1953 when Richard Klingler and his father built a boxy little 13-foot trailer in their garage. It might not have been much to look at, but it had all the necessary furnishings for a family getaway: bunk beds, dinette, hot plate, icebox, and heater. Klingler and the company he founded, however, were not satisfied with bare necessities. In the past 40 years Holiday Rambler has introduced both style and technological innovations, such as aerodynamic radius corners and aluminum frames, to the RV industry. Since 1986, HR has been a subsidiary of Harley-Davidson, Inc.

After your guide tells you about the company's history and the production of premium recreational vehicles, you'll visit the factory floor to watch the construction of motorized and towable RVs. Over 800 employees work on the RVs as they move down the line. HR is especially proud of its Alumaframe construction; all Holiday Ramblers are built with this durable, lightweight frame. Workers carefully interlock C-channel aluminum studs at the joints, then double-weld each joint together.

Further down the line you may see a fifth wheel or travel trailer being tipped over onto its back so workers can install the welded steel undercarriage, water pipes, and heating ducts. Once this step is completed, the unit is turned right side up and sent down the line to receive its sidewalls. Notice how employees fit two layers of insulation and a moisture barrier into the frame before adding aluminum skin on the outside and paneling on the inside. Equal care is taken with the roof. Workers busily rivet and seal the roof together and onto the frame to prevent leakage.

All cabinets and furnishings are made on the premises. Peek inside at the wooden cabinets and stylish upholstery—you'll be reminded more of a luxury hotel than wilderness. Enjoying the great outdoors does not have to include "roughing it"!

Cost: Free

Freebies: Holiday Rambler pen and product literature

Video Shown: Optional 15-minute video about HR production.

Reservations Needed: No, except for groups larger than 20 people.

Days and Hours: Mon-Fri, 10:00 AM and 1:30 PM; Winter months (November through April), 1:30 PM only. Closed holidays, week between Christmas and New Year's, and first 2 weeks in July.

Plan to Stay: 2 hours

Minimum Age: No small children

Disabled Access: Yes

Group Requirements: Groups over 20 people should call 1 month in advance; will be split into smaller groups.

Special Information: HR is currently revamping its tour; will announce changes by the end of 1994. Information available about the Holiday Rambler RV Club, the oldest company-sponsored enthusiast organization in the industry.

Gift Shop: No

Directions: From the west, take Tollroad 80/90 East to the first South Bend exit. Take Hwy. 20 Bypass East to SR 19 South, then go south 7 miles to Wakarusa. Holiday Rambler corporate headquarters is at the intersection of SR 19 and County Road 40. From the east, take Tollroad 80/90 West to Elkhart exit. Take SR 19 South. Proceed as above.

Nearby Attractions: Elkhart County is the RV manufacturing capital of the world. Local Convention & Visitors Bureau lists companies that give tours (call 800-262-8161). The RV/MH Heritage Foundation (call 219-293-2344) features museum, library, exhibition hall, and Hall of Fame dedicated to recreational vehicle and manufactured housing industries.

See color photos, page 151

Jayco ⟨⟩ *recreational vehicles*
58075 State Road 13 South
Middlebury, IN 46540
(219) 825-5861

Since the mid-1960s when Jayco founder Lloyd Bontrager first built his "pop-up camper" prototypes in a converted chicken coop, family members and friends have been an integral part of Jayco's success. Watching the construction of fifth-wheel travel trailers, the RVs that fit into the back of a pickup truck, you still sense that family feeling, even though Jayco is now one of the five largest RV manufacturers in the country.

Every Jayco trailer begins as a tubular steel frame built by a firm that specializes in RV frames. Workers lay an insulated tongue-in-groove plywood floor with fiberglass fabric on the bottom. Following these steps, you'll see the entire trailer flipped upside down, like an immense turtle on its back. Workers attach axles and wheels to the underbelly, and install a fresh-water tank. The unit is turned back over and placed on dollies that run down a track to various workstations in the plant.

Workers attach white-pine sidewalls, cover the wood with glue, and install the inside paneling. Next, they lay the carpeting and linoleum. Look up and you'll see the cabinet shops above the plant floor. Wood from the mill room is assembled into cabinets. Each line of Jayco trailers—the economy Eagle, the mid-range Jay, and the top-of-the-line Designer series—has its own cabinet shop. Carpenters slide the finished cabinets down a ramp to the production area.

Toward the end of the trailer's construction, workers attach the roof. They screw on tapered two-by-fours for the rafters, then stretch a rubber or aluminum roof over them. The area resounds with whining drills. The trailer's "skin" of .024-gauge aluminum (fiberglass on the Designer series) is drilled into position. Once the trailer's body is complete, appliances, drawer and cabinet fronts, and windows are added. Your tour's final highlight is the sewing department where the trailer's curtains and upholstery are designed and produced. About 80 percent of Jayco's 1,000 workers are Amish, and their dedica-

tion to quality will be evident to you as you travel through the factory.

Cost: Free

Freebies: Product brochures. A follow-up letter includes a Jayco keychain.

Video Shown: 15-minute video on the company's history and production methods.

Reservations Needed: No, except for groups larger than 15 people.

Days and Hours: Mon-Fri at 1:30 PM; from June-August there is also a 9:30 AM tour. Closed holidays, 4th of July week, and the week between Christmas and New Year's.

Plan to Stay: 1½ hours for video and tour, plus time for gift counter.

Minimum Age: None

Disabled Access: Yes

Group Requirements: Groups larger than 15 people need to make reservations 10 days in advance. Maximum group size is 50.

Special Information: No video cameras allowed. Upon request, tours available of the mini-motor home and fold-down production buildings.

Gift Shop: Customer service center sells logoed items including mugs, hats, and license plates. Open Mon-Fri 8:00 AM to 5:00 PM. Closed holidays.

Directions: From I-80/90 (Indiana Toll Road) take Exit 107 for SR 13 South to Middlebury. The Jayco complex is on the right, just south of the intersection with U.S. Rt. 20.

Nearby Attractions: Holiday Rambler factory tour (see page 59). Elkhart County is the RV manufacturing capital of the world. Local Convention & Visitors Bureau lists companies that give tours (call 800-262-8161). The RV/MH Heritage Foundation (call 219-293-2344) features museum, library, exhibition hall, and Hall of Fame dedicated to recreational vehicle and manufactured housing industries.

Perfection Bakeries ⟿ *bread*

350 Pearl Street
Fort Wayne, IN 46802
(219) 424-8245 / (800) 347-7373 (ext. 89)

Food manufacturing can be highly automated in big bakeries with lopsided ratios of workers-to-units-produced. Perfection Bakeries has about 30 production people who make 180,000 loaves per day of such well-known breads as Sunbeam, Aunt Millie's, Country Hearth, and Holsum. This tour shows you high-speed bread-making at its most mechanized, with techniques very different from those used in 1901, when the company started baking wafers.

As you would do at home, Perfection combines ingredients in the mixer, bakes dough in the oven, and slices the bread before eating. But there the comparison ends, since Perfection's process is much bigger, faster, and more intensely aromatic. About every 10 minutes a trough filled with 2,000 pounds of dough rises above a "J" divider and drops a mushy blob of dough into a machine, which separates it into softball-size portions. A "rounder" machine then rounds and flours the dough before it heads for the "proofer."

Once the dough comes out of the overhead proofer, it moves through a "sheeter," which rolls it flat to remove gases and air bubbles. Then it falls into pans on five-across trays. Even the ovens seem to be in constant motion, welcoming and expelling loaves after an 18-minute baking. The depanners magically lift the hot bread from the pans, using small suction cups. The baked loaves cool on a 1-mile overhead conveyor-belt cooling system. While cooling, the bread is inspected for foreign objects; occasionally you'll see a loaf almost mysteriously flying off the line.

Slicing and packaging must be done quickly, while the bread is still warm; otherwise, the slices lose moisture that keeps the loaf fresh. The tour guide explains some nuances of slicing bread, such as why pumpernickel is sliced thinnest. The bagging process is like inflating a balloon, except that the loaf follows the air into a bag which is then automatically tied. After watching state-of-the-art mass bread production, you'll never again take for granted that bread in your local supermarket.

Cost: Free
Freebies: Samples of warm bread with jam and margarine; gift bag of promotional items.
Video Shown: 11-minute video on bread production.
Reservations Needed: Yes. Individuals and families need to join scheduled group tours or form a group of at least 7 people.
Days and Hours: Mon and Wed 9:00 AM and 11:00 AM; Thurs. and Fri at 9:00 AM. Closed holidays.
Plan to Stay: 1½ hours for talk on nutrition and company history, video, tour, and sampling.
Minimum Age: 10
Disabled Access: Yes
Group Requirements: Minimum of 7 people, maximum of 35. Two weeks' advance notice required.
Special Information: No photography. Warm during summer tours.
Thrift Store: Located on the west side of building. Sells 2-day-old breads at discount. Open Mon-Fri 9:00 AM-5:30 PM and Sat 8:30 AM-4:00 PM. Closed holidays.
Directions: Atop the bakery is a unique billboard of bread slices continuously spilling from a bag of Sunbeam bread. More than 750 million slices have "fallen" from the yellow wrapper. Find this billboard and bakery from I-69 by taking Exit 102 (Hwy. 24 W) to the east. This becomes Jefferson Blvd. Follow Jefferson Blvd. into the city. Turn left (north) onto Ewing St., right onto Main St., and immediate left into the Light & Breuning parking lot.
Nearby Attractions: Seyfert's snack food tour (see page 63); Fort Wayne Newspapers tour (call 219-461-8274); Botanical Gardens.

Sechler's   ~   *pickles*

5686 State Route 1
St. Joe, IN 46785
(219) 337-5461

Like all pickles, Sechler's start out as cucumbers, salt, and water. Now in its third generation, Sechler's started making pickles in 1921. The first packing was done in the basement of Ralph Sechler's home, now the plant's office. A tour of Sechler's shows you how farm-fresh cucumbers become flavored sliced pickles.

Trucks full of fresh cucumbers are unloaded into grading machines. From a 20-foot elevation, the cucumbers fall into slats; smaller cukes roll through the first slats and larger ones fall through slats at the end. Once sorted into seven sizes, the cukes are weighed in 20-bushel (1,000 pounds) boxes. Farmers are paid by number of pounds of each size cucumber, with the midgets (known as "gherkins") being the most expensive.

In the tank yard, 120 wooden 8-foot-deep and 10-foot-wide pickle vats, in neat rows, hold up to 750 bushels (or 37,000 pounds) of pickles. The cucumbers are placed in these tanks by size, salt brine is added, and the tanks are closed with wooden lids. The pickles are usually in these tanks for at least 10 weeks, but may stay as long as 1½ years, depending on demand and the cycle relative to next year's crop.

In the processing room, pickles cook in 110°-140° water for 24 hours to remove some of the salt. Cutting machines slice, dice, chip, grind, and chop the inspected pickles into numerous shapes and sizes. The pickles marinate for 1 to 2 days in dill brine or 7 to 10 days in vinegar and spices for sweet flavoring. Smells of hot peppers, raisins, or oranges fill the air, depending on the variety in production.

Workers stand at a stainless steel table hand-packing whole pickles, spears, and large bottles. Machines pack relishes and hamburger chips. Jars move along the conveyor belt single-file, filling with pickles. The excess rolls into a cylinder below and recirculates back to the top of the machine. Down the line, the "juicer" overflows the jars with juice or brine. As the cap is put on, a burst of steam shoots across it, cooling, condensing, and pulling down the center of the lid to form a pressure seal. The "dud" detector measures the jar's resulting vacuum level by measuring the recess in the lid. If the center isn't pulled down enough, the machine rejects the jar and sends it back through the line.

Cost: Free

Freebies: Jar of pickles and samples of all varieties in the showroom.

Video Shown: No

Reservations Needed: No, except for groups over 6 people.

Days and Hours: Tours only April 1-October 31. Mon-Fri 9:00 AM-11:00 AM and 12:30 PM-3:00 PM, every half hour. Closed holidays.

Plan to Stay: 30 minutes for tour and tasting, plus time in showroom.

Minimum Age: None

Disabled Access: Yes

Group Requirements: Groups larger than 6 people should call 2 days in advance. No maximum group size.

Special Information: Wear comfortable shoes.

Showroom: Sells over 30 varieties of pickles, in pint to gallon containers. Offers specialty pickles such as orange-flavored spears, jalapeño slices, and candied raisin crispies. Display cases show company history. Open year-round Mon-Fri 8:30 AM-4:30 PM, Sat 8:30 AM-12:00 PM. Closed major holidays. Mail-order form available from (800) 332-5461.

Directions: From Fort Wayne, take I-69 North to Dupont exit. Turn right on Dupont. Go straight through traffic right onto SR 1 North. Sechler's is 20 miles ahead on your left. From Auburn, take SR 8 East to SR 1 South. Sechler's is on your right.

Nearby Attractions: Auburn Cord-Duesenberg Museum; Fort Wayne's attractions, including Perfection Bakeries tour (see page 61) and Seyfert's snack food tour (see page 63), are 20 miles away.

Seyfert's ⟾ *potato chips and pretzels*

1001 Paramount Road
Fort Wayne, IN 46808
(219) 483-9521

When Charles Seyfert left his Pennsylvania farm for the Chicago World's Fair, he expected to earn his fortune from selling pretzels. His dreams ended rather quickly, however, when only a handful of fairgoers dared to try his snacks. Discouraged, he headed back to Pennsylvania, stopping only in Fort Wayne for one more try. The pretzels failed again but his potato chips were a hit, especially in bars and saloons. Seyfert stayed in Fort Wayne and opened Seyfert Foods in 1934. Today, producing snack foods at a 3-acre plant not far from the original site, Seyfert's is owned by Bordens.

Charles Seyfert once said he would retire only when his business reached a production level of 500 pounds of chips a week. Today, the business produces 9,000 pounds of chips *an hour*. The pretzel machines, which finally began production in 1976, turn out almost 100,000 pretzels each hour.

You will first be greeted by your tour guide, usually Myrtle Young, who has been on several talk shows displaying her famous potato-chip collection. One of the industry's foremost experts on potato-chip lore, Myrtle shows you each step involved in making chips and pretzels. She encourages questions and loves to discuss her unique collection before you head out to watch production from a long, narrow, windowed corridor.

In the pretzel-making area, the newest part of the factory, watch the ingredients being mixed and sent through machines that twist and spurt out pretzels at unbelievable speeds. Pretzel sticks are produced at even faster speeds before joining their three-ring cousins for the next step. They all travel by conveyor belt to the cookers and salters, then head for packaging. Pretzels dive into bags and boxes and are stored in the warehouse before heading out to stores.

In the potato-chip section, spuds arrive in tractor-trailers driven onto hydraulic lifts. As the lifts tip the trucks back, hordes of potatoes come barreling down into the factory, where bins catch them and take them to the washers. Here you can first view the potatoes as they are scrubbed, inspected, and mechanically peeled and sliced. For every pound of potatoes that enters the washer and peelers, only about 3.2 ounces leave. The rest is discarded in the form of skin, starch, and water. Potato slivers travel by conveyor to the cookers and salters. After inspection for imperfections, the chips travel a maze of conveyor highways to be machine-packed for shipping.

Cost: Free
Freebies: Sample bags of pretzels and potato chips
Video Shown: No
Reservations Needed: Yes. Individuals and families will usually be combined into larger groups.
Days and Hours: Mon-Thur 9:00 AM-3:00 PM. Closed holidays.
Plan to Stay: 45 minutes
Minimum Age: None, although the 400 feet of walking may not be suitable for very young children.
Disabled Access: Yes, but let reservations operator know ahead of time so appropriate accommodations can be made.
Group Requirements: Maximum group size is 30 people. Groups should make reservations at least 1 day in advance. Groups with more than 15 people will be divided into smaller groups.
Special Information: No photography
Gift Shop: No
Directions: Take I-69 to Exit 111A. Seyfert's is straight ahead in the industrial park.
Nearby Attractions: Perfection Bakeries tour (see page 61); Fort Wayne Newspapers tour (call 219-461-8274); Botanical Gardens; Lincoln Museum; Franke Park Zoo; Diehm Museum; Cord-Duesenberg Museum 20 miles away in Auburn.

Ertl   ⟶   *farm toys, model kits, and die-cast vehicles*

Highways 136 and 20
Dyersville, IA 52040-0500
(319) 875-2000

Dyersville, Iowa, home to three of the premiere farm toy manufacturers, prides itself on being the "Farm Toy Capital Of The World." Started in 1945 by Fred Ertl, Sr. in his Dubuque, Iowa basement, Ertl is now the largest of the three and the only one to offer regular public tours. With thousands of die-cast trucks, cars, and tractors coming off its production lines daily, Ertl makes more tractors than any tractor manufacturer and more trucks than the largest truck manufacturer. This factory floor tour shows what's involved in making and packaging their large-scale die-cast replica toy tractors, as well as replica cars, trucks, banks, and plastic model kits.

The metal parts come from the nearby foundry building (not on the standard tour). It takes more steps than you imagine to produce a 1/16th-scale tractor, truck, or car from start to finish. Everywhere you look in the replica assembly and model packaging areas it seems that miniature parts are moving along conveyor belts. Quick hands apply decals, paint parts, assemble metal pieces, or box together plastic model parts, tires, and instructions.

Rows of injection molding machines, which look like giant cannons loaded with small plastic pellets instead of shells, pop out more plastic model pieces in one hour than you can assemble in ten years. Each machine injects heated plastic pellets into a custom-designed mold, which forms all the model parts. In the vacuum metalizing area, silver-colored lacquer is first oven-baked onto the plastic parts. Then thousands of these parts, filling the inside of a 5-foot-high hollow cylinder, are placed into a vacuum chamber. When vacuum conditions are reached, electricity shoots through aluminum filaments, which vaporize and cover the plastic parts to produce the shiny chrome appearance. If you've toured factories that make real tractors, cars, and, trucks, you'll appreciate Ertl's efforts to produce toys that are "Just Like The Real Thing, Only Smaller."

Cost: Free

Freebies: Ertl commemorative coin good for $1 discount at the nearby outlet store. Brochure includes information and statistics you see on the poster-size boards throughout tour.

Video Shown: No

Reservations Needed: Yes, however, can take a few walk-ins if space allows.

Days and Hours: May 1 through September 30 Mon-Fri 10:00 AM, 11:00 AM, 1:00 PM, 2:00 PM. October 1 through April 30 Mon-Fri 10:00 AM and 1:00 PM. Closed holidays.

Plan to Stay: 45 minutes

Minimum Age: None, but children should be at least 6 to appreciate the tour and not be afraid of the machines.

Disabled Access: Yes

Group Requirements: With 3 days' advance notice can handle groups up to 60 people, split into groups of 10 for each tour guide. Can give group tours at 9:00 AM. Minimum group size is 40.

Special Information: No photography. Be alert for forklift trucks.

Outlet Store: Located ¼-mile away on Hwy. 136. Sells entire Ertl line of die-cast replicas, plastic model kits, miniature action figures, and items produced at other Ertl plants worldwide. Many specials and some factory seconds are red-tagged. Mon-Fri 10:00 AM-5:00 PM, Sat 10:00 AM-2:00 PM. Longer hours in summer.

Directions: From Dubuque, take Hwy. 20 West. Take the exit for Hwy. 136 in Dyersville. Turn left onto Hwy. 136. The factory is on your left.

Nearby Attractions: *Field Of Dreams* movie site; National Farm Toy Museum; Basilica of St. Francis Xavier; Becker Wood Carver Museum; Heritage Trail; Dyer/Botsford Doll Museum.

John Deere ⌒ *tractors*

Waterloo Works
3500 East Donald Street
Waterloo, IA 50701
(319) 292-7801

Deere began building tractors in downtown Waterloo in 1918 and moved to the current location in 1981. Many of the old two-cylinder John Deere tractors, manufactured from 1918 to 1960 and affectionately known as "Johnny Poppers," are still in active use. The tour shows you manufacturing techniques that produce the tractors which *Fortune* magazine called one of the "100 Products That America Makes Best."

Your tour through the tractor assembly building (48 acres under one roof) will be guided by a company retiree. The air is filled with the scent of machine oil and the sound of presses and conveyors. A computer system guides the tractors through assembly, keeping tabs on parts drawn from some 40,000 storage bins. Tractor-building requires many subassembly steps, such as constructing the cab, before the main assembly lines put it all comes together. Hydraulic presses, with a force of nearly 2,000 tons, form pre-sized sheet steel blanks into tractor frames, fenders, and other parts. Lasers cut out plates for the sides of fuel tanks. Robotic welders join parts with impressive consistency and rainbows of sparks.

An overhead conveyor carries completed parts on a 2-mile journey through paint operations. An electrocoat process bonds the paint to each part's metal surface. A computer directs parts and subassemblies to the proper assembly area at the right time. Three chassis lines and three final assembly lines move at a measured pace. In about two hours the tractor frames become complete machines. Notice how carefully the cab and other parts are lowered from an overhead conveyor hoist and mounted on the tractor frame. Near the end of the line, after fluids are added, workers test wheel-less tractors for such features as engine start-up, speed and power levels, and brake and park/lock security.

Unlike row-crop tractors, the heavy-duty four-wheel-drive tractors are assembled using a modular, team concept. The production area is arranged in process groups called "cells," with each cell's operators responsible for assembling a related family of parts. Once a cell's work is completed and checked, the tractor moves to the next cell.

Cost: Free
Freebies: Brochure on tractor production
Video Shown: 18-minute video overviews the entire John Deere Waterloo Works.
Reservations Needed: Preferred for individuals and families. Required for groups larger than 10 people.
Days and Hours: Mon-Fri 9:00 AM and 1:00 PM. Closed major holidays and week between Christmas and New Year's. Summer shutdown last week of July through first week of August. (Call about more extended summer shut-down.)
Plan to Stay: 2½ hours
Minimum Age: 12
Disabled Access: Yes
Group Requirements: Groups larger than 20 people should make reservations 10 days in advance.
Special Information: No photography. For information on John Deere factory tours nationwide (including Davenport, Dubuque, Des Moines, and Ottumwa, IA), call Visitors' Services in Moline, IL (309-765-4235). East Moline, IL, plant produces harvesters (see page 52).
Gift Shop: No
Directions: From Dubuque, take Hwy. 20 West to Exit 68 North in Waterloo. Follow exit road north. Turn left onto Gilbertville Rd. Turn right onto North Elk Run Rd. Turn left onto East Donald St., which leads directly to John Deere's Waterloo Tractor Assembly Division. From Des Moines , take I-80 East to Hwy. 63 North. Exit at Hwy. 20 East to Waterloo Exit 68 North. Follow the directions above.
Nearby Attractions: Other John Deere tours in Waterloo available at the Foundry, Component, and Engine Works (call 319-292-7801 for information); Wonder Bread bakery tour (call 319-234-4447); Groute Museum of History and Science; Waterloo Recreation and Arts Center; George Wyth Memorial Park.

Krauss Furniture Shop ⟋ *furniture*

Highway 6
South Amana, IA 52334
(319) 622-3223

Krauss Furniture is located in Iowa's Amana Colonies, which were founded in 1855 by German immigrants escaping religious persecution. The Amana Colonies offer an abundance of family activities, including many craftswork tours. The moment you walk in the company's door, the smell of walnut, cherry, and oak woods mixed with the odor of fresh varnish will tell you this is a furniture factory. As you saunter between the yellow lines on this self-guided tour, you watch as many as 15 craftsmen building custom-made tables, chairs, cupboards, bedroom sets, rockers, and clock cabinets. Krauss completes up to 1,000 pieces per year.

You'll see many different types of woodworking tools, some brand new and other over eighty years old. In the cutting area, workers dry, machine, glue, and rough sand all the lumber used. A lathe-worker, covered head-to-toe with sawdust and chips, turns spindles to make the furniture legs. Planers reduce the boards to equal thickness. They are then glued into panels, rough sanded, and cut into rough lengths.

Krauss does not use an assembly line to make furniture. Each craftsman has his own workbench and builds the furniture, one piece at a time, from start to finish. The method is the old-time hand-fitted, dovetailed or mortise-and-tenon joinery. Woodworker hobbyists will covet these craftsmen's tools, time, and skill in building furniture. In the finishing area, the workers sand and finish the pieces. The finish, Krauss Furniture's pride, is painstakingly sprayed and brushed on (as many as seven coats) and sanded off until it is completely smooth. When the oil is finally applied for a hand-rubbed finish, workers show the same affection as parents brushing their children's hair.

Cost: Free
Freebies: Product brochure
Video Shown: No
Reservations Needed: No, except for bus tours

Days and Hours: Mon-Fri 7:00 AM-4:00 PM, Sat 8:00 AM-4:00 PM. Not always in full production on Saturday, so call ahead. Closed major holidays.
Plan to Stay: 15 minutes for the self-guided tour, plus time for the showroom.
Minimum Age: None
Disabled Access: Yes
Group Requirements: Bus tour groups can get guided tour. Call 1 week in advance.
Special Information: Sawdusty setting.
Showroom: Sells all Krauss wood pieces, from large furniture to smaller gift items. Most smaller wooden items, such as magazine racks and picture frames, are made by local retired people. Picture albums show custom-designed furniture that can be built to order. Open Mon-Sat 8:00 AM-5:00 PM, plus Sundays 1:00 PM-4:00 PM (May-December). Catalog available.
Directions: From I-80, take Exit 225 for Hwy. 151 North. At the T-intersection with Hwy. 6, go left 2 miles. Krauss Furniture is on the north side of Hwy. 6 (large clock outside building). From Hwy. 6 West, Krauss is about 1 mile east of South Amana.
Nearby Attractions: The Amana Colonies have a number of attractions and a worldwide tradition of craftsmanship. Some other local businesses which offer tours or work-area viewings include Amana Woolen Mill (call 319-622-3432), Schanz Furniture and Refinishing (call 319-622-3529), Amana Furniture and Clock Shop (call 319-622-3291), and Ehrle Brothers Winery (call 319-622-3241).

Winnebago ⟿ *motor homes*
1416 South 4th Street
Forest City, IA 50436
(515) 582-6936

Winnebago Industries was born in 1958 when a group of local businesses, worried about Iowa's depressed farm economy, persuaded Modernistic Industries of California to build a travel-trailer factory in Forest City. Local businessmen soon bought the factory and in 1960 named it Winnebago Industries after the county in which it is located. Since 1966, when the company started making motor homes, the name Winnebago has become synonymous with "motor home."

You will not doubt Winnebago's self-proclaimed position as an industry leader after touring the world's largest RV production plant. The company prides itself on its interlocking joint construction and on the fact that it produces almost everything in-house, including fabric covers for its seats and sofas. The 200-acre factory includes the chassis prep and main assembly areas (which you'll see on the tour), metal stamping division, plastics facility, sawmill and cabinet shop, and sewing and design department.

Your tour begins in the chassis prep building. Parts of the all-steel frame are stamped out on the "Dinosaur." Sparks fly as workers weld floor joints and storage compartment to the chassis. The completed RV (including windshield wipers and doors) will be set into this steel frame. The front end drops from a mezzanine onto the chassis and is aligned by laser beams.

The motor home production lines are in a building employees affectionately call "Big Bertha." From your vantage point on the catwalk, you'll see the developing motor homes creep down three 900-foot-long assembly lines at 21 inches per minute. First, workers install a heat-resistant plywood floor. Next they screw the Thermal-Panel sidewalls, made of Styrofoam embedded with an aluminum frame and steel supports, onto steel outriggers extending from the floor of the motor home. Further down the line, interior paneling is installed, along with the furniture and cabinets. Finally the entire unit receives a fiberglass skin and a one-piece, fiberglass-covered roof. As your tour guide explains, the completed motor home is rigorously inspected in the test chambers, where it "travels" through rainstorms and over potholes—while standing still.

Cost: Free

Freebies: Winnebago brochures

Video Shown: 20-minute video "Experiencing America: The Winnebago Lifestyle" follows a couple as they travel America in their Winnebago. When no factory tours, visitors can watch a 15-minute promotional video, "American Pride: The Winnebago Difference," featuring Don and Susan Meredith.

Reservations Needed: No, except for groups larger than 12 people.

Days and Hours: April through October Mon-Fri 9:00 AM and 1:00 PM; November through mid-December 1:00 PM. No tours mid-December through March 31. Closed holidays and 1 week in July.

Plan to Stay: 1½ hours for video and tour, plus time for Visitors Center motor-home exhibits and wall displays.

Minimum Age: No, but small children must be accompanied by an adult.

Disabled Access: Factory tour includes three staircases. The Visitors Center is accessible.

Group Requirements: Groups larger than 12 people should make reservations 2 weeks in advance.

Special Information: Photography allowed in Visitors Center, but not in plant.

Gift Shop: Winnebago-Itasca Travelers Club office sells logoed items including jackets, belt buckles, and caps. Open 8:30 AM-4:00 PM year-round. Closed holidays.

Directions: From I-35, exit at Hwy. 9 West. At the junction of Hwy. 9 and Hwy. 69, take Hwy. 69 South. Turn right on 4th St. in Forest City. The Visitors Center is on the right.

Nearby Attractions: Pammel RV Park; Pilot Knob State Park.

Binney & Smith

2000 Liquitex Lane
Winfield, KS 67156
(316) 221-4200

Crayola crayons, markers, and Liquitex paints

Even though there are now more than 100 Crayola crayon colors, the two most popular are still red and black, which are used to outline drawings. Binney & Smith (founded in 1903), makers of Crayola and Liquitex products, takes fun seriously, producing more than 2 billion crayons, 200 million markers, and 6 million Silly Putty eggs each year, as well as colored pencils, chalk, Crayola and Liquitex paints, and more.

The Winfield facility is the exclusive producer of Liquitex paints. In four separate expansions this plant grew to the size of nine football fields, yet still encompasses the original 1952 building and Crayola sign. In 1990, the U.S. Postal Service officially designated the streets leading to the plant as Crayola Drive and Liquitex Lane.

As at the Easton, Pennsylvania plant (see page 202), here you'll watch B&S assembling markers and learn the automatic and flat-bed molding processes of producing crayons. A special feature of this tour is watching Liquitex paints being made. Each year, B&S mixes 100,000 pounds of oil paints, 3½ million pounds of acrylics, and almost 8 million pounds of Crayola tempera and finger paints. As if making a milkshake, a high-speed industrial-size kitchen mixer in a 300-gallon silver tub blends the basic ingredients in artists' acrylic paints. The sharp blades break up pigment particles into a thick buttery texture; the finer the pigment particles, the brighter and more intense the color becomes. For oil paints, three-roll mills grind the ingredients until the paint is smooth.

Paint is pumped through a long pipe and funnels into the machine that fills 2-ounce plastic tubes. These tubes, sealed by ultrasound waves, are crimped at the ends like toothpaste tubes and stamped with a freshness date. Bottles and jars, made at the Winfield plant, are also filled with paint, packaged, and shipped all over the world. You leave agreeing that the name Crayola has become synonymous with childhood, creativity, and fun.

Cost: Free

Freebies: Box of 16 crayons; "Welcome to Crayola Product Tours" coloring book.

Video Shown: 18-minute "Crayola Products Wonderful World of Color" video narrated by two children, Peter and Amanda. Animated characters Tip and Professor Markeroni share a colorful adventure showing crayon, marker, and Liquitex production, and company history.

Reservations Needed: Yes. Tours can be filled 1 year in advance. Since maximum per tour is 30 people, individuals and families will find it easier to schedule summer tours and not compete with school groups.

Days and Hours: Mon-Thur 10:30 AM and 1:00 PM. May add Friday tours. Closed holidays. No tours November 15 through January 31.

Plan to Stay: 1½ hours for tour and video.

Minimum Age: 7

Disabled Access: Yes

Group Requirements: Maximum size is 30 people. No minimum group size. Due to tour's popularity, groups should call 1 year in advance.

Special Information: Photography allowed only in products display area. The Easton, PA factory currently gives tours (see page 202) but plans to replace tour with a Visitor Center in future.

Gift Area: Sells logoed items from T-shirts to lunch sacks and more.

Directions: From Wichita, take K-15 East to Hwy. 77, and go south through Winfield to 19th St. Turn left onto 19th St. Binney & Smith is located 1 mile ahead on the left. From Oklahoma City, take I-35 North to Wellington, KS. Take Hwy. 160 East into Winfield. Turn right at Main St., then left onto 19th St. Follow above directions.

Nearby Attractions: Crayola Park, across the street, offers a covered pavilion and restrooms; Henry's "Better Made" Candies tour (call 316-876-5423); September Walnut Valley Bluegrass Festival; Chaplain Nature Center; Cherokee Strip Landrush Museum in Arkansas City.

Country Critters   ⬯   *plush toys and puppets*

217 Neosho
Burlington, KS 66839
(316) 364-8623 / (800) 369-8623

In 1977, self-described "country boys" Lawrence "Bud" and Jim Strawder acquired some Korean puppets from a bankrupt company to sell in their S&S Bargain Center. The puppets sold well when the Strawders "wore" them and made them come alive. But they would sell better, the Strawders reasoned, if they were more realistic, better quality, and—most importantly—made in the U.S.A. Today, though Country Critters is one of the world's largest puppet manufacturers, you may still find Bud demonstrating a 3-week-old baby-pig puppet himself. You'll wonder if the pig really is alive as Bud remarks, "I've been feeding him out of a bottle, but I sure would like to teach him to drink out of a glass."

Acrylic fabric used in quality imitation-fur coats is specially designed for these life-like puppets: pink for tongues and insides of ears; shiny black for skunks, baby pigs, bears, puppies, and kittens; and striped for raccoon tails. In the cutting room, four people cut, clean, and sort parts fast enough to keep 75 people sewing. The 30-ton computer-controlled hydraulic press cuts up to six rolls of material at once. Many machines have been adapted or converted from other uses. Look for the "cleaner" Bud made from an old piano, plywood, microwave, furnace, and wire screen. It cleans the excess fuzz off freshly cut plush pieces.

Sewing machines designed for fur-coat production stitch a more secure seam. Parts are turned inside out and a converted button machine secures eyes into place. A converted farm grinder fluffs up the animal stuffing. Arriving in big bales, the polyester fibers are torn apart to make them softer, then pumped through a pipe to stuff each animal. Sewers hand- or machine-sew the final hole closed.

Then the animal puppets head for the beauty shop for brushing and grooming—even for haircuts and decoration with ribbons. To ensure that their new owners give the puppets continued loving care, workers include hang tags explaining what to feed the animals and how to care for them.

Puppets are then shipped from this 3,000-person town all over the U.S. and even overseas.

Cost: Free
Freebies: No
Video Shown: No
Reservations Needed: No, except for groups larger than 20 people.
Days and Hours: Mon-Fri 9:00 AM and 1:30 PM. Closed major holidays.
Plan to Stay: 1 hour, plus time for showroom; 2 hours for large groups, since Bud often leads these anecdote-filled tours himself.
Minimum Age: None
Disabled Access: Yes
Group Requirements: Groups larger than 20 people should make reservations 1 week in advance. Reserved tours of 10 or more people receive a 25% discount in the showroom. Maximum group size is 50.
Showroom: Sells all Country Critter plush toys and puppets. Look for the entire bear family, from 8" Tipsy to 66" Grandpa bear. The assortment ranges from the popular raccoon, pig, and skunk hand puppets to ride-on giant plush horses and cows. Also sells pocket-size stuffed toys called "Cottage Critters," made by home sewers. Bargain area sells imperfect or discounted items. Open Mon-Fri 8:00 AM-4:30 PM; from Thanksgiving to Christmas, usually open Sat 8:00 AM-4:30 PM. Catalog available from nearby "Made In Kansas" store (call 800-728-1332).
Directions: From Kansas City, take I-35 South to Beto Junction. Take U.S. 75 South to Burlington. Turn left onto Neosho St. Country Critters is on your right.
Nearby Attractions: Coffey County Museum

Reuter ⟋ *pipe organs*

612 New Hampshire
Lawrence, KS 66044
(913) 843-2622

Since 1917, Reuter Organ Company has produced custom-built organs for churches, universities, and homes. Housed in an 1880 building (originally a shirt factory), 50 organ-builders and craftsmen build 15-30 pipe organs per year. Construction of each organ takes two to four months, so you'll see several in progress during your tour.

Each organ's size depends on its site, so engineers draw individualized musical and architectural plans. Musical plans incorporate the setting's size and other aspects that affect acoustics. Architectural plans specify arrangement of the parts and perhaps a rendering of the finished and installed organ. Guided by these plans, workers cut raw lumber, metal for pipes, and electrical cables.

In the pipe department, workers cut sheets of zinc, copper, and spotted metal (a tin-lead alloy), to each pipe's size and shape. Metal is rolled on mandrels to form the pipes, then pipes are hand-soldered or tig-welded. Pipes range from 32 feet to pencil size, and actually look more like missiles than organ pipes. The number of pipes varies from four or five ranks, each with 61 pipes, to 100 ranks—over 6,000 pipes! Each rank is analogous to an orchestral instrument. "Voicers" allow these new organ pipes to "sing," then refine their sound so each rank's pipes sound identical.

As you tour this four-story factory building, notice the skilled woodworkers and metalsmiths meticulously hand-fashioning organ parts. As you smell the raw wood and hear the drills and saws, appreciate the more easy-going pace that handwork allows over machinery. The console mechanism of switches, keys, combination action, and expression controls is installed into the console case. The wood used for the console case, organist's bench, pedal keys, and decorative case matches the purchaser's decor.

Everything comes together in the assembly room. Here, workers assemble the wind chest and build the framework which supports the organ. They test the organ musically, in the same arrangement as its final destination. Now, you hear the full "color of sounds" that the different organ ranks create. Once you see the fully assembled organ, you'll understand why some larger organs require two 45-foot-long trucks to transport them to their final destinations.

Cost: Free
Freebies: Brochures and postcards
Video Shown: Short videos of manufacturing process
Reservations Needed: Preferred for individuals. Required for groups (see below).
Days and Hours: Mon-Fri 9:00 AM-2:00 PM, lunch break from 12:00 PM-1:00 PM. Closed holidays and Christmas through New Year's week.
Plan to Stay: 1 hour
Minimum Age: No, for families; age 12 for groups.
Disabled Access: Yes, via freight elevator.
Group Requirements: Groups larger than 15 people will be divided into smaller groups, each with its own guide. Call 2 weeks in advance for reservations. Maximum group is 40 people.
Special Information: Recommends walking shoes. Finished organs are not tested on every tour, because an organ is completed every 2 to 6 weeks. Call ahead to arrange your tour accordingly.
Gift Shop: No, but can purchase concert recital CDs from the office.
Directions: From Kansas City, take I-70 West to East Lawrence exit. Go left onto North Second St. Cross Kansas River, and turn left immediately after bridge onto 6th St. As you go around curve, factory is on the left. From Topeka, take I-70 East to East Lawrence exit, and follow above directions.
Nearby Attractions: Riverfront Mall; Kansas University; Haskell Indian Nations University; NCAA Hall of Fame. Kansas City's attractions, including the Hallmark Cards Visitors Center (see page 119), about 45 minutes away.

Coca-Cola Bottling ⌒ *soda*
Schmidt's Coca-Cola Museum
1201 North Dixie
Elizabethtown, KY 42702
(502) 737-4000

Visiting this bottling plant and adjoining Coca-Cola museum takes you from the present to the past, from the lightning speed and clamoring action of the bottling line to the serenity of the extensive memorabilia collection. Fountains grace the bottling plant entrance. A colorful stained-glass mural reflects in the lobby's Japanese carp (koi) pool. Hidden Coca-Cola bottle and can shapes create a fascinating optical illusion in this mural.

On a self-guided tour, watch the bottling and canning of Coca-Cola products from an observation gallery. The filler shoots 12 ounces of soda into 1,350 aluminum cans per minute. Once the cans depart this roaring carousel, they twirl single-file along the line so fast that the writing on their labels blurs. This noisy, busy freeway has no honking or bottlenecks. Instead, cans and bottles simply squeeze their way from four lanes to one.

After the fast-moving machines, you'll appreciate the museum's calm. The world's largest privately-owned collection of Coke memorabilia begins with a mirror dated 1885, one year older than Coca-Cola itself, and continues to 1969. Beautiful "Coca-Cola Girl" calendars identify the dates of the memorabilia below them. It's fun to see what was fashionable in the year you were born. You'll find yourself exclaiming, "I wore that!" or "That's my first car!"

The Schmidts, now in their third and fourth generations of bottling Coca-Cola in Kentucky, have filled the floors with old vending machines, coolers, and street signs. There's even a full-scale 1890s soda fountain. Painstaking care over the years has preserved the picturesque paper festoons which used to hang in soda fountains.

In tracing Coca-Cola's history, the museum also illustrates the history of advertising in the U.S. The recognizable red script Coca-Cola trademark appears on many familiar, everyday objects, such as beverage glasses, playing cards, trays, and dishes. The logo was placed nearly anywhere it would fit—even on ax handles!

Cost: Plant: free; Museum: adults, $2; seniors and tour groups, $1.50; students, 50¢; preschoolers, free.
Freebies: A cup of Coke, Sprite, or Diet Coke in the lobby area.
Video Shown: No
Reservations Needed: No, except for bus groups.
Days and Hours: Museum: Mon-Fri 9:00 AM-4:00 PM. Plant: 8:00 AM-5:00 PM. Closed holidays.
Plan to Stay: 1 hour for self-guided tour and museum.
Minimum Age: None
Disabled Access: Flight of stairs into building lobby and up to production-area balcony and museum. Part of the bottling and canning visible from the lobby area.
Group Requirements: Bus groups should call in advance. Group discount on museum admission. Groups of 15 people or more can get guided tours if booked a few days in advance.
Special Information: Frequently no canning or bottling on winter Fridays.
Gift Counter: A small counter in the museum sells Coca-Cola paraphernalia, from the standard (postcards, key rings, T-shirts) to the unusual/collectible (clocks, trays, breakdancing Coke can), and also *Schmidt's Museum Collection Book*. Call the above number for mail orders.
Directions: From the north, follow I-65 South to Exit 94. Take U.S. 62 to Ring Road to U.S. 31W. Go south 1 mile to Coca-Cola plant. From the south, take I-65 North to Exit 91, and take Western Kentucky Pkwy. to U.S. 31W Bypass. This goes directly to the plant. Look for fountains in front.
Nearby Attractions: Freeman Lake Park; Patton Museum at Fort Knox; Abraham Lincoln Birthplace.

Churchill Weavers

blankets, throws, scarves

100 Churchill Drive
Lorraine Court
Berea, KY 40403
(606) 986-3127

It takes hard work and heritage to hand-weave a beautiful Churchill Weavers blanket or throw. Churchill Weavers, nestled in a small college town where Kentucky's Bluegrass meets its Cumberland Mountains, encompasses history, pride and craftsman-ship. MIT graduate and industrial engineer Carroll Churchill and his wife Eleanor, an English schoolteacher, returned from missionary work in India to found Churchill Weavers in 1922. Richard and Lila Bellando, personally selected by Eleanor, continue Churchill's legacy of making fine handcrafted items while updating the colors and yarns for current fashion trends.

Your self-guided tour includes the historic loomhouse, residence to almost 50 looms. Notice that the weathered brown of the looms matches the building's ceilings, walls and wooden plank floors. In the loomhouse is the water-wheel-like "warper." Threads are wrapped around it according to a written pattern, then wound onto a warp drum which fits into the back of a loom.

The highlight of the tour is watching wooden looms in action as women weave baby blankets, throws, table linens, scarves, and fabric for neckties. Watch an agile weaver alternate between pulling the beater forward with her left hand and "throwing" the shuttle with her right. At the same time, as if playing an organ, she steps on foot pedals to create a pattern. The rhythm of the weavers at their looms sounds like the hoof-beats of galloping horses. The rhythm breaks only when a weaver stops to replace a yarn-filled bobbin in the shuttle, then it begins again.

Menders check newly-woven cloth on light boards and repair flaws. From warping to weaving to tying the fringes, you will observe this timeless, hands-on process of "constructing" fabrics. These beautiful "high-touch" items, made by loving hands, help balance the "high-tech," fast-paced world in which we live.

Cost: Free

Freebies: No

Video Shown: 4-minute optional video in gift shop shows the company's history and its weaving process.

Reservations Needed: No for self-guided tour. Yes if groups want tour guide.

Days and Hours: Mon-Fri 9:00 AM-12:00 PM, 1:00 PM-4:00 PM. Loomhouse hours vary seasonally. Closed Christmas and New Year's.

Plan to Stay: 20 minutes for tour plus time for video and gift shop.

Minimum Age: None

Disabled Access: Yes

Group Requirements: Maximum group is 40 people. Tour guide can be arranged if booked 3-4 days in advance.

Special Information: Due to the intense concentration required by the weaving process, please do not disturb the weavers at work.

Retail Store: Sells baby blankets, scarves, stoles, throws, and neckties made by Churchill Weavers, and pottery, candles, baskets, and woodcrafts from all over the U.S.A. The outlet room sells woven seconds and overruns by well-known craftspeople. Open Mon-Sat 9:00 AM-6:00 PM, Sun 12:00 PM-6:00 PM. Catalog available from the above number.

Directions: From Lexington, take I-75 South to Exit 77. Follow Walnut Meadow Rd. past four-way stop light to traffic light at Berea College campus. Turn left onto Rt. 25 North and pass Berea Hospital. Bear right onto Hwy. 1016. Follow the signs to Churchill Weavers. From the south, take I-75 North to Exit 76. Stay on Rt. 25 North through town, past Berea Hospital. Continue with above directions.

Nearby Attractions: Berea is the folk arts and crafts capital of Kentucky. You can purchase the works of local craftspeople while observing them in their studios scattered throughout the town. At Berea College you can watch students produce a variety of crafts.

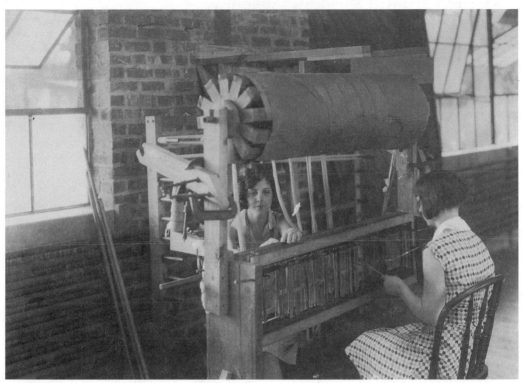

In this 1930s photograph, employees wrap a warp before placing it on a loom at Churchill Weavers, Berea, Kentucky

Silent loomhouse awaits the "click-click-click" sounds of production at Churchill Weavers

Colonel Harland Sanders Museum   *fast food*

KFC International Headquarters
1441 Gardiner Lane
Louisville, KY 40213
(502) 456-8607

In Japan, Colonel Sanders is *Ohji-san*, or "Grandfather," and his statue stands near every one of the restaurants he inspired. A life-size statue also graces the entrance to this small museum, which honors the man who above all else demonstrated that the little guy can succeed in America.

An old-style black-and-white movie called "Portrait of a Legend" shows how Harland Sanders, born in 1890, held many jobs to support his family—streetcar conductor, cook, justice of the peace, and automobile mechanic. After the historic film, stroll around the museum and enjoy the many photographs and mementos.

Some of the rare photos show Sanders' Court Restaurant. About 1930, Sanders began cooking chicken for customers at his auto service station (later a restaurant) along busy U.S. 25. At Sanders' Court he perfected his famous secret blend of 11 herbs and spices, and developed the innovation of frying chicken in a pressure cooker. Here at the museum you'll see the original cooker and learn why it made such a difference. In 1935, Governor Ruby Laffon made Sanders an honorary Kentucky Colonel for his contribution to the state's cuisine.

Unfortunately, a highway bypass closed the restaurant in the early 1950s. After paying his bills, Sanders had nothing to live on except his social security check. With his wife Claudia, he hit the road, making samples of his chicken and offering franchise deals to restaurant owners. The idea was so successful that in 1964 he sold his interest in Kentucky Fried Chicken and became the company's spokesman, wearing his now-famous white suit (one is displayed at the museum).

The pictures on the wall show that the Colonel traveled extensively around the world, met many dignitaries and celebrities, and gave millions of dollars to charities. Watch classic U.S. and foreign television commercials and clips of the Colonel's other television appearances. You'll also see the Colonel's favorite award, a wire chicken presented to him by the National Restaurant Association. Today a subsidiary of PepsiCo, KFC is the world's second-largest restaurant chain—8,700-plus restaurants in 60-plus countries. But after touring this compact museum you'll forever associate KFC with the 66-year-old man who began an empire with a $105 social security check.

Cost: Free
Freebies: No
Video Shown: An optional 25-minute film about Sanders and history of KFC; 8-minute video of commercials and interviews.
Reservations Needed: No, except for groups larger than 15 people.
Days and Hours: Mon-Thur 8:00 AM-5:00 PM, Fri 8:00 AM-3:00 PM (closes at 1:00 PM June-August and on Derby Friday). Closed standard holidays.
Plan to Stay: 40 minutes
Minimum Age: 8
Disabled Access: Yes
Group Requirements: Groups of 15 people or more should call at least 2 weeks in advance. Maximum group size is 40.
Special Information: Museum is in the lobby of the KFC corporate headquarters, so dress appropriately. The cafe and motel in Harland, Kentucky, where the Colonel concocted his secret recipe, has been restored to its mid-1940s glory (call 606-528-2163).
Gift Shop: No, but the closest KFC is on Bardstown Rd.
Directions: Take I-264 to Newburg Rd. Exit. Go south and turn right onto Bishop Ln. Turn right onto Gardiner Rd. Museum is in KFC corporate headquarters, which has an antebellum plantation facade.
Nearby Attractions: Ford Truck and Louisville Stoneware tours (see pages 76 and 77); Hadley Pottery tour (call 502-584-2171) and American Printing House for the Blind tour (call 502-895-2405); Louisville's attractions include J.B. Speed Art Museum, Churchill Downs/Kentucky Derby Museum, and Kentucky Art and Craft Center.

Corvette ⌒ *sports cars*

Corvette Drive
Bowling Green, KY 42101
(502) 745-8419 / (502) 781-7973

Since it was first built in 1953, GM's Corvette has become an American automotive icon, representing muscle, fantasy, and youth. The television series "Route 66," about two bachelors who traveled American highways in their 'Vette, increased the car's popularity. In 1981, GM moved Corvette assembly to a Bowling Green complex the size of 22 football fields.

You know this tour is going to be fun when you look up and see half of a 1983 Corvette above the tour entrance door. Led by a guide who points out the car's special features, you'll walk on the plant floor to witness the major steps in the sports car's production. See the frame and body take shape, the engine and drive train go together, the windshields attached, and the joining of the chassis and body.

Computerized robots weld the steel frame together before the Corvette receives its signature fiberglass body panels. Once the car is painted, it returns to the main assembly floor where workers install other parts such as dashboard, wheels, and removable roof. While the car's body is being assembled in the plant, the engine and drive train are assembled along the plant's back area. When the two come together it's called "body marriage," with workers scampering underneath the car to connect the chassis and body.

Almost everywhere you look, Corvettes in some stage of assembly move past on a multi-level network of conveyors that cover more than 6 miles. Only when the car is fully built do all four wheels touch the ground for the first time. A worker sits in the car and starts the engine. Like a baby's first cry, the engine makes its initial roar. It may take a couple of seconds for the car to start but once running, it idles for some time while workers make various checks throughout the car and add such fluids as antifreeze. Even if you didn't arrive as a diehard Corvette enthusiast, you'll leave as one.

Cost: Free

Freebies: No

Video Shown: 15-minute video on the car's proud history and production, including steps not on the tour, such as body painting.

Reservations Needed: No, except for groups of 10 people or more.

Days and Hours: Mon-Fri 9:00 AM and 1:00 PM. Closed holidays, week between Christmas and New Year's, 2 weeks in summer (usually starting early July), and for model changes. Tour schedule may increase in Fall 1994, when the National Corvette Museum opens, so call ahead.

Plan to Stay: 1¼ hours for tour and video, plus time in gift shop.

Minimum Age: None, but children under 6 may be intimidated by the noise.

Disabled Access: Yes.

Group Requirements: For groups larger than 10 people, call (502) 745-8228 for reservations 1 week in advance. Maximum group size is 50 people.

Special Information: No photography on tour. 1 mile of walking. GM plans an extensive redesign of the Corvette to appear in 1996, which may change the tour.

Gift Shop: Sells Corvette memorabilia including T-shirts, hats, and key chains. Open during tour hours. When National Corvette Museum officially opens, merchandise may be sold only at museum. Call (502) 781-7973.

Directions: From I-65 take Exit 28. For plant, turn right at Corvette Dr., then right after entering the gate. Follow signs to tour parking. For museum, turn left at Corvette Dr.

Nearby Attractions: National Corvette Museum (scheduled to open Fall 1994); Beech Bend Raceway Park; Mammoth Cave National Park.

Ford ⟷ *trucks*

3001 Chamberlain Lane
Louisville, KY 40232
(502) 429-2146

Many of the big trucks barreling by on the highway come from this plant, the largest heavy-truck assembly plant in the western world. In a site larger than 400 football fields, Ford manufactures medium, heavy, and extra heavy-duty trucks along 9½ miles of conveyor belts. With a recent expansion, they now also build commercial light trucks.

For most of the standard tour, you'll walk next to the final chassis assembly lines where the truck's pieces all come together. Every truck is made for a specific order, so you may see a bright yellow school bus being built next to an olive-green army truck. Since the major components attached to a frame are so heavy, the frame is built upside down and everything is laid on top of it for mounting. After turning right-side-up, the frame travels by overhead conveyor through a robotic frame-paint booth and paint-baking oven. The chassis frame "touches down" from an overhead sloping conveyer at the start of the final chassis line. The cabs reach the chassis lines in job sequence from the four-level automated cab-stackers. Overhead hoists lower the cabs onto the chassis and they are bolted down in a process called "cab decking." The hood assemblies, front ends, and engines are also decked into place, with the trucks soon ready to drive off the assembly line.

Notice how the heavy-truck engines travel around the plant on their own magic carpets, the computer-controlled automatic guided vehicles (AGVs). From the receiving sections to engine build-up and final assembly lines, the yellow AGVs transport the engines along a guide path in the plant's floor, using sonar to direct its journey. In the tire/wheel mounting area, a rotary mounting machine has automated the difficult process of putting tubeless truck tires around metal rims and then inflating them.

The assembly line moves at a slow enough speed that you can study the making and installing of up to 27,000 truck parts. Workers are very friendly; many have been assembling Ford trucks for over 20 years.

Truck owners like to shake hands with the people who actually produce their rigs, so the workers are used to talking with visitors. If something interests you, take a closer look (safety permitting) and ask questions. Don't be surprised if next time you see trucks on the highway you find yourself looking for the medallion logos of the company that built them.

Cost: Free
Freebies: Brochure describing the plant and its main production areas.
Video Shown: No
Reservations Needed: Yes
Days and Hours: Mon-Fri when the tour coordinator is available. Ford likes giving public tours but focuses on customer tours. Public tours are scheduled in available time slots. Closed the week between Christmas and New Year's and usually the first 2-3 weeks of July.
Plan to Stay: 1 hour
Minimum Age: 10
Disabled Access: Yes
Group Requirements: 2 weeks' advance notice. Call tour coordinator for size restrictions.
Special Information: No photography. Tour involves at least 1 mile of walking. Standard tour can be modified to meet special interests. Plant is hot during the summer.
Gift Shop: No
Directions: Take I-71 North to I-265 South. Get off at West Port Rd./Chamberlain Ln. exit. Head in the direction of Chamberlain Ln. Enter plant through Gate 3.
Nearby Attractions: Ford Explorer and Ranger tours (Monday mornings by reservation, call 502-364-3728); Louisville's attractions include Louisville Stoneware tour (see page 77), Colonel Harland Sanders Museum (see page 74), and Churchill Downs/Kentucky Derby Museum.

Louisville Stoneware ～ *pottery*

731 Brent Street
Louisville, KY 40204
(502) 582-1900

Raw clay, mined from Western Indiana, forms a small hill against the back wall of the clay-making room. Since 1905, this has been the main ingredient for the artistic, durable, authentic American pottery made by Louisville Stoneware. Upon request, your tour can include the clay-making room, where clay dirt is vigorously mixed with water to make a clay "soup." Under high pressure, a press pushes liquid clay through filters with water dripping out the bottom. In the pug mill, the resulting firm "cakes" of fine clay are chopped into stiff or soft mud or turned into pourable liquid "slip" clay. In a process called "slip casting," this fluid slip is poured into angular, geometric-shaped, plaster molds to form items like bird feeders and birdhouses.

The standard tour begins with "jiggering," another process of romancing the clay, used for more concentric shapes. Leaning over a spinning pottery wheel, a potter places clay onto a concave plaster mold (shaped like the inside of a bowl) and then lowers the jigger handle to form the plate or bowl. The potter uses a water-drenched sponge to smooth the clay's surface. Each plate hardens on its individual plaster mold. Throughout the factory, you will see earthenware drying on 6-to-10-foot-high storage conveyors whose shelves can be rotated or advanced when full.

Traditional patterns are hand-painted directly onto the dried clay piece. At first appearing pastel, the final underglaze colors reveal themselves only after a white translucent glaze is applied and the piece is fired at a high temperature. You will feel the heat emerging from the three kilns, which hold 1,000 pieces each. The whole firing process takes almost a full day—10 hours to reach 2350°F, and then 12 hours to cool.

Cost: Free
Freebies: No
Video Shown: No
Reservations Needed: No, except for groups larger than 15 people.

Days and Hours: Mon-Fri 10:30 AM and 2:30 PM. Closed holidays. Additional tours usually possible if a guide is available.
Plan to Stay: 15-25 minutes for the tour, depending on whether you see the clay-making process, plus time for the factory sales room.
Minimum Age: None
Disabled Access: Yes
Group Requirements: Groups larger than 15 people should call 1 day in advance for desired time. Large groups will be split into smaller groups.
Special Information: Since there are three firing kilns, the factory can be hot.
Outlet Store: Sells factory seconds at 30-40% off regular prices, and firsts of Kentucky-related items (mugs with horse designs, etc.). Product line includes colorful dinnerware, outdoor products (birdhouses, etc.), and stoneware. Look for the big "Night Before Christmas" soup tureen with the entire poem written on its outside. Open Mon-Sat 8:00 AM-5:00 PM. At the annual tent sale, in July, seconds sell at additional savings. Catalog available from (800) 626-1800.
Directions: From Lexington, take Rt. 64 West to 3rd St. South (one way). Turn left onto Broadway, then right onto Brent St. Located 2½ blocks ahead on left. From the Louisville area, take Rt. 65 North to Broadway exit. Turn right onto Broadway, then right onto Brent St.
Nearby Attractions: Colonel Harland Sanders Museum (see page 74); Ford Truck tour (see page 76); Hadley Pottery tour (call 502-584-2171); American Printing House for the Blind tour (call 502-895-2405); J.B. Speed Art Museum; Churchill Downs/Kentucky Derby Museum; Kentucky Art and Craft Center.

Maker's Mark ⟶ *bourbon*
3350 Burks Spring Road
Loretto, KY 40037
(502) 865-2099

An illustration of the Maker's Mark distillery appears on its bottles, and the label invites you to visit "any time you're in the neighborhood," so you know the place must be special. Just as Bill Samuels, Sr. wanted to create his own distinctive bourbon by using gentle winter wheat instead of rye, he wanted to restore a historic distillery complex into the home of Maker's Mark. His efforts and those of his son, Bill Jr., made the distillery a National Historic Landmark that produces award-winning bourbon.

The tour begins near the stone-walled creek that runs through the peaceful, landscaped grounds, where you'll hear a brief history of the distillery. Its black buildings feature bright red shutters with a Maker's Mark bottle cutout. Unlike larger distilleries' 600-barrel-per-day production, Maker's Mark crafts about 40 per day.

In the still house you'll smell corn, wheat, and malted barley cooking. The bubbling yellow mash ferments in century-old cypress vats. Vaporization of the mash in the shiny copper still separates out the whiskey, which is placed in charred oak casks for aging. When you enter the aging warehouse's ground floor, the aromas alone tell you what's in the barrels. Barrels reach maturity only after completing a rotation system in which the newest barrels are placed on the warehouse's hot upper floors and are gradually moved to the cooler lower levels.

Only in the bottling house does the production pace quicken. Near the end of the line, two women dip each bottle's glass neck into red sealing wax and then twist the bottle out to allow the excess to drip off and run down the neck. Notice each worker's distinctive dipping and twisting technique.

Cost: Free
Freebies: Iced tea and lemonade; bottle labels; smells.
Video Shown: No
Reservations Needed: No, except for groups larger than 25 people.

Days and Hours: Mon-Sat 10:30 AM, 11:30 AM, 12:30 PM, 1:30 PM, 2:30 PM, 3:30 PM. No production from mid-August to mid-September, but tour still runs. Closed Saturdays in January and February. Closed Thanksgiving, Christmas Eve, Christmas, and New Year's.

Plan to Stay: 40 minutes for the tour, plus time for visitors center, Quart House, and Gift Gallery. Once a pre-Civil War distiller's home, the visitors center has items from the Samuels' collection of early-1800s furniture, a set of old cooper's tools, and other historical and crafts items. The Quart House is a restored pre-Prohibition retail package store.

Minimum Age: Recommends that children under 10 be accompanied by an adult.

Disabled Access: Visitors center fully accessible. Bottling house and aging warehouse have a few steps. Distillery building has a flight of stairs. Gravel walking paths between buildings.

Group Requirements: At least 2 weeks' notice for groups of 25 people or more. Maximum group size is 50, but can handle larger groups in special situations.

Special Information: Wax dipping of bottles does not occur every day, but tour guide will demonstrate.

Gift Shop: The Gift Gallery in the visitor center sells logoed and craft items, including shirts, sweaters, jackets, key chains, and shot glasses. Also gourmet sauces and candies made with Maker's Mark. Open Mon-Sat 10:00 AM-4:30 PM. Call number above for mail order product list.

Directions: From Bardstown, take KY 49 South and follow signs to distillery. You're there when you see the sign that says "You've Just Found The Home Of Maker's Mark."

Nearby Bourbon-Related Attractions: Heaven Hill Distillery tour (call 502-348-3921); Oscar Getz Museum of Whiskey History (call 502-348-2999); Jim Beam's American Outpost (call 502-543-9877); Annual Bardstown September Bourbon Festival.

———— *See color photos, page 143* ————

Old Kentucky Candies   ~   *chocolates*

450 Southland Drive
Lexington, KY 40503
(800) 786-0579

Bourbon Chocolates, Bourbon Cherries, Chocolate Thoroughbreds, and Kentucky Derby Mints—the names alone are enough to attract you to this candy-factory tour. Combine the tour with plentiful free samples before, after, and even right off the assembly line, and you have the makings of a tasty experience.

The chocolate in these famous Kentucky candies starts as 10-pound bars of Guittard Chocolate. In the molding area, melted chocolate sits in a mixer while a rotating blade slowly turns it into a creamy paste. While the tour guide is pointing to overhead photographs and explaining how cocoa beans are harvested and the chocolate is made, you'll be tempted to sneak your finger into the mixer for a taste. Nearby are stacks of Old Kentucky's popular molds, including a 75-pound Easter bunny, dentures, and a horse's behind.

As you stroll through the candy "kitchen," you often see 8-foot-by-3-foot slabs of fudge and candy centers cooling before they are cut with a ridged rolling pin. In the production room, glass jars of maraschino cherries may be marinating in 101-proof Jim Beam Bourbon. Stand next to the conveyor belt while the candies receive a bottom chocolate base, then go through a "chocolate car wash" that coats them in chocolate. Looped chains drop down to caress the tops of the candies, creating a swirl design. After the candies exit the cooling tunnel, workers carefully hand-pack the chocolates—a job that must require great willpower to prevent constant nibbling.

Cost: Free
Freebies: Plentiful candy samples, including a candy directly off the assembly line.
Video Shown: No
Reservations Needed: Yes. Individuals and families must join a group tour.
Days and Hours: Mon-Thur 10:30 AM-3:30 PM, with other times available upon request. Closed holidays.
Plan to Stay: 20 minutes for tour, plus time for gift shop.

Minimum Age: None
Disabled Access: Yes
Group Requirements: 1 day's advance notice for groups. No maximum size. Large groups split into groups of 25 people.
Special Information: If interested in seeing specific candies made, ask when you book the tour.
Retail Store: Sells all of the company's different kinds and shapes of candies. Look for gift baskets shaped like horse heads, horseshoes, and Kentucky maps. Glass showcases filled with truffles sit next to canisters of various free samples. On the store's front table, notice the upside-down mushroom-shaped jar filled with cherries aging in bourbon. (Unfortunately, once the cherries are aged, Kentucky liquor laws do not allow the sale of this cherry-flavored bourbon.) Open Mon-Fri 9:00 AM-6:00 PM, Sat 9:30 AM-5:30 PM, Sun 1:00 PM-5:00 PM. Catalog available from above number.
Directions: From Cincinnati, take I-75 South to Exit 115 for Newtown Pike. Go west on Circle 4 (New Circle Rd.). Take exit for Harrodsburg Rd. toward Lexington. Turn right onto Lane Allen Rd., which becomes Rosemont Garden. Turn right onto Southland Dr. Old Kentucky is on the right. Factory is in the back of its retail store, in a shopping center. From Louisville, take Rt. 64 West to I-75 South. Continue with above directions.
Nearby Attractions: Toyota tour (see page 81); Three Chimneys horse farm tour (see page 80); Kentucky Horse Park; Boonesborough State Park; Fort Harrod State Park.

Three Chimneys ~ *horse breeding farm*

Rt. 1, Old Frankfort Pike
Versailles, KY 40383
(606) 873-7053

Although a tour of a horse breeding farm is a slight diversion from the other companies in this book, we decided to include Three Chimneys because the thoroughbred industry is the third largest industry and the number one tourist attraction in the state of Kentucky. In fact, Kentucky-bred horses are a majority among winners of the world-famous Kentucky Derby.

As you leave the city of Lexington and drive along the Old Frankfort Pike, you will be calmed by the gently rolling hills, and the black or white ribbons of fencing that zigzag across green pastures dotted with sleek brown horses. Enjoy this scenic drive past other horse farms while watching for the low, forest-green sign that identifies Three Chimneys.

Walk along the red brick walkway to the office, poshly decorated with colonial furniture and oriental rugs. Further down the red-brick path, past the great oaks, is the limestone stallion barn. This five-star equine hotel, lined with oak panels, trimmed with palladium windows and topped with a skylight in a cupola ceiling, is home to champion racehorses, now studs worth millions of dollars. Each 16-foot-square stall has black bars with black-and-gold engraved name plates. Grooms attend to the stallions' every need.

These knowledgeable grooms are available to answer all your questions and list each of their charges' accomplishments; for example, Seattle Slew won the Triple Crown in 1977 and has sired six champion racehorses and stakes winners. His foals have won millions of dollars in purse money. Seattle Slew's son Slew O' Gold, who lives two stalls away, has produced four Grade One winners in his first foal crop.

Every day, the stallions graze and stretch their legs in their individual 1-to-2-acre paddocks. They are also ridden or walked daily for exercise. Twice daily, February through July, you can observe thoroughbreds in the breeding shed. To ensure the safety of mares and stallions the round walls are lined with foam-rubber-padded vinyl, the floor is covered with wood chips and a raised cocoa mat, and five grooms assist with the breeding—a brief act, but one that can be worth $120,000 to Seattle Slew's owners.

Cost: Free. Tips to grooms are appreciated.
Freebies: No
Video Shown: No
Reservations Needed: Yes. For tours in April, July, and September through November call 2-3 months in advance; other times of the year, call 2 weeks ahead of time.
Days and Hours: Mon-Sun 10:00 AM and 1:00 PM. Call about breeding times. No tours the week before the Kentucky Derby (first Saturday in May). Closed holidays.
Plan to Stay: 30 minutes
Minimum Age: None
Disabled Access: Yes
Group Requirements: Standard bus tours are discouraged.
Special Information: Please respect the grounds and horses. This is neither a zoo nor a public riding stable.
Gift Shop: No
Directions: From Lexington, take Rt. 4 (New Circle Rd.) to Old Frankfort Pike. Drive west for 8 miles, passing a red brick church on your right. The farm is ½-mile ahead on your left. From Cincinnati, take I-75 South to I-64 West to Midway exit. Follow signs on Rt. 62 West through Midway to a four-way stop. Turn left onto Old Frankfort Pike. Farm is 2 miles ahead on your right.
Nearby Attractions: Toyota tour (see page 81); Kentucky Horse Park; Keeneland Racecourse; Calumet Farm tour (organized through Historical Tours at 606-268-2906).

Toyota ~ *cars*
1001 Cherry Blossom Way
Georgetown, KY 40324
(502) 868-3027

In 1988, Toyota began building its popular Camry in this small Kentucky town. Since then the factory has won awards for producing cars with the fewest problems. When the current expansion is completed, up to 420,000 Kentucky-made Toyotas, produced by over 6,000 workers, can roll off its assembly lines each year. The tour shows the process and pride of Toyota Motor Manufacturing, U.S.A. (TMM) and its uniformed team members (TMM employees).

The Camry begins in the stamping area as a gleaming steel coil. The steel is cleaned, straightened, and stamped into more than 50 sheet-metal components that make up the Camry body. With loud thumps, automated presses shape metal, bend edges, pierce holes, and trim excesses.

In the body-welding area, robotic and human arms hold the equipment that welds together a body shell. Sparks fly, as computer-controlled robots perform thousands of welds in synchronized unison. Cameras, lasers, and team members check the new Camry bodies before they travel by overhead conveyors to the Paint Shop. As the cars move slowly down the trim, chassis, and final assembly lines, you'll see a silhouette become an operating automobile.

The factory is modeled after the Tsutsumi Plant in Toyota City, Japan. As you tour this facility in an electric tram, your guide points out specialties of the Toyota Production System, including *kaizen* (continuous improvement), just-in-time parts delivery, and the Andon Cord (any team member can pull it to stop the line for quality concerns).

An example of *kaizen* is the mechanical arm that automatically installs the spare tire in the trunk, once a difficult manual process. Just-in-time delivery is vividly demonstrated by the different-colored car bodies moving down the assembly line. Instead of producing all cars of a certain color at one time, each color body shell represents a recent order; a nearby seat manufacturer delivers the correct color seats as the body emerges from the paint area. With all this automation, loud machines, and sophisticated engineering, it's soothing to see team members transporting parts around this massive plant on bicycles equipped with bells and wire baskets.

Cost: Free

Freebies: Key chain and brochure on TMM and Camry manufacturing.

Video Shown: 15-minute video, "Our Pride Is On The Line," gives a brief plant overview, some production steps not on the tour, and interviews with team members about TMM and its impact on the local community.

Reservations Needed: Yes

Days and Hours: Tue and Thur 8:30 AM, 10:00 AM, 12:00 PM, 2:00 PM, 6:00 PM. Closed holidays, July 4th week, and 2 weeks around Christmas.

Plan to Stay: 1½ hours, including tour, video, Q&A, and visitor center. The visitor center includes displays and interactive exhibits that explain the Toyota Production System.

Minimum Age: 8

Disabled Access: Yes

Group Requirements: Maximum group size is 80 people. At least 2 months' advance notice for large groups.

Special Information: No photography. Minimal walking and loud noise, since you tour the plant in an electric tram and wear headphones to hear the guide.

Gift Shop: No. Possibly in future.

Directions: From Lexington, take I-75 North (toward Cincinnati) to Exit 126 (Georgetown/Cynthiana). Turn right on U.S. 62 (Cherry Blossom Way). Visitors' Gate 2 is on the left, 2 miles after exit. From Cincinnati, take I-75 South to Exit 126. Turn left onto U.S. 62 and follow above directions.

Nearby Attractions: Three Chimneys horse farm (see page 80); Rebecca Ruth Candies tour (call 800-444-3766); Carolina Pottery Outlet Center; Georgetown College; Elkhorn Creek.

Wild Turkey   *bourbon*

1525 Tyrone Road
Lawrenceburg, KY 40342
(502) 839-4544

Wild Turkey Distillery sits on a hill next to the Kentucky River. Water from this naturally filtered limestone riverbed and corn from nearby farmers are the main ingredients in bourbon, a uniquely American whiskey. This tour shows almost all steps in crafting the bourbon named after founder Thomas McCarthy's private stock taken on a wild turkey hunt.

The first surprise is the metal-barred windows on the big, gray, square warehouses throughout the grounds. What could be mistaken for jailhouses are actually rack houses where the bourbon ages. The tax-hungry government once required installation of the bars to prevent any barrels from leaving without proper fees being paid.

The initial step in producing bourbon is mixing corn, rye, and water. The mix is cooked and cooled, then malted barley is added. With special yeast added, this sour mash ferments in cypress-wood or stainless-steel tanks. Watch the slow, gentle swirl of the thick yellow mash in the vats; carbon-dioxide bubbles rise to the surface as the yeast changes sugar to alcohol, called "distiller's beer." Stand next to the 40-foot-high copper still where the alcohol is separated in a vaporization process.

Charred white-oak barrels then become the colorless whiskey's home. The tour guide explains that the burnt layers of wood inside the barrel give bourbon its distinctive flavor and color (whiskey must be aged in new, charred-oak barrels for two years to be legally called "bourbon"). Inside a cool warehouse amid racks of barrels on wood planks, you'll enjoy the sweet bourbon smell. Wild Turkey calls this the "angels' share" because one-third of each barrel's contents evaporates over the bourbon's 8 years of aging. It's not until you walk through the quality control lab and the bottling area that the process seems any different from what it must have been 100 years ago.

Cost: Free

Freebies: Food made with Wild Turkey, such as a bourbon brownie; a barrel bung; lemonade; coffee; and recipes that use Wild Turkey; smells.

Video Shown: No

Reservations Needed: No, except for groups of 20 or more people.

Days and Hours: Mon-Fri 9:00 AM, 10:30 AM, 12:30 PM, 2:30 PM. Closed holidays.

Plan to Stay: 45 minutes for tour plus time for snacks and visitors center. The visitors center is in a restored building with a small display of ceramic Wild Turkey decanters, historical mementos, a scale model of the bourbon production process, and a gift shop.

Minimum Age: No

Disabled Access: Visitors center is fully accessible. Remainder of the facility has gravel paths and flights of stairs to some areas.

Group Requirements: Advance notice requested for groups of 20 or more. No maximum size.

Special Information: Wear comfortable walking shoes. Tour runs all year, but not all areas are in production during certain weeks in July and August.

Gift Shop: Sells hats and clothes, including T-shirts and shorts with the Wild Turkey logo and popular "Too Good To Gobble" slogan (Bruce gave this to his mom!), other logoed items, and barbecue sauce. Open Mon-Fri 8:30 AM-4:00 PM. Catalog available from (800) BUY-TRKY.

Directions: From Louisville, take I-64 East to Rt. 151 South to Rt. 127 South. Turn left on Rt. 44, which turns into U.S. 62 East. Bear right onto Tyrone Rd. (Rt. 1510) to distillery. From Lexington, take U.S. 60 West (take Business Route at split) to Versailles to U.S. 62 West to distillery. You're almost there when you see billboards announcing "Bird Sanctuary Ahead" and "Home of Wild Turkey."

Nearby Attractions: Beaver Lake and Taylorville Lake; Ripplewood Estate.

See color photos, page 148

Bruce Foods   *pepper sauces and Cajun foods*

1653 Old Spanish Trail
St. Martinville, LA 70582
(318) 365-8101 (ext. 261)

BRUCE FOODS CORPORATION

Bruce Foods, discreetly located on a country highway between Lafayette and New Iberia, is the quiet giant of food factories in the South. Its success has grown exponentially in recent years. The company which began over 60 years ago with one product, a pepper sauce, today has more than 300 products marketed to 75 countries around the world. Bruce Foods now produces everything from Cajun seasonings to Mexican mixes, in addition to its well-known pepper sauces (Louisiana Gold).

After seeing the offices and conference room, where new product marketing strategies are discussed, you'll tour the factory. In one room, empty bottles ride around a carousel where they're filled with colorful red pepper sauce. In another area, the pungent smell of several varieties of cured peppers fills the air as the peppers are mashed to make different sauces. The coarse pepper mash is mechanically cut over and over again until it is liquid-fine. The residue, or "chaff," from the peppers looks like wet, red sand. You can feel it between your fingers, but this "sand" isn't for playing with at the beach. It's so combustible it can ignite on its own if left in the sun. The chaff is sold to area restaurants for pepper seasoning in crab boil.

The factory also has an open-air production area where you'll see a gargantuan colander that rinses freshly cut jalapeño slices. You'll also stare at a field's worth of sky-high, 23,650-gallon tanks—64 in all—that look like they could hold oil or gas reserves. Actually, they store concentrated pepper mash that will age like fine wine for six months to a year. All this concentrated mash is needed to make the famous hot sauces that will fill everything from Bruce's 2-ounce souvenir bottles to its tanker trucks.

Cost: Free
Freebies: Product brochures
Video Shown: No
Reservations Needed: Yes. Individuals and families need to join scheduled group tours.

Days and Hours: Mon-Fri 8:00 AM-5:00 PM, although tours are limited. Closed holidays and the week between Christmas and New Year's.
Plan to Stay: 30-45 minutes
Minimum Age: 6
Disabled Access: Cramped quarters make access difficult for wheelchairs.
Group Requirements: Maximum group size is 10 people. Groups should call 1 week in advance.
Special Information: The company recently started giving public tours, so requirements and tour route are still evolving. No photography. Factory floor may be wet, so wear sneakers. Strong pepper smell.
Gift Shop: No. Catalog available for full line of food products, Chef John Folse's cookbooks and black iron pots (call 800-299-9082).
Directions: From New Orleans, take I-10 West. Exit at 103A. Follow U.S. 90 through Lafayette to Cade/St. Martinville exit. Turn left off exit onto Hwy. 182 (Old Spanish Trail). Factory is on the left.
Nearby Attractions: Konriko and McIlhenny tours (see pages 84 and 85); Steamboat House; Shadows-On-The-Teche; Delcambre Shrimp Boat Landing; Vermilionville and Acadian Village in Lafayette.

Konriko <small>∼</small> *rice and Cajun seasonings*

309 Ann Street
New Iberia, LA 70560
(800) 551-3245

The best place to start a tour of the Konriko Rice Mill is in the Konriko Company Store, a replica of an old plantation company store located adjacent to the mill. While you wait for a tour to begin, the friendly Cajun staff offers you a cup of strong, flavorful South Louisiana-style coffee. Something is always cooking for visitors in the store, too: one day it might be Konriko red beans and rice; another day, Konriko's jambalaya mix with rice. Once you've sampled some good Cajun coffee and cooking, the tour officially begins.

After watching a video, you move next door to America's oldest rice mill. Konriko's mill was built by founder Philip Conrad in 1912, and has been in continuous operation ever since. Made of wood and corrugated tin, it's loud and rickety when in operation. But it has great character and is on the National Register of Historic Places.

Before entering the mill, you'll see the outdoor scale and dryer that weighs and dries the unmilled rough rice local farmers deliver. An average truckload of rice is about 30,000 pounds. Next to the dryer is a bin that stores the rice before it is processed. When full, the bin holds 1 million pounds of rice—about $100,000 worth. And don't overlook Konriko, the company's "guard" dog, usually sleeping in the sun.

Inside the mill, a visual aid explains how different varieties of rice are milled. No part of the milled rice is wasted. You'll see several rooms where workers package Konriko rice and seasonings and make rice cakes. You're not allowed in the rice-cake room, but you can watch the assembly line from a window. If you're lucky, your tour guide will give you a hot rice cake fresh from the oven to top off the tour.

Cost: Adults, $2.75; seniors 62 and over, $2.25; children under 12, $1.25.

Freebies: Fresh, hot coffee; cooked Konriko products; and recipes. Hot rice cakes may be given out during the tour.

Video Shown: 20-minute "historically correct" slide presentation on Cajun culture and Konriko development.

Reservations Needed: No, except for groups.

Days and Hours: Mon-Sat at 10:00 AM, 11:00 AM, 1:00 PM, 2:00 PM and 3:00 PM. No production on Saturdays and holidays, but tours usually run.

Plan to Stay: Approximately 40 minutes for video and tour, plus time for gift shop.

Minimum Age: None

Disabled Access: Access to Konriko Company Store, but not to the mill.

Group Requirements: Groups over 15 people should call 2 weeks in advance. 50 is maximum group size. Group rates available for 40 or more.

Special Information: Mill can be loud. Hot in the summer.

Gift Shop: Konriko Company Store sells local foods and condiments, complete assortment of Konriko products and mixes, T-shirts, novelty items, even Cajun dance video and music tapes. Open Mon-Sat, 9:00 AM–5:00 PM. Closed Thanksgiving, Christmas, New Year's, and July 4th. Catalog available at the above number.

Directions: From I-10, take Lafayette/U.S. Hwy. 90 exit (Exit 103), and follow U.S. 90 through Lafayette toward New Iberia. At LA 14 (Center St.) in New Iberia, exit and turn left. Turn right on St. Peter St., then right on Ann St. Rice mill and company store are both on left.

Nearby Attractions: McIlhenny and Bruce Foods tours (see pages 85 and 83); Shadows-On-The-Teche; Live Oak Gardens, Jefferson Island; Delcambre Shrimp Boat Landing; Vermilionville and Acadian Village in Lafayette.

McIlhenny Company ∼ *Tabasco brand pepper sauce*
Avery Island, LA 70513
(318) 365-8173

The concentrated hot pepper sauce, first created after the Civil War on the McIlhenny family's exotic 2,300-acre island in the South Louisiana bayou country, has such a lively flavor that it is now sold in more than 100 countries around the world and its labels are printed in 15 foreign languages. McIlhenny Company grows the *Capsicum frutescens* peppers (tabasco peppers) in several countries to insure a good harvest. But there is only one Tabasco sauce factory, and you'll recognize it as soon as you open your car door and whiff the piquant pepper aroma.

After seeing the historical gallery's Avery Island photo mural and collage of Tabasco sauce and Avery Island artifacts, you officially begin your tour by viewing a brief film. You learn that the sauce, basically unchanged over the years, was created by Edmund McIlhenny from his vegetable gardening hobby and his love of spicy food. McIlhenny planted hot peppers seeds a friend brought from Mexico. He created his famous hot sauce (brand-named Tabasco, a Central-American Indian word) by mashing the peppers with Avery Island salt, aging the mash in wooden barrels, adding vinegar, and then straining the mixture.

The tour guide leads you down a long corridor in the modern factory, where you view Tabasco sauce bottling from behind a glass wall. The smell here isn't nearly as strong as it must be inside the packaging room, where workers oversee four production lines. Some lines produce over 300 bottles of Tabasco sauce a minute, helping the factory produce over 300,000 bottles a day.

Naked bottles of the hot red sauce stream down the assembly line, where they are mechanically clothed with the familiar green foil neckbands, diamond-shaped labels, and bright red octagonal caps. The dressed bottles are then mechanically packed in boxes, ready to travel. Their final destination will be dining tables from Pennsylvania to Peking, where their red caps will be removed and they will "drop in" to spice up a meal.

Cost: Free

Freebies: Miniature Tabasco sauce bottle, recipes, and samples of other McIlhenny products.

Video Shown: 8-minute overview of McIlhenny's history and operations, as well as Tabasco brand pepper sauce origins and processing.

Reservations Needed: No, except for groups over 20 people.

Days and Hours: Mon-Fri 9:00 AM-4:00 PM; Sat 9:00 AM-12:00 PM. Last tour ½ hour before closing. May not see production on Saturdays. Closed standard holidays and long holiday weekends.

Plan to Stay: 25 minutes for video and self-guided tour, plus time for gift shop and grounds.

Minimum Age: None

Disabled Access: Yes

Group Requirements: Groups larger than 20 should make advance reservations. One week's notice appreciated.

Special Information: Some production process details are in photos and captions above the viewing window.

Gift Shop: Tabasco Country Store sells a wide variety of Tabasco brand specialty foods and novelty items, from pepper earrings to lithographs, toys, cookware, cookbooks, and spices. Open same hours as tour. Catalog available at (800) 634-9599.

Directions: From New Orleans, take I-10 West to Exit 103A. Follow U.S. 90 through Lafayette toward New Iberia. Exit at LA 14 and turn left. At LA 329 junction, turn right. Stay on LA 329 approximately 6 miles. The road dead-ends at Avery Island. Signs will direct you to factory.

Nearby attractions: Jungle Gardens and Bird City on Avery Island; Konriko and Bruce Foods tours (see pages 84 and 83); Live Oak Gardens on Jefferson Island.

Trappey's ~ *pepper sauces and pickled peppers*

900 E. Main Street
New Iberia, LA 70562-3610
(800) 365-8727

If you want to understand the literal meaning behind the popular slogan "Cajun Hot," visit Trappey's, one of the oldest food plants in the U.S., and discover the real taste of Cajun country (known locally as Acadiana). Trappey's has manufactured premium quality pepper sauces and pickled peppers for nearly 100 years, and you'll experience first-hand these peppers' potency. At the beginning of the tour, the guide gives each guest a tissue. The unsuspecting visitor might imagine the tissue is for a free sample to be given out during the tour. Not so! The tissue is to cover your nose and mouth when you enter the open-air production area where peppers and pepper sauces are bottled.

Trappey's products originated in 1898 from Mr. Trappey's experiments with his home-grown pepper plants. Although Trappey's was acquired in 1991 by former competitor McIlhenny Company, the maker of Tabasco brand pepper sauce, Trappey's products haven't changed. The Trappey plant processes 6 million pounds of peppers a year, though not all these peppers are grown in Louisiana. In the production area—where your throat and nose will tingle from the peppers' aroma—you may find several different varieties being bottled, including chili, jalapeño, cherry, and banana peppers.

Outside the production area, in an open shed, are more than 200 10-foot-deep vats, filled with salt water and vinegar that pickle 10,000 pounds of peppers and okra for up to three months. (Okra is Trappey's only cooked product.) If you tour the plant in late June you'll see farm-fresh okra being cooked in jars, but peppers are processed year-round. By the end of the tour, you'll understand how peppers become guaranteed mouth-watering, and sometimes eye-watering, treats.

Cost: Adults, $1.75; seniors over 50 years, $1; children under 17, 75¢.
Freebies: Samples of Trappey's products. (And, of course, free sinus clearing in the pepper production room!)

Video Shown: Short video explains Trappey's history and gives a brief introduction to Cajun culture.
Reservations Needed: *Unfortunately, this tour was discontinued just as we went to press. For a similar tour, see McIlhenny, page 85.*
Days and Hours: Mon-Fri 9:00 AM, 9:45 AM, 10:30 AM, 1:00 PM, 1:45 PM, and 2:30 PM. Closed holidays.
Plan to Stay: 25 minutes for video and tour, plus time for gift shop.
Minimum Age: None
Disabled Access: Yes
Group Requirements: Admission for groups of 10 or more is $1.25 per person. Groups should call 1 week in advance; and as far in advance as possible in March, April, and May—these are the busiest months and group tours fill very quickly. Larger groups should allow 1 hour for the tour.
Special Information: Strong pepper smell in most areas; not recommended for anyone with a breathing problem, such as emphysema. Factory can be noisy.
Gift Shop: Cajun Shop sells Trappey's food products, local arts and crafts, and souvenirs unique to South Louisiana. Open Mon-Sat 9:00 AM-4:30 PM. Closed holidays. Catalog available from above number.
Directions: From New Orleans, take I-10 West to Exit 103A. Follow U.S. Hwy. 90 through Lafayette to New Iberia. Turn left onto LA 14 (Center St.). Follow Center St. to St. Peter St. and turn right (one-way street). Turn left at Lewis St. and left at E. Main St. Plant is on your right.
Nearby Attractions: Konriko, McIlhenny, and Bruce Foods tours (see pages 84, 85,and 83); Shadows-On-The-Teche; Avery Island; Jefferson Island; Live Oak Gardens; Vermilionville and Acadian Village in Lafayette.

International Paper   ~~ *paper*

Androscoggin Mill
Jay, ME 04239
(207) 897-1589

Maine's lush forests and rivers provide a natural home for the paper industry. Founded in Maine in 1898, International Paper is the world's largest paper company and the nation's largest private landowner. After experiencing the sights and sounds of the Androscoggin mill, you will re-examine how you use, waste, and recycle paper.

Even before you enter the mill building, the tour guide emphasizes how much wood and water are used to make paper. As the tour leader drives you around the woodyard, you'll stare at logs piled four stories high across a 20-acre area. This is only a six-week supply of wood for the mill, with about 5,000 tons of wood used every day (fortunately, IP plants five trees for every tree used). Giant, dinosaur-like cranes use their claws to pick up the logs and place them on a water flume for the trip to the debarking drums. An extensive water treatment area, including a 37-acre lagoon, recycles nearly 40 million gallons of water each day. The waste and sludge from the papermaking process provide energy for the mill.

For safety reasons the tours cannot visit all areas inside the mill, such as where the logs are debarked and reduced into 1-inch square chips before heading into the "digester." However, you'll see what's involved in making and bleaching "pulp," the goopy wood-fiber soup that is the intermediate stage between wood and paper. Then watch the pulp, which is 99 percent water, enter one of the mill's five enormous papermaking machines. At a speed of up to 32 miles per hour, the rumbling machines systematically reduce the water content to 5 percent through gravity and heavy, rotating cylinders that press and then dry out the liquid. At the end of this machine, at least a football field away from where the pulp entered, the paper is wound onto reels 20 feet long and 6 feet wide—about a thousand times bigger than a standard paper roll.

Cost: Free

Freebies: Colorful brochure on how paper is made. Small samples of scrap paper from the giant rolls. School-age children receive a pad of paper.

Video: No

Reservations Needed: Yes

Days and Hours: Wed 10:00 AM, with other times for groups upon special request. Mill shuts down for certain weeks in May and October.

Plan to Stay: 1½ hours

Minimum Age: 12

Disabled Access: No. Tour involves a lot of walking and climbing.

Group Requirements: Can accommodate any size group with 30 days' advance notice. Tour guide's van fits 10 people. Larger groups need own bus for outside part of tour.

Special Information: No photography. Be aware that papermaking involves intense smells of cut logs, pulp, and wet paper. Earplugs and eye protection required and provided.

Gift Shop: No

Directions: Take I-95 to I-495 (Maine Tpke.) to Exit 12 for Auburn. Take Rt. 4 North. About 2 miles after going though Livermore Falls, turn left at Riley Rd. (there's a blinking light and a gas station on the corner). Follow this road across the river and to the right. The "Big Andy" mill is ahead on the left.

Nearby Attractions: Sugarloaf and Sunday River ski areas; for a list of other Maine paper industry tours write to the Paper Industry Information Office, P.O. Box 5670, Augusta, ME 04332-0570.

Tom's of Maine ~~ *natural toothpaste*

Railroad Avenue
Kennebunk, ME 04043
(207) 985-2944

Over 20 years ago, Kate and Tom Chappell moved to Maine to live a simpler life and to create a company committed to developing all-natural personal hygiene products, such as toothpaste, mouthwash, and deodorant. While we don't know if they found a simpler life, they have created a successful, socially conscious, environmentally committed company. In fact, their tasty toothpaste—made without artificial preservatives, sweeteners, or coloring—is the top-selling brand in many major stores.

All Tom's of Maine products are made in a restored railroad station, a very different setting from most successful companies' plants. On the first floor, toothpaste ingredients are mixed in a 3,000-pound vat. Ingredients for liquid products such as mouthwash or shampoo have a second mixing area.

As you walk upstairs to the second floor, you'll know what products the toothpaste and liquid lines are packaging. If you smell cinnamon, they're packaging that flavor toothpaste or mouthwash. An intense coriander smell usually means deodorant. You cannot miss the machine that pumps the still-warm toothpaste into recyclable tubes and clamps the backs closed. Notice how the company tries to reduce the amount of product packaging. For the deodorants, the outer paper carton has been replaced with a thin leaflet that folds into the back of the recyclable plastic container.

What's most interesting about this tour isn't so much the production process, but the sense that the workers enjoy their jobs and take seriously their responsibility for quality control. The smiles you see just aren't to show off good teeth. About every 15 minutes, most workers on the packaging line switch positions. A worker who just put the tubes into the filler machine now boxes toothpaste. While you may be bored brushing your teeth, the people who make your toothpaste aren't!

Cost: Free

Freebies: Samples of products packaged that day, often straight off the line. Fresh fruit in the lobby area.

Video Shown: 12-minute video, "Common Good: The Story of Tom's of Maine," covers company history and production. Video shown in the outlet store.

Reservations Needed: Yes

Days and Hours: Summer months only. Call for hours since the tour is being restructured. Closed holidays. When tours not available, you can watch video of production in the nearby outlet store.

Plan to Stay: 1 hour for the tour and a talk about the company and its philosophy, plus time for video and outlet store.

Minimum Age: 7

Disabled Access: Flight of stairs leads to factory. Can view video in fully accessible outlet store.

Group Requirements: Groups larger than 10 people should call 1 month ahead. Groups larger than 15 people will be split into smaller ones (some groups go to the outlet store before the tour).

Special Information: No photography. The company is committed to public tours, however its tour program is being restructured.

Outlet Store:. Located about 1 mile away on Main St. (call 207-985-3874). Sells all Tom's natural personal-hygiene products, including discounted, partially-damaged factory seconds. Open Mon-Sat 9:30 AM-5:00 PM. Closed holidays.

Directions: Tours meet at the Tom's of Maine Outlet store. From I-95, take Exit 3. Turn left onto Rt. 35. At fork just past school, bear right. The outlet store is in the Lafayette Center (a renovated brick factory along the Mousam River) approximately half-mile ahead on right.

Nearby Attractions: Kennebunkport Brewing Co. tour (call 207-967-4311); Wedding Cake House; Brick Store Museum; Kennebunkport.

Bartley Collection ⟿ *wooden furniture reproductions*
29060 Airpark Drive
Easton, MD 21601
(800) 787-2800

Have you ever yearned for a magnificent Queen Anne sideboard or an 18th-century Chippendale night stand? If you are at all handy with woodworking, use Bartley antique reproduction kits to make your own highboys, four-poster beds, dining tables, chairside tables, jewelry boxes, and more. With the plant manager as your guide, you can tour the one-acre factory where these antique reproductions are designed, created, and packed.

Pass the hardware department, where you may see a worker assemble each kit's perfectly reproduced brass fittings. When Bartley designers find desirable antiques to reproduce, they make rubberized castings of the original hardware and intricate moldings. These castings become the foundations for brass pourings and guide workers in reconfiguring their machines.

As you enter the rough mill, the scent of lumber and sound of ripsaws prevail. Bundles of 8-to-16-foot-long rough-cut boards crowd the aisle. Workers plane the rough-cut lumber, revealing the grain and color. Different saws cut the boards to the proper dimensions. Despite a dust collection system, a faint film of sawdust clings to everything in the plant, an unavoidable mark of the woodworker's craft.

The wide sections of wood are matched by grain and color; edges are aligned (or recut), and glued. Notice the radio-frequency gluer: it sends energy through the wood, activating a catalyst in the glue that cures it. The wide belt-sander's five sanding heads, with progressively finer grades of sandpaper, then smooth the surfaces.

Amid conventional routers, bandsaws, drill presses, and shapers are two computerized routers. A vacuum sucks air through holes in the tabletop, holding the board in place. The router's patterns are programmed by a designer in the main office, and it runs automatically, without a worker's intervention. The table moves forward and back as the six router heads spin. Before seeing the showroom, watch the cabinetmakers in the sample shop create prototypes, following the designers' sketches and building reproductions from scratch.

Cost: Free
Freebies: No
Video Shown: No
Reservations Needed: Yes, since tours not often given.
Days and Hours: Mon-Thur 9:00 AM-4:00 PM. Closed holidays, Christmas week, and certain floating holidays.
Plan to Stay: 1 hour for tour and showroom.
Minimum Age: 12
Disabled Access: Limited aisle space and sawdust on floors makes it unsuitable for wheelchairs and walkers.
Group Requirements: Groups should call 1 week in advance. No more than 6 people can be accommodated at a time.
Special Information: Wear sneakers and clothing that will not be harmed by sawdust. Parts of plant can be noisy.
Showroom: Most of the reproductions are on display in the showroom. Kits can be purchased or ordered. Open Mon-Fri 9:00 AM-5:00 PM. Catalog available from above number.
Directions: From Annapolis, MD, and points west, cross the Bay Bridge and take Rt. 50 South to Easton. Take Rt. 322 to the first traffic light. Turn right onto Old Centerville Rd., which goes straight into the Industrial Park. Bartley is second building on the right. From Norfolk, VA, take Rt. 13 North to Salisbury, MD. Take Rt. 50 North into Easton and follow Rt. 322. Turn left at fifth traffic light onto Old Centerville Rd.
Nearby Attractions: St. Michaels and Oxford, old ship-building towns with antique shops, restored buildings, and boat-builders; Black Water Wildlife Refuge, Wild Goose Brewery tour (call 410-221-1121), and Brooks Barrel Company tour (410-228-0790) in Cambridge, 20 minutes away; Atlantic Ocean beaches 1 hour away.

Moore's Candies   *chocolates*

3004 Pinewood Avenue
Baltimore, MD 21214
(410) 426-2705

How often have you been on a tour where the company owner accompanies you, introduces you to the employees (many of whom are immediate family members), and lets you make your own candy? Here's the place! Don't look for a factory or industrial park—this plant is in the 1,500-square-foot basement of the family residence. The company has produced treats from this same space since 1929. In fact, one employee has been dipping Moore's chocolates since the 1920s.

Owner Jim Heyl grew up in the house's upper level. When young Jim needed to raise money for his Cub Scout pack, his parents worked for and eventually bought Moore's Candies, known for helping groups with fund-raising. These fund-raising sales are still important to Moore's Candies' business.

The tour is an informal look at this small, hands-on candy-making operation. Tour guide Jim enthusiastically describes the chocolate "waterfall," the home nut-roaster, and the fillings prepared by his candy-makers. Rich aromas draw you from one table to the next, where caramel or vanilla butter cream fillings are prepared for their chocolate bath, or special-order chocolate swans are filled with home-dry-roasted cashews.

Watch one worker hand-dip chocolates while another uses a wooden paddle to stir bubbling caramel in a copper cauldron. Cherries roll around in rotating kettles, getting a sugar coating before their journey through the enrobing machine for a chocolate cover. This chocolate coating seals in the cherries, whose natural citrus acid reacts with the sugar coating to form the liquid inside a chocolate-coated cherry. Before you leave, be sure to run your own pretzel through the enrobing machine and eat the rewards of your efforts.

Cost: Free

Freebies: Sample chocolate right off the packing line; Official Candymaker Certificate.

Video Shown: No

Reservations Needed: Suggested for under 5 people. Required for larger groups.

(Individuals or groups of fewer than 5 can observe production from the edge of the factory floor without reservations, although you should still call ahead to see if in production.)

Days and Hours: Mon-Fri 10:00 AM-2:00 PM. Lunch break from 12:00 PM to 1:00 PM. Closed holidays, 1 week in July, and between Christmas and New Year's.

Plan to Stay: 20 minutes, plus time in sales area.

Minimum Age: None for families. Recommended minimum for school groups is 6. Due to the small area, children need to be well supervised.

Disabled Access: Yes

Group Requirements: Minimum group size is 5; maximum is 40; 3-5 days' notice required. Special tours may be arranged. For groups larger than 15, with 5 days' advance request, 10-minute slide presentation covers origins of the cocoa bean, harvesting, roasting, and how chocolate is made.

Special Information: Production is most active in fall, winter, and early spring. No photography.

Gift Area: Assorted candies available in small retail space at the entrance including Maryland chocolate and confection specialties (Crabs by the Bushel, Crab Pop, and Chesapeake Chocolates). Open Mon-Fri 9:00 AM-4:00 PM and Sat 10:00 AM-3:00 PM. Closed holidays. Mail-order price list available.

Directions: From Baltimore Beltway (Rt. 695), take Exit 31A. Take Rt. 147 East for 2 miles. Turn left onto Pinewood Ave. Factory is the first building on the left, a brick house that looks like a residence. Park in rear and use building's rear entrance.

Nearby Attractions: Pompeian Olive Oil tour (see page 91); Seagram's tour (call 410-247-6012); GM Minivan tour (call 410-276-6900); White Marsh Shopping Mall; Fire Museum; Baltimore's attractions include Museum of Industry, Fort McHenry, Inner Harbor Area, Lexington Market, and National Aquarium.

Pompeian Olive Oil ⟨⟩ *olive oil and*
red wine vinegar

4201 Pulaski Highway
Baltimore, MD 21224
(410) 276-6900 / (800) 638-1224

Did you know that it takes 2,000 olives to make 1 quart of olive oil? Or that olive oil was one of the earliest products traded internationally? Do you know the differences between types of olive oil, the recommended way to toss a salad, or the uses of olive oil (even in desserts)? Discover these and other interesting historical, gastronomical, and international business facts on a tour of Pompeian, headquartered in East Baltimore since 1906. The company is America's oldest and largest importer, bottler, and distributor of olive oil and red wine vinegar.

Pompeian prides itself on tailoring its educational tour to each group's specific interests. Though there is no "typical tour," the basic tour includes the historic mill, tank storage system, quality control, and bottling process. The 200-year-old, 22-ton granite mill in front of the plant was found in pieces in Spain, restored, and shipped to Baltimore for permanent display at Pompeian. Although earlier mills were human-powered, this mill was originally steam-operated to produce olive oil, a natural fruit juice. Notice the four cone-shaped grinding stones on a 15-foot-wide base. This mill is the only one of its kind in America.

The tour highlight is going underground to see the extensive storage tank system, which covers the length of a football field. The 18 tanks hold 1.5 million gallons of extra-virgin olive oil. The underground temperature naturally maintains itself around 64°. In Spain, the oil is pressed from olive fruit within 72 hours after picking; it's then shipped to Baltimore for storage in these tanks. In the quality control area, learn about the different types of tests performed, the chemical composition of olive oil, and the fundamentals of general nutrition. In the bottling areas, you may see oil pouring into 4-ounce bottles or gallon jugs. From another bottling line, smell the pungent aroma of red wine vinegar aged in casks in Spain for 15 years. The tour ends with a culinary treat, ranging from light snacks to an olive-oil tasting.

Cost: Free

Freebies: Nutrition literature and recipes, light snacks.

Video Shown: 17-minute video, "Olive Oil: From Tree To Table," sent out to groups in advance. Provides overview of olive oil production in Spain and at Baltimore plant.

Reservations Needed: Yes. Provides group tours only (individuals and families join scheduled group tours).

Days and Hours: Mon, Wed, Thur 10:00 AM and 1:00 PM. Closed holidays. Reduced production during Christmas week.

Plan To Stay: 1½ hours for tour and snacks

Minimum Age: 8. Because of the high level of tour's educational content, company's recommended minimum age is 12.

Disabled Access: Yes

Group Requirements: Minimum group is 10 people; maximum is 40. Groups should call 2 weeks in advance for reservations.

Special Information: Vinegar aroma can be strong. Open houses are scheduled based on demand. Spanish language tours are available. For a tour of an olive processing company, see the feature on Graber Olive House, Ontario, CA (page 14).

Gift Shop: No, but can purchase cases of 16-ounce bottles at a discount.

Directions: From I-695 (Beltway), take Rt. 40 toward Baltimore (Rt. 40 is Pulaski Hwy.). Pompeian is on the left at their billboard.

Nearby Attractions: Moore's Candies tour (see page 90); GM Minivan tour (call 410-276-6900); Fells Point; Inner Harbor Area; Baltimore Museum of Industry; Fort McHenry; National Aquarium.

Boston Beer Co. ⌁ *Samuel Adams beer*

30 Germania Street
Boston, MA 02130
(617) 522-9080

In 1985, founder Jim Koch revived his great-great-grandfather's beer recipe and launched the Boston Beer Company. Almost immediately, the company's full-bodied Samuel Adams beers started winning awards. To ensure freshness, Samuel Adams brews most of its beer at larger brewers' facilities which are located nearer to retailers nationwide. It develops its new beers in a part of this urban development park that once housed the Haffenreffer Brewery. Lining the walls of the beer museum are lithographs tracing the history of this urban brewery site; illustrated plaques describing the history of beer, the brewer's art and the family of beer; and other beer memorabilia.

The tour guide, often a brewer, begins by handing out tastes of barley malt and hops. As you chew on barley malt, which tastes like Grape Nuts cereal, your guide explains that the use of only these ingredients (plus yeast and water) makes Samuel Adams one of the few beers to pass Germany's purity laws; thus it can be sold and brewed in Germany.

All the shiny tubs, vats, and kettles of the brewhouse are viewed in one small area, providing a good introduction to the steps involved in brewing beer. Each vessel is labeled so you can identify the mash tub, copper brew kettle, or glass-lined stainless-steel aging tank. Although Samuel Adams makes only a small percentage of its output at this Boston site, you'll leave with the full story of the company and its beer.

Cost: $1, which is donated to the Boys and Girls Club of Greater Boston.
Freebies: 7-oz. logoed tasting glass. Free postage for Samuel Adams postcard to friends or family. In the tap room, glasses of beer and perhaps a taste of seasonal ale brewed only at this location.
Video Shown: In the tasting room, a short video tells why Jim Koch, a sixth-generation brewer, started the company and how it operates.

Reservations Needed: No, except for groups larger than 25 people.
Days and Hours: Thur 2:00 PM; Fri 2:00 PM; Sat 12:00 PM, 1:00 PM, 2:00 PM. Call above number for schedule changes. No beer production during Saturday tours. Closed holidays.
Plan to Stay: 1 hour for tour and tasting, plus time for souvenir shop and beer museum.
Minimum Age: None. Children are welcome. Root beer is available for minors.
Disabled Access: Yes
Group Requirements: Groups larger than 25 people should call 2 weeks in advance for reservations (call 617-497-3209).
Special Information: For safety reasons, you will not see bottling line in operation.
Gift Shop: Sells half-yard and yard glasses, hats, T-shirts, and baseball jackets with the company's logo. Displays paraphernalia and collectors items, such as coasters, bottles, serving trays, and clocks from extinct Massachusetts breweries. Open during tour time periods.
Directions: Take I-93 to Exit 18 (Massachusetts Ave.). Go straight off the ramp onto Melnea Cass Blvd. Turn left onto Tremont St. (eventually becomes Columbus Ave.). Turn right onto Washington St., then right onto Boylston St. Turn left onto Bismark St. and watch for Samuel Adams Brewery signs. Recording at above number gives directions from other routes, including by subway.
Nearby Attractions: Mass Bay Brewing Co. tour (call 617-455-1935); Doyle's restaurant, a nearby pub full of Irish family history, has all Samuel Adams beers fresh on tap; National Braille Press tour (see page 99); Wm. S. Haynes flutes tour (see page 102); *Boston Globe* newspaper tour (call 617-929-2653); Jamaica Pond; Franklin Park Zoo; Arnold Arboretum; Boston's downtown attractions are only a few miles away.

Cape Cod Potato Chips ∼ *potato chips*

Breeds Hill Road
Hyannis, MA 02601
(508) 775-3206

Cape Cod Potato Chips still follows the company's original intent—"to make the best potato chip possible." Just as when Steve Bernard founded it in 1980, the company still kettle-cooks its potato chips one batch at a time. Cape Cod's 1980 production of 200 bags per day is now 150,000-200,000 a day, using 28 million pounds of potatoes each year.

From the plaques in the entranceway, you'll learn that 4 pounds of potatoes yield 1 pound of potato chips and that, depending on the month, the potatoes come from different eastern seaboard states. Each truckload of 45,000-50,000 pounds of potatoes is unloaded into its own silo, since the potatoes must be inspected for solid mass (or "gravity"), external defects, size, and color before farmers receive payment. Different rollers and brushes, depending on the skins' thickness, wash and peel the inspected spuds, which then tumble down to the trim table for further inspection and halving of large potatoes.

Through glass windows you watch sliced potatoes feed into one of the three production lines, each with six gas-fired cooking kettles. Raw potatoes sizzle in hot oil, creating clouds of steam. In the midst of this steam, workers rake the potatoes back and forth in the 8-foot-by-3-foot vats with stainless-steel rakes. The steam subsides as the cooking cycle ends. A worker tilts a scoop into the kettle for the cooked batch of potato chips. Oil drips back into the kettle through the scoop's screen bottom. The worker tilts the scoop back to its original position, allowing the potato chips to slide into a white basket with holes. This centrifuge spins for 4 minutes, allowing excess oil to drain through the holes. Other workers pour the drained chips onto a long cooling conveyor belt.

As you walk along the production line, read the plaques that describe potato-chip making. Along the opposite wall of the corridor, a schematic diagram explains how popcorn is produced. Further down the corridor, workers inspect the cooled chips along a vibrating table which moves them forward without breaking them. The chips pass under the salter box and are transported by "bucket elevator" to the next room for packaging. On each packaging line a carousel of 14 hoppers weighs and releases the correct amount of chips into the bagging machine. Workers hand-pack bags into cardboard boxes, which are shrink-wrapped for shipment or storage in the warehouse.

Cost: Free
Freebies: Sample bag of potato chips
Video Shown: No
Reservations Needed: No
Days and Hours: Mon-Fri 10:00 AM-4:00 PM. Closed holidays.
Plan to Stay: 15 minutes for self-guided tour, plus time in gift shop.
Minimum Age: None, except difficult for small children to see activity beyond cooling chip conveyor.
Disabled Access: Yes
Group Requirements: None
Special Information: No photography. On rainy summer days, allow for waiting time to enter the tour.
Gift Shop: Sells all Cape Cod potato chips, popcorn, logoed caps, and T-shirts. Open Mon-Fri 10:00 AM-5:00 PM. Closed holidays.
Directions: From Rt. 6, take Exit 6 for Rt. 132 South. At fourth traffic light, turn left into Independence Park. Factory is on the right after the airport.
Nearby Attractions: Pairpoint Crystal tour (see page 100); Cape Cod Mall; JFK Museum; Hyannis waterfront and beaches; Thornton Burgess Museum.

Continental Bakery ⟋ *Wonder breads and Hostess snack cakes*

330 Speen Street
Natick, MA 01760
(508) 655-2150

Did you ever wonder how the sweet cream gets into the Hostess Twinkies (invented in 1930) or the seven-loop cupcakes (invented in 1919)? You can witness the sweet cream in action, as Continental Bakery fills thousands per minute! Over one million giant Wonder bread loaves (sliced bread was invented in 1924) per week flow out of its ovens and into the colorful balloon-pictured plastic bags.

As you stroll through this 6-acre bakery, leaving footprints on the lightly floured floor, you follow the making of bread and cakes. They start as ingredients in 50-to-100-pound bags and end as finished goods in a maze of hundreds of 7-foot, 14-shelf high shipping racks. Surprisingly, the aroma isn't much more intense than at your local bakery, except that the whiff hits you a half-mile down the road and lingers in your nostrils for a few hours after the tour.

Wherever you look, future baked goods in some stage of production roll by on conveyors. Dough sits in big troughs waiting to be dropped into bread pans. Giant ovens swallow 2,700 loaves in five-pan rows for their 22-minute transformation from dough to bread. Suction cups gently pull the hot baked loaves from their pans for an overhead cooling-off journey above and across the factory floor four times, until ready for slicing at 110°. Quality control workers grab rejects from the line and toss them into bins headed for the pig farm. At mind-boggling speed, loaves are sliced and packaged into plastic bags. On the cake side of the factory, injection machines shoot sweet cream into the behinds of newborn Twinkies and cupcakes.

Cost: Free
Freebies: Samples of the freshest Wonder bread and Hostess snack cakes you've ever eaten.
Video Shown: No
Reservations Needed: Yes. Since production schedules change, call at beginning of month to schedule tours for that month. Individuals and families need to join a scheduled group tour.

Days and Hours: Mon, Wed, Fri 9:00 AM-4:00 PM. Because of the heat from the ovens, no tours between the end of May and the beginning of September. Closed holidays.
Plan to Stay: Approximately 1 hour, depending on what is in production.
Minimum Age: 4, with one adult required for every four children.
Disabled Access: Yes. Advance notice required for people with wheelchairs.
Group Requirements: Groups must call at beginning of month to schedule tours for that month. No maximum group size.
Special Information: Wear sneakers or rubber-soled shoes, as floor can be slippery. For sanitation and noise reasons, the bakery provides hair nets and earplugs that must be used.
Thrift Store: Sells Hostess cupcakes, Twinkies, and Wonder breads at discounted prices. Open Mon-Fri 9:00 AM-8:00 PM, Sat 9:00 AM-7:00 PM, and Sun 10:00 AM-5:00 PM.
Directions: From I-90 (Mass Pike), take Exit 13. Take Rt. 30 East. Turn right on Speen St. Follow your nose and park in the Wonder Bread Thrift Store parking lot.
Nearby Attractions: Garden in the Woods; Lake Cochituate; Shoppers World; Boston's attractions, including Boston Beer Co. (Samuel Adams beer) and Wm. S. Haynes (flutes) tours (see pages 92 and 102), Back Bay, and Fanueil Hall, are about 15 miles away.

Cranberry World ~ *cranberry juice and related products*

Ocean Spray Cranberries, Inc.
225 Water Street
Plymouth, MA 02360
(508) 747-2350

Cranberries were named because the plant's blossom resembles a crane's head—a "craneberry," which eventually became "cranberry." This native North American fruit is grown only in Massachusetts, Wisconsin, New Jersey, Oregon, Washington, and parts of Canada. Cranberry World offers these and other "berry" unusual facts, along with exhibits and interactive audio-visual displays tracing cranberry cultivation from pre-Pilgrim times to the present. You'll also sample Ocean Spray juice drinks and taste cranberry treats fresh from the demonstration kitchen.

Along the short boardwalk to the entrance, notice the two small cranberry bogs and the flags of the states in the cranberry and citrus farmers' cooperative known as Ocean Spray Cranberries, Inc. Once inside, look for the "rocker" scoop, a wooden cranberry-harvesting implement used from the late 1800s to 1950s. On hands and knees, a grower-harvester put the scoop into the cranberry vines. The scoop's long wooden teeth gently tugged the berries off the vine, then the farmer rocked the scoop onto its curved side and the berries rolled back. At best, the scoop method yielded an average of 400 pounds per day; today's mechanical picking machines average 5,800 pounds daily.

Other highlights include the wooden one-third-scale model of the "bounce machine," a quality control device that tests "bounceability." Ask a guide to put wooden beads into this machine to simulate cranberries. Good berries bounce and are sold as fresh fruit; bad berries are discarded.

Downstairs, a display shows Ocean Spray packaging designs for various products from 1912 to the present. Push-buttons activate brief videos on cranberry sauce and cranberry juice production, and television commercials dating back to 1955. Learn tricks of the trade (like: freezing cranberries makes them easier to slice) and watch a cook whip up a cranberry delicacy in the demonstration kitchen.

Cost: Free

Freebies: Tastes of Ocean Spray juice drinks, treats prepared in kitchen; recipe leaflet.

Video Shown: Brief videos throughout the museum: history of immigrants' role in cranberry industry; old commercials; "Ask" videos on harvesting and on sauce and juice production.

Reservations Needed: No, except for groups of 10 or more people.

Days and Hours: Open May 1-November 30 only. Mon-Sun 9:30 AM-5:00 PM. Demonstration kitchen open for one-hour intervals at 9:30 AM, 11:30 AM, 1:30 PM, and 3:30 PM.

Plan to Stay: 45 minutes-1 hour for museum, videos, and kitchen, plus time for the gift counter.

Minimum Age: None

Disabled Access: Yes

Group Requirements: Groups of 10 or more must call in advance to arrange guided tour.

Special Information: Henderson, Nevada plant and visitors center scheduled to open in early 1995. Will be able to view actual juice-making process through glass windows in visitors center. Call (702) 435-5868 for tour information.

Gift Counter: Sells cranberry-related items (such as cranberry honey, cranberry wine vinegar, and cranberry-colored glass); also Ocean Spray products and pencils. Open same hours as visitors' center.

Directions: From Boston, take I-93 South to Rt. 3 South to Rt. 44 East. Cross Rt. 3A and continue to waterfront. Turn left around rotary onto Water St. Cranberry World is on the right. From Cape Cod, take Rt. 6. Cross Sagamore Bridge. Take Rt. 3 North to Rt. 44 East. Follow the above directions.

Nearby Attractions: The Massachusetts Cranberry Harvest Festival held Columbus Day Weekend features operation of harvesting equipment, historical displays, and cranberry-related cooking and crafts demonstrations; Plymouth Rock; Mayflower II; Whale Watch Cruises; Plymouth National Wax Museum; Plimoth Plantation; beaches.

See color photos, page 153

Crane & Co. ~ *paper*

Crane Museum
Routes 8 & 9
Dalton, MA 01226
(413) 684-2600

Crane's fine papers are used by the White House for stationery and by the Bureau of Engraving and Printing for currency (see page 34). Since 1801, Crane has produced 100 percent cotton paper that offers strength, durability, and surface texture unsurpassed by paper made from wood. The company has even started using denim scraps from Levi Strauss jeans and worn dollar bills to make recycled paper. This family-owned company's mills are in Dalton, in western Massachusetts. The Crane Museum, housed in the company's Old Stone Mill (built in 1844), has welcomed visitors since 1930.

The museum sits on the banks of the Housatonic River, which supplied water to wash the rags and drive the machines of the early Crane paper mills. This ivy-covered stone building has a completely different feel from the modern, multimedia-filled company museums built recently. The museum's interior resembles the Old Ship Church in Hingham, Mass., with rough-hewn oak beams, colonial chandeliers, many-paned windows, and wide oak floorboards. The ceiling looks like an upside-down ship's hull, possibly because the structure was built by shipbuilders instead of carpenters.

After you watch the video on Crane's modern paper-production techniques, walk through exhibits on the history of the company and of papermaking since the Revolutionary War. A scale model of the vat house in the original Crane mill shows the laborious process of hand-making paper one sheet at a time. This process, used by company founder Zenas Crane, contrasts with the modern method of making long continuous rolls of paper.

Among the many different kinds of paper displayed in glass cases are those used for currency, American Express checques, stock certificates, and the stationery of presidents and movie stars. One exhibit of corporate innovation features Crane's paper collars, which the company made after the Civil War. At the time these disposable collars were fashionable and very profitable.

Cost: Free

Freebies: Package of Crane stationery papers.

Video Shown: 20-minute video on company's history and papermaking methods.

Reservations Needed: No, except for groups larger than 15 people.

Days and Hours: Open June through mid-October only. Mon-Fri 2:00 PM-5:00 PM. Closed major holidays.

Plan to Stay: 30 minutes for exhibits, plus time for video.

Minimum Age: None

Disabled Access: Museum is all on one ground-level floor. However, there are a couple of steps to reach it.

Group Requirements: With 1 week's notice, Crane can handle groups up to 50 people.

Special Information: Can visit museum before 2:00 PM if call a few days ahead. Company retirees run museum; they answer questions and offer interesting anecdotes.

Gift Shop: No

Directions: From I-90 (Mass Pike), take the Lee Exit. Follow Rts. 7 and 20 North through Pittsfield. Take Rts. 8 and 9 East about 5 miles. Turn right onto Housatonic St. At bottom is Pioneer Mill. Museum is on the right at the end of Mill.

Nearby Attractions: Berkshire attractions include Clark Art Museum, Mt. Greylock, Berkshire Museum, and Tanglewood.

Harbor Sweets ⟶ *chocolates*

Palmer Cove
85 Leavitt Street
Salem, MA 01970
(508) 745-7648 / (800) 234-4860

While Salem is known for its witches' potions, Harbor Sweets brews only the sweet variety. Their most popular nautical New England theme candies include: "Sweet Sloops," white chocolate-coated almond butter crunch sailboats with dark chocolate and crushed pecan trim; "Sand Dollars," pecan halves soaked in caramel and dark chocolate; and "Marblehead Mints," sailboat-embossed round chocolates with crushed peppermint. The company's key players are its 150 part-time/flex-time employees (many disabled, elderly, or foreign-born) and its innovative founder, Ben Strohecker, the former Schrafft's Candy marketing director who launched Harbor Sweets in 1975.

While the company has expanded into three connected brick buildings, visitors see only the first room. From the slightly raised gift-shop platform, you can observe the labor-intensive production of Sweet Sloops in front of you and molded candies at the far end. Even though you do not enter the production areas, workers will gladly answer your questions. The air is rich with the smell of caramel, toffee, and chocolate.

Notice the home-style, four-burner gas stove in the back. Leaning over copper cauldrons, workers stir batches of almond butter crunch and caramel with wooden paddles. The butter crunch is poured onto a cooling table and then smoothed. With a bladed metal rolling pin, a worker scores the crunch into squares and then triangles. A helper breaks the triangles apart. The triangles proceed through the "enrober" for a coating of white chocolate. With a long metal ice-cream spoon, a worker draws lines representing the mast and jib. After the cooling tunnel, workers hand-dip the Sweet Sloops into melted chocolate and chopped pecans, often a tough job—they must eat their mistakes.

All other candies are molded. Some shapes are specially designed for such organizations as the Boston Symphony Orchestra and the Smithsonian. Depending on the candies being made, melters contain milk or dark chocolate, some with crushed orange or peppermint crunch. A worker holds a 16-cavity plastic mold while the "depositor" drops a specially timed amount of chocolate into each cavity. Another worker inserts dollops of raspberry/cranberry gnache and white chocolate from a hand-held funnel. Once chilled, the candies are individually foil-wrapped before being gift-boxed.

Cost: Free
Freebies: Chocolate sample from a silver serving platter.
Video Shown: No
Reservations Needed: No, except for groups over 6 people.
Days and Hours: Mon-Fri 8:30 AM-4:30 PM. Call about Saturday hours preceding candy-giving holidays. Closed holidays and 2 weeks in July. Limited production May–August.
Plan to Stay: 10–15 minutes for self-guided viewing, plus time in gift shop.
Minimum Age: None
Disabled Access: Yes
Group Requirements: Groups larger than 6 people call 1 week in advance to arrange a tour guide. Groups over 12 will be split into smaller groups. No maximum group size.
Special Information: Best time to see production is September 1 to Easter.
Gift Shop: Sells Harbor Sweet's six varieties of nautical New England theme candies in a variety of gift boxes sizes. Open Mon-Fri 8:30 AM-4:30 PM, Sat 9:00 AM-3:00 PM, with extended hours before holidays and shorter hours in summer. Catalog available from (800) 243-2115.
Directions: From Rt. 128, take Rt. 114 East to Salem. Turn left onto Leavitt St. Harbor Sweets is the last building on the left. From 1A North, follow Rt. 1A as it meanders to Salem. Turn right onto Leavitt St.
Nearby Attractions: Stowaway Sweets self-guided candy tour in Marblehead (call 800-432-0304); Saugus Iron Works blacksmith demonstrations (call 617-233-0050); Salem's attractions, including Pickering Wharf, Salem Witch Museum, House of Seven Gables, and Peabody/Essex Maritime Museum.

Milton Bradley 〜 *board games and puzzles*

443 Shaker Road
East Longmeadow, MA 01028
(413) 525-6411

Abraham Lincoln's beard launched the world's most successful toy manufacturer. According to company folklore, Mr. Milton Bradley needed new work for his lithographic press after sales of his beardless-Lincoln portraits declined. So in this early example of corporate diversification, he created a game: "The Checkered Game of Life."

A part of Hasbro since 1984, the company that bears Bradley's name now builds many best-selling games at this 1-million-square-foot plant, including THE GAME OF LIFE, OPERATION, CHUTES & LADDERS, and SCRABBLE. The plant also builds games by Parker Brothers (bought by Hasbro in 1991), such as MONOPOLY, CLUE, and RISK. After walking this factory floor (the world's largest games and puzzle manufacturing plant), you will never again open a game without recalling how the board, spinner, cards, dice, pad of paper, and fake money found their way into the box.

The plant's printing area hums as high-speed six-color presses spin out freshly painted board sheets for games from CANDYLAND, a child's first game, to the sophisticated, adult SCATTERGORIES. As you tour a football-field-sized holding area filled with 6-foot piles of soon-to-be game covers and boards, childhood memories return and stacks of $100 and $500 MONOPOLY bills catch your eye.

You will not know beforehand what game will be in production during your tour. Ten stations can each assemble up to 1,800 games per hour. An electric-eye machine or a worker places a cardboard-box bottom onto a glued bottom sheet. The bottom is conveyed past workers lined up like BATTLESHIP pegs, each depositing a specific game piece. The top then goes on the box and it's sealed with plastic shrinkwrap.

Jigsaw puzzles from 12 to 3,000 pieces have their own production area, with 10-foot-high pallets of BIG BEN puzzle boxtops waiting for contents. Giant cookie-cutter-like machines chop up the pictures pasted on cardboard, drop the pieces through an over-

sized funnel into a box, and seal it so no piece is lost. The puzzle that you need weeks to assemble takes less than one minute from cutting to sealed package.

Cost: Free
Freebies: Games or puzzles sometimes given to children's groups.
Video Shown: No
Reservations Needed: Yes, at least 12 months in advance. Limited number of tours available. Small groups only. First priority to local children's groups.
Days and Hours: September-November and January-June Wed 9:30 AM.
Plan to Stay: 45 minutes-1 hour for display cases and tour.
Minimum Age: 7
Disabled Access: Due to safety regulations, many factory areas are off-limits to all visitors.
Group Requirements: Minimum group size is 12 people; maximum is 25, with priority to local kids' groups. Reserve tours at least 12 months in advance. Cannot accommodate standard bus-tour groups.
Special Information: This is one of the hardest tours in the book for individuals and families to take. Because the tour is very interesting and the products so well-known, we included it after lengthy discussions with the company about the description of their tour requirements. We recommend you form a group *before* calling about reservations.
Gift Shop: No
Directions: From Boston/Worcester, take I-90 (Mass Pike) West to Exit 6. Take I-291 West to I-91 South Exit 1. Make the first left at the light onto Forest Glen Rd., then a left at Converse St., follow Converse until it ends. Turn right onto Dwight Rd. Go two traffic lights and in about 1 mile turn left onto Industrial Dr. Turn right onto Shaker Rd. and right onto Denslow Rd. Park in first lot. Enter into Human Resources department.
Nearby Attractions: Riverside Amusement Park; Basketball Hall of Fame; Springfield Science Museum.

National Braille Press ⟿ *Braille publications*

88 St. Stephen Street
Boston, MA 02115
(617) 266-6160

National Braille Press

National Braille Press, founded in 1927, is one of only five companies in the U.S. that mass-produce Braille materials, and the only one that publishes original self-help books for the blind. The company prides itself on its leading-edge position in computer-assisted production of Braille publications and on hiring people with disabilities (almost half of its 35-person in-house staff).

The company produces approximately 23 million Braille pages per year from this four-story converted piano-factory on a tree-lined street in the Northeastern University area. Specialized translation software helps workers transcribe the written word into Braille pages. To find any errors in the transcription, blind proofreaders listen to an audio tape of what should be written while following the Braille version with their hands. The proofreading room chatters with the sound of the Braille typewriters that proofreaders use to note mistakes.

Once the pages are corrected, a software version of the publication to be printed directs the computerized plate-embossing machines which punch the raised dots of the Braille alphabet onto zinc printing plates. For any new errors, a small hammer knocks dots out or in on the zinc plates. In the cluttered printing area, you'll watch and hear reconditioned Heidelberg cylinder presses spin out up to 8,000 Braille pages per hour. Workers then hand-collate Braille versions of well-known magazines such as *Parenting* or *Book World*, computer manuals for Microsoft, or popular children's books, before stitch-binding completes the production process.

Cost: Free
Freebies: Samples of Braille materials
Video Shown: No
Reservations Needed: Yes
Days and Hours: Mon-Fri 8:30 AM-5:00 PM. Usually Tue and Thur 10:30 AM and 2:30 PM. Closed holidays.
Plan to Stay: 1 hour
Minimum Age: While there is no official minimum age, children should be at least 6 years old to appreciate the tour. The company tries to make the tour more interactive for children. Watching blind people and those with disabilities working at productive jobs provides kids with a lasting impression.
Disabled Access: Yes, enter from bottom floor.
Group Requirements: Can handle groups up to 12 people with 5 days' advance notice
Special Information: Carefully supervise children around the printing presses. Tours also available at the American Printing House for the Blind in Louisville, KY, the largest and oldest (1859) publishing house for the blind (call 502-895-2405).
Gift Shop: No
Directions: By subway, take the "E" train on the Green Line to the Northeastern University stop on Huntington Ave. Cross Huntington onto Opera Place and turn right onto St. Stephen St. The building is a block ahead on your right. By car, take the Massachusetts Ave. exit on I-93 (Southeast Expwy.). Turn right on Massachusetts Ave. and go straight until you cross Huntington Ave. At Symphony Hall (on your left), turn left on St. Stephen St. National Braille Press is ahead on your left.
Nearby Attractions: Wm. S. Haynes flute tour (see page 102); Boston Beer (Samuel Adams) tour (see page 92); *Boston Globe* newspaper tour (call 617-929-2653); Symphony Hall; Christian Science Center; Northeastern University; Boston's museums and attractions, including the Museum of Science and the Back Bay.

Pairpoint Crystal Company ~ *glass*

851 Sandwich Road
Sagamore, MA 02561
(508) 888-2344 / (800) 899-0953

Since Pairpoint's philosophy is "made in America the old-fashioned way," it utilizes the same hand tools and processes as when Deming Jarves founded the company in 1837. Pairpoint makes cup plates (many are collectors' items), limited editions, and other fine pieces for such museums as New York City's Metropolitan Museum of Art and Boston's Museum of Fine Arts.

Though the observation window shields you from the furnaces' 2500° heat, you know the factory below is hot—the artisans wear shorts year-round. Watch a "gaffer," the most experienced glassblower on the five-person team, fill his cheeks with air and blow into the blowpipe. Once the glass at the other end of the pipe reaches the desired size, he twirls the rod like a baton to elongate the glass.

Using another rod, a team member gathers glass from the furnaces and brings it to the gaffer, who attaches it to the original piece, snips it with shears, then shapes the piece with wooden and metal hand tools. Eventually, the piece is transferred to the "pontil" rod and cracked off from its original blowpipe. The gaffer inserts the work, perhaps a vase or a flask, into a reheating furnace called a "glory hole" and then shapes its opening.

Cup plates, widely used in the mid-1800s as plates for handle-less cups of hot tea, have increased in popularity since Pairpoint started pressing cup plates in the early 1970s. A "gob" of 34 percent lead crystal glass is placed in a mold and an artisan pulls on a lever to exert just the right amount of pressure. While the standard patterns on these 2-inch-diameter cup plates include endangered species, birds, and geometric shapes, you will also want to see the gift-shop display of collector's cup plates commissioned by companies, clubs, and towns.

Cost: Free
Freebies: Product brochures

Video Shown: 20-minute continuously running video covers company history and the glassmaking process. Shown in gift shop.
Reservations Needed: No, unless guided factory-floor tour desired.
Days and Hours: Mon-Fri 9:00 AM-12:00 PM and 1:00 PM-4:30 PM. Closed holidays and for 5 weeks starting January 1.
Plan to Stay: 20 minutes for self-guided tour, plus time for video and gift shop.
Minimum Age: None for gallery, 6 for floor tour.
Disabled Access: Yes
Group Requirements: Maximum group size for factory-floor tour is 20. Call 2 days in advance for reservations.
Special Information: Call to find out about production on weekends or during the January break. Although factory-floor tours can get quite hot, you are closer to the action and also see inspecting and packing areas.
Retail Store: Sells works by the artists, including museum reproductions, vases, candlesticks, and cup plates. Look for the display case with the Barbara Bush Volunteerism Award that Pairpoint makes each year for a deserving Wellesley College student. Can see engraver at work. Open Mon-Sat 9:00 AM-6:00 PM and Sun 10:00 AM-6:00 PM. Closed holidays. Catalog available from (800) 899-0953.
Directions: From Boston, take I-93 South to Rt. 3 South to Sagamore Bridge. After bridge, take first exit onto Rt. 6A. Pairpoint is on your left. From Hyannis, take Rt. 6 West. Take last exit before bridge. Turn left onto Adams St. and left onto 6A. Pairpoint is on your right.
Nearby Attractions: Sandwich Glass Museum; Thornton Burgess Museum; Sandwich Boardwalk (look for nearby plaque designating site of original Boston and Sandwich Glass Co., also founded by Jarvis); Old Grist Mill; Cape Cod Canal Bike Trail; beaches.

Visitors from Winterthur Museum watch gaffers attaching handle to a glass pitcher at Pairpoint Crystal, Sagamore, Massachusetts

Glassblowing at Pairpoint Crystal

Wm. S. Haynes ⁓ *flutes and piccolos*

12 Piedmont Street
Boston, MA 02116
(617) 482-7456

THE HAYNES FLUTE
MFD BY
WM. S. HAYNES CO
BOSTON, MASS

Flutists from all over the world travel to Boston just to visit this famous flute factory. Since 1888, when William S. Haynes opened his flute-making shop in the heart of downtown Boston, legendary artists like Jean-Pierre Rampal have refused to play anything but Haynes flutes.

After viewing the dozens of autographed photos of famous musicians in the front office, you will be guided to the first floor of the factory. Every part of a Haynes flute is made by hand on the premises except for the hollow silver tube body, purchased prefabricated from a precious-metal supplier. If the diameter of this tube is off by more than 1/1000th of an inch (less than the thickness of a human hair) it is returned.

The first stages of flute-making begin in this downstairs workshop, where artisans learn the basics of their craft in what looks more like a machine shop than the birthplace of these beautiful instruments. Drill machines line the walls in a corner where your guide explains Haynes' method of "drop forging," which is more precise and laborious than the casting process used by other flute-makers. The craftsmen hunch over their tables, laboring on the precise placement of the "tone holes" on the body.

The upstairs workshop resembles a jewelry shop, where trained artisans work with tiny silver keys. Each craftsman serves a five-year apprenticeship next to a 20-year veteran in order to learn the craft of hand-finishing the keys. Behind a glass window, watch an artisan polish the flutes to their shiny final appearance with the delicacy and accuracy of a surgeon. You understand why artists around the world proudly send the company records and CDs on which they play their beloved Haynes instruments.

Cost: Free
Freebies: Catalog, price list, and literature.
Video Shown: No video shown on the tour. "The Haynes Story," a brief video on flute-making and Haynes' history, is available for sale.

Reservations Needed: No, except for groups of 6 people or more.
Days and Hours: Mon-Fri 9:00 AM-3:00 PM. Closed holidays.
Plan to Stay: 30 minutes. Flutists should allow extra time at the end of the tour to try out the gold flutes.
Minimum Age: No minimum age, but to best appreciate the tour, a child should be of high-school age or play the flute.
Disabled Access: Yes
Group Requirements: Groups of 6 or more should call 1 week in advance.
Special Information: Best time to tour is Tue or Thur 11:00 AM-2:00 PM, when the tester plays the flutes to check their quality. Parts of the tour can be loud.
Gift Area: Videos, posters, and Haynes logo T-shirts available in the front office during office hours.
Directions: By subway, travel to Arlington Stop on the Green Line. Walk in the direction of traffic down Arlington St. Piedmont St. is the third street on the left. By car from the west, take I-90 (Mass Pike) East to Prudential Center exit. Go towards Copley Square. Follow ramp onto Stuart St. Turn right onto Arlington St. and left onto Piedmont St.
Nearby Attractions: National Braille Press (see page 99); Boston Beer (Samuel Adams) tour (see page 92); *Boston Globe* newspaper tour (call 617-929-2653); Downtown Boston's attractions include Boston Symphony Hall, Carl Fisher Music Store, Berklee School of Music, Faneuil Hall, Boston Common, Public Garden, and the Back Bay.

Yankee Candle   ⌒   *candles*

Route 5
South Deerfield, MA 01373
(413) 665-8306

Yankee Candle Company

If you ever made candles by melting wax and crayons, you have something in common with Mike Kittredge, founder of Yankee Candle. This tour starts where it all began, at the antique Queen Atlantic gas stove Mike used to melt wax in his parents' cellar at age 17 in 1969. The walls display a pictorial history of the company's development from his parents' house to a renovated paper mill in 1974 to the current Yankee Candle complex in 1983.

T-shirted employees who work with piped-in music describe the place as a huge craft studio that smells like a spice rack. Through glass windows, you'll see almost all the steps involved in making taper, jar, pillar, and sampler candles. Overhead videos and plaques describe the manufacturing process at each viewing station. The automatic taper-candle-dipping machine, resembling a chandelier with wicks instead of light bulbs, dips up to 2 miles of wicks per day. To create the standard ⅞-inch taper candle, the machine dips braided cotton wicks into liquid wax (as many as 30 times), alternating with dips into a cooling water bath. Workers then hand-dip the final, harder wax layers to create smooth, dripless candles.

Textured pillar candles start as colorful solid-wax cylinders. Workers place four smooth pillar candles on pedestals to begin their transformation. The candles, pushed up through 300°-hot grooved rings, emerge from the top of the press as ionic (vertically grooved) or twist (spirally grooved) pillars. The making of jar candles will remind you of jello molding: a machine fills eight glass containers at a time with hot, colorful, fragrant wax.

While you watch the candle-making, grab a "sampler menu" and test-sniff some of the 120 sample scents along the "Wall of Samplers" that lines the glass observation windows. Fragrances include the traditional (cranberry), the unexpected (autumn leaves), the delicious (vanilla cookie), and the inspirational (mountain stream).

Cost: Free

Freebies: "Fun Sheet" for kids tests candle-making knowledge.

Video Shown: Continuously running videos above viewing windows provide close-up shots of the processes occurring at each station.

Reservations Needed: No, except for groups of 10 or more.

Days and Hours: Guided tours (still through windows) Mon-Sun 11:30 AM, 1:00 PM, and 3:00 PM. Self-guided tours during store hours. Best tour time is 1:00 PM because all areas are in full production. May not see production on weekends. When not in production you can watch the overhead videos and look at the candle-making machines. Closed Thanksgiving and Christmas.

Plan to Stay: 20 minutes for tour and videos, plus time for gift shop and any special events on the grounds.

Minimum Age: None

Disabled Access: Yes

Group Requirements: Groups of 10 or more should call at least 1 day ahead for guided tours. Call (413) 665-8306, ext. 206. Bus-tour participants receive a pair of half tapers and a logo button.

Special Information: Company has plans to take people onto the factory floor in a specially designed tunnel.

Retail Store: Sells country-kitchen jar candles, aromatic samplers, and scented and unscented tapers. Upstairs "Seconds Room" has overruns and flawed candles at marked-down prices. Open Mon-Sun 9:30 AM-5:30 PM; longer hours during Christmas season. Catalog available from (800) 243-1776. Also a 13,000-square-foot Christmas store, including 14 individual shops with a European fairyland feeling.

Directions: Take I-90 (Mass Pike) to I-91 North to Exit 24. Turn right on Rtes. 5 and 10. Yankee Candle is on your left.

Nearby Attractions: Mt. Sugarloaf State Reservation; Sugarloaf Shoppes; Historic Deerfield; Mohawk Trail Autoroad.

Amway ⟿ *household and personal care products*

7575 E. Fulton Street East
Ada, MI 49355
(616) 676-6701

Amway believes hard work and diligence give individuals the power to control their own destinies by owning their own businesses. In the headquarters lobby is a 16-foot sculpture, "Building Together The American Way," showing how the Amway network marketing system works. Beside the sculpture are statues of Amway's founders, Rich De Vos and Jay Van Andel. The 3.5-million-square-foot manufacturing and distribution center supplies merchandise and support that make individual distributors' dreams of owning their own businesses a reality.

The tour winds through hallways lined with products in display cases and plaques identifying individual distributors' accomplishments. Near the new-product labs, notice the plaques for each of Amway's patents. In the Michigan Regional Distribution Center, hear the cacophony produced by hundreds of thousands of wheels in the network of conveyors. This conveyor maze carries merchandise from the warehouse shelves to the staging area, where it is packed and shipped to supply much of the Midwest. As you would expect, the whole operation is computerized and each box is labeled with the recipient's name and address before being loaded into the appropriate semi-trailer.

After a short bus ride, still within the confines of the city-like Amway complex, the tour takes you through one of the largest private printing operations in the Midwest. With rivers of multicolored paper running up down and around at a mind-boggling rate, these gargantuan printing presses produce much of Amway's letterhead, catalogues, and promotional materials. They print some 2,300 different pieces in all and use 500 to 800 rolls of paper per day. You leave understanding more about the attitude that built Amway into a successful direct-marketing business.

Cost: Free

Freebies: Travel-size bottles of body lotion, shampoo, conditioner and other Amway products.

Video Shown: 11-minute video introduces the company and details some processes used in manufacturing soap powder and other household products.

Reservations Needed: No, except for groups of 10 or more.

Days and Hours: Mon-Fri 9:00 AM, 11:00 AM, 1:00 PM, and 3:00 PM. Closed for long holiday weekends and 1 week in June for annual convention.

Plan to Stay: 1-1¼ hours for tour and video.

Minimum Age: None, although all children under 16 must be accompanied by an adult.

Disabled Access: Since part of the tour is conducted on a mini-bus, Amway prefers advance notice to arrange for a mini-bus with a lift.

Group Requirements: Groups of 10 or more require 2-4 weeks' advance booking. Maximum group size is 50.

Special Information: Plan to arrive 15 minutes prior to tour time. Wear comfortable walking shoes for the almost 1-mile walking tour, which includes steps.

Gift Shop: No. Catalog available from (800) 544-7167.

Directions: From Detroit, follow I-96 West toward Lansing and Grand Rapids. Pass Lansing on I-96 and continue to Exit 52 (Lowell). Follow the signs into the town of Lowell. Turn left onto Main St. (M-21). Follow M-21 out of Lowell for about 6 miles. Turn right into the Amway World Headquarters Building and park immediately in front. The tour desk is located in the back of the main lobby. From Chicago, follow I-94 East to I-196 East (Gerald R. Ford Freeway) toward Grand Rapids. Stay on I-196 through Grand Rapids (becomes I-96 just east of Grand Rapids) to Exit 39. The exit road becomes Fulton Rd. In about 5 miles, turn left into the Amway World Headquarters Building.

Nearby Attractions: Public Museum of Grand Rapids; Grand Rapids Art Museum; Gerald R. Ford Museum; Grand Rapids Symphony Orchestra.

AutoAlliance *Ford and Mazda cars*

1 International Drive
Flat Rock, MI 48134
(313) 782-7128

While you may not recognize a car company named "AutoAlliance," you do know the cars they build: Ford Probe, Mazda 626, and Mazda MX-6. Originally, Mazda Motor Manufacturing (USA) owned the plant, with its first cars rolling off the line in September 1987. Ford bought into the facility in July 1992, which resulted in a name change and a 50/50 joint venture between the two auto manufacturers.

The tour showcases current robotics and automation used to build cars under a Japanese production system with UAW-represented workers. After an introductory briefing and video, you walk through most of the plant's major production operations. In the stamping area, automated guided vehicles (AGVs) deliver metal sheets to the thundering presses that produce major body parts, such as the roofs, side panels, and fenders. Workers in company-logoed uniforms unload and stack the stamped panels for delivery to body assembly.

Robots perform the most physically demanding tasks in body-shell construction. The body's silver-gray metal pieces slide together and a frame holds them in place while robotic arms apply precise welds. Although the conveyor belt and robots are fenced in, you'll see sparks fly as the frame moves down the line, stopping at different stages so the 400 robots can perform 97 percent of the required body welds. In the paint area, workers apply different coatings for corrosion protection and leak prevention. Robots then apply the top coat and perform sealer and under-coating operations.

The trim and final assembly lines combine more robotics with some novel ergonomic methods. Notice how the car is tilted above the worker to a 30° angle. This allows workers to install underbody parts, such as the fuel tank, without bending and twisting their backs. Long robot arms with suction fingers pick up and install the front and rear windshields. Engine and transmission installation are also automated. By the time the car reaches the quality control and testing areas, it has traveled 13 miles in the course of its production. Here human workers' eyes, hands, and ears again take over, making you realize the different roles that machines and humans play in building cars.

Cost: Free
Freebies: Information folder that includes a brochure with highlights of the production process.
Video Shown: 15-minute video on AutoAlliance and its production methods and 8-minute video on the paint department (not on the tour).
Reservations Needed: Yes. Individuals and families need to join scheduled group tours.
Days and Hours: Thur 8:30 AM and 1:00 PM. Closed holidays, week between Christmas and New Year's, and week of July 4th.
Plan to Stay: 2 hours for videos and tour.
Minimum Age: 14 (9th grade and above)
Disabled Access: Yes
Group Requirements: Minimum group is 10 people; maximum is 30. Make reservations as far ahead as possible, at least 3 months ahead for summer reservations.
Special Information: No photography. No shorts. Limited tours available at Ford luxury car plant in Wixom, MI (call 313-344-5358).
Gift Shop: No
Directions: From I-75 South, take Exit 29B (Flat Rock). Turn right onto Gibraltar Rd. and right onto International Dr. AutoAlliance is on your right. Enter S-3. From I-75 North, take Exit 29. Turn left onto Gibraltar Rd. and follow above directions.
Nearby Attractions: Henry Ford Museum and Greenfield Village are about 20 minutes away, in Dearborn (call 313-271-1620). Henry Ford built this 245-acre, indoor-outdoor complex as a tribute to the culture, resourcefulness, famous inventors, and technology of the U.S.A. Look for multimedia "Made In America" exhibit of how things are manufactured and the people who manufacture them. Detroit's attractions, including Greektown, Detroit Science Center, and the Motown Historical Museum, are about 30 minutes away.

Brooks Beverages

7-Up, Canada Dry, other sodas

777 Brooks Avenue
Holland, MI 49423
(616) 396-1281

Brooks Beverage Management, Inc.

Gleaming, stainless-steel tanks holding the essence of some of your favorite refreshments—Canada Dry, Squirt, Hires, 7-Up, Hawaiian Punch, Tahitian Treat—fill the syrup room, your first sight on one of the few soda-bottling plant tours you can take without reservations. Phillips Brooks founded the company in 1934, producing 7-Up in his basement. The company has remained family-owned, and is now run by Phil's grandson. A handout explains the processes you'll see through windows on the plant's observation deck.

Each unit of the highly concentrated extract in the syrup room produces 400 cases of soda! Nutra Sweet or corn sweetener combine with the extract to form syrup, which fills even larger tanks (some hold enough syrup for 20,000 cases). In the filling room, a larger area crammed with oversized equipment and speeding conveyor belts, the blender machines mix syrup into fresh, purified, charcoal-filtered water before the mixture is cooled to 35°. Injecting the mixture with carbon dioxide completes the recipe, and the "pop" is ready for bottling.

Glass bottles, plastic containers, and cans race at dizzying speeds along three filling lines. Cans are not filled through the holes from which you drink. Rather, a machine fills them through the top, seals on the flip-top lid, then flips the cans over to heat them and check for leaks. The white foam all over the floor isn't "escaped" soda pop—it's a soap lubricant that keeps the conveyors whirling at high speed without overheating and jamming. The can line fills almost 1,200 cans per minute, nearly 27,000 cases per 8-hour shift.

The packaging room holds empty cans and bottles awaiting their turns to be filled. Through a viewing window you can follow the bottles' conveyor-belt passage through the wall into and out of the filling room. Steam clouds hover over warmers, which bring the filled cans and bottles up to room temperature to avoid condensation damage to the cartons. Filled cases climb the belt to stack themselves on pallets for storing or

shipping. Every month, Brooks produces over one million cases of refreshment. During your tour alone, 25,000 containers will finish the bottling journey.

Cost: Free
Freebies: Beverages
Video Shown: No
Reservations Needed: No, except for groups larger than 10 people who want a guided tour.
Days and Hours: Open Mon-Thur 8:00 AM-5:00 PM. Call ahead, since production shuts down once every few weeks for a short inventory. Closed holidays.
Plan to Stay: 15-20 minutes for self-guided tour.
Minimum Age: None
Disabled Access: Observation deck is up one flight of stairs.
Group Requirements: Groups larger than 10 people can request guided tour by calling 1 week in advance.
Special Information: No photography. Production is heaviest in the summer and before holidays. Avoid starting your tour in late afternoon, when the bottling lines may be closing down.
Gift Shop: No
Directions: From Grand Rapids, take I-196 West to Exit 52. Turn right onto 16th St. Turn left onto Waverly Rd. Turn right onto 32nd St. The plant is ahead on the left, at the corner of 32nd St. and Brooks Ave.
Nearby Attractions: Original Wooden Shoe Factory tour (see page 111); DeKlomp/Veldheer tour (see page 107); Annual Tulip Time Festival (in May); Hope College; Lake Michigan shorefront; Holland State Park (campgrounds).

DeKlomp/Veldheer   *wooden shoes and delftware*

12755 Quincy St. & U.S. 31
Holland, MI 49424
(616) 399-1900

Holland, Michigan, is full of Dutch treats. The Tulip Time Festival (usually the second or third week of May) will pleasantly overwhelm you with the dazzling colors of millions of tulips in full bloom. At DeKlomp, the only delftware factory in the U.S., watch delftware and wooden shoes being made. Also enjoy Veldheer's tulip farm and show garden.

Delftware originated with pottery brought to the Netherlands from the Orient in the 13th century. In 1310, Dutch artists in the village of Delft adapted the oriental patterns, giving birth to the familiar blue-and-white handpainted floral designs and Dutch scenery. Much of what passes for delftware in this country is actually mass-produced and stencil-decorated. However, DeKlomp's artisians paint each individual piece with the blue-and-white designs.

Dressed in traditional Dutch costume during Tulip Time, the artisans happily discuss each step of the production process, from molding the clay to decorating the final product. All materials—clay, molds, and machinery—are imported from the Netherlands. Walk through the pour room where liquid clay ("slip") is poured into plaster molds, the kiln room where dried pottery is fired, and the paint room where pottery is hand-painted and signed on the bottom.

In the next room, watch the creation of wooden shoes. Using a "dual-action" shaper machine and a pattern, workers make the left and right shoes simultaneously. By rotating a block counterclockwise the machine traces a mirror image, thus producing a matched pair. Notice the narrow shelves along the wall which contain wooden shoe patterns. A worker places one of these patterns on the center rod of the dual-action carving machine. The right rod carves the right shoe and the left rod, the left shoe. You will also see the only automated wooden shoe carving machine in the U.S. and a shaper machine that makes souvenir 3.5-to-12.5-cm. shoes—sometimes as many as five in a row, resembling a totem pole.

Cost: Free
Freebies: No
Video Shown: No
Reservations Needed: No, except for groups over 20.
Days and Hours: June-December: Mon-Fri 8:00 AM-6:00 PM, Sat-Sun 9:00 AM-5:00 PM. December-April: Mon-Fri 9:00 AM-5:00 PM. During Tulip Time Festival (May): Mon-Sun 8:00 AM-dusk. Closed Thanksgiving, Christmas, and New Year's. Wooden shoes not carved January-March.
Plan to Stay: 20-30 minutes for self-guided tour, plus time for gift shop and Veldheer's Tulip Gardens. During April and May, you'll see millions of tulips and daffodils in bloom among windmills, Dutch drawbridges, and canals.
Minimum Age: None
Disabled Access: Yes
Group Requirements: Groups over 20 should call in advance to arrange a guided tour. No maximum group size.
Gift Shop: Carries all of the shoes and delftware made in the factory, including delft canister sets and Christmas ornaments, and a wide variety of Dutch gifts. Open same hours as tour. Catalog available from above number.
Directions: From Chicago, take I-94 East to I-196 North to Exit 44. Bear left at Exit 44. Take U.S. 31 North (don't take Business Rt.) through Holland. From Grand Rapids, take I-196 West to Exit 55. Take Business Rt. 196 West. Turn right onto U.S. 31 North and follow it to Quincy St. The factory is on Quincy St. just east of U.S. 31.
Nearby Attractions: During Tulip Time Festival in May, the entire town is alive with color and activities. Original Wooden Shoe Factory tour (see page 111); Brooks Beverages tour (see page 106); Dutch Village; Windmill Island; Saugatuck, an artists' colony.

General Motors ～ *Buick cars*

Buick City
902 E. Hamilton Ave.
Flint, MI 48550
(810) 236-4494

From the outside, Buick City looks just as you would expect any other 1905-vintage factory to look—big and brown, with lots of smokestacks. This early-1900s exterior, however, conceals one of GM's most sophisticated automobile assembly facilities. Starting in 1982, GM and UAW Local 599 worked together to turn this old factory into a competitive modern plant. The tour allows you to see many of the major steps in manufacturing a Buick. While workers are important to most of the assembly steps, it's the extensive use of robotics you'll remember most.

After body parts—the side frames, underbody, roof, and other steel parts—have been stamped, the car begins to come together in the Robogate Station, where computerized body-welding robots move with surgical precision. A throng of the long-necked, reptilian robots simultaneously dances in and out of each vehicle. They weld each section of the body frame, producing a brilliant fountain of sparks with each weld. On another part of the seemingly endless assembly line, robots automatically install and seal windshields and rear windows. A robot arm picks up the glass with vacuum suction cups and sets it precisely into place. Other robots apply adhesive and primer and even clean the glass.

The seat installation process shows the latest in just-in-time manufacturing. At the loading docks, a line of trucks brings the prefabricated seats into Buick City. There is never more than a one-hour supply of seats in the plant at any time. As each truck pulls up, a robot reaches into the trailer, pulls out the correct color seat, and delivers it directly to the appropriate place on the assembly line, where it is installed by a worker. The engine, which travels by trailer from the adjoining engine plant, is attached to drivetrain components such as the transaxle and exhaust system. Automatic Guided Vehicles (AGVs) place the assembled drivetrain beneath the car body and workers bolt drivetrain and body together. When you see workers do a detailed quality check of the

car, you appreciate how robots have become the autoworker's best helper.

Cost: Free
Freebies: Safety glasses provided at the start of the tour; brochure on Buick City and production process.
Video Shown: No
Reservations Needed: Yes
Days and Hours: Normally Thur 9:30 AM and 12:00 PM. Closed holidays and 2 weeks in July, usually at end of month. *Because of the addition of a third assembly line to manufacture the Buick Park Avenue, tours were suspended just as we finished writing this book. GM plans to continue tours after the new line is constructed.*
Plan to Stay: 1½-2 hours for tour and Q&A.
Minimum Age: 6
Disabled Access: Yes
Group Requirements: Maximum group size is 40. Make reservations at least 1 month in advance for summer tours.
Special Information: No photography. Tour does not include paint department. Buick tours also available at Warren, OH plant (call 216-824-5000)
Gift Shop: No
Directions: From Detroit, take I-75 North to I-475 North (at Flint) to Exit 8B (Stevers-Broadway). From the exit you can drive only one way on Stevers until Broadway. Turn left on Broadway. At the river, Broadway becomes Hamilton. Continue on Hamilton to North St. and turn right. Enter the plant grounds at the second entrance gate.
Nearby Attractions: Crossroads Village/Huckleberry Railroad; Flint Institute of Arts; Children's Museum; For-Mar Nature Preserve and Arboretum; Frankenmuth's attractions (known as "Michigan's Little Bavaria") include the Frankenmuth Pretzel Company tour (call 517-652-9171) about 20 miles away.

Hoegh Industries ~ *pet caskets*

317 Delta Avenue
Gladstone, MI 49837
(906) 428-2151

Hoegh Industries is the world's largest manufacturer of pet caskets, cremation urns, and memorial plaques. Dennis Hoegh began the business in 1966 after meeting a dog owner who could not find a casket worthy of his beloved sled dog. The company now produces over 30,000 caskets annually in eight sizes and 22 styles, ranging from a hamster-sized 10-inch case to a 52-inch box fit for the grandest Great Dane. Molded of high-impact styrene plastic and equipped with a padded cloth interior, the caskets are made by a crew of eight workers.

Your tour starts near the computerized ovens; each one heats and softens four pieces of plastic simultaneously. Plastic sheets in different sizes, some pink, some blue, most buff, line the corridor awaiting their turn in the ovens. Entering the oven as a rigid sheet clamped into a metal frame, the plastic undergoes a startling transformation. The rigid sheets become flexible, clothlike membranes, vibrating and jiggling as they're pulled out of the oven. As a plastic sheet hovers in the air, a mold rises up to meet it. Vacuum pumps suck all the air from the space between plastic and mold, and a pet casket forms.

Once cool, molded bottoms are lifted out of the frame so a worker can cut off the flashing and scrape the edges. One worker collects this excess plastic and feeds it into a waist-high grinder, creating tiny plastic pebbles. Beyond the grinder machine you can see where the polyurethane foam is added. The casket bottom sits in a wooden support while a worker sprays a thin stream of superheated chemicals along the bottom inside edge. The worker must quickly insert, brace, and clamp down the interior wall, since the chemicals immediately begin to expand like exploding meringue. Confined by the interior and exterior casket walls, the foam expands within the cavity into a sturdy insulation, creating a double-walled, eternal vessel. Home workers sew the cloth interiors for the caskets.

Step outside to admire the model pet cemetery. Most intriguing is a wall of remembrance plaques. A pet's photograph can be engraved onto a durable metal plaque, along with a name, dates, and a brief comment. Look for the plaques for Chuck the lizard, Fruit Loops the toucan, and the pet turkey who died at age 13 and would walk on a leash.

Cost: Free
Freebies: Postcards, brochures, rulers, pencils, pens, occasionally calendars.
Video Shown: Optional 17-minute video highlights the production process and shows a model pet cemetery. Video usually shown in winter or bad weather; also can be sent to groups, upon request.
Reservations Needed: No, however preferred for groups larger than 10 people. Individuals and families may want to call ahead (same day) to give the factory notice.
Days and Hours: Open Mon-Fri 8:00 AM-4:00 PM. Lunch break from 12:00 PM-12:30 PM. Closed holidays.
Plan to Stay: 30-45 minutes
Minimum Age: No minimum if accompanied by a parent. Children in groups should be 10 years old.
Disabled Access: Yes
Group Requirements: Groups larger than 10 people should call at least 1 day in advance.
Special Information: Umbrella tables are available for picnicking in the outdoor area.
Gift Shop: No
Directions: Take I-75 North. At the Mackinaw Bridge, follow U.S. 2 West. When you reach Gladstone, turn left on Delta Ave. The factory is on the right.
Nearby Attractions: Iverson Snowshoes tour (call 906-452-6370); DeLoughary's Sugar Bush maple syrup and cream tour (call 906-466-2305); Fayette State Park; Seney National Wildlife Refuge; Hiawatha National Forest.

Lionel Trains   ~   *model trains*
26750 Twenty-Three Mile Road
Mt. Clemens, MI 48045
(810) 949-4100, ext. 1211

Just about every American over 35 recognizes the Lionel Train brand name. Back in 1949, people of all ages used to stop by the company's showroom on East 26th Street in New York City to see the famous miniature railroad display. Store buyers and collectors would come to watch as small locomotives pulled freight cars through pretend towns and over imitation mountains. But in 1964, the showroom closed its doors. Today, thanks to the hard work, dedication, and volunteer efforts of the employees at Lionel Trains' Michigan headquarters, you can once again enjoy seeing Lionel trains in action and learning the story behind the company that started in 1900.

Your visit begins with a video about Lionel and its heritage. Then you enter the showroom. Lights slowly rise over the 14-by-40-foot railroad display, illuminating a fascinating arrangement of trains, tracks, and scenery that will remind kids (and kids at heart) why they love collecting model trains.

The classic display maintains ties to the famed 1949 showroom layout but adds its own personality and modern design. It features three levels of tracks with four different rail lines. Buttons around the display allow visitors to operate accessories themselves, including trains on a smaller layout just for young kids. The design of the bottom level includes elements from the original 1949 layout, such as the underground passenger platform and the yard and roundhouse area. The next level reveals more modern-era trains, including more freight cars and diesel-powered engines. The top level uses the American Flyer line which, although different in size than the other model trains, seems to fit in perfectly with the rest of the display atop the imposing mountain range.

While gazing at the moving trains, don't forget to explore the impressive scenery. Kits and landscape sets made of painted wood and foam were pieced together to make a small, semi-real city. The workers who created this extraordinary display thought of every detail, right down to the park statues, railyard

workers, and store signs. Also notice the company timeline on the wall, illustrating over nine decades of model train history; it includes rare and unique prototype train models and historic ads and photos.

Cost: Free
Freebies: Souvenir pin and product catalog.
Video Shown: 10-minute video on company history and manufacturing, narrated by Lionel Chairman and CEO Richard Kughn.
Reservations Needed: Yes
Days and Hours: Tue 10:00 AM; Wed 3:00 PM and 4:00 PM; Thur 10:00 AM, 3:00 PM, and 4:00 PM; Fri 1:30 PM and 2:30 PM; Sat 9:00 AM, 10:00 AM, 11:00 AM; Sun 11:00 AM, 12:00 PM, 1:00 PM. Additional times added seasonally. Closed holidays.
Plan to Stay: 1 hour for video and tour, plus time for gift shop.
Minimum Age: None
Disabled Access: Yes
Group Requirements: For groups of 20 or more, additional tour times may be available. Maximum group size is 60 people.
Special Information: Information available about Railroader Club membership.
Gift Shop: Sells the Visitors Center Boxcar (available only at this store) and logoed items including T-shirts, signs, and clocks. Discount for Railroader Club members. Open around tour hours.
Directions: From I-94, take Exit 243 (Twenty-Three Mile Road/New Baltimore Exit). Veer left at exit if coming from Detroit. Turn left at second light. Turn right at second drive.
Nearby Attractions: Morley Candy factory tour (groups only, call 810-468-4300); Detroit's attractions, including Greektown, Detroit Science Center, and Motown Historical Museum, are about 30 minutes away.

Original Wooden Shoe Factory

447 U.S. 31 at 16th Street ⌒ *wooden shoes*
Holland, MI 49423
(616) 396-6513

No trip to this quaint Dutch village near Lake Michigan is complete without a visit to a wooden shoe factory. Opened in 1926, Original Wooden Shoe is the oldest such factory in North America, and the only factory still using early-1900s, European-made wooden-shoe-making machines which turn out the shoes one at a time.

As you walk onto the shoe factory's sawdust-covered floor you smell the poplar and aspen wood and hear the sounds of the old machines at work. Behind a protective screen sits a pile of logs, first sawed into lengths determined by shoe size and then quartered according to the width of the shoe. The "roughing" machine, dated 1908, strips off the logs' bark and imperfections. A worker clamps wood onto the "shaping" machine as you would put a chicken on a rotisserie spit. This machine gives shoes their basic shape.

A few steps further down the line a worker strains with the "boring" machine. This contraption, made in France in 1914, uses a pattern shoe to bore out the front of the new shoe to the desired specifications, just as the hardware store's key-cutting machine uses your old key as a guide to create an exact duplicate. With his drawknife fastened to a ring at the end of his cutting log, a worker skillfully hand-carves and trims the outside of the shoe and smoothes the edges. Finally, artists personalize the finished product by painting or wood-burning traditional Dutch decorations and your name onto each shoe. Whether you call their wooden shoes *klompen* (Dutch) or *sabots* (French), you can leave with a pair fitted just for you.

Cost: 25¢ per person
Freebies: No
Video Shown: No
Reservations Needed: No, but best to call ahead to ensure production in off-season (December through March).
Days and Hours: Mon-Sat 8:00 AM-4:30 PM. Tulip Time Festival (10 days in May, starting the week before Mother's Day): Mon-Sun 8:00 AM-6:00 PM. Limited tours December through March. Closed Thanksgiving, Christmas, and New Year's.
Plan to Stay: 20 minutes for self-guided tour, plus time for gift shop.
Minimum Age: None
Disabled Access: Yes
Group Requirements: Groups larger than 25 people are asked to call 1 or 2 hours in advance of arrival. No maximum group size. No admission charge for bus tours
Special Information: In addition to the early-1900s machines which are the major attraction, the factory also operates relatively modern "dual-action" machines which make both shoes at the same time. In addition, hand-carving demonstrations are conducted frequently during Tulip Time Festival, and by appointment the rest of the year.
Gift Shop: Sells a wide variety of Dutch gifts, including wooden shoes (produced on-site or mass-produced in Europe) and hardwood salad bowls (made on-site in a non-public factory). Mon-Sun 8:00 AM-6:00 PM. Tulip Time Festival and July 4th–Labor Day: Mon-Sun 8:00 AM-8:00 PM. Price list available from above number.
Directions: From Grand Rapids, take I-96 West to Exit 52. Turn right onto 16th St. The factory is 2 miles ahead on the left. From Chicago, take I-94 East to I-96 (U.S. 31) North to Holland. Stay on U.S. 31 Bypass toward Muskegan. Factory is on your right.
Nearby Attractions: During Tulip Time Festival in May, the entire town is alive with color and activities. DeKlomp/Veldheer tour (see page 107); Brooks Beverages tour (see page 106); Dutch Village; Windmill Island; Saugatuck, an artists' colony 8 miles away.

Arctco ~ *Arctic Cat snowmobiles and*
personal watercraft

600 Brooks Avenue South
Thief River Falls, MN 56701
(218) 681-8558

The Arctic Cat snowmobile has often set the standards for the North American snowmobile industry. In 1962, the Arctic Cat was the first front-engine snowmobile ever produced in this country; in the early 1970s it was the top selling snowmobile. Tough times for the industry and the U.S. economy in the late 1970s halted production. During the early 1980s the "Boys From Thief River" restructured the company; now, once again, it manufactures award-winning racing and touring snowmobiles (one-millionth model built in July 1993). The company also started producing Tigershark-brand personal watercraft.

Depending on the month, your tour shows what's involved in making the Arctic Cat or Tigershark (although not in sequential assembly order) and numerous subassembly steps. The first thing you see is a line hanging with parts that have been through the powder paint shed, on their way to an oven that bakes the paint into the metal parts. Throughout the tour, you often see parts on conveyors moving in and out of cleaning, priming, and painting booths.

Robots and workers weld together the chassis. Workers put the parts in the "jig," a frame that holds them together during assembly. With sparks flying, a robotic arm moves from spot to spot welding the chassis. Down the line, workers bolt some parts and robotic arms weld others to the chassis, including the skis. As your guide explains in the Tigershark production area, the fiberglass bodies are made from the outside in, with chopped-up fiberglass and resin shot into molds.

The foam cushion seats start as liquid chemicals, with the mix determining the desired plushness. This mixture is squirted into preheated molds and within a few minutes, out pops a cushion. After the vinyl is stretched around it, the seat is ready for the silk-screened logo. In the main assembly area, each chassis moves down the line with a parts cage that contains all its pieces; workers pull out parts as needed. When they test the engine, you think about the fun of riding the machine on the nearby Thief River.

Cost: Free
Freebies: Balloons, bumper stickers, decals, product literature.
Video Shown: No
Reservations Needed: No, except for groups larger than 15 people.
Days and Hours: Mon-Fri 1:00 PM. Closed holidays. Special arrangements possible for other tour times. Not always in full production December-March and occasional shutdowns when waiting for parts, so call ahead about the day you want to visit.
Plan to Stay: 1 hour for tour, plus time for gift counter.
Minimum Age: None
Disabled Access: Yes
Group Requirements: 1 week's advance notice for groups larger than 15 people. Maximum group size is 25.
Special Information: No photography. Other than during spring months, snowmobiles and personal watercraft are not in production simultaneously.
Gift Shop: Sells logoed items, including T-shirts, caps, mugs, and scale-model Arctic Cats and trucks. Open Mon-Fri 1:00 PM-5:00 PM or after tour, if earlier. Catalog with full line of clothes and accessories available at above number. Information about Cat's Pride, the world's largest organized snowmobile owners club, available from (800) 279-8558 (800-461-1987 in Canada).
Directions: From Hwy. 2, take Hwy. 59 North through center of Thief River Falls. Turn left onto Brooks Ave. (Bowling Center on the corner). Arctco is on your right. From Hwy. 32, turn left at Brooks Ave.
Nearby Attractions: Christian Brothers hockey stick factory tour in Warroad (see page 114); Polaris snowmobile tour (call 218-463-2312) in Roseau; Red Lake River; Pioneer Park; Agassiz Wildlife Reserve.

Blandin Paper ⟶ *paper*

115 S.W. First Street
Grand Rapids, MN 55744
(218) 327-6682

BLANDIN PAPER

Since pioneer days, northern Minnesota has depended on the forest products industry. Today, sophisticated machinery replaces late 1800s logging camps. Blandin Paper specializes in making coated paper for such magazines as *Time, Forbes,* and *Sports Illustrated,* and Spiegel and Eddie Bauer catalogs.

The huge, new No. 6 paper machine—375 feet long, 35 feet wide, and 60 feet high—fills your view as the guided tour begins. It produces 4,000 feet of paper per minute (45 mph) with only a few people driving it. The pulp, 99.3 percent water, flows in at the machine's "wet end." Paper is initially formed on a wire screen; the water content is decreased by suction, gravity, and presses. The paper then enters the dryer, where it takes a roller-coaster ride through 40 heated cylinders that reduce the moisture content to less than 3 percent. Look for the electronic hole-detectors that find flaws in the paper as it runs around the cylinders. The machine marks the edge of the web with blue dye where it senses holes, which are patched when the paper is re-wound.

The 20-ton rolls (45 miles of paper) then go through the coater machine for a thin layer of coating formula, consisting mostly of clay. The running web is immersed in a coating bath, and excess is scraped off with blades. Air foils, steam-heated dryer cans, and gas-fired infrared burners dry the coating on one side, then the other side goes through the same processes.

Next, the roll goes through the "supercalenders" to receive its glossy shine. The paper spins rapidly between vertical stacks of fiber and metal rolls to polish the coated surface. The space between the rollers determines the amount of gloss. Winder machines cut the jumbo rolls and rewind them into smaller-diameter rolls, though each still averages the size of two men. This process produces up to 1,370 tons per day.

Cost: Free
Freebies: Brochure illustrating the paper-making process.

Video Shown: 8-minute video about the company, its commitment to quality, the foresting of trees, and the mill.
Reservations Needed: No, except for groups larger than 12 people.
Days and Hours: Tours from the first Monday in June through the Friday before Labor Day. Mon, Wed, Fri 9:00 AM-4:00 PM. Closed July 4th. Call (218) 327-6226 about tours at other times of the year.
Plan to Stay: 45 minutes for video and tour
Minimum Age: 10. Children ages 10-14 must be accompanied by an adult.
Disabled Access: Mostly accessible, although a few steps lead to the control room and tour involves a lot of walking.
Group Requirements: Groups larger than 12 people need 1 week's advance notice; call (218) 327-6226.
Special Information: No photography. Will be 10-15° warmer than outside air temperature. Machines are loud. The chemically-produced kraft pulp needed for paper production is not manufactured at the mill, so there's none of the sour odor that bothers some people at paper mills.

Gift Shop: No
Directions: From the intersection of Hwy. 169 and Hwy. 2 (at Central School), go 1 block south on Pokegama Ave. Turn right at 3rd St. N.W. Tour information center is 1½ blocks ahead on the left.
Nearby Attractions: Blandin Forest tour (9-mile self-guided tour of tree plantations and logging operations; call above number for map); Blandin Tree Nursery tour; Forest History Center; Gunn Park; Judy Garland Museum. Other Minnesota paper industry tours include Lake Superior Paper Industries in Duluth (call 218-628-5100) and Boise Cascade in International Falls (call 218-285-5011).

Christian Brothers ⟋ *hockey sticks*

Highway 11
Warroad, MN 56763
(800) 346-5055

Who is better equipped to make hockey sticks than a former hockey star and Olympic Gold medalist, or two? Brothers Roger and Billy Christian combined their hockey acumen— honed during the 1960 (U.S.A.'s first Olympic gold in hockey) and 1964 Winter Olympics— and their carpentry skills to found Christian Brothers in 1964. Today the company is one of the world's best-known hockey stick manufacturers, only two of which are in the U.S.A. Your tour guide explains some of the company history.

Particularly during winter, you can follow along as workers create sticks for National Hockey League (NHL) professional hockey players and silkscreen the famous players' names onto the shafts. Whether the sticks are for a schoolyard team or the NHL, they start as ash and elm blanks, cut to the general length and width of a handle. A grader, using a specially designed bending machine, tests the wood for strength and integrity. (In fact, all of the factory's machines were custom-designed for the Christians, several are one-of-a-kind inventions.) Workers then add a block of wood to the handles, slice the block, and glue the blade form together. A carousel-like machine heats the sticks two by two, setting the glue and bonding blade and handle together. Each time the machine turns, workers add two more sticks.

After going through a sander machine so powerful that its operation literally shakes the ground around it, the sticks enter the steamer for softening. Workers handpress the curve into the blades. Each NHL pro who uses a Christian stick has sent the factory a sample stick with a blade curve that lies on the ice just the way he likes. New sticks are made with the exact dimensions of this template.

Christian Brothers' best playmaker is a machine that forces a fiberglass-like tube over the blade and cuts it off, edge-free, with air scissors. After another hand-smoothing and an epoxy bath, 1,200 sticks per hour pass through the silkscreener, which affixes the company's name (and, for custom orders, the player's name) to three sides of each handle.

Cost: Free

Freebies: Posters, brochures, sometimes miniature hockey sticks (drink stirrers).

Video Shown: No

Reservations Needed: No, except for groups over 40 people

Days and Hours: Mon-Fri 10:30 AM and 3:00 PM. Closed holidays, week between Christmas and New Year's.

Plan to Stay: 20 minutes

Minimum Age: None

Disabled Access: Yes. A few aisles may be too narrow for wheelchairs.

Group Requirements: Groups larger than 40 people should call 1 week ahead. Large groups will be split into groups of 15.

Special Information: No photography. Sawdusty factory. Winter visits are the best time for seeing NHL pros' custom orders. Plant busiest with retail stock orders April through June.

Gift Shop: No, however Christian Brothers hockey sticks and athletic wear are available at retail stores in Warroad.

Directions: From the east, take Hwy. 11 West to Warroad, which lies 6 miles south of the U.S./Canada border. Christian Brothers sits prominently on your left. From I-29, take Hwy. 11 East to Warroad.

Nearby Attractions: Polaris snowmobile tour (call 218-463-2312) in Roseau; Arctic Cat snowmobile tour in Thief River Falls (see page 112); Warroad Library & Heritage Center; Lake of the Woods Recreational Area.

Faribo ⌒ *wool blankets and throws*

1819 N.W. 2nd Avenue
Faribault, MN 55021
(507) 334-1644

Long ago, 800 central-U.S. mills made woolen blankets. Today only three carry on, the largest being Faribo Woolens. Faribo produces more than half the wool blankets made in the United States. It is one of the few "fully vertical" mills left (that is, a soup-to-nuts mill, starting with raw wool and ending with a finished blanket). Although automated machines help with the weaving, the process is still labor-intensive. Workers handle fibers, comb batting, spin yarn, and finish and bind woven pieces—human touches that machines cannot replicate.

In the wool stock area, huge bales of raw wool await your inspection. You may catch the scent of wet wool. Touch Faribo blankets' three component fibers: domestic wool, merino wool, and acrylic. Each fiber feels softer than the next. Scouring and blending operations clean the wool stock before the dyeing vats color it. In carding, the fibers are combed into huge fluffy sheets of batting. Workers slice the batting into strips of roving, which will then be spun into yarn. Your tour guide may let you feel how soft and weak the roving is, easily torn by the gentlest tug. Then try tearing the spun yarn apart—you'll hurt your hand before you succeed!

In the weaving room, elephantine computerized looms transform the yarns into blankets. Shuttles fly from side to side on the looms so rapidly that the human eye cannot follow. Horizontal "packing bars" move back and forth to pack in the just-woven yarns. Faribo's 26 automated looms can create over 2,000 items a day. Watch the careful inspectors at the burling station, where each woven piece is backlit and inspected, inch by inch, for snags, flaws, and finished quality, then measured and sized.

The final stop is the finishing area. Massive presses pull the blankets and throws, squaring them, truing the edges, and preparing them for the sewers. Using yarn as thread, the sewers add silken tapes to bind blankets' edges or overstitch the edges with sergers. These laborious personal touches continue as the final products are carefully prepared for shipment worldwide.

Cost: Free
Freebies: Logoed souvenir key ring
Video Shown: 15-minute video runs continuously in the retail store. Features a mother sheep describing the blanket-making process to her lamb.
Reservations Needed: No, except for groups over 10 people.
Days and Hours: Mon-Fri 10:00 AM and 2:00 PM. Closed New Year's, Easter, Thanksgiving, last week in June, and the first 2 weeks in July, and 2 weeks around Christmas. Plan to arrive 15 minutes before tour.
Plan to Stay: 40 minutes for tour, plus time for retail store.
Minimum Age: None for families; 12 for groups.
Disabled Access: Only to the first floor of the factory (can see everything except the first and last production steps).
Group Requirements: Groups larger than 10 people should make reservations at least 1 or 2 weeks in advance. Large groups will be split into groups of 12-14.
Special Information: Automated looms in the weaving area are loud and portions of the tour can be hot during summer.
Retail Store: Sells Faribo first-quality blankets and throws as well as discontinued lines and irregulars, various manufacturers' all-season clothing for men, women, and children, and one-of-a-kind antique bobbins. Open Mon-Sat 9:00 AM-5:30 PM, Sun 12:00 PM-4:00 PM (until 5:00 PM in summer). Closed holidays. Catalog available from above number.
Directions: From Minneapolis, take Rt. 35 South to Faribault. Then follow billboards directing you to factory and store.
Nearby Attractions: Rice County Historical Museum; Alexander Faribault Park; Cannon River Dam.

Peavey Electronics ⟋ *music amplifiers and electric guitars*

Peavey Visitors Center and Museum
4886 Peavey Drive
Meridian, MS 39302
(601) 486-1460

Hartley Peavey, founder of the world's largest music and sound equipment manufacturer, grew up in this eastern Mississippi railroad town. As a teenager in 1965, he constructed his first guitar "amp" in his parents' basement. Today, his company employs 2,000 workers in Mississippi, Alabama, and England, and markets amplifiers, guitars, keyboards, and sound systems in 103 countries. Every form of music—from punk to polka, from country to classical—has been touched by Hartley Peavey's products.

Though its factories are not open for tours, the company celebrates its history—R&D and manufacturing—at the Visitors Center. In its first life, the building was a U.S. Department of Agriculture research facility, specializing in sugar-producing crops. Peavey lovingly restored the exterior to its original Federalist style. But the interior is now strongly post-modern, with splashes of chrome, teal, yellow, and black—colors found on many Peavey's products.

Called The Peavey World Tour, the center presents exhibits and video programs and has become a mecca for musicians of all types who trust their stylings only to equipment bearing the Peavey logo. The first-floor galleries provide a personal view of the company's founder. Look for a 1901 photograph of Hartley Peavey's grandfather and the original lightning-bolt logo drawn on notebook paper. One room recreates the basement where Hartley made his first amplifier, complete with tools and old issues of *Popular Mechanics* and *Popular Science*. Upstairs galleries chronicle the company's growth from this basement workshop to 19 facilities.

Follow the yellow banister downstairs to today's "world of Peavey" and make your own music on some of the world's most sophisticated and coveted sound systems. Test the full Peavey line, including electric guitars, electronic keyboards, amplifiers, and complex studio mixing equipment. Peavey Electronics designed this hands-on space for visitors of all ages. Several guitars are mounted on the floor, giving toddlers a chance to pluck away at the taut steel strings.

Cost: Free

Freebies: Copy of *Monitor*, the company magazine.

Video Shown: 18-minute video details company history and goals; 35-minute optional video covers history until the 1992 Peavey family's acceptance of Literacy Award at the White House.

Reservations Needed: No, except for groups of 50 or more.

Days and Hours: Open Mon-Fri 10:00 AM-4:00 PM, Sat-Sun 1:00 PM-4:00 PM. Closed holidays.

Plan to Stay: 1 hour for video, museum, and playing instruments, plus time in gift shop.

Minimum Age: None

Disabled Access: 5 steps to first-floor historical exhibits. Staircase down to video theater and hands-on equipment display.

Group Requirements: Groups of 50 or more need reservations at (601) 484-1460.

Special Information: Center is set up for self-guided tours, but guided visits can be arranged.

Gift Shop: Axcess shop sells Peavey-related items from $2 keychains to $100-plus satin "tour" jackets. Open center hours. Catalog available from (800) 752-7896.

Directions: From Jackson, take I-20 East through Meridian as it changes to I-20/59. Take Exit 157B for Hwy. 45 North. Take the first exit (for Sonny Montgomery Industrial Park). At bottom of ramp, turn right onto Marion Russel Rd. After you cross railroad track (about 1 mile), turn right into the center's parking lot.

Nearby Attractions: The Jimmie Rodgers Museum (Meridian is the birthplace of Jimmie Rodgers, the father of country music); Annual Jimmie Rodgers Country Music Festival; Grand Opera House of Mississippi (tours of "The Lady" are available; call 601-693-LADY); Merrehope Mansion; Dunn's Falls Water Park; The Dentzel Carousel.

Anheuser-Busch   ✑   *Budweiser beer*

1127 Pestalozzi Street
St. Louis, MO 63118
(314) 577-2333

This tour of Anheuser-Busch's headquarters and birthplace (founded 1852) puts a face on the world's largest brewer. The facility offers historical and architectural delights that nicely complement the beer-making. As the tour guide leads you from the Budweiser Clydesdale Stables to the lager cellar and the packaging plant, a sense of history and the smell of hops surround you. Three of the tall red-brick buildings are on the National Historic Register. The world-famous horses, a corporate symbol, seem comfortable in their wood-and-wrought-iron stables.

The beechwood-aging process distinguishes Budweiser from other major brewers. It's part of the second fermentation, a step most brewers do not follow. In the new lager cellar, silver lager tanks have layers of beechwood chips spread on the bottoms. The chips provide more surface area for the action of the yeast, which settles on the chips and continues to work until the beer is completely fermented. Each of these tanks holds enough beer to fill 200,000 six-packs.

It's the 10-foot-tall, whimsical fox sculptures perched on each corner of the bottling plant that really amuse you. The foxes are munching on chicken legs and drinking mugs of Bevo, a non-alcoholic cereal beverage manufactured between 1916 and 1929. The Bevo Bottling Plant, which now bottles beer, was built in 1917. Its 27 acres of floor space make it the world's largest bottling facility under one roof—it can produce 23.5 million 12-ounce bottles per day. Inside the building, watch the bottles speed through the machines that rinse, fill, cap, label, and box them.

During the short trolley ride back to the Tour Center from the packaging plant, look up at the six-story brewhouse, with its ornate trim and dominant clock tower. Although you cannot enter until renovations are completed (scheduled for 1995), you can imagine the glistening copper kettles and massive chandelier. You leave understanding how Anheuser-Busch, which now also manufactures snack foods and baked goods, and runs

entertainment parks, has come to symbolize much of America's brewing heritage.

Cost: Free
Freebies: Beer, soda, and Eagle brand pretzel snacks
Video Shown: 6-minute video on brewing process.
Reservations Needed: No, except for groups of 15 or more.
Days and Hours: January through May and September through December Mon-Sat 9:00 AM-4:00 PM; June through August Mon-Sat 9:00 AM-5:00 PM. Closed holidays.
Plan to Stay: 1¼ hours for tour, video, and sampling, plus time for gift shop and Tour Center (look for the display of beautiful beer steins).
Minimum Age: Under age 18 must be accompanied by adult.
Disabled Access: Yes
Group Requirements: Groups larger than 15 should call 1 week ahead. No maximum group size.
Special Information: Anheuser-Busch also gives tours in Columbus, OH; Baldwinsville, NY; Merrimack, NH; Williamsburg, VA; Jacksonville, FL; Tampa, FL; Houston, TX; Fort Collins, CO; and Fairfield, CA. For general information on all tours, call (800) 765-1055. See page 130 for feature on Merrimack, NH tour.
Gift Shop: Sells logoed items and beer paraphernalia, including T-shirts, mirrors, dart boards, beer steins, and a Bud-can-shaped cooler. Open 1½ hours later than tours.
Directions: Take I-55 to Arsenal St. Exit. Follow signs to Tour Center (on 13th & Pestalozzi).
Nearby Attractions: St. Louis area attractions include the McDonnell Douglas Museum (see page 124), St. Louis Zoo, Gateway Arch, Union Station, Botanical Gardens, St. Louis Science Center, and National Bowling Hall of Fame and Museum. Tour Center front desk has information sheet with directions and hours for nearby attractions.

See color photos, pages 139, 140, and 141

Chrysler ~~⟩ *minivans*
1050 Dodge Drive
Fenton, MO 63026
(314) 349-4000

Since Chrysler introduced the minivan to the market in 1984, its minivans have earned many awards and the number-one position in sales. Since 1987, its St. Louis Assembly Plant II has built the long-wheelbase minivan. In 1992, this factory became the first North American assembly plant to successfully initiate a three-shift schedule, operating three 7-hour production shifts five days a week and two 9-hour shifts on Saturday.

Building the skeleton frame in the metal shop starts the production process. Parts arrive by train and truck from the stamping plant. Fenders, doors, and roofs are attached on the assembly line to create the gray frame. Chrysler is proud of its extensive use of robotics. Look for the robotic arm that uses large suction cups to pick up the roof panel and, with workers' guidance, precisely place it. The minivan then heads through a tunnel that automatically welds the roof joints.

Sparks fly when the entire frame heads down a row of robots, each with an assigned place to spot-weld the body frame. Once the frame is assembled and its dimensions tested, it receives a primer coat bath. The entire frame is immersed in 73,600 gallons of paint (resembling a whale as it's lowered into the vat), then moved through the rinsers. By negatively charging the body and positively charging the paint, the primer bakes into the frame's smallest corners.

From the paint area, the shiny frame travels through the assembly lines that bring the minivans to life. Some lines install the interior electric systems, others the engine and axles, and ergonomic robot arms help with steps such as seat and windshield installation. Ask the tour guide to explain the Joint UAW/Chrysler Product Quality Improvement Partnership and point out worker suggestions that have been successfully implemented. Notice the overhead signs at different assembly stations that say "Critical Buzz, Squeak, and Rattle Operation." At the tour's end, peek into the test booth where the minivan "travels" (on rollers) up to 65 miles per hour while a worker analyzes the electrical systems, transmission, and engine.

Cost: Free

Freebies: Brochure with production pictures and statistics.

Video Shown: 15-minute slide show on Chrysler's changing corporate culture.

Reservations Needed: Yes. Company prefers that individuals and families join a scheduled group tour.

Days and Hours: Wed 9:00 AM, 11:00 AM, 1:30 PM, 5:30 PM. Subject to change based on shift schedule and model changes. Closed holidays.

Plan to Stay: 1½-2 hours for tour and slide show.

Minimum Age: 16

Disabled Access: Wheelchairs and walkers not allowed on factory floor. Special arrangements can be made for physically challenged if a cart is available.

Group Requirements: Groups of 10 or more get a plant retiree as a tour guide. No maximum group size with 1 week's advance notice.

Special Information: You will walk at least 1 mile on tour. Plant is undergoing a $578-million renovation to launch new generation minivans in January 1995. Tour at this state-of-the-art assembly plant, which will have almost 400 robots, may be suspended during the transition.

Gift Shop: No

Directions: From I-44 West, take Exit 275 onto North Highway Dr., which runs parallel to I-44. Turn right before overpass onto Marez Ln. Plant entrance is last driveway on the left. You must drive a UAW-made car to park in the visitor's lot.

Nearby Attractions: St. Louis attractions, including the Anheuser-Busch (Budweiser) brewery tour (see page 117), are about 25 minutes away. Limited tours at Ford minivan plant in Hazelwood (call 314-731-6365).

Hallmark Visitors Center ⟷ *greeting cards*

Crown Center Complex
25th and Grand Avenue
Kansas City, MO 64141
(816) 274-5672

Hallmark's slogan, "When You Care Enough To Send The Very Best," applies to its visitors center. You're surrounded by the world of Hallmark (founded by Joyce Hall in 1910) as you walk through 14 exhibits that tell the story of the world's largest greeting-card company. Your activities vary: see a 40-foot historical time-line with memorabilia from Hallmark's history intertwined with world events; view classic commercials or clips from Hallmark Hall of Fame television dramas; watch a Hallmark technician create dies for die-cutting or embossing cards; and even make your own star-bow on the automatic bow-making machine.

One of the most popular exhibits expresses the creativity involved in developing new cards. Step through a giant keyhole into a room filled with 6-foot pencils, markers, brushes, paint tubes, and jars, all on a floor that resembles an artist's drawing board. You'll think you're on the movie set from *Honey, I Shrunk the Kids.* Sit on oversized paint jars and view a video on how Hallmark artists draw, letter, paint, sculpt, and stitch designs.

Many things you take for granted about greeting cards come alive in exhibits on graphic arts, manufacturing, and distribution. The color separation display explains how Hallmark turns the original artwork into a product. Hallmark plant employees operate two presses that produce greeting cards: one applies colored foil and the other cuts unusual card shapes.

Exhibits also show other Hallmark products, including gift wrap, art supplies, candles, jigsaw puzzles, plush toys, collectibles, and Crayola crayons. Hallmark employees' affection for company founder Hall shows in a display of Christmas trees that employees gave Hall from 1966 to 1982. Each tree's decorations reflect a theme of importance to the company during that year. To experience Hallmark's international appeal (cards sell in more than 100 countries), rub Snoopy's nose on one of the cards to hear birthday greetings in twelve languages.

Cost: Free

Freebies: Postcard and a bow

Video Shown: 13-minute film, "Coming From The Heart," follows Hallmark artists and photographers during a week-long creativity retreat on a picturesque rural-Missouri farm. Shown on the hour. Throughout the visitors center are other short videos on topics related to the exhibits.

Reservations Needed: No, except for groups of 10 or more.

Days and Hours: Mon-Fri 9:00 AM-5:00 PM and Sat 9:30 AM-4:30 PM. Closed Thanksgiving, Christmas, and New Year's. Also usually closed the first 2 weeks in January for yearly renovations.

Plan to Stay: 1 hour for exhibits, plus time for videos.

Minimum Age: None

Disabled Access: Yes

Group Requirements: Groups of 10 or more should make reservations 2 to 4 weeks in advance. Guided tours available. School/youth groups need 1 adult for every 7 children. Call (816) 274-3613.

Special Information: Braille available on all major exhibits. Some Hallmark Production Centers conduct tours by advance reservation. Visitors center provides this information.

Gift Shop: Not in visitors center. The closest of the 21,000 independently owned Hallmark stores is in Crown Center.

Directions: Located in Crown Center Complex, about 1 mile south of downtown Kansas City. Take Grand Ave. to 25th St. and park in the Crown Center Parking Garage. Proceed to third level of Crown Center shops. The visitors center is located outside Halls department store.

Nearby Attractions: Kansas City's downtown attractions include Crown Center; Kaleidoscope children's interactive exhibit (reservations only, call 816-274-8301); Arabia Steamboat Museum; Toy and Miniature Museum, Marion Merrell Dow Visitor Center (see page 122); Ford tour (call 816-459-1356).

——*See color photos, page 150*——

Purina Farms   *pet food*

Ralston Purina Company
Route 2
Gray Summit, MO 63039
(314) 982-3232

From its 1894 beginnings as a horse- and mule-feed store to its position today as the world's largest producer of pet food, Ralston Purina Company remains focused on animal care and nutrition. Located on the grounds of the oldest and largest animal nutrition center in the world, Purina Farms wants visitors to gain a greater appreciation and understanding of their pets. While the Visitor Center has a few displays about Ralston Purina and its products, the complex resembles a family-oriented petting zoo more than a promotion-laden company museum.

With the company celebrating its 100-year anniversary in 1994, Purina Farms plans to add new exhibits over five years. A new timeline will trace the company's history and product development. Other business-related exhibits will show how pet food is manufactured and play classic Ralston Purina commercials for products such as Dog Chow, the nation's leading dry dog food. Interactive displays teach the basics of pet nutrition and the remarkable sensory and physical abilities of domestic animals. Scent boxes help you experience how a dog smells things, while other displays show the differences between your vision and that of dogs and cats.

The Farm Animal Barn contains sheep, cows, horses, hogs, rabbits, and turkeys. Roll up your sleeves here to romp in the hayloft, pull a rope to determine your "horsepower," pet piglets, or milk a cow. Inside the Pet Center, home for different breeds of dogs, cats, puppies, and kittens, you'll see cats lounging and climbing on a five-story Victorian mansion, complete with special windowsills, stairways, and mantelpieces. Petting windows and outdoor areas for dogs let you cuddle and play with them. The Pet Center also features videos and newsletters with tips on pet care. You leave having learned more about your favorite pets and about Ralston Purina's efforts to keep them well-fed.

Cost: Free

Freebies: Brochures, by request from front desk, on pet care and the company's products.

Video Shown: Two videos shown in a converted 48-foot grain barn: one provides a brief history of Ralston Purina; the second captures the special role animals play in human lives. Other short videos shown at selected exhibits.

Reservations Needed: Yes, although can usually accommodate a large number of visitors.

Days and Hours: Open mid-March to mid-November only. Spring and Fall: Wed-Fri 9:30 AM-1:00 PM and Sat-Sun 9:30 AM-3:00 PM. Summer: Tue-Sun 9:30 AM-3:00 PM. Closed holidays.

Plan to Stay: 2 hours for displays in main building, videos, Farm Animal Barn, animal demonstrations, and Pet Center, plus additional time for fish ponds, children's play areas, picnic area, and gift shop.

Minimum Age: None

Disabled Access: Yes

Group Requirements: No maximum group size. Requests 1 week's advance notice for large groups.

Special Information: New exhibits will be phased in over five years. Special events scheduled throughout the year include Kids' Catfish Derby, St. Louis City Police Canine Training, and the very popular Haunted Hayloft. Call for schedule.

Gift Shop: Sells animal-decorated items including mugs, cards, pencils, and banks; also logoed clothes and hats. Open same hours as visitors center.

Directions: From St. Louis, take I-44 West. Pass Six Flags Over Mid-America. Take the Gray Summit exit and turn right onto Hwy. 100. Turn left on Country Road MM. Follow signs to Purina Farms.

Nearby Attractions: Shaws Arboretum; Six Flags Over Mid-America.

Play with dogs and cats at the Pet Center, Purina Farms, Gray Summit, Missouri

Purina Farms includes a Farm Animal Barn, Pet Center, theater, and exhibits

Marion Merrell Dow   ～ *pharmaceuticals*

Visitors Center
10245 Marion Park Drive
Kansas City, MO 64137
(816) 966-7333 / (816) 966-4253

This company museum captures the spirit of Ewing Marion Kauffman, founder of Marion Laboratories, and the success of Marion Merrell Dow (Mr. K's company merged with Merrell Dow Pharmaceuticals in 1989). Colorful, interactive displays show how this company began and grew and how pharmaceutical companies develop and manufacture new drugs. Like many newer corporate visitor centers, this one extensively uses clever videos and larger-than-life displays to explain complex topics.

In the spacious wood and slate-tiled entranceway, spend a few minutes looking at the company's products and history. Unless you're a doctor or pharmacist you may not be aware of Marion Merrell Dow's range of products, including Cardizem, Seldane, Nicoderm/Nicorette, and Carafate. In the room on manufacturing, you'll almost think you're in a factory. A mannequin stands inside the entranceway and floor-to-ceiling pictures show machines and workers making, packaging, and distributing the company's drugs. To discover more about each of these processes, such as tablet and capsule production, you simply push a button to see a video.

The drug research and development room depicts the stages through which a compound moves in becoming a new drug. The product lifeline begins with displays about drug sources, such as plants. The lifeline continues to scenes of post-FDA-approval activities. In a unique exhibit called the "Product Experience," you discover how an antihistamine works to control allergies. The exhibit combines animation with sound-and-surround visual techniques.

Another portion of the Visitors Center is devoted to Mr. K. This airy, windowed gallery overlooks a small lake and landscaped grounds. You can "interview" Mr. K by selecting from a menu of questions and viewing his refreshing videotaped responses. Additional displays highlight specific Kauffman Foundation projects, including Project Choice, Project Star, and Project Early.

An 8-by-24-foot colorful mural of Royals Stadium during the 1986 World Series highlights his ownership of the baseball team. As you look at the display of his actual office, with the pipe on his desk, the private phone line for baseball business, and the frayed black chairs, you understand a little more of this company's roots.

Cost: Free
Freebies: Postcard; "Portrait Of A Leader" booklet about Mr. K available upon request, if supply on hand
Video Shown: At start of visit, 8-minute video on company and its products. Other videos on a different topics throughout the museum.
Reservations Needed: Yes
Days and Hours: Tue and Thur 8:00 AM-4:30 PM. Other days available. Closed holidays and week between Christmas and New Year's.
Plan to Stay: 1 hour
Minimum Age: None, but company suggests 5th grade and some interest in science.
Disabled Access: Yes
Group Requirements: 1 week's advance notice required for groups larger than 25. No maximum group size.
Special Information: Ask the Visitors Center director for materials on Ewing Marion Kauffman Foundation.
Gift Shop: No
Directions: Take I-435 to exit for Hickman Mills Rd. Turn left at exit. Turn left on 103rd St. and left again onto Marion Park Dr. After the guard station, the Visitors Center is on your immediate right (follow the lake). Can also take Wornall Rd. to Bannister Rd., which is 95th St. Turn left onto Bannister to Hickman Mills Rd. Turn right on Hickman Mills Rd. and follow above directions
Nearby Attractions: NCAA Visitors Center (call 913-339-0000); Country Club Plaza; Kansas City Board of Trade (816-753-7500); Ford Motor Plant tour (816-459-1356); Kansas City's downtown area attractions, including Hallmark Visitors Center (see page 119), about 20 miles away.

McCormick Distilling Co.

One McCormick Lane
Weston, MO 64098
(816) 640-2276 / (800) 825-0377

bourbon, whiskey, other alcoholic beverages

As the oldest continually active distillery in the U.S.A. and the only distillery west of the Mississippi, McCormick's history runs deep—so deep that you'll enter the cave where founder Ben Holladay (1856) stored his whiskey. Meriwether Lewis and William Clark charted the property's limestone springs, a crucial ingredient in fine whiskey, during their 1804 expedition. The springs and distillery are on the National Historic Register.

In 1985 McCormick stopped distilling here and focused the facility's activities on bottling, aging, and distribution. The tour visits the now-quiet fermentation and still rooms, with their 17,000-gallon fermentation tanks and 46-foot worn copper still, while your guide describes whiskey-making. You can imagine what it was like when mash bubbled in the fermenters and alcohol vapors rose in the still condenser.

It's a peaceful walk up to three silver-painted aging warehouses, set on a small hill to capture cool breezes. In the entrance, the sweet whiskey aroma hits you. Whiskey ages in rows of white-oak barrels on the rack house's six floors. Changes in weather make the liquid expand and contract into the barrels' charcoal linings, flavoring and coloring the whiskey while it's aging.

In the bottling house McCormick packages all of its products, including whiskey, bourbon, gin, brandy, rum, vodka, and tequila. With up to three lines in operation it's often a noisy place. From a small raised platform, watch the synchronized bottling process. Bottles travel single-file to the filling unit, where they are injected with liquor and spun around to the capping machine. A suction device affixes brand labels. The rattling sound comes from the case-packing machine, which operates and sounds like a pin-setter in a bowling alley, lifting filled bottles from the conveyer belt and mechanically guiding them into even rows in cardboard cartons.

Cost: Free
Freebies: Samples (10¢) for visitors who have aged at least 21 years.
Video Shown: 10-minute slide show on distillery's history and company's products.
Reservations Needed: No, except for groups larger than 15.
Days and Hours: March through November Mon-Sat 9:30 AM-4:00 PM and Sun 10:30 AM-4:00 PM. Closed Thanksgiving. No tours December-February.
Plan to Stay: 45 minutes for tour and slide show, plus time for pavilion, picnic area, and Country Store.
Minimum Age: None
Disabled Access: The cave and first level of fermentation and still house are accessible. Small flight of stairs into the bottling house and warehouse.
Group Requirements: Groups larger than 15 should call at least 3 days in advance. No maximum group size.
Special Information: Best time to see production is Mon-Fri before 3:00 PM, during bottling house operation.
Gift Shop: Country Store sells memorabilia and logoed items, including key chains, T-shirts, jackets, long johns and shot glasses, and all McCormick Distilling products. Open year-round. March through November Mon-Sat 9:00 AM-5:00 PM, Sun 10:00 AM-5:00 PM; December Mon-Sat 9:00 AM-5:00 PM; January and February Mon-Fri 9:00 AM-5:00 PM. Catalog available from above number.
Directions: From Kansas City, take I-29 North to Platte City exit (Exit 20). Go west on Hwy. 92 to Hwy. 273 West. Follow signs to Weston. When Hwy. 273, Hwy. 45, and Rt. JJ join at stop sign and blinking light, continue straight and you'll be on Rt. JJ West. Distillery is ahead on the left.
Nearby Attractions: Pirtle's Winery (call 816-386-5728); Weston's historic attractions include Weston Historical Museum and restored 1840s downtown area.

McDonnell Douglas

Prologue Room   ➦   *airplanes, missiles, and spacecraft*
McDonnell Boulevard and Airport Road
St. Louis, MO 63134
(314) 232-5421

McDonnell Douglas Corporation (MDC) calls its company museum the Prologue Room, after William Shakespeare's comment that "what is past is prologue." To MDC, its past achievements are not history but the beginning of each new technical advancement. As you stand on the steps overlooking the museum room you'll realize MDC's part in aviation's past, present, and future. Models of commercial planes, missiles, spacecraft, and fighter jets of all sizes and colors seem to be everywhere.

MDC aircraft downed every enemy fighter shot down during Operation Desert Storm. With this track record, the display of military planes will pique your curiosity. A wide, oval glass case shows the evolution of MDC military planes from aviation's golden age in the 1930s to the most current technology. In the center of the oval are 1/7th scale models of the F/A-18 Hornet, F-15 Eagle, and AV-8B Harrier combat fighters, and the AH-64 Apache helicopter. Nearby is a full-scale mock-up of a Harpoon missile. A glass oval in the front of the museum has a similar display for the generations of the company's commercial aircraft, from the DC-1 (the first successful commercial passenger plane) to the MD-11.

Although the museum does not show how MDC builds its products, displays do provide a complete history of its aviation products. Aviation buffs can study aircraft and fighter plane lineage charts and display cases depicting MDC's numerous firsts, such as building the first planes to land at the North and South poles. The center of the museum contains full-size engineering mock-ups of the Mercury and Gemini spacecraft that carried America's early astronauts into space. In the era before computer-aided design, engineers had to build these full-scale models to test the practicality of their hand-drawn designs.

Notice the aviation-art gallery, which features oil paintings by several artists whose work is also displayed in the National Air and Space Museum in Washington, DC. You leave understanding how MDC products since 1920 have affected wars' outcomes, made worldwide travel possible, and helped explore the universe.

Cost: Free

Freebies: No

Video Shown: Optional video in gallery area runs for 2 hours. Consists of shorter videos, presenting company history, building of jet fighters, and MDC planes in flight accompanied by music. Can watch 5 minutes of it or the entire video.

Reservations Needed: No, except for groups larger than 20 people.

Days and Hours: June through August only, except for school programs. Tue-Sat 9:00 AM-4:00 PM. Closed July 4th.

Plan to Stay: 45 minutes for museum, plus time for video.

Minimum Age: None, but 6 years old recommended to appreciate displays.

Disabled Access: Yes

Group Requirements: Groups larger than 20 should call ahead to arrange a guided tour. During school year, programs available for 4th, 5th, and 6th graders with maximum group size of 40.

Special Information: Special summer program available for schools and camps.

Retail Store: Located 5 minutes away at 5900 N. Lindbergh Blvd. (314-895-7019), corner of Lindbergh and McDonnell Blvd. Sells aviation posters, photos, and models, plus MDC logoed items including T-shirts, caps, jackets, mugs, and key chains. Open Tue-Fri 10:00 AM-6:00 PM and Sat 10:00 AM-3:00 PM year-round.

Directions: From downtown St. Louis, take I-70 West to I-170 North and exit at Airport Rd. Turn left onto Airport Rd. Enter through MDC World Headquarters gate 2 blocks ahead on the left. Look for large black glass building.

Nearby Attractions: St. Louis' downtown attractions, including Anheuser-Busch (Budweiser) Brewery tour (see page 117), are 20 minutes away.

Weaver's   ～   *snack food*
1600 Center Park Road
Lincoln, NE 68512
(402) 423-6625 / (800) 456-3445

Since 1932, Weaver's Potato Chips has used home-grown potatoes to produce some of the most popular potato chips in its area of the Midwest. It started on Mr. Ed Weaver, Sr.'s stove with a scrub brush, knife, and kettle. Weaver's still uses the same equipment, only much bigger. Over 90 percent of Weaver's potato-chip ingredients come straight from Nebraska. Every day, 100,000 pounds of these potatoes are trucked into the factory, where they are dumped into large bins and sent on a short trip through the plant, then a longer trip to stores in 14 states as potato chips.

Unlike most snack-food companies, Weaver's currently allows you to view the process up close, sometimes only five feet away from the machines, instead of seeing it from an observation deck or overhead walkway. You can watch as the whole, uncooked potatoes jump into the washers for a hot bath and scrub-down (they always scrub, rather than peel, the potatoes to retain the vitamins). The clean potatoes are then sent to the slicers, where razor-sharp blades quickly slice the potatoes into pieces 1/100th of an inch thin. A spiked roller pierces little holes in the chips to prevent blistering while they cook. The slices move to the 35-foot fryer and cook until crispy. You and the cooked chips then move ahead to the packaging room.

The potato chips enter a very modern, high-tech piece of chip-making machinery: an optic sorter. Although you will not be able to see this particular process up close, your tour guide will explain it to you. The optic sorter takes photographs of the chips as they move past the camera's lens. Dark brown, green, and other imperfect potato chips are actually blown off the conveyor by air jets. The rest of the chips move on to the packaging room. Chips are gently conveyed to the sophisticated packaging equipment that automatically weighs, fills, and seals bags. Workers inspect the bags and then hand-pack them into cardboard boxes for storage in the warehouse. Delivery trucks pick them up and deliver them to stores all across the Midwest. Be sure to taste your free sample on the way out.

Cost: Free

Freebies: Half-ounce bag of potato chips

Video Shown: No, although company plans to include video displays in the future.

Reservations Needed: Yes

Days and Hours: Mon-Thur 9:00 AM-11:00 AM and 12:00 PM-1:30 PM. Closed holidays.

Plan to Stay: 30-40 minutes

Minimum Age: No

Disabled Access: Yes

Group Requirements: Groups larger than 20 people should call 5 days in advance. Groups larger than 20 people will be split into smaller groups.

Special Information: Wear comfortable shoes, since there is a lot of standing and walking on the factory floor. Weaver's plans to expand tour to other production areas, including popcorn, cheese puffs, and Puffins, and possibly to add a visitor center.

Gift Shop: No

Directions: From I-80, exit at Hwy. 2 in Lincoln. Follow Hwy. 2 West to Rt. 77 South. Take second left into the industrial park. Plant is red-white-and-blue building on the left.

Nearby Attractions: State Capitol; University of Nebraska.

Fisher Space Pen ～ *pens*

711 Yucca Street
Boulder City, NV 89005
(702) 293-3011

What writes at any angle, including upside-down, under water, and even in outer space? A Fisher Space Pen. Only a dream in 1948, the Fisher Space Pen has accompanied Neil Armstrong, Buzz Aldrin, and all subsequent astronauts to the moon. In the 1950s, Paul Fisher (engineer, inventor, and occasional politician) designed a pressurized ink cartridge that withstands gravity and developed the AG-7 model whose thick ink won't ooze—even under 100-pounds-per-square-inch pressure created by nitrogen gas inside the cartridge.

In the entrance to Fisher Space Pen Co., located in the only Nevada town that prohibits gambling, you begin to understand Paul Fisher's link with outer space. Hanging on a wall is a Limited Edition collection of NASA photographs especially designed for Paul Fisher as a tribute to the space shuttle Challenger and its heroic crew. Look for the AG-7 pen and crew patch which flew aboard the Orbiter Atlantis in May 1989. As you enter the factory, notice the wall murals (painted by Paul's daughter) of a space ship and the first man on the moon.

Walk on the factory floor right next to the workers who, with the assistance of specially designed equipment, hand-assemble the 12-plus parts of the pens. Each cap moves down the line and eventually meets up with its bottom. At the first station along each row, clips are attached to pen caps. Next, a worker operates a die press to punch out the hole for the mechanism spring. With a tray of 500 pen barrels in his lap, another worker inserts a spring into each one. At the end of the row, refills are placed in the barrels and tops and bottoms are screwed together. Along the row, air-driven machinery hisses.

Into skinny empty metal tubes, the refill-making machine inserts white plastic bb-size balls that act as floats to push the ink down. Nitrogen gas and ink are injected. Different color inks, made by the company, are as thick as tar. A special machine tests how many feet of ink are in refills. Resembling a spirograph, the machine rotates the refills to draw circles on white paper below—ideally, enough circles to equal three miles of writing ink. You leave recognizing that NASA put humans on the moon but Fisher, the grandfather of the ball-point pen, made sure they could write home.

Cost: Free
Freebies: No
Video Shown: No
Reservations Needed: Yes
Days and Hours: Fri 9:00 AM-3:00 PM (usually at 9:45 AM and 12:15 PM). Closed holidays. Call to find out about Christmas shutdown.
Plan to Stay: 20 minutes for guided tour, plus time in retail store.
Minimum Age: None
Disabled Access: Yes
Group Requirements: Groups larger than 10 people should call 2 weeks in advance. No maximum group size.
Special Information: Summer temperatures reach 110°.
Retail Area: Sells all 27 models of Fisher Space Pens, official Star Trek Series pens, and silver-bullet pens on silver necklace chains, at 20% discount. Open Mon-Fri 9:00 AM-3:00 PM. Closed holidays. Catalog available.
Directions: From Las Vegas, take Boulder Hwy. South to Boulder City. Turn left onto Yucca St. (first street in Boulder City on left side). Look for orange building on the right. From Hoover Dam, take I-93/95 North to Boulder Hwy. Turn right onto Industrial Rd. and then left onto Yucca St. Look for orange building.
Nearby Attractions: Ethel M Chocolates and Kidd's Marshmallow tours (see pages 126 and 129); Ocean Spray Cranberry Plant tour (opening early 1995; call 702-435-5868); Hoover Dam; Lake Mead.

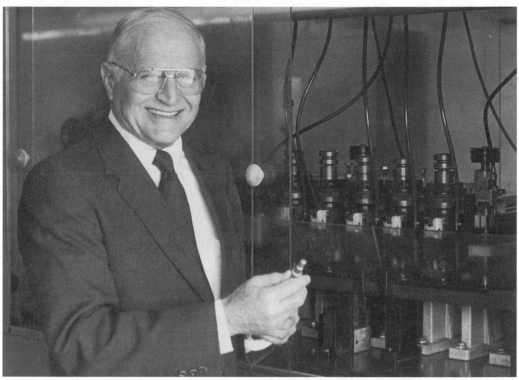

Paul Fisher inspecting ball point pen production at a machine he invented, Fisher Space Pen, Boulder City, Nevada

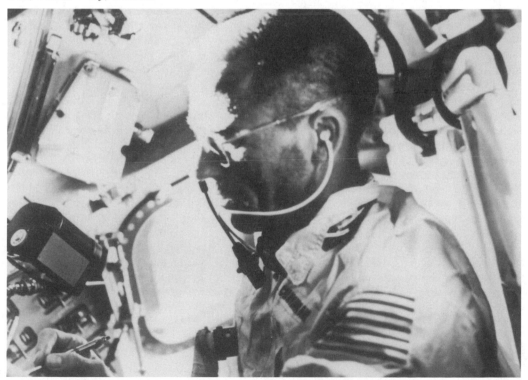

Astronaut Walter Cunningham uses a Fisher Space Pen during Apollo 7 mission

Ethel M Chocolates   ⟜   *chocolates*

Two Cactus Garden Drive
Henderson, NV 89014
(702) 433-2500

Only in Las Vegas would a candy factory identify its product lines with flashing red neon signs. Thousands of people come here daily as a diversion from Las Vegas' casinos. Ethel M began in 1981 with one shop and now has around 20 in three states. A tour of Ethel M not only shows you how premium chocolates are made, but also offers you relaxation in their cactus garden.

Stroll along pathways that meander through the Ethel M cactus garden's 350 varieties of shrubs, succulents, and cacti. Species collected from South Africa, the Red Sea, South America, and Japan are up to 60 years old. The garden blossoms with red, orange, and purple flowers from late March to May, but the stone benches soothe visitors year-round.

Start your self-guided factory tour at the kitchen. From a corridor, observe the chocolate-making through glass windows. Depending on when you visit, you'll see different production steps. Batches of toffee bubble in copper kettles, then workers pour this Almond Butter Krisp onto cooling tables. Butter creams (maybe raspberry or chocolate) or liqueur creams (perhaps Amaretto) swirl slowly in shallow, round mixers. Metal blades stir these candy "centers" until they're smooth.

Further along the corridor, notice the two massive pale-yellow machines. Since most of these machines' action occurs on the inside, an overhead video explains the process. Empty plastic coin-shaped molds, patterned after a U.S. 1904 Series, methodically move along the conveyor belt through the long machine. Liquid milk- or dark chocolate pours through spigots to fill the molds. Some even get mint cream centers. The molds are vibrated to shake out air bubbles, conveyed through a cooling tunnel, and then flipped over to release the chocolate coins. You exit the tour into the retail store, where you are greeted with a sample chocolate of the day.

Cost: Free
Freebies: Sample chocolate of the day

Video Shown: Short overhead videos explain chocolate-making.
Reservations Needed: No
Days and Hours: Mon-Sun 8:30 AM-7:00 PM. Closed Christmas. No production for 1 week in July, but can visit cactus garden and view videos.
Plan to Stay: 15 minutes for self-guided tour and videos, plus cactus garden and shops.
Minimum Age: None
Disabled Access: Yes
Group Requirements: Can accommodate very large groups; those larger than 200 people need to call (702) 435-2641 in advance for special tour times.
Special Information: Best times to see production are Mon-Sun 9:00 AM-2:00 PM. Guided cactus-garden tours available for groups of 10 or more with 1 day's advance notice to (702) 435-2641.
Gift Shops: Chocolate Shoppe sells entire Ethel M line—over 60 varieties of chocolates. Offers 1-pound assortment gift boxes and the popular 29-ounce "Taste of Las Vegas" assortment with a photograph of Las Vegas's neon lights on the cover. Design your own chocolates assortment from the display cases. Look for silver boxes shaped like Las Vegas slot machines, filled with chocolate coins. Open same hours as tour. Closed Christmas and shorter hours on Thanksgiving Day. Courtesy phones provided for placing catalog orders. Catalog available from (800) 4-ETHEL M. Cactus Shoppe offerings include cactus plants, books, and T-shirts.
Directions: From Las Vegas strip, drive east on Tropicana. Turn right onto Mountain Vista. Turn left onto Sunset Way (Green Valley Business Park) and follow signs. From Hoover Dam, take Boulder Hwy. to Sunset Rd. Turn left onto Sunset Rd. Turn right onto Sunset Way. Follow above directions.
Nearby Attractions: Kidd's Marshmallow tour (see page 129); Ocean Spray Cranberries Plant tour (opening early 1995; call 702-435-5868); "The Strip"; Hoover Dam; Lake Mead.

——————*See color photos, page 136*——————

Kidd's ⟋ *marshmallows*

8203 Gibson Road
Henderson, NV 89015
(702) 564-5400

Welcome to the magical world of marshmallows, including Marshall, a stuffed 5-foot talking marshmallow, and more white than a hospital room or a six-inch snowstorm. Kidd & Co. is the second-largest producer of marshmallows, the leader in private-label marshmallows, and a manufacturer of specialty marshmallow products—are you surprised that the factory is located on Marshmallow Lane? The Kidd family has been making this soft fun stuff for nearly 100 years, and now produces 3.2 billion marshmallows a year in its two factories.

Overhead signs briefly explain the process as you take your self-guided tour. In the kitchen, corn syrup and sugar cook in big stainless-steel kettles. A mixture of gelatin and water meet the corn syrup and sugar in another enclosed metal vat, where vanilla flavoring is added. Air is injected to puff up the mixture—marshmallows consist of 80 percent air.

Walk along the corridor, looking through the glass windows, and follow the marshmallows' journey. The marshmallow mixture is forced through the "extruder," which contains a pipe with a series of holes in it. The resulting ropes of marshmallows slowly flow along the conveyor belt under a snowfall of cornstarch. A blade chops the ropes into uniform lengths, producing bite-size marshmallows. Once cut, the marshmallows drop into a rotating cylindrical tunnel and bounce around to absorb more cornstarch, which prevents sticking and gives them a smooth skin. The conveyor belts and revolving cylindrical drums provide the only silver color in this otherwise entirely white room.

The marshmallows eventually move to the next room for bagging into 200-plus private-label brands. After being heat-sealed for freshness, the plastic bags are hand-packed into boxes and shipped to customers. Whatever the season, you'll leave longing for campfires with roasted marshmallows and s'mores or hot chocolate with mini-marshmallows.

Cost: Free
Freebies: 1.5-ounce bag of marshmallows
Video Shown: No
Reservations Needed: No, except for groups that want guided tour.
Days and Hours: Mon-Sun 9:00 AM-4:30 PM. Closed Thanksgiving, Christmas Eve, Christmas, New Year's, and Easter. Best time to see production is Mon-Fri.
Plan to Stay: 15 minutes for self-guided tour, plus time for gift shop.
Minimum Age: None
Disabled Access: Yes; wheelchair available upon request.
Group Requirements: Groups should call 1 day in advance for guided tour. No maximum group size.
Gift Shop: Sells marshmallows and logoed items such as T-shirts, sweatshirts, mugs, and baby clothes. Open same hours as tour.
Directions: From Las Vegas, take I-95 South to Sunset exit. Turn left on Sunset and right on Gibson Rd. Turn right onto Mary Crest Rd. and continue onto Marshmallow Ln. Look for building with copper roof. From Hoover Dam/Boulder City, take Boulder Hwy. to Lake Mead Blvd. Turn left onto Lake Mead and right on Gibson Rd. Turn left onto Mary Crest Rd. Follow above directions.
Nearby Attractions: Ethel M Chocolates tour (see page 126); Ocean Spray Cranberries Plant tour (opening early 1995; call 702-435-5868); Wholesale Clothing Outlet; Lied Discovery Children's Museum; Clark County Heritage Museum; Hoover Dam; Lake Mead.

Anheuser-Busch   ⌁   *Budweiser beer*

221 Daniel Webster Hwy.
Merrimack, NH 03054
(603) 595-1202

Although this is the second smallest of Anheuser-Busch's 13 U.S. breweries, it can package 8 million 12-ounce servings in 24 hours. Throughout this tour, you will be bombarded with other impressive statistics, such as: almost one of every two beers consumed in America is made by Anheuser-Busch. You'll also learn about the company's diverse business interests.

Your tour guide will lead you to the brewery, built in 1970, past a life-size replica of a Clydesdale horse. In the brewhouse, a mixture of water and rice or corn fills three stainless-steel mash tanks. Malt enzymes break the starch in the corn or rice into fermentable sugars. Once strained, the remaining liquid ("wort") is boiled and hops are added. After cooling, the liquid is pumped into 45° fermentation cellars. On the ground floor of this four-story cellar, you may see a worker climb into the stainless-steel tanks to place a layer of beechwood chips. These chips provide surface area on which yeast settles during secondary fermentation.

On your way to the packaging area, notice the 8-foot carved mahogany mural of the Anheuser-Busch corporate trademark. Through glass windows, watch the tightly woven maze of filling lines. Once rinsed, bottles proceed to the rotating bottle-filler carousel, speeding up and slowing down on their way into cardboard cartons. After the brewery tour, don't miss the Clydesdale Hamlet, modeled after an 18th-century German Bauernhof. This barn and courtyard are home base for the traveling East Coast Clydesdale eight-horse show hitch. This close-up look at the Budweiser Clydesdales is a highlight of the tour.

Cost: Free
Freebies: Beer, soda, and Eagle brand pretzel snacks
Video Shown: If packaging line isn't operating, 15-minute film shown in hospitality room. Also, 3-minute video about responsible drinking on "Know When to Say When" display.

Reservations Needed: No, except for groups larger than 15.
Days and Hours: November through April Wed-Sun 10:00 AM-4:00 PM; May through October Mon-Sun 9:30 AM-5:00 PM. No bottling on weekends or holidays. Generally closed day before and day of: Thanksgiving, Christmas, and New Year's.
Plan to Stay: 1¼ hours for tour, hospitality room, and Clydesdale Hamlet, plus time for gift shop and tour assembly-room displays.
Minimum Age: Under age 18 must be accompanied by adult.
Disabled Access: Yes, some freight elevators utilized.
Group Requirements: Groups larger than 15 should call 1 day in advance. Groups of more than 35 people will be split into smaller groups. No maximum group size.
Special Information: No photography inside brewery. Tour includes indoor and outdoor walking, with three double flights of stairs. See page 117 for St. Louis feature and information about other Anheuser-Busch brewery tours.
Gift Shop: Sells logoed items including T-shirts, bathing suits, steins, neon signs, and jackets. Look for Budman and other signature steins. Open one hour later than tours.
Directions: From Boston, take Rt. 93 North to I-95 South to Rt. 3 North. In New Hampshire, Rt. 3 becomes Everett Tpke. Get off at Exit 10. At end of ramp, go right. At the next set of lights, turn left onto Daniel Webster Hwy. At the next traffic light, turn right into the brewery. Park in second lot on right. From Rt. 101, take Everett Tpke. South to Exit 10 in Merrimack. At end of ramp, turn left. At the second set of lights, turn left onto Daniel Webster Hwy. Follow to next traffic light and turn right into brewery.
Nearby Attractions: Stonyfield Farm Yogurt tour (see page 132).

See color photos, pages 140 and 141

Hampshire Pewter

9 Mill Street
Wolfeboro, NH 03894
(603) 569-4944

pewter tableware, ornaments, and gifts

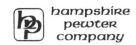

Using skilled craftspeople and modern machines, Hampshire Pewter has revived the craft of colonial pewter-making and practices the centuries-old art of handcrafting fine pewter into candlesticks, vases, goblets, and Christmas ornaments. As high-tech manufacturers strive to develop lighter, stronger, and more durable metals, it's good to know that pewter is still valued.

On your guided tour, watch craftspeople mix pure tin with other fine metals to create Queens Metal; Hampshire Pewter is the only U.S. company that uses this special alloy. You probably don't think of metal as a liquid. But to combine the metals, workers liquefy them at over 1900° in the foundry, "cool" the mixture to 600°, then pour it into specially designed bronze molds to form shapes. The crafter carefully judges when the pewter has solidified enough to be cautiously knocked from the mold. The different castings that make up an item, such as the stem and bowl of a goblet, must be soldered together skillfully and quickly—otherwise, the flame's heat may melt or scorch the joined pieces.

Craftspeople called "finishers" then "turn" the pewter piece on a lathe, using chisels to chip away all the rough, gray metal. As a piece spins, the finishers artfully and gently carve the fine details of traditional designs. Delicately holding the pewter pieces, craftspeople buff them on cotton wheels to obtain the soft pewter luster. When you see workers finish the process by stamping each piece with the distinctive "touchmark" that identifies a Hampshire Pewter original, you know that the trademark is well deserved.

Cost: Free
Freebies: No
Video Shown: 10-minute video on history of pewter and Hampshire production process.
Reservations Needed: No reservations needed June through mid-October, except for groups of 15 or more. Reservations are needed mid-October through May.
Days and Hours: Memorial Day to Labor Day Mon-Fri 9:00 AM; 10:00 AM; 11:00 AM; 1:00 PM; 2:00 PM; 3:00 PM; Labor Day to Columbus Day Mon-Fri 9:30 AM, 11:00 AM, 1:30 PM; and 3:00 PM. Call for hours and reservations mid-October through May. Closed holidays.
Plan to Stay: 30 minutes for tour and video, plus time for gift shop.
Minimum Age: None
Disabled Access: Yes
Group Requirements: 10 days' advance notice for groups of 15 or more.
Special Information: No photography.
Retail Store: Tabletop Shop sells full selection of 200 different handcast pewter items, ranging from teddy bear and bunny birthday-candle holders to flower vases and classic goblets. Personal engraving available. Open Mon-Sat 9:00 AM-5:00 PM and July through mid-October also Sun 11:00 AM-4:00 PM. Closed Memorial Day, Thanksgiving, Christmas, and New Year's. Catalog available from (800) 639-7704.
Directions: From Boston and Southern New Hampshire, take I-93 North. Take Exit 9 North, which turns into Rt. 28 North. Stay on this road into Wolfeboro. Soon after the center of town, turn right on Mill St. Hampshire Pewter is in a red barn-like building on your right.
Nearby Attractions: Pepi Herrman Crystal tour (call 603-528-1020); Annalee Dolls Museum (call 800-43-DOLLS); Castle Springs bottling plant and castle tour (call 800-729-2468); Lake Winnipesaukee; Libby Museum.

Stonyfield Farm   ~   *yogurt*

10 Burton Drive
Londonderry, NH 03053
(603) 437-4040

As the name suggests, Stonyfield Farm Yogurt began on a farm. But meteoric growth forced this award-winning company off the small farm to its present location in Londonderry. Developed in 1983 by two environmentalists, the all-natural yogurt can now be found in grocery stores nationwide. Their original mission hasn't changed—to demonstrate that a company can do good in the world and still be profitable. The tour shows you how they work their "magic" and live their corporate mission.

Follow your enthusiastic tour guide down the hall lined with laminated "love letters" from consumers. In the Yogurt Works area, watch the pasteurization of milk as it travels through a network of pipes to a tank where Stonyfield's secret concoction of healthy yogurt bacteria (or culture) is added. The milk moves through a big funnel and a tangle of yellow tubes to fill plastic cups containing a predetermined amount of fruit. Next, the safety sealer machine, acting like a cookie cutter, punches out circles from clear plastic sheets to form the cups' safety seals. Once filled and packaged, the containers may appear ready to ship to the stores, but actually they are still filled with warm milk.

Next, you walk inside to "experience" the warm incubator. While it may appear calm, there is plenty of activity. Inside each yogurt cup, the yogurt cultures are multiplying, digesting the milk and turning it into yogurt. Once the yogurt reaches the correct pH level, it is moved into the "chill cells"—the most popular spot on the tour. After the hot incubator, the Arctic wind inside each cell will cool you right off. Then return to the visitors' center to sample some frozen yogurt.

Cost: $1 for visitors between 12 and 60. All others, free. Half is donated to family farmers or farm organizations.

Freebies: Frozen yogurt sample, grocery coupons, and Moos-letter.

Video Shown: 12-minute video covers company history and close-up views of production process.

Reservations Needed: No, except for groups larger than 6 people.

Days And Hours: Tue-Sat 10:00 AM-4:00 PM on the hour. During July, August, and school vacations, frequency increases. Closed holidays and special Stonyfield days.

Plan To Stay: 45 minutes for tour, video, and sampling, plus time in gift shop.

Minimum Age: Recommended minimum age is 4; however, strollers welcome.

Disabled Access: Yes

Group Requirements: Groups over 6 people should call in advance. No reservations accepted for July and August. Maximum group size is 50 people, with groups over 20 split into smaller groups. $1 per person regardless of age.

Special Information: In the summer, there is often production on Saturdays. No photography. Stonyfield is developing a demonstration farm.

Gift Shop: Sells logoed and cow-motif products such as bibs, mugs, and MOO-LA-LA T-shirts and sweatshirts. Refrigerated case stocks discounted yogurts. Sells *Stonyfield Farm Yogurt Cookbook* and pancake mix. Moochandise cowtalogue available from above number. Open Tue-Sat 9:30 AM-5:00 PM. Closed holidays and special Stonyfield days.

Directions: From Boston, take I-93 North to Exit 5. Turn left onto Rt. 28 North. Go a little over 2 miles. Turn left onto Page Rd. Take second left onto Webster Rd. Turn left at stop sign and go 1 mile. Turn right onto Burton Dr. From Everett Turnpike, take Rt. 101 East to S. Willow St. Turn right onto Rt. 28 South. At fork, bear right onto Harvey Rd. (follow as it turns right in 1 mile). Turn right onto Burton Dr.

Nearby Attractions: Anheuser-Busch (Budweiser) Brewery tour (see page 130); Currier Gallery of Art; Canobie Lake Park; The Met Children's Museum.

See color photos, page 146

Ford  *Ranger pickup truck*

Edison Assembly Plant
939 U.S. Highway 1
Edison, NJ 08818
(908) 632-5930 ext. 5306

The Big Three auto companies owe part of their resurgence to the mushrooming popularity of non-car cars: pickups, minivans, and sport-utility vehicles. Classified as "trucks" for purposes of energy and safety regulations, this is one of the few vehicle segments that Japanese manufacturers were slow to exploit. In 1993, the Ford Ranger compact pickups made at this plant ranked as the fourth most popular vehicle sold in the U.S.A., behind the Ford full-size pickup, the Chevrolet full-size pickup, and the Ford Taurus.

As Ford's second smallest assembly plant, the Edison facility produced only cars from the 1947 Lincoln up to the Ford Escort in the late 1980s. In 1990, Ford switched the plant to making pickups, extensively retooling the factory and retraining the workers. Production went from 85 percent manual to about 85 percent robotic, so here you'll see the latest in automation and robotics. The tour begins on the final trim lines where workers install small pieces like the mirrors, instrument panel, and back windshield as the pickups move by on the ubiquitous conveyors.

Robots do over 90 percent of the body welding. No people seem to be nearby as the steel body shell moves down the line in a synchronized pattern, allowing the robotic welding arms to do their jobs hundreds of times the exact same way every day. If you're not too startled or amazed by the waterfall of sparks generated by each weld, study the different role each robot plays in building the body.

Another part of the plant constructs the frame that supports the engine, cab, and other truck parts. Watch how the engine is "decked" to the frame and, later, how the frame (at this point resembling a giant go-cart more than a pickup) is decked with the body cab. "Pit" workers test the pickup's features such as brake and gas lines. More robots help with the front windshield and seat installation. Giant praying-mantis-like arms pick up the glass and slap it into place. With all the advanced technology you see during the tour, you'll enjoy debating your fellow visitors about what was the coolest thing you saw.

Cost: Free
Freebies: Pins or pens, when availabile
Video Shown: No
Reservations Needed: Yes. Individuals and families are either joined with a scheduled group tour or formed into a group.
Days and Hours: Mon 10:00 AM and sometimes Fri 10:00 AM. Closed holidays, 2 weeks around Christmas, and 3 weeks in July.
Plan to Stay: 1¼ hours
Minimum Age: 15
Disabled Access: Yes
Group Requirements: Minimum group size is 15 people; maximum, 35. Call 4-6 weeks in advance to schedule tour.
Special Information: No photography. Tour does not visit paint department, although tour guide explains the process. About every year or so the plant has an open house that offers tours all day, a look at new pickup models, and food.
Gift Shop: No
Directions: From the New Jersey Tpke., take Exit 10. Take 287 North to Hwy. 1 South. Plant is on right.
Nearby Attractions: Edison National Historic Site in West Orange, featuring Thomas Edison's house, laboratory complex, and exhibits on his inventions and life (call 201-736-5050); Cybis Porcelain tour (call 609-392-6074); American Labor Museum in Haledon tells the story of American workers, their unions, and their diverse ethnic heritage (call 201-595-7953); Delaware and Raritan Canal State Park.

Wheaton Village   *glass and other crafts*

1501 Glasstown Road
Millville, NJ 08332-1566
(609) 825-6800 / (800) 99-VILLAGE

In 1888 Dr. T.C. Wheaton, interested in making medicine bottles, purchased a Millville glass factory which burned down in 1889. A working replica of this original factory is the centerpiece of Wheaton Village, a cultural center for glass, crafts, folklife, and art which was established in 1968.

At set times, workers demonstrate traditional glassblowing. One worker narrates as another gathers molten glass onto a long rod (a "punty"). To make a paperweight, the "gaffer" inverts the "gob" of glass onto a mold, perhaps flower-shaped. The gob absorbs colored powdered glass from inside the mold. At other times, you can also observe these workers without narration.

Sharing the floor are glassworkers on fellowship from all over the world, making contemporary sculptures. While casting, workers wear protective outfits and face protection. With a saucepan-size ladle, a worker pours 30-50 pounds of molten glass into a sand-casting (made in sand) mold.

The Museum of American Glass houses the largest collection of entirely American-made glass. Its 7,500-plus objects include paperweights, chandeliers, prisms, and Mason jars—and the nearly-9-foot-tall, 193-gallon *Guinness-Book-of-World-Records* largest bottle. The museum covers the glass industry from the first factory (1739), through the 1800s when South Jersey was a major glass-making center, to today. The glass whimsy exhibit contains objects such as walking canes that workers made from leftover glass.

The Crafts and Trades Row building contains several studios and historical exhibits. Two potters transform clay into pots as pottery wheels spin. Over a torch, a lampworker manipulates glass rods of various colors and diameters to create marbles. Each colored swirl requires a separate rod. You may see a worker forming miniature animals or people at a tiny tea table. Elsewhere, a woodcarver uses a sharp knife to carve feathers or bird feet. Afterwards, enjoy the peaceful, 60-plus-acre grounds' picnic tables,

shrubs, shady pine trees, scampering squirrels, and flocks of birds and Canada geese— or browse the numerous shops.

Cost: Adults, $6; seniors, $5.50; family, $12; students, $3.50; under 5, free.
Freebies: No
Video Shown: No
Reservations Needed: No. Groups see below.
Days and Hours: Village hours: January through March Wed-Sun 10:00 AM-5:00 PM (Crafts and Trade Row closed); April through December Mon-Sun 10:00 AM-5:00 PM. Glass demonstrations: 11:30 AM, 1:30 PM, and 3:30 PM, when village is open. Closed Easter, Thanksgiving, and Christmas.
Plan to Stay: 2½ hours, plus time in shops.
Minimum Age: None
Disabled Access: Yes
Group Requirements: Groups of more than 25 adults or 10 schoolchildren need reservations 1 month in advance. Craft Sampler Days (provide hands-on crafts participation for school groups) must be arranged 4-6 months in advance.
Special Information: Make Your Own Paperweight Program available to individuals and groups over age 21 with 1 week's advance notice. Call (800) 99-VILLAGE for special events calendar or more information.
Gift Shops: Shops sell works made at Wheaton Village and by other American glassmakers; also crafts, books, and even penny candy. Open same hours as village.
Directions: From Philadelphia, take Walt Whitman Bridge (follow signs to Atlantic City) to Rt. 42 South. Take Rt. 55 South to Exit 26. Signs lead to main entrance. From Atlantic City, take Atlantic City Expwy. West to Exit 12. Take Rt. 40 West. Turn left onto Rt. 552 West. At first traffic light in Millville, turn right onto Wade Blvd. Follow the signs.
Nearby Attractions: Parvin State Park; Atlantic City's beaches and casinos, 35 miles away; Cape May's beaches and Victorian homes, 40 miles away.

See description on page 45

The dramatic entrance to the World of Coca-Cola, Atlanta, Georgia

Club Coca-Cola features free exotic soda flavors at World of Coca-Cola

See description on page 128

The 2½-acre cactus garden in colorful bloom at Ethel M Chocolates, Henderson, Nevada

The march of candies through the chocolate enrober at Ethel M Chocolates

See description on page 227

Hand decorating the tops of Deluxe Fruitcakes with pecans, Collin Street Bakery, Corsicana, Texas

A baker inspects a few of the 1.5 million fruitcakes made each year at Collin Street Bakery

Boehms Chocolates

138

See description on page 254

Candymakers show off the sweet stuff at Boehms Chocolates, Issaquah, Washington (Photo © Journal American)

Dr. Pepper Bottling

See description on page 228

Bill Kloster, owner, and grandson Mark Kloster inspect bottling line at the oldest Dr. Pepper bottling plant, Dublin, Texas

See description on page 117

The Historic Clock Tower, one of the unique landmarks at Anheuser-Busch headquarters in St. Louis, Missouri

See descriptions on pages 117 and 130

At Anheuser-Busch tour sites nationwide, you can see brewing control rooms from the viewing galleries

Quality Insurance tests product samples throughout the brewing process at Anheuser-Busch

See descriptions on pages 117 and 130

The final step of the high-speed packaging process at Anheuser-Busch

At the end of the high-speed packaging process, a palletizer prepares Budweiser cases for distribution, Anheuser-Busch

See description on page 46

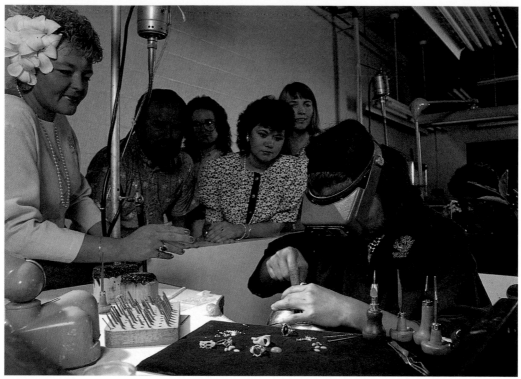

A jeweler carefully sets diamonds as the final step in jewelry design at Maui Divers, Honolulu, Hawaii

Precious black coral, diamond, and 14-karat gold Yin and Yang ring, Maui Divers

See description on page 78

Bubbling corn mash ferments in cypress wood vats at Maker's Mark Distillery, Loretto, Kentucky

The National Historic Landmark buildings and grounds of Maker's Mark Distillery

See description on page 197

Custom 4 manual console made by Rodgers Instrument Corporation, Hillsboro, Oregon

Rodgers Instrument employees build traditional organs and contemporary keyboards

See description on page 246

Glassblowing at Simon Pearce, Windsor, Vermont

See description on page 132

Watch up close how milk turns to yogurt. The packaging line at Stonyfield Farm, Londonderry, New Hampshire.

Experience the Arctic-like winds in the yogurt "chill cells" at Stonyfield Farm

See description on page 245

Enthusiastic Bear Ambassadors guide tours at Vermont Teddy Bear, Shelburne, Vermont

Mother and baby bear sunning themselves at Vermont Teddy Bear

Wild Turkey Distillery

See description on page 82

Bourbon ages for at least eight years in white oak barrels at Wild Turkey Distillery, Lawrenceburg, Kentucky

Master Distiller Jimmy Russell samples a batch of bourbon at Wild Turkey Distillery

See description on page 166

Glassmaking in Steuben Factory at Corning Glass Center, Corning, New York

Ancient glass found in a 2,000-year-old Roman tomb, Corning Museum of Glass at Corning Glass Center

See description on page 119

A press operator demonstrates the process of foil stamping on greeting cards at Hallmark Visitors Center, Kansas City, Missouri (Photo © Hallmark Cards, Inc.)

Push a button to make your own bow at Hallmark Visitors Center (Photo © Hallmark Cards, Inc.)

See description on page 59

The Navigator hits the open road headed for a factory tour, Holiday Rambler, Wakarusa, Indiana

Motorhome assembly line production at Holiday Rambler

Pennsylvania Dutch Candies

See description on page 208

Sampling of candy made by Pennsylvania Dutch Candies, Mt. Holly Springs, Pennsylvania

Rowena's

See description on page 250

Almond Pound Cake and Lemon Curd, made and sold by catalog at Rowena's, Norfolk, Virginia

Taste cranberry treats in the demonstration kitchen at Cranberry World Visitor Center, Plymouth, Massachusetts (Photo © David C. Bitters)

View cranberry harvesting on videos and at Cranberry Harvest Festival, Cranberry World Visitor Center (Photo © Ocean Spray Cranberries, Inc.)

See description on page 206

Applying the supportive "X" bracing, invented by C. F. Martin, Sr. in the 1850s, Martin Guitar, Nazareth, Pennsylvania

See description on page 269

Tractor assembly line at J I Case, Racine, Wisconsin

J I Case workers in front of factory display their first 7200 Series MAGNUM tractor

See description on page 26

Tea packaging line at Celestial Seasonings, Boulder, Colorado

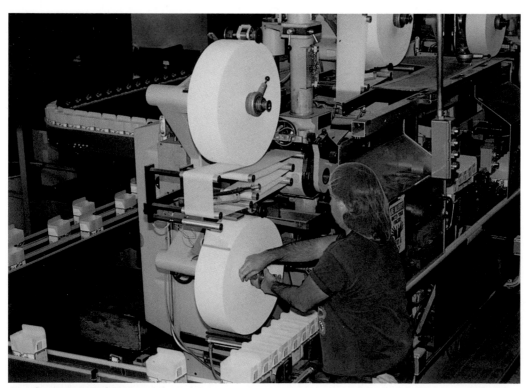

Tea bagging machine at Celestial Seasonings

Basic Brown Bear

See description on page 8

Merilee Woods, owner, with her furry friends at Basic Brown Bear, San Francisco, California

Stuff your own bear on a tour of Basic Brown Bear

From freshly peeled potatoes to tasty chips. The packaging line at Herr's, Nottingham, Pennsylvania

See pretzels shaped, then baked golden brown at Herr's

Heart of the Desert ～ *pistachios*

Eagle Ranch
7288 Highway 54/70
Alamogordo, NM 88310
(505) 434-0035

According to ancient Turkish legend, young lovers walked through moonlit pistachio groves to test their love. If they heard pistachios splitting open on the trees, they knew their love was indeed true. Centuries later, in another desert thousands of miles away, the Schweers family may have had this romantic legend in mind when they chose Heart of the Desert Pistachios as their trademark. As owners/operators of Eagle Ranch Groves, New Mexico's first and largest pistachio farm, the Schweers have put years of love and hard work into producing these delicious nuts.

Tours are offered year-round, but if you visit Eagle Ranch in September you can watch the mechanical shaking machines harvest the pistachios. The shakers clasp and vibrate the trees, releasing showers of nuts that are then transported into bins by conveyor belt. The pistachios move past a group of "gals" who remove blemished or deformed nuts. The good pistachios enter a needle sorter, a 6-foot-diameter barrel open at both ends. The needles that line the inside of the barrel hook into the split nuts' green meat, leaving the unsplit pistachios to roll out the bottom. The unsplit nuts are shelled and these nut meats are flavored, roasted, and packaged.

The split nuts, meanwhile, flow across a sloped, vibrating sizing machine comprised of flat plates with various-size holes. As the pistachios jump along the vibrating plates, the smaller nuts fall through the tiniest holes into bins underneath. The remaining nuts continue along the machine, dropping into openings of increasing size until each bin along the way holds larger-sized pistachios.

In another process, pistachios move downhill on a hopper that feeds into a seemingly benign color-sorting machine. Suddenly, you may hear a machine gun-like blast as nuts shoot out of the color sorter. A jet of air kicks out on a trajectory those nuts whose hue does not match the machine's prescribed color standards. The remaining pistachios are either sprayed with chile flavors or salted, then roasted in a huge oven.

Workers insert and remove 40-pound trays of nuts from the 10-foot-tall roaster in a nonstop workout. Meanwhile, you can take a relaxed stroll into the gift shop, where you can sample and go "nuts" over Heart of the Desert pistachios.

Cost: Free
Freebies: Pistachio samples
Video Shown: No
Reservations Needed: No, unless groups larger than 10 people want different tour times.
Days and Hours: Memorial Day through Labor Day Mon-Fri 10:00 AM and 1:30 PM. Labor Day through Memorial Day Mon-Fri 1:30 PM. Closed Thanksgiving and Christmas.
Plan to Stay: 45 minutes for tour, plus time for gift shop, visitors' center, and art gallery.
Minimum Age: None
Disabled Access: Yes
Group Requirements: Groups larger than 10 people should call 1 week in advance for alternative tour times. No maximum group size.
Special Information: Adjacent to gift shop is a visitors' center with background information on the farm and pistachios, and an art gallery.
Retail Store: Sells pistachios, southwestern Indian jewelry, gourmet items, gift baskets, pottery, and T-shirts with southwestern themes. Open Mon-Sun 9:00 AM-6:00 PM. Mail order brochure available from (800) 432-0999.
Directions: From I-25 or I-10, take Hwy. 70 North. Eagle Ranch is 4 miles north of Alamogordo on Hwys. 54/70.
Nearby Attractions: Apache Trail attractions include White Sands National Monument, Space Hall of Fame, Ruidoso Downs Race Track, Lincoln National Forest, Museum of the Horse, Valley of Fires State Recreation Park, and Lincoln Historical District (Billy the Kid Museum and Lincoln Heritage Center).

George Schweers, owner, checking a pistachio tree near harvest time at Heart of the Desert Pistachios, Alamogordo, New Mexico

Bin of ripe pistachios on its way to the huller at Heart of the Desert Pistachios

George Eastman House ~ *photography*

900 East Avenue
Rochester, NY 14607
(716) 271-3361

In the 1980s, Eastman Kodak stopped giving public plant tours. While this book wouldn't normally include a company founder's home, the extensive $1.7 million restoration completed in 1990 and the exhibits and videos on George Eastman and Kodak provide a personal look at the company's roots. America's great companies begin and grow with individuals, and Kodak owes its existence to this hardworking inventor and businessman. (He probably would also have loved this book.)

George Eastman lived in this house from 1905 to 1932. The 50-room mansion and grounds have been authentically restored. Your guide's amusing gossip and anecdotes give you a sense of this great American entrepreneur, inventor, and marketer. In the conservatory, stand under a huge replica of an elephant's head and tusks while you listen to the story about why Eastman stood his ground to take a photo of an onrushing rhino. It provides a lesson on how he built his successful business.

Colorful displays in two second-floor rooms capture his personality, lifestyle, philanthropy, management techniques, and marketing strategy. Kodak's early history is intertwined with George Eastman's life, so the displays also show the company's development. You'll learn many tidbits, including why Eastman named his company "Kodak," why he gave away 500,000 "Brownie" cameras—one to every child who turned 12 in 1930—and see early Kodak advertising campaigns featuring themes still used today. You'll leave with a taste of how Eastman turned new scientific inventions into enormously popular products—a trait American companies have re-learned.

Cost: Adults, $6; seniors and students, $4.50; children 5-12, $2.50; children 4 and under, free.
Freebies: No
Video Shown: A second-floor room continuously screens videos about George Eastman and Kodak. The Kodak video shows manu-facturing process and overviews company's new products and direction.

Reservations Needed: No, except for groups larger than 30 people.
Days and Hours: Museum: Tue-Sat 10:00 AM-4:30 PM, Sun 1:30 PM-4:30 PM. Closed holidays. During May (Lilac Festival in Rochester), open Mon-Sun 10:00 AM-4:30 PM. Tours: Tue-Sat 10:30 AM and 2:00 PM, Sun at 2:00 PM.
Plan to Stay: 2 hours for house and gardens tour (which can be self-guided), watching most of both videos and visiting second-floor exhibits, and seeing the excellent International Museum of Photography and Film attached to the house (one of the world's greatest collections of photography, film, technology, and literature).
Minimum Age: None
Disabled Access: Yes
Group Requirements: Groups larger than 30 people must schedule tours in advance by calling (716) 271-3361, ext. 238. Group rates available.
Gift Shop: Books, posters, collectors' items and other photography-related gifts available in museum's gift shop. Open same hours as museum.
Special Information: Devices available to assist hearing-impaired.
Directions: Take New York State Thrwy. to Exit 45 and go north on Rt. 490 towards Rochester. At Exit 19, go north on Culver Rd., then left on East Ave. The museum is on the right.
Nearby Attractions: Memorial Art Gallery; Strong Museum; Rochester Museum and Science Center; Highland Park (annual May Lilac Festival); Seneca Park Zoo; Susan B. Anthony House.

The dining room after restoration, George Eastman House, Rochester, New York

George Eastman, founder of Kodak, lived here from 1905 to 1932 (Photo: Barbara Puorro Galasso)

NBC Studios ~~~ *television programs*
30 Rockefeller Plaza
New York, NY 10112
(212) 664-4000

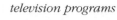

NBC prides itself on being the first radio network (1926), the first coast-to-coast television network (1951), and the first to broadcast in color (1953, "Kukla, Fran & Ollie"). This tour of the network headquarters (NBC employees call it "30 Rock") reflects that spirit. After seeing the behind-the-scenes hardware that helps edit, select, and broadcast shows to millions of homes, you appreciate what's involved when you flick on your TV.

While you will see neat technical TV hardware such as the Automated Record Playback System, the tour's highlight is visiting the sets of well-known shows or possibly meeting a TV star in hallways lined with NBC promotional posters. With your guide, you may explore the versatile Studio 3K used for several NBC sports and entertainment programs. Discover how small the set really is and examine the imitation wood, plants, and other background materials that look so realistic on television.

Up to 12 different sets appear simultaneously in "Saturday Night Live" ("SNL" in TV jargon) Studio 8-H, with the band and monologue sets the only two "permanents." During the show, actors jump between stages and workers move walls and props preparing for upcoming skits. If you're here the week a new SNL is taped, you can briefly watch a rehearsal through glass walls, with the casually clothed director, guest host, cameramen, and production assistants going over segments. But don't let the relaxed dress fool you. As employees briskly walk by, you'll sense the pressures and deadlines of live television.

Cost: $8.25
Freebies: Small "NBC Studio Tour" sticker and the possibility of meeting a TV star.
Video Shown: 10-minute video explains NBC history and the television production process.
Reservations Needed: No, except for groups larger than 10 people.
Days and Hours: Mon-Sat 9:30 AM-4:30 PM, every 15 minutes. Call about Sunday hours

during busy December and summer seasons. Closed Thanksgiving, Christmas, New Year's, and Labor Day.
Plan to Stay: 1 hour for video and tour, plus time for gift shop.
Minimum Age: 6
Disabled Access: Yes
Group Requirements: Groups larger than 10 people need at least 1 week's advance reservations (call 212-664-7174). Maximum group size is 80. Group rates available.
Special Information: No photography. Purchase tickets early in the day; they can sell out by mid-morning, especially during holidays. The tour varies with fast-breaking news or broadcast schedule changes. For show tickets, write NBC Tickets at the address above. NBC Burbank (818-840-4444) also gives tours.
NBC Page Program: Tour guides are part of the NBC Page Program that gives people an opportunity to break into broadcasting. Besides conducting tours, pages seat audiences at show tapings and also work within departments. For more information, contact NBC Page Program, Employee Relations #1678, at above address.
Gift Shop: Sells T-shirts, caps, mugs and other novelty items, many with logos of your favorite shows and NBC Sports. Open Mon-Fri 9:00 AM-7:00 PM, Sat 9:00 AM-11:00 PM (closes at 5:00 PM in summer), and usually Sundays when tours run. Call (212) 664-5354.
Directions: Located in GE Building on 50th St. between 5th & 6th Aves. Subway stops below building, so take B, D, or F subway. Get off at the 47-50th St., Rockefeller Plaza station, then walk up a few flights to building lobby.
Nearby Attractions: Radio City Music Hall tour (call 212-632-4041); Maidenform Museum (call 212-953-1400); IBM Gallery of Science and Art (call 212-745-5214); Museum of Television and Radio; 5th Ave shopping; Museum of Modern Art.

Play weatherperson using technology similar to the pros' at NBC Studios, New York, New York (Photo © NBC, Inc./Alan Singer)

NBC Studios headquarters at Rockefeller Plaza in New York City (Photo © NBC, Inc.)

Corning Glass Center   〰   *glass*

151 Centerway
Corning, NY 14831
(607) 974-8271

Like a glass prism, a visit to the Corning Glass Center is multi-faceted. The complete experience of The Corning Museum of Glass, the Hall of Science and Industry, and the Steuben Factory illuminates the history of glass, optical-fiber communications, and glassmaking. The Museum's world-famous collection of more than 26,000 glass objects traces 35 centuries of human experience with glass, starting in ancient Egypt's 18th Dynasty when the search for perfectly clear crystal glass began. You will be amazed that the 11-foot-high Tiffany window, now in the museum's permanent collection, was originally part of a private residence destined for destruction.

Learn how light transmits information through optical fibers in "Master of Light," one of the Hall's interactive educational exhibits. Also notice the 200-inch mirror disk, one of the most massive glass pourings ever, planned for the Mt. Palomar telescope. In the Hall, watch a craftsman melt rods of glass tubing over a single gas-flamed jet and form tiny glass animals.

While the Museum and Hall are interesting, the real fascination is watching the production of world-renowned Steuben glass. During a self-guided tour you sit on wide, carpet-covered steps in front of a glass wall to watch master glassworkers perform their art. Gaffers collect gobs of red-hot glass from a central tank. Glassblowers' cheeks resemble Louis Armstrong playing the trumpet as they blow into the long blowpipes. They shape each piece with wooden and metal hand tools.

Along a walkway you see the engraving process that makes Steuben glass so unique and valuable. The engraver first coats the glass with protective shellac, then transfers an image onto its surface with India ink. To cut the design, the engraver presses the glass upward against as many as 50 different fine copper wheels on a rotating lathe. Intricate designs may require as many as 300 hours to engrave. You will leave with respect and admiration for the Steuben glassmakers' skills and the technological advances of glass in science.

Cost: Adults, $6; senior citizens, $5; ages 6-17, $4; children under 6, free. Families with children 6-17 years old are charged $14 family rate regardless of number in family.

Freebies: No

Video Shown: Overhead videos during self-guided tour of Steuben factory explain glassblowing. Overhead videos in museum illustrate glassmaking methods.

Reservations Needed: No, except for groups larger than 20 people.

Days and Hours: Open Mon-Sun 9:00 AM-5:00 PM; July and August Mon-Sun 9:00 AM-8:00 PM. Closed Thanksgiving, Christmas Eve and Day, and New Year's. Best time to see Steuben factory production is Mon-Fri 9:00 AM-5:00 PM.

Plan to Stay: 2 hours

Minimum Age: None

Disabled Access: Yes

Group Requirements: Groups of 20 or more should call 2 weeks in advance for special group rates and reservations (call 607-974-2000). No maximum group size.

Special Information: No photography in Steuben factory visitor's gallery.

Gift Shop: Glass Center features five shops selling Steuben and other glass objects, glass-related books, souvenirs, and Corning tabletop and cookware products. Open same hours as Center. July and August "Just Uncrated" sale offers discounted Corning products, "how to use Corningware" presentations, ongoing food demonstrations, and recipes from local restaurants.

Directions: From New York City, take Rt. 17 West. Take Corning exit and follow signs. From Rochester, take I-390 South to Rt. 17 East. Follow above directions.

Nearby Attractions: At Historic Market Street shopping district, watch live demonstrations at glass studios; Rockwell Museum; Taylor Winery Visitor Center (call 607-569-6111); Benjamin Patterson Inn; Glenn Curtiss National Soaring Museum.

See color photos, page 149

New York Stock Exchange ⌒ *stocks and bonds*

20 Broad Street
New York, NY 10005
(212) 656-5167

While the New York Stock Exchange (NYSE) isn't a factory, it is the place many companies in this book rely on to raise money. Over 250 million shares are traded on an average day at this world's-largest stock exchange. Even if you have no background in finance, the video, architecture, and action on the trading floor give you an enlightened view of our economic system.

At your first look through the visitor gallery's glass windows, there seems to be nothing but confusion on the trading floor below. People wearing suits, dresses, and jackets of various colors move about briskly. Arms wave, voices shout, and scraps of paper drop onto the floor. But once you concentrate on the activities at the individual trading posts, listen to the continuously playing audiotaped explanation, and look at the diagrams, the activities begin to make sense.

The trading posts teem with the latest high-tech data-communications equipment, with glowing green monitors sticking out like spider legs—very different in appearance from the old oak-and-brass posts they replaced. The brokers and specialists (NYSE-assigned dealers) buy and sell stock in a continuous process according to orders received via their computer screens and by phones around the floor's perimeter. Before you leave the gallery, examine the room's beautiful architecture, with its ornate gilded ceiling, marble walls. and famous wall of windows directly opposite the viewing gallery.

Displays describe the NYSE's function, workings, and development since it was founded in 1792 to trade New York banks' stocks and bonds that covered Revolutionary War debts. The exhibits teach financial neophytes about stock and bond trading and answer common questions. Other displays show more-experienced investors how to retrieve computerized information on stocks, bonds, futures, and options. The newspaper's stock price tables will have new meaning after your visit.

Cost: Free

Freebies: NYSE literature at information desk.

Video Shown: 11-minute video in the Experience Theater, "NYSE: A Portrait," features interesting historical footage and close-ups that take you onto today's trading floor.

Reservations Needed: No, except for groups of 10 or more.

Days and Hours: Mon-Fri 9:15 AM-4:00 PM. Outside the building, tickets are distributed daily starting at 9:00 AM and often run out by mid-morning. Open the day after Thanksgiving only until 1:00 PM (this is the most popular day of the year for visitors). Closed holidays.

Plan to Stay: 40 minutes for trading floor viewing gallery, video, and displays, plus time for gift counter.

Minimum Age: None

Disabled Access: Yes

Group Requirements: Groups of 10 or more need reservations at least 1 month in advance. Maximum group size is 25. Call (212) 656-5168. Groups receive a special presentation at "The Market Today" exhibit. Financial district "trail map" with quiz available for school groups.

Special Information: No photography. Tight security. Taped explanation in viewing gallery available in major foreign languages.

Gift Counter: Sells NYSE publications and logoed items including caps, T-shirts, Christmas ornaments, cufflinks, and key rings. Catalog available from (212) 656-5166.

Directions: Take the No. 2, 3, 4, or 5 subway to Wall St. stop. Look for the six-Corinthian-column facade of building's Broad St. entrance. Directions for driving (very challenging with many one-way streets) and from other subway lines available by calling (212) 656-5168.

Nearby Financial Attractions: Museum of American Financial History (call 212-908-4110); Commodities Exchange Visitors Gallery (call 212-938-2025); New York Federal Reserve Bank tour (call 212-720-6130). South Street Seaport also nearby.

The Original American Kazoo Company

8703 South Main Street   ⌇   *kazoos*
Eden, NY 14057
(716) 992-3960

"If you can hum . . . you can play the kazoo" is the motto of the Original American Kazoo Company, the only metal-kazoo factory in the world. The kazoo is truly an American instrument, invented in the U.S. in the 1840s. Since kazoos are made the same way today as when the company started in 1916, we can say some things never change.

Pass through the toy and gift shop into the museum and factory. Wander around the small museum area looking at exhibits of kazoo trivia, history, and memorabilia. Learn that "Kazoo" was once a brand name for underwear and that the navy ship USS *Kalamazoo* was nicknamed "the Kazoo"—its sailors owned kazoos printed with the ship's real name. Display cases show a variety of creative kazoos. Look for the liquor-bottle-shaped kazoo (made in 1934 to "Kazelebrate" the end of Prohibition) and even a Woody Woodpecker model.

An 18-step process transforms sheets of metal into the classic submarine-shaped kazoo, without soldering, welding, or gluing. Pieces are joined by shaping and crimping metal. From behind a railing, you watch as workers operate individual presses (built in 1907) that flange edges, curve bottoms and tops, and stamp out the air hole. Parts are "seamed" together over a sword-shaped mold, then workers hand-insert the resonator and screw on the cap. Notice the single 10-horsepower motor that drives all of the presses as you listen to the rhythmic thump of the metal blanks being transformed into kazoos.

Don't blow off this place because the manufacturing steps sound confusing—posters describe how the company makes kazoos to the tune of about 35,000 per week. In fact, you'll probably leave playing your favorite song on a kazoo.

Cost: Free
Freebies: No
Video Shown: 10-minute video in the museum area shows news clips about the company.

Reservations Needed: No, except for groups larger than 12 people.
Days and Hours: Mon-Sat 10:00 AM-5:00 PM, Sun 12:00 PM-5:00 PM. Production takes place Mon-Fri until 3:30 PM. Closed holidays, week between Christmas and New Year's, and inventory days.
Plan to Stay: 20 minutes for self-guided tour, video, and the museum displays, plus time for gift shop.
Minimum Age: None for families. 6 for school groups.
Disabled Access: Yes
Groups Requirements: Reservations required 2 days in advance for group tours given Mon-Fri 10:15 AM-2:30 PM. Minimum group size is 12. Groups larger than 20 people are split into shifts. Minimum age is 6 for school groups. Groups receive a discount on one kazoo per customer.
Special Information: The tour does not take you onto factory floor. As you stand behind the viewing area railing, a worker describes the manufacturing process and answers questions.
Gift Store: Sells kazoos of all kinds, toys, wind chimes, cards, hand-crafted instruments, and children's books. Also sells jewelry, glassware, and other gift items. Open Mon-Sat 10:00 AM-5:00 PM; Sun 12:00 PM-5:00 PM. Closed holidays.
Directions: Take New York State Thrwy. to Exit 57A. Turn left onto Eden-Evans Center Rd. When you reach the first traffic light, turn right onto Main St. (Rt. 62). The company is 2 blocks ahead on the left.
Nearby Attractions: Leon, NY, an Amish community, is 20 minutes away. Perry's Ice Cream (see page 170) and Buffalo's attractions, including QRS Music Rolls tour (see page 171), are about 45 minutes away.

Pepsi-Cola Bottling ~ *soda, iced tea, fruit juice*

2770 Walden Avenue
Buffalo, NY 14225
(716) 684-4900

This plant seems to bottle or distribute almost every existing non-alcoholic drink . . . except those marketed by Coca-Cola. As you walk through the plant you see large stacks of cases filled with your favorite beverages. Pepsi, 7-Up, Dr. Pepper, A&W Root Beer, Vernors, Mountain Dew, and Squirt are just a few of the products bottled here, for which an average of two tankers of liquid sugar per day make the base syrups. When you've stopped being amazed at this range of brands, you'll see how two filling lines fill all those bottles, and how aluminum cans, plastic bottles, and glass bottles are recycled.

This independently owned bottling company prides itself on being one of the few Pepsi bottlers that still use 16-ounce refillable glass bottles (they also bottle the 2-liter size). The uncaser automatically takes empty bottles from cases and places them on a conveyor belt that moves through the washer/rinser. After both visual and electronic inspections the bottles march into the filler. This noisy machine is a wheel-shaped bowl with a series of valves. As bottles whirl around the machine, a tube inserts itself into each one and quickly fills it to the appropriate level. Caps then drop down to seal the bottles before they are automatically packed into cases, stacked, and placed on pallets.

Try to follow one bottle's journey through the filler and capper machine. Since this plant bottles 5,000 cases of 16-ounce refillable bottles per day, you'd better not blink or your bottle will get lost in the crowd. The bottling process has come a long way from when Caleb Bradham, a young pharmacist, invented Pepsi-Cola from kola nuts in 1898 to sell at his drugstore soda fountain. The other line, which bottles 2-liter beverages, follows a similarly mind-boggling process. You can guess the flavors and brands in production just by the smells.

The recycling area is filled with cans in bags and cardboard boxes. A dumpster receives the cans and crushes them into a work of modern art that looks like a giant metal haystack. When you walk through the vending area where workers are repairing and painting dozens of vending machines, you don't need to reach inside to grab a can or bottle—your thirst from this tour will soon be quenched.

Cost: Free
Freebies: Beverage sample
Video Shown: No
Reservations Needed: Yes
Days and Hours: Mon, Wed, and Fri 9:30 AM. Closed holidays.
Plan to Stay: 1 hour
Minimum Age: 6
Disabled Access: Not encouraged. Narrow areas and stairs.
Group Requirements: Can handle groups up to 35 people with at least 1 week's notice.
Special Information: No photography. You may hear an occasional explosion—every so often a bottle on the line may explode due to weakened glass. Most local bottling plants no longer give public tours. Contact bottlers in your area for more information. Pepsi corporate headquarters in Purchase, NY has a public art exhibit/rock garden.
Gift Shop: No
Directions: From Downtown Buffalo, take I-90 to Exit 52 East. Plant is 1½ miles ahead on the left. From Buffalo Airport, turn right on Genesee St. and left on Dick Rd. Go 1½ miles and turn right onto Walden Ave. Plant is second building on right.
Nearby Attractions: QRS Music Rolls tour (see page 171); New Galleria Mall; Buffalo's attractions 7-10 miles away.

Perry's Ice Cream — *ice cream*

One Ice Cream Plaza
Akron, NY 14001
(716) 542-5492 / (800) 8-PERRYS

When H. Morton Perry started his business in 1918, he bottled milk for dairy farmers in the Akron area. Every so often he made small batches of ice cream for his family and friends—to rave reviews. By 1932 he began selling his ice cream to the public, and Perry's Ice Cream Company was born. H. Morton's grandchildren now run the business. You'll see that modern freezers have taken the place of ice-cooled storerooms, and a fleet of trucks has replaced horse-drawn wagons. You'll view an impressive manufacturing facility that makes millions of gallons of ice cream and related frozen treats every year.

After watching a video that covers Perry's proud history and the production of its quality ice cream, you'll walk up to a mezzanine area and peer through glass walls that survey the production floor. To your right are vats that hold the base mixes for ice cream and yogurt. In the center are the ever-moving machines that make ice cream and "novelty items," what they call treats like ice-cream sandwiches and cones. In this area, up to eight movable production lines may be in action. To the left are freezers for the finished products. While you're taking in the view, you'll munch on a free novelty item.

The various ice cream flavors start as base mixes and then journey through enclosed machines and pipes that add goodies like pecan halves, caramel sauce, chocolate chips, or strawberries. Look for the line that makes ice-cream sandwiches. The vanilla ice cream is piped in and squirted between two traveling chocolate wafers. The ice cream and wafers come together in a continuous stream that makes and packages 120 sandwiches per minute.

Perry's can make cones a lot faster than your local ice-cream parlor. The cones are loaded into one end of the production line. Ice cream is shot inside, then chocolate sauce and nuts drop on top. Quicker then you can say "another scoop, please," the cones are packaged and off to the massive freezer.

Cost: Free

Freebies: Ice-cream novelty item of your choice.

Video Shown: 12-minute video on Perry's history and production process.

Reservations Needed: Yes

Days and Hours: Mon-Fri 9:00 AM, 10:30 AM, 12:00 PM, 1:00 PM. Closed holidays.

Plan to Stay: 45 minutes for video and tour

Minimum Age: No

Disabled Access: Stairs lead to production viewing area.

Group Requirements: Maximum group size is 40 people. Should call 1 month in advance.

Special Information: No photography of production floor.

Gift Counter: Sells logoed T-shirts, mugs, and key chains from a cabinet in the room where you watch the video. Open after tour.

Directions: From the east, take I-90 West to Exit 48A (Pembroke). Take Rt. 77 South. Turn right onto Rt. 5 West, then right onto Rt. 93 North. Follow Rt. 93 as it turns and curves through Akron. Turn right at Ice Cream Plaza. From the west, take I-90 East to Exit 49 (Depew). Turn left on Rt. 78, then right on Rt. 5 East. Turn left on Rt. 93 North to Ice Cream Plaza.

Nearby Attractions: Original American Kazoo Company tour (see page 168); Eric County Park; Octagon House; Niagara Falls is 35 miles away.

QRS Music Rolls   ~~~ *player-piano rolls*

1026 Niagara Street
Buffalo, NY 14213-2099
(716) 885-4600

At the world's oldest and largest mass manufacturer of player-piano rolls, you see how computer technology now makes a product whose prime was in the Roaring Twenties. You've gotta love a tour that begins by letting a nostalgic visitor play a popular tune on a player piano. Enter the memorabilia-filled waiting area where old ads and letters from Jackie Gleason and Princess Grace of Monaco adorn the walls. In the corner sits a 1912 QRS "marking piano" which produces master rolls by recording an actual performer. The modified piano keys are pneumatically connected to a stylus that makes small markings on a roll of paper in the recorder.

Upstairs, look through glass windows at the predecessor of today's high-tech recording studio. To make the master roll, the "arranger" played a song beat-by-beat on a "recording piano" that put holes directly on a master sheet. With this time-consuming process (8 hours to make a 3-minute song) the roll could not be played back until the recording was finished. Now, a computerized process produces the master roll. Watch the arranger enter keystrokes on the computer and instantly play them back for accuracy. The floppy disk, not holes in paper, creates the master.

In the manufacturing area, a worker feeds the disk into a perforator machine that cuts a pattern on sheets of paper according to computer code. Nearby, another worker handles the printer that puts song lyrics and other information onto the rolls. Look for the device that slurps up the sheets into finished piano rolls. As the tour ends, you're happy that our world of CD players and digital audio tapes still has room for player-piano music.

Cost: Adults, $2; children over 6, $1.
Freebies: No
Video Shown: 12-minute slide show on company history and how player-piano music is created.

Reservations Needed: No, except for groups larger than 8 people.
Days and Hours: Mon-Fri 10:00 AM and 2:00 PM (two tours daily). Closed holidays.
Plan to Stay: 1 hour for slide show and tour, plus time to look at items in waiting area and seconds area.
Minimum Age: 7. Children should have some interest in music to enjoy the tour.
Disabled Access: Small flight of stairs to the exhibits in the waiting area. However, most of tour is not wheelchair accessible.
Group Requirements: Groups larger than 8 people should call 2 weeks in advance. Maximum group size is 20.
Special Information: The tour is a mecca for people with player pianos, and will be most interesting for people with some player-piano experience. For an interesting comparison to the production of CDs, the most modern form of recorded music, see the feature on Disc Manufacturing, Huntsville, AL on page 1.
Gift Shop: Sells 2,500 QRS songs in stock, including children's music, Broadway and movie musicals, country and western hits, and rock 'n' roll hits. Seconds are half price, but you must sift through individual boxed and unboxed rolls for the song titles. Tour admission is redeemable toward purchase. Open Mon-Fri 8:00 AM-4:00 PM. Catalog available from above number.
Directions: From Rt. 33, take Rt. 198 West to Rt. 266. Turn left on Rt. 266, which is Niagara St. Company is about 1 mile ahead on the right.
Nearby Attractions: Original American Kazoo Company and Pepsi-Cola Bottling tours (see pages 168 and 169); Rich Products History Exhibit in Rich Renaissance Niagara building (call 716-878-8000); Buffalo area attractions, including Buffalo Museum of Science and Albright Gallery. Niagara Falls is approximately 20 miles away.

Steinway & Sons ~~ *pianos*

1 Steinway Place
Long Island City, NY 11105
(718) 721-2600

STEINWAY & SONS

A piano mecca exists inside a four-story building in urban Queens, New York. Part lumberyard, woodshop, fine-cabinet studio, music-playing room, and back-office operation, Steinway & Sons is a world microcosm, with 33 different nationalities of workers. Over 300 craftspeople, trained by apprenticeship, handbuild 2,500 pianos each year. Since it takes one year and approximately 12,000 parts to make a Steinway piano, you will be amazed by the number of pianos in progress.

One tour highlight is the rim bending. Six men carry a laminated, rock-maple board (often with 18 layers) to one of the piano-shaped presses, the same ones invented 100 years ago by the founder's son. They wrestle the wood, bending it around the press, then hammer, screw, and clamp the wood into place. Each rim stays one day on the press. Once removed, rims rest calmly for at least six weeks in a sauna-hot, dark room. Here you appreciate the range of piano sizes, as the rims stand from 5 to 9 feet tall.

The belly department is rumored to be named after the original beer-drinking workers whose bellies hung over the pianos as they worked here. Sound boards are custom-fit into each piano. Workers hammer in the bridge to which strings will be attached. Saws hiss and the floors vibrate with the rhythmic banging and drilling. Cast-iron plates suspended in air wait for installation into rims. In the stringing department, you'll watch with fascination as a worker attaches each metal string to the plate (or "harp"), loops it tightly around the bridge, and then clamps it around the tuning pin. This process is skillfully repeated until all strings are installed.

The final stage is tuning. Master voicers in soundproof rooms regulate the "action," which is how piano-makers refer to the key/hammer mechanism. To ensure that all hammers rise to the same height, voicers hit each key and watch the corresponding hammer bob like a woodpecker's head. Once the action is regulated, the voicer inserts it into

the front of the piano and tests its musical quality, adjusting its tuning and brightness before the piano's first performance in Carnegie Hall or your living room.

Cost: Free
Freebies: Catalog and refreshments at end of tour.
Video Shown: No, but can purchase 15-minute video which alternates between factory and pianists' performances.
Reservations Needed: Yes
Days and Hours: Most Fri (possibly Thur) 9:00 AM. No tours July and August. Closed holidays and week between Christmas and New Year's.
Plan to Stay: 2½ hours
Minimum Age: 16
Disabled Access: Yes, via freight elevators.
Group Requirements: Maximum group size is 25 people. Call several weeks in advance for reservations.
Gift Area: Can order books, videos, posters, and logoed items including mugs, T-shirts, and pens, with delivery in 7-10 days. Product listing available at above number.
Special Information: Since factory covers 450,000 square feet and four floors which may be sawdusty, wear comfortable walking shoes.
Directions: From LaGuardia airport, take Grand Central Pkwy. West. Take first exit and turn right onto Steinway St. to 19th Ave. Steinway & Sons is on your left. From Manhattan, take Triboro Bridge toward Queens. Take first exit in Queens. Stay in right lane to get onto Astoria Blvd. Turn left onto Steinway St. Follow above directions. Call for subway directions. (N to Ditmars Blvd.)
Nearby Attractions: Shea Stadium; Manhattan's music attractions include Lincoln Center, Carnegie Hall, nearby Steinway Hall (company's piano showroom and museum—call 212-246-1100), Radio City Music Hall tour (call 212-632-4041).

Fieldcrest Cannon ~~ *sheets*

Cannon Village Visitors Center
200 West Avenue
Kannapolis, NC 28081
(704) 938-3200

You cannot help noticing the tall, red brick smokestack, bearing the Fieldcrest Cannon name, that towers against the background as you drive into Kannapolis. (Appropriately, the town's name combines two Greek words meaning "City of Looms.") You'll pass some of the 1,600 "mill houses" constructed for employees in the early 1900s. Here, on land that was once a 600-acre cotton plantation, farming and textiles are interwoven with the history of the land. The museum, with its old wooden looms and textile artifacts, is located in the Cannon Village Visitor's Center and provides an introduction to the textile industry. The museum includes photographic history of the plant, early-to-modern towels made by Fieldcrest Cannon, other displays, and a video about the process of producing towels and sheets.

You will learn that when bales of fresh cotton are received, the dirty cotton is cleaned to remove lumps and alien fibers. Enormous barrels of spun, coiled cotton ropes wait to be processed. In the card room, large, noisy card machines align webs of soft cotton side by side.

To make the famous cotton/poly 50/50 blend, a drawing machine processes four barrels each of cotton and polyester. Over 550 looms in the nearby plant weave threads into muslin and percale sheeting; another plant bleaches, prints, and dyes it. At a Concord, North Carolina facility the sheet is cut, hemmed, labeled and packaged.

Cost: Free
Freebies: Coupon booklet for discounts at various Cannon Village shops, including a coupon for a complimentary item from the Fieldcrest Cannon outlet store.
Video Shown: 20-minute video covers history of the town and company. Shows towel manufacturing process.
Reservations Needed: No
Days and Hours: Mon-Sat 10:00 AM-5:00 PM, Sun 1:00 PM-6:00 PM. Closed Thanksgiving, Christmas, and Easter.

Plan to Stay: 1 hour for museum, plus time for Cannon Village shops.
Minimum Age: None
Disabled Access: Yes
Group Requirements: Groups of 10 or more should call 1 week in advance for reservations. Maximum group size is 40 people.
Special Information: Due to insurance reasons, plant tour was recently discontinued.
Outlet Store: Fieldcrest Cannon Bed & Bath is in Cannon Village (call 800-237-3209 or 704-939-2869). Open Mon-Sat 9:00 AM-7:00 PM, Sun 1:00 PM-6:00 PM, with extended hours around Christmas. Closed Christmas and New Year's.
Directions: From I-85 North, take Exit 58 for Kannapolis. Take Hwys. 29 & 601 North. Travel under bridge. Take first right, onto 1st St. and into Village. Go to Cannon Village Visitor's Center. From I-85 South, take Exit 63. Follow Lane St. into Kannapolis.
Nearby Attractions: Cannon Village has many specialty shops, factory outlet stores, and restaurants; Charlotte Motor Speedway.

Replacements ~ *china, crystal, and flatware*
1089 Knox Road
Greensboro, NC 27420
(910) 697-3000 / (800) 562-4462

REPLACEMENTS, LTD.

For a special dinner party, you carefully set the table with the fragile bone china Aunt Millie willed you. But a guest accidentally dropped a precious teacup while helping clear the table. Once you see Replacements, Ltd.'s rows of shelves (62,000, to be exact!) stacked 16 feet high with 46,000 different patterns of china and crystal, you will feel confident about matching Aunt Millie's teacup. Replacements, the world's largest supplier of obsolete, active, and inactive china, crystal, and flatware, receives 15,000 pattern requests every month.

In the research department, "detectives" identify discontinued china, crystal, and flatware patterns for desperate customers, who send pictures, photocopies, or pencil rubbings of their treasures. The researchers use old catalogs (one prize possession is a 1936 Fostoria Catalog) and pictures to identify patterns. Antique dealers and a 2,000-buyer network receive Replacements' 600-page bimonthly "wish list" of customer requests. Buyers scour auctions, estate sales, and flea markets worldwide in search for specific patterns.

Wearing goggles that protect their eyes, skilled restoration-area workers carefully smooth out small (less than ⅛-inch) chips in crystal. Besides restoring crystal to its original beauty, workers reglaze and fire certain china pieces to remove scratches. Paintbrushes in hand, these artists expertly dab special paint onto the gold and platinum trim on ornate, elegant porcelain.

One tour highlight comes when your guide leads you down an aisle of the 1.6-million-piece warehouse. Looking but not touching is difficult—but required—as you peer into one of the towering shelves and spot anything from the elegant stem of a Baccarat crystal to a Limoges dessert plate. Equally impressive is the flatware department. Here you see gleaming silver serving spoons and shiny butter knives being inspected, identified, inventoried, and most importantly, measured. Workers polish precious pieces on high-speed buffing machines, then seal them in their own plastic bags to retard tarnishing. You leave with a true appreciation of the effort and dedication involved in researching, restoring, and replacing the "irreplaceable."

Cost: Free
Freebies: Logoed key chains and calendars
Video Shown: No
Reservations Needed: No, except for groups larger than 25.
Days and Hours: Mon-Fri 8:00 AM-5:00 PM (possibly later), Sat 9:00 AM-5:00 PM, Sun 1:00 PM-5:00 PM; every 30 minutes. Closed Thanksgiving, Christmas, New Year's, and July 4th.
Plan to Stay: 20-30 minutes, plus time in showroom.
Minimum Age: None
Disabled Access: Yes
Group Requirements: Groups larger than 25 should call 2 days ahead; will be split into smaller groups.
Special Information: Wear comfortable shoes. Opening of 2,400-square-foot museum adjacent to showroom planned for late 1994. Will focus on Ohio River Valley's early-20th-Century glass industry.
Retail Store: Showroom displays porcelain, crystal, and metal collectibles in antique mahogany, oak, and walnut showcases (some dating back to the 1800s, and many with their original glass!). Also Masons' lamps (Wedgewood), crystal perfume bottles, and jewelry. Open Mon-Fri 8:00 AM-8:00 PM, Sat 9:00 AM-6:00 PM, and Sun 1:00 PM-6:00 PM. Closed holidays.
Directions: Take I-85/40 and get off at Exit 132. Go north (left if coming from Greensboro, right from Burlington) on Mt. Hope Church Rd. and turn left on Knox Rd. Replacements is on the left.
Nearby Attractions: Greensboro's attractions include Colonial Heritage Center, Greensboro Arboretum, Greensboro Cultural Center at Festival Park; Burlington Factory Outlets; Winston-Salem's attractions, including Stroh Brewery tour (see page 176), are 25 miles away. Seagrove, largest community of potters in the U.S.A. (call 910-873-7887) is located about 40 miles away.

Example of china pattern, the classic Moss Rose by Rosenthal, which is replaceable by Replacements, Greensboro, North Carolina

Warehouse packed with 46,000 patterns of china, crystal, and flatware at Replacements

Stroh Brewery Company 〜 *beer*

4791 Schlitz Avenue
Winston-Salem, NC 27107
(910) 788-6710

STROH

Founded by Bernhard Stroh in 1850, the Stroh Brewery Company is the fourth-largest brewer in the U.S.A. The Winston-Salem plant is the company's largest facility, brewing such well-known brands as Stroh's, Old Milwaukee, Schlitz, and Schaefer. The brewery tour takes you through the highly automated packaging center and brewhouse, and—like all good brewery tours—ends with an opportunity to sample products in the attractive Strohaus Hospitality Center.

The shiny stainless-steel vessels and tubs in the brewhouse convert the malted barley, hops, yeast, and water into beer. The computerized instrument panel across from the observation area controls the entire operation. Your guide explains the roles of the different tubs in making the mash, wort, and then beer, according to different recipes for each brand. Stroh's produces the only commercially fire-brewed beer in the country; other beers are steam-brewed. With fire-brewing, a special boiler called a "Flammkessel" shoots open flames around coiling copper tubes containing wort. After fermentation, aging, and inspections, the beer heads off to be bottled, canned, or kegged.

The roaring packaging area fills more cans and bottles of beer in one minute than you and your family will drink in the next 10 years. Walking above the lines, you get end-zone and sideline views of the action. Four of the six canning lines fill 1,600 cans per minute by using an elaborate conveyor system. Empty cans are filled in one rotation of the filler machine and move to the seamer that applies the lids. After traveling through the pasteurizer and electronic inspectors, the packer combines the cans into 4-, 6-, or 8-packs and then in various combinations to produce 24-can cases. The three bottling machines spin around to fill as many as 900 bottles per minute from their 100 spouts. The bottles go through the crowner and then are inspected, pasteurized, labeled, and packed.

The long dark-wood tables and exposed wood beams of the Bavarian-style Strohaus provide an appropriate place to discuss the company's major brands and reminisce about your favorite Stroh TV commercials. Large photos of the company's original brewery in Detroit line the walls, and a fireplace creates a beer-hall feeling worthy of the Stroh family's European heritage.

Cost: Free

Freebies: Beer for visitors at least 21, soda, and pretzels

Video Shown: No

Reservations Needed: No, except for groups of 15 or more.

Days and Hours: Mon-Fri 1:00 PM-4:00 PM, on the hour. Closed holidays and week between Christmas and New Year's.

Plan to Stay: 30 minutes, plus time for hospitality room and gift shop.

Minimum Age: None

Disabled Access: Yes

Group Requirements: Groups over 15 people need to give 1 day's advance notice at (910) 650-8102. No maximum group size.

Special Information: No photography in production areas. Can be hot in the summer. Plant also brews and bottles iced tea. Hospitality room available by reservation. Tours also available at Stroh's Allentown, PA brewery (call 610-395-7515).

Gift Shop: Sells logoed items including mugs, pitchers, T-shirts, caps, and popular beer-can-shaped mints. Open Mon-Fri 12:30 PM-5:00 PM. Closed holidays and week between Christmas and New Year's.

Directions: From I-40, exit at Hwy. 52 South. On Hwy. 52 take the S. Main St. exit, turn on South Main St., turn left on Barnes Rd. and left again onto Schlitz Ave. Recording provides directions from other routes.

Nearby Attractions: Old Salem; Reynolda House Museum; and Sci-Works.

Young/Spangle ~ *furniture*
1150 Tryon Road
High Point, NC 27260
(910) 884-4535 / (800) 962-3694

North Carolina is known for furniture-making, and High Point is the furniture capital of the world. The large factories do not give public tours. However, Young/Spangle, a small family-owned and -operated business that has been manufacturing custom furniture since 1941, graciously opens its doors to visitors. Instead of the hustle-bustle and noisy atmosphere of many manufacturers, you hear the steady hum of sewing machines and intermittent hammering and stapling. Rolls upon rolls of different colored and patterned fabric catch your eye.

Seated at sewing machines, several women stitch together hand-cut pieces of upholstery fabric. The common work area is one large open space that has a folksy, informal feeling. In one spot, a worker staples or hammers fabric to a wooden frame, carefully matching the fabric to make sure all the petals of a flower, for example, align correctly. In another space, a worker fills a cushion with fiberfill, feathers, or down.

Since the company specializes in custom pieces (they can even reproduce something from a magazine photograph!), you will see different types of furniture. The introductory video and your tour guide, one of the company owners, explain processes which you may not see. Furniture pieces, such as overstuffed mauve chairsleepers, receive final touches before being shipped. For the company's regular line of leather furniture, workers cut hides according to certain patterns and sew cushions and other upholstery parts.

The guide turns over a chair and explains the quality craftsmanship that goes into making each piece. She points out the double-dowel and corner block joint frame construction which is sturdier than stapling. "Eight-way hand tying," a manual process of tying string in eight different directions around the furniture's springs and frame, makes furniture more durable and prevents sagging springs. The company prides itself on manufacturing comfortable and sturdy made-to-order furniture which can be passed down and reupholstered through generations. Upon personally testing one of these chairs, you will certainly agree that Young/Spangle deserves its reputation.

Cost: Free
Freebies: No
Video Shown: 14-minute video on how company makes furniture.
Plan to Stay: 30 minutes
Reservations Needed: Yes. Individuals can call for same-day reservations. Groups see below.
Days and Hours: Mon-Fri 9:00 AM-2:30 PM. Closed holidays and week between Christmas and New Year's.
Minimum Age: None
Disabled Access: Yes
Group Requirements: Groups larger than 20 people should call 1 week in advance; will be split into smaller groups.
Special Information: Groups larger than 15 people can arrange tours of other furniture factories and showrooms by calling High Point Convention & Visitors Bureau 1 month in advance (910-884-5255).
Retail Store: No, but can place catalog or custom orders. Open for ordering Mon-Fri 9:00 AM-3:30 PM.
Directions: From I-85, look for High Point sign and take Business I-85. Take West Green Dr. Turn left onto Tryon Ave. Look for brick building on the right at the end of street. From I-40, take Hwy. 68 South. Turn left onto Ward St. Turn left onto Prospect St. and right onto Courtesy Rd. Young/Spangle is at corner of Courtesy Rd. and Tryon Ave.
Nearby Attractions: The Furniture Discovery Center (call 910-887-3876) is an interactive museum that simulates a furniture factory. Follow the "flow of production" from design to wood species, carving, assembly, finishing, upholstery, and fabrics. Exhibits include Furniture Hall of Fame and Serta Miniature Bedroom Collection; Atrium Furniture Mall.

Pipestem Creek

sunflower bird-feeders and wreaths

7060 Highway 9
Carrington, ND 58421
(701) 652-2623

Named for the beautiful, pristine stream that flows through the nearby prairie, Pipestem Creek makes an unusual natural product. Ann Hoffert, a former nurse-practitioner, established Pipestem Creek in 1991 at her dad's 7,500-acre farm. Her wreaths and birdfeeders are made of home-grown sunflowers, millet, barley, ornamental corn, burgundy amaranths, and everlasting flowers. They are carefully dried, preserved, and hand-fashioned into large and small edible wreaths, suitable for bird-feeders or home decorations. The wreaths, called SunFeeders, and the home decorations, called SunFlorals, sell through national mail-order catalogs as well as specialty shops and direct orders.

The drive to Pipestem Creek takes you past acres of planted fields, towering grain elevators, and rumbling tractor/combines, which service the feed business run by Ann Hoffert's father and her husband on the family farm. Several red, wooden, old-fashioned granary buildings house Pipestem Creek's drying, shipping, and gift-shop facilities. In the production building, a white building bedecked with vines in the summer and surrounded by flowering beds, workers at large tables carefully assemble the sweet-smelling sunflower heads, corn husks, amaranths, and sheaths of millet or green barley. It can take a worker up to an hour to create one of the largest wreaths.

The head gardener comes and goes with armfuls of dried materials, distributing fragrant supplies to the workers. Some assemblers are neighborhood farmwives, who take home raw materials and return later with finished components. One wall is covered with pictures and informational materials, spelling out Pipestem Creek's history and illustrating its varied marketing methods.

If you visit during summer, your tour guide (probably Ann herself, perhaps accompanied by one of her daughters) will walk you past a big farmhouse and through the maintained private gardens to admire the 1,500 feet of rainbow-colored beds planted in everlastings. The shipping granary is a tall, red, wooden building that houses the crops while they're drying. Cast your gaze upward at the ceiling—a cornucopia of sunflower heads, each one bound with wire and hung separately to dry, head down, free from destructive mold and hungry critters. Other edible grains, along with sparkling burgundy amaranths and colorful heads of Indian corn, fill every blank space. Large catalog orders are assembled and crated in this area, but its primary appeal is the upside-down Eden drying overhead.

Cost: $2.50; free for children under 12.
Freebies: No
Video Shown: No
Reservations Needed: Yes
Days and Hours: Mon-Fri 8:30 AM-4:30 PM, weekends by appointment.
Plan to Stay: 1 hour, plus time for gift shop.
Minimum Age: None. Youngsters who are bored watching the production can play with the four Hoffert girls, feed the farm horses, or pet the kittens and bunnies.
Disabled Access: Grounds and gift shop accessible. Stairs in production areas.
Group Requirements: Groups larger than 10 people should call 1 week in advance. No maximum group size.
Special Information: August is the best month for viewing sunflower fields. To see the everlasting flower fields, specialty crops, and gardens also, tour from May to October.
Gift Shop: Features sunflower-based products, SunFeeders, SunFlorals, and dried flower arrangements. Housed in a ten-sided wooden granary. Open same hours as tour. Catalog available at above address for $2.
Directions: From I-94, take Hwy. 281 North. Turn right onto Hwy. 9 East. Pipestem Creek is about 1 mile ahead on the right.
Nearby Attractions: Putnam House; Arrowwood National Wildlife Refuge; Foster County Museum; Hawksnest Ridge; McHenry Railroad Loop.

American Whistle ~ *whistles*
6540 Huntley Road
Columbus, OH 43229
(614) 846-2918

"How does that little ball get into the whistle?" is the question asked by most curious children (and adults) who tour the American Whistle Corporation. The answer is, "The corking machine does it." The little solid-cork ball is squeezed and then shot by air compression through a clear plastic tube into each already-assembled whistle.

The corking machine is just one of the many whistle-making steps you'll see at the only metal-whistle manufacturer in the U.S.A. As you journey through the factory's work stations, with the din of the press in the background, you'll be amazed to learn from your tour guide that over one million whistles are manufactured each year in this neat, compact facility. Watch whistles being cut, stamped, soldered, baked, bathed, polished, and packaged.

The press is your first stop, after an initial briefing by your tour guide. Here, in rapid succession, a large, overhanging piece of machinery fitted with a die (a piece similar to a cookie cutter) stamps down on each small brass square with 78,000 pounds of compressed air pressure. One after another, brass cut-outs resembling miniature sets of Mickey Mouse ears are punched out. In a later process, the ears fold upward to become the sides of the whistle.

During another part of the tour, you are privileged to view the whistles in their own private bathing area—a tiny room off the main factory floor. Here, in a large, open, circular trough called a vibratory, the whistles take a stone bath. The stones resemble rough jade pieces and are placed in with the whistles and a tiny bit of liquid. Then the vibratory actually vibrates for 7 hours to smooth any rough edges off the whistles. The finished, bright, shiny whistles, lined side-by-side for inspection and packaging, are the same whistles you probably see being tooted by a policeman at a busy traffic intersection or by a referee at the Super Bowl.

Cost: $3 per person
Freebies: New "American Classic" chrome whistle
Video Shown: No
Reservations Needed: Yes. Individuals and families must join scheduled group tour.
Days and Hours: Mon-Fri 9:00 AM-4:00 PM. Closed holidays.
Plan to Stay: 1 hour for tour
Minimum Age: None
Disabled Access: Yes
Group Requirements: Minimum group size of 15 people or $45. Call at least 1 week in advance. Maximum 45 people per group.
Special Information: Photography restricted in parts of the factory.
Gift Counter: Display case is located in the factory at the end of the tour. Whistles (metal, plastic, and even 24-karat gold), lanyards, and mouthpiece covers available in many colors. Catalog available from above number.
Directions: From I-71, exit for Rt. 161 (Dublin-Granville Rd.) Go west on Rt. 161 to Huntley Rd. Turn right onto Huntley Rd. Factory is on the right in about 1 mile—roughly halfway between Rt. 161 and Schrock Rd.
Nearby Attractions: Anheuser-Busch (Budweiser) Brewery tour (call 614-888-6644); Tropical Fruits and Nuts tour (call 614-431-7233); Krema Peanut Butter tour (call 614-299-4131); other Columbus attractions include Columbus Zoo and Center of Science and Industry.

Ballreich's   *potato chips*

186 Ohio Avenue
Tiffin, OH 44883
(419) 447-1814 / (800) 323-CHIP

Potato Chips

When Fred Ballreich was working as a baker in the Army during WWI, he never expected to make a career out of it. Unable to find a job to support himself and his wife Ethel, he opened his own potato-chip business in an unfinished garage. While Fred fried potatoes in a copper kettle, Ethel packaged the finished chips. On a good day, they produced 14 pounds of chips. Before the evening ended, Fred loaded his truck with the day's supply of chips and sold them to anyone who wanted them. That was in 1920.

Ballreich Brothers has come a long way since then. Today, the modern factory produces about 2,000 pounds of chips every hour, sending bags, boxes, and cans to stores across the United States and even the world. The company's marcelled chips, with big, wavy ridges, have fans everywhere. It takes only 18 minutes for a raw potato to become a potato chip. And with machines taking Ethel's place in the packing room, 80 1⅛-ounce bags or 22 11-ounce bags are filled in one minute.

Your Ballreich tour takes you onto the factory floor, past almost every part of the chip-making process. Potatoes arrive on the factory's second floor from an enormous bin located at ground level. An automatic abrasive peeler washes and peels the spuds before they travel past workers who remove spots and eyes. Conveyors carry potatoes to the slicers, where razor-sharp blades rapidly chop them. The slices are washed and dumped into a long rectangular fryer, which begins the day with 2,000 pounds of soybean shortening and receives 1,250 pounds more every hour. Paddles move the slices around the fryer through the shortening.

Potato slices exit the fryer by conveyor and head for the salter, drying out during the trip. The chips leave the salter and fall into buckets, which carry them to the packaging room. Bags of chips are automatically filled, measured, and sealed before being chuted to the shipping area. From here they are trucked to warehouses all over Ohio, and they reach the stores by the next day.

Cost: Free
Freebies: Sample bag of potato chips
Video Shown: No
Reservations Needed: No, except for groups larger than 10 people.
Days and Hours: Mon, Tue, Thur, and Fri 8:00 AM-10:00 AM. Closed holidays.
Plan to Stay: 45 minutes for the tour, plus time for gift counter.
Minimum Age: None
Disabled Access: Yes
Group Requirements: Groups larger than 10 should call 1 week ahead to schedule a tour. No maximum group size.
Special Information: No photography. Floor can be slippery.
Gift Counter: Sells all varieties of chips in different size bags and boxes. Open Mon-Fri 8:00 AM-4:00 PM. Price list available from above number.
Directions: From I-20, take SR 53 South into Tiffin. Turn left on Huss St. Bear right after bridge onto Ohio Ave. Plant is ahead on the left. From I-75, take Rt. 224 to the intersection of State Rtes. 224 and 18. Follow SR 18 through town. After Heidelburg College, go straight on SR 101. Turn left on Dwight St. and then right onto Ohio Ave.
Nearby Attractions: Maxwell Crystal tour (call 419-448-4286); Seneca County Museum.

Creegan Company   ~ *animated figures and costume characters*

510 Washington Street
Steubenville, OH 43952
(614) 283-3708

The coal and steel industry problems in this tri-state area of West Virginia, Pennsylvania, and Ohio may have left a void in Steubenville. However, few places have more vigor than the family-owned and -operated Creegan Company, the nation's largest manufacturer of animated and costume characters. You may recognize Beary Bear, Plentiful Penguin, Strawberry Bunny, and The Gamuffins from your local retail store windows and seasonal mall displays. Creegan also designs characters for Sea World, Hershey's Chocolate World, and Disney World. Inside the former Montgomery Ward department store, Creegan employees bring an array of characters to life. The three-floor factory/craft showcase teems with creativity as artists and craftspeople design, sculpt, decorate, and mechanize hundreds of animated creatures.

Inside the factory, your guide leads you into a virtual craft heaven containing what must be thousands of spools of ribbon of every color, pattern, and texture. Puppet heads, scenery, and props lurk behind silk flowers and craft paraphernalia. A large, life-like white gorilla stands beside three rosy-cheeked elves. An employee dressed as Beary Bear wanders around. Up a wide staircase is the art shop where workers make costumes and paint faces on molded plastic heads. On the main floor, a huge vacuum-form machine presses out the puppets' faces. Here, you may see sheets of stark white plastic being pressed over molds into various facial configurations.

Downstairs in the sculpting area, one woman sculpts all of the character-head molds. Shelves contain hundreds of plaster molds shaped like heads, feet, hands, and animals. Further along is the mechanics/electronics department, full of workbenches laden with toolboxes, hand saws, lathes, vises and drillpresses. Peek inside some headless mechanized bodies to discover some figures' detailed electronic insides and to see how the parts unite to produce a character's body movements. After a tour of the Creegan Company, you will agree with their motto: "We make things move."

Cost: Free

Freebies: Cake, candy, or cookie samples from Fancy Food Dept.

Video Shown: No, however some are for sale.

Reservations Needed: Preferred

Days and Hours: Mon-Fri 10:00 AM-4:00 PM, Sat 10:00 AM-2:00 PM (tours by request on Saturdays during summer). Call for extended tour hours November 1 through December 31. Closed Easter, Christmas, and New Year's.

Plan to Stay: 45 minutes-1 hour, plus time for shops.

Minimum Age: None

Disabled Access: Yes

Group Requirements: 1 day's advance notice is requested for groups larger than 10 people. Inquire about group discounts on store merchandise.

Special Information: Individuals not part of a group may walk through the factory on their own, or may join a group led by one of the entertaining tour guides.

Retail Store: Showroom displays and sells Creegan's most recent animated figures and scenery. Year-round Christmas shop offers ornaments, gifts, and novelties. Retail store carries cake decorating and candy-making supplies and seasonal decor items. Open Mon-Fri 10:00 AM-5:00 PM, Sat 10:00 AM-2:00 PM, Sun by appointment; November 1 through December 31 Mon-Thur 9:00 AM-6:00 PM, Fri-Sun 10:00 AM-5:00 PM. Catalog available from above number.

Directions: From I-70, take SR 7 North to Steubenville. Turn left on Washington St., then left on Fifth St. Creegan's is on the corner of Washington and Fifth Sts.

Nearby Attractions: Hall China and Homer Laughlin China tours (see pages 183 and 264); Steubenville is the "City of Murals," with 21 beautifully painted historic murals throughout the city. Welsh Jaguar Classic Car Museum; Jefferson County Historical Museum; New Cumberland Locks and Dam.

Goodyear World of Rubber

tires and rubber

Goodyear Tire & Rubber Company
1201 E. Market Street
Akron, OH 44316
(216) 796-7117

Akron, Ohio is so closely identified with the beginnings and growth of the rubber industry that it is acknowledged as the rubber capital of the world. Most of the rubber and tire factories have moved out of Akron, however, so the closest you can get is to visit the Goodyear World of Rubber. This traditional company museum's exhibits trace the history of the company and the rubber industry.

Enter the museum through a small grove of rubber trees that gives you the ambiance of a rubber plantation. When you look up at the lush tree leaves and down at the rubber trunk, you'll imagine yourself in a tropical setting. Now that you have gained respect for nature's role in rubber production, bounce through the other exhibits, which describe synthetic rubber, the evolution of tires, the history of the blimp (with models), rubber-making and tire-building processes, and the interstate trucking industry. Short, informative videos accompany many exhibits.

The museum includes a replica of Charles Goodyear's workshop, where he discovered a process for vulcanizing rubber to give it elasticity. The workshop looks like a kitchen because it really was one. Legend has it that Goodyear accidentally discovered his rubber-curing process when he stuck the rubber recipe in the oven to hide it from his wife. The Goodyear Memorial Collection features paintings and many personal mementos acquired from heirs of this famous inventor. You'll also be surprised to learn that the Goodyear Tire & Rubber Company is connected to Charles Goodyear in name only. The company was founded in 1898 by Frank A. Seiberling, 38 years after Charles Goodyear's death.

The museum displays many Goodyear products, including some that may intrigue you—like the artificial heart and moon-tire displays. Finally, two Indianapolis 500 racecars with Goodyear tires illustrate the company's strength: making world class, high quality tires.

Cost: Free

Freebies: No

Video Shown: Optional 25-minute video on tire production process shown in theater. If not playing, ask museum staff to start it. Other short videos throughout museum complement the displays.

Reservations Needed: No, except for groups of 20 or more people.

Days and Hours: Mon-Fri 8:30 AM-4:30 PM. Closed holidays.

Plan to Stay: 1 hour for museum and main video.

Minimum Age: None, but children should be at least 6 to appreciate the displays.

Disabled Access: Yes

Group Requirements: Groups of 20 or more need to call for reservations; special guided tours available by calling 1 month in advance.

Special Information: No photography.

Gift Shop: Gift Center sells Goodyear logoed items, including miniature blimps, jewelry, and clothing. Open same hours as museum.

Directions: Expressway is being reconfigured, so call to confirm directions and exits. From I-76 West, take Martha Ave./Goodyear Tech Center exit and turn right (north). From Martha Ave., go north, and turn left on East Market. Visitors' parking lot is on the right before you reach the red brick building, Goodyear Hall. From I-76 East, take Martha Ave. exit going south, turn around at the Tech Center, and proceed north on Martha. Follow above directions.

Nearby Attractions: Stan Hywet Hall; Hale Farm and Village; Akron Art Museum; John Brown Home; Quaker Square.

Hall China ~ *china*

Anna Avenue
East Liverpool, OH 43920
(216) 385-2900

What seems to be a small cluster of red brick buildings on the outskirts of East Liverpool is actually eleven acres of production, retail, and office space for Hall China, founded in 1903. Since its early years, Hall has been recognized as an industry leader in hotel and restaurant china production. Hall produced the first lead-free glazed chinaware, which requires only one firing at 2400°.

Walk up the steps into the 1940s-style foyer and the receptionist will point you in the direction of yellow arrows that lead you into the factory and on your way through the self-guided tour. Immediately, you see stacks of bowls and pitchers as you hear the clinking of china being hand-packed. Next, you're surrounded by tall, free-standing, wheeled racks loaded with unfinished gray clay pottery pieces ranging from pasta bowls to mugs, waiting to be glazed and fired.

The facility's ambiance is friendly and easy-going. When asked questions, workers eagerly explain the pottery-making process. Some workers sit at potter's wheels while others, bent over wooden work benches, hand-sponge and trim away seams to smooth the just-formed mugs and bowls.

Glance over into the plant's interior to see workers making bowls out of hunks of raw clay. A long, stout log of gray clay is mechanically sliced into thick rounds. A worker places each slice into a bowl-shaped mold. The jiggering machines mechanically spin and shape each hunk of raw clay into a bowl. The inverted wet clay bowls are placed on conveyors fitted with 149 horizontal shelves, which rotate upward into a dryer for 1¼ hours.

As you near the tour's end, you smell the wax and glaze mixtures that will coat the clay pieces. You may see a woman stirring a large cauldron of glaze with a long wooden paddle. Before each piece is glazed, a worker air-sprays it to remove any dust or particles. Watch as a worker places both hands inside two crocks to lift them, then simultaneously dips them into the pot of glaze. Slowly and carefully, she twists her wrists to uniformly cover each piece with glaze. The two crocks are then set upon a grate to dry. Kiln firing at 2400° fuses the clay with the glaze and gives each piece its shiny color.

Cost: Free

Freebies: No

Video Shown: No

Reservations Needed: No, except for groups larger than 10 people.

Days and Hours: Mon-Fri 9:15 AM-2:00 PM. Lunch break 12:00 PM-12:30 PM. Closed holidays. Minimal production week between Christmas and New Year's.

Plan to Stay: 20 minutes for self-guided tour, plus time in Hall Closet.

Minimum Age: None. Children must be accompanied by adult.

Disabled Access: Yes

Group Requirements: Call at least 3 weeks ahead to reserve guided tour for groups of 10 or more.

Special Information: Wear comfortable shoes and lightweight clothing, since factory is warm.

Gift Shop: Hall Closet offers overruns of first-quality Hall China products, such as cookware and bowls, at slightly discounted prices. Open Mon-Sat 9:00 AM-5:00 PM.

Directions: Take Rt. 7 North, which becomes SR 39. Follow it east until it takes a sharp 90-degree turn. Immediately after the turn, look for Boise Church sign and make a left onto Anna Ave. At the cluster of red brick buildings, turn right into parking lot.

Nearby Attractions: Homer Laughlin China and Creegan Animation tours (see pages 264 and 181); Sterling China tour (call 216-532-4907) in Welsville, WV; Museum of Ceramics; Beaver Creek State Park; Thompson Park.

Honda ~~~ *cars and motorcycles*

Honda Parkway
Marysville, OH 43040
(513) 642-5000

HONDA

Honda is the first Japanese automaker to build cars (1982), motorcycles (1979), lawn mowers (1984), and engines (1985) in the U.S.A. It also is the first to export its U.S.A.-made cars to overseas markets Taiwan (1987) and Japan (1988). Its five U.S. plants (Accord and motorcycles in Marysville, OH; Civic in East Liberty, OH; engines in Anna, OH; power equipment in Swepsonville, NC), employ over 10,500 workers, or "associates." For many years, Accord has been the best-selling American-made car. By 1996, Honda plans North-American production of all Accord and Civic automobiles sold in the U.S.A.

Honda offers no regular factory tours, but does have a visitor center ("Welcome Center") in the lobby of its Associate Development Center. Honda motorcycle enthusiasts will find more to explore than fans of its cars will. Behind the glass entrance are 14 motorcycles, dating back to Honda's first U.S.A.-built bikes.

The exhibit featuring the Gold Wing motorcycle, Honda's luxury touring bike made only in the U.S.A. and exported to over 20 countries, is the Welcome Center highlight. The Gold Wing sits on a pedestal, bathed in spotlights. When the Welcome Center associate touches a button, the Gold Wing "talks," explaining and showing the bike's features. When the tape mentions the windshield, up it goes. Saddle bag and trunk quickly snap open and shut, the engine starts, and the wheels spin in reverse when the tape discusses them.

Two monitors in a kiosk play a selection of videos geared to your interest. Tell the Welcome Center host that you're interested in engineering or auto racing and you'll soon watch a video on the topic. In another area, a shiny Accord and Civic wait peacefully. Under the large "Honda Of America Manufacturing" sign are pictures of associates involved in manufacturing and the products or parts they built. Notice the photos on Honda's international auto and motorcycle racing championships. Honda uses racing as a training ground for its engineers. While the center does not hold the excitement of a factory tour, it provides some insight into Honda's history, production process, and commitment to manufacturing in the U.S.A.

Cost: Free

Freebies: Company brochures

Video Shown: Different videos available, ranging from history to basics of car manufacturing. Tell the Welcome Center associate what you want to see.

Reservations Needed: Not for Welcome Center. No public plant tour currently available.

Days and Hours: Mon-Fri 7:30 AM-4:00 PM. Closed holidays, week between Christmas and New Year's, and week of July 4th.

Plan to Stay: 30 minutes for displays and selected videos.

Minimum Age: None

Disabled Access: Yes

Group Requirements: No maximum group size, although advance notice appreciated for large groups.

Special Information: Factory tours available on special request, but not open to regular public tours. Information on auto and motorcycle plant tours available from Corporate Communications Department at above address, or call (513) 642-5000, ext. 1334.

Gift Shop: No

Directions: From Rt. 33 East, take second Honda Pkwy. exit. Turn left, drive over Rt. 33 and enter through first gate (East). From Columbus, take Rt. 33 West past Marysville. Exit at first Honda Pkwy. exit and turn right. Plant is on the right.

Nearby Attractions: Navistar International truck plant tour (see page 189); Mad River Mountain; Piatt Castles; Ohio Caverns; Columbus attractions, including American Motorcycle Association Heritage Museum, are about 30 miles away.

Lee Middleton Original Dolls  *baby dolls*

1301 Washington Boulevard
Belpre, OH 45714
(614) 423-1481 / (800) 233-7479

Lee Middleton began creating dolls at her kitchen table in 1978, using her children as the first models. While the kitchen table may have given way to a 37,000-square-foot "dollhouse" factory (hidden behind a pastel-colored Victorian "gingerbread" facade), the same detailed, labor-intensive production process continues. The tour, led by guides dressed like Lee's most popular dolls, shows the intricacy involved in making her vinyl and porcelain collectible baby dolls and clothing.

All dolls start with molds for heads, forearms, and lower legs. A measured amount of liquid vinyl fills metal mold trays. The vinyl "cures" to a solid state in rotational molding ovens. After the molds cool, workers pull a small plug from each one. Then they use pliers to magically yank warm, hollow vinyl parts from each mold's tiny opening. For porcelain doll heads, arms, and legs, liquid porcelain ("slip") is poured into plaster molds to produce soft "greenware." After it dries, workers delicately hand-sand the surface to remove all seams and bumps. Kilns then fire the pieces at 2300°, changing the consistency from white chalk to flesh-colored, silky porcelain.

Stencils based on Lee's prototypes are used in painting vinyl doll faces. One head may require different stencils for eyebrows, lips, and teeth, while blush on the cheeks is done freehand. Air is pumped into the head, temporarily expanding it like a balloon and enlarging the eye sockets. Workers then insert eyes into the openings and focus them, before delicately applying eyelash strips. Even more painstaking steps are involved in creating porcelain doll faces. Eyelashes, for example, must be inserted individually, in groups of four or five hairs at a time. When the heads, arms, and legs are attached to polyfill-stuffed bodies to complete the dolls, you appreciate the "labor" involved in their birth.

Cost: Free
Freebies: Miniature Bible that comes with each doll. Lee includes a Bible with each of

her "babies" because she wants to thank God for giving her the talents that make her collectible dolls so special. Also fudge samples from Little Sweet Shoppe.
Video Shown: No
Reservations Needed: No, except for groups.
Days and Hours: Mon-Fri 9:00 AM, 10:15 AM, 11:00 AM, 12:30 PM, 1:15 PM, 2:15 PM, 3:00 PM; summer hours: Tue-Sat 9:00 AM-3:00 PM (same schedule). Will try to accommodate tours at other times until 3:00 PM. Closed holidays and week between Christmas and New Year's.
Plan to Stay: 30 minutes for tour, plus time for gift shop and Little Sweet Shoppe.
Minimum Age: None
Disabled Access: Yes
Group Requirements: Large groups should call in advance. No maximum group size.
Special Information: No photography. May not always see porcelain-doll production.
Gift Shop: Sells "less than perfect" Lee Middleton Original Dolls, limited-edition "first quality" dolls, designer doll accessories (including clothing and nursery furnishings), and other gift and souvenir items. Little Sweet Shoppe sells homemade fudge, popcorn, and soft drinks. Open Mon-Sat 9:00 AM-5:00 PM. Catalog available from above number.
Directions: From I-77, take Parkersburg, WV, exit for Rt. 50. Head west across Ohio River. Once over the bridge, road becomes Washington Blvd./Rt. 618. Look for large building with gingerbread front, ¾ mile ahead on left. From the east, take Rtes. 7 & 50. Turn right on Farson Ave. and left on Washington Blvd. Signs guide you to factory (on the right).
Nearby Attractions: Fenton Art Glass tour (see page 262); Stahl's Christmas Shop; Children's Toy and Doll museum; Doll Showcase store; Historic Marietta, OH; Blennerhassett Island and Museum.

Longaberger   ~ *baskets*
5563 Raider Road (State Route 16)
Dresden, OH 43821-0073
(614) 754-6330

Tree-lined streets and beautifully restored Victorian houses create historic charm in Dresden, Ohio, also home to Longaberger Baskets. Housed in the former Dresden 1852 Bakery building, the Longaberger Museum offers a perfect introduction to basket-making. Original baskets displayed in farm-kitchen surroundings will make you want to gather apples and fill a basket for apple pies.

A short drive from Dresden's center is the world's largest basket-making plant (6½ acres under one roof!). Upon entering, you are struck with the fresh outdoor aroma of damp wood. From the mezzanine, gaze down at hundreds of workers and listen to the clicking, hammering, and tapping. The maple logs used to make the baskets are first "cooked" for 8 hours and cut before they reach the manufacturing facility. In the saw area, the wood strips are cut and metered to the proper length for each style of basket.

Weavers' fingers nimbly maneuver the moist, flexible maple strips in and out, in and out, to create the mosaic of the weave. The basket gradually takes shape as the craftsperson weaves, then taps the weave with a hammer to ensure a secure, tight, durable result. Near the end of the process, the basket receives a "haircut" to trim away excess upsplints (the basket's vertical strips of wood). The weaver wraps the last band of wood around the circumference of the basket, hand-tacks it into place, then dates and signs the completed artwork.

One of the few automated processes you'll see at Longaberger occurs in the staining chamber. Here, baskets are hooked onto circular overhead racks called "spinners." As the spinners rotate them, the baskets move down a conveyor belt through the chamber where they are doused with stain. You leave with the image of row upon row of wooden baskets waiting to be filled with strawberries, fresh-baked bread, just-picked daisies or even today's newspaper.

Cost: Free
Freebies: No
Video Shown: 13-minute optional video gives history of Longaberger and describes basket-making process; may be seen at Museum or at plant (by special arrangement).
Reservations Needed: No, except for groups larger than 15 people.
Days and Hours: Tours: Mon-Fri 8:30 AM-2:00 PM, Sat 10:00 AM-2:00 PM. Tours every 15 minutes. To see weaving, tour plant Mon-Fri before 12:30 PM. No weaving on Saturdays. Closed holidays. Museum: Mon-Sat 9:00 AM-6:00 PM, Sun 12:00 PM-6:00 PM.
Plan to Stay: 1 hour for plant tour; 2 hours if visiting museum and viewing video there first.
Minimum Age: None
Disabled Access: Yes
Group Requirements: Call 1 day ahead for groups larger than 15 to arrange tour and video at plant. No maximum group size.
Special Information: Shuttle bus provided to museum.
Gift Shop: Just For Fun Shop, on plant's mezzanine, sells Dresden Tour Basket—the only style basket available without contacting a Longaberger Sales Consultant. Logoed T-shirts, basket stationery, and jewelry available here and in Museum. Shop open Mon-Fri 9:00 AM-2:00 PM, Sat 10:00 AM-2:00 PM. "Wish List" catalog with entire Longaberger basket and pottery line is available from a consultant at (800) 966-0374.
Directions: Take I-70 to Zanesville, then SR 60 North. Turn left onto SR 16. Plant is ahead 2.8 miles on your right. Stop at guardhouse for directions.
Nearby Attractions: The World's Largest Basket; Station House and Depot; Leslie Cope Museum; Triple Locks and Side-Cut Canal; Longaberger Family Restaurant, with baskets everywhere!

Malley's Chocolates ⟶ *chocolates*

13400 Brookpark Road
Cleveland, OH 44135
(216) 362-8700

You cannot miss the enormous ice-cream sundae that adorns the top of Malley's Chocolates' 60,000-square-foot building. This landmark commemorates Malley's first ice-cream and chocolate shop, opened in 1935. Like the best candy-factory tours, this one begins with a sample, great chocolate smells, and a brief introduction to chocolate-making. To put you in the right mood, they pipe in sounds of the tropical rainforest. The immediate landscape is festooned with banana and cocoa trees hand-painted in lively pastels. Temporarily, you return to the very origins of chocolate—to the tropics where cocoa beans grow.

As you gaze out over the expansive, modern candy kitchen, your tour guide describes chocolate's journey from its birth in the cocoa plantations to the creamy liquid that you see swirling and churning in the 500-pound chocolate melter. This is Malley's secret chocolate recipe, which is kept under lock and key. Meanwhile in the center's kitchen, anything from strawberry to caramel centers may be bubbling away in copper kettles on gas stoves. Amid all this modern equipment, look for the antique gas stove dating back to the company's inception.

Your attention is drawn to the center of the room, where the automated kettle-lift pours 60 pounds of chewy, gooey hot caramel onto one of several cooling tables. Like a construction worker hurrying to smooth out a layer of concrete before it hardens, a chocolatier uses a huge spatula to quickly spread and smooth the thick caramel. A large rolling-and-cutting instrument is used to cut the still-soft caramel into pieces.

In another area, you see the enrober automatically coating the candy centers with chocolate. Before your tour concludes, you pass by the design center to glimpse some of Malley's specialty items.

Cost: $2 per adult; $1 per child.
Freebies: Samples at beginning and end of tour, and a take-home treat.

Video Shown: 3-minute video describes hand-packing process.
Reservations Needed: Yes. Individuals and families must join scheduled group tour.
Days and Hours: Mon-Fri 10:00 AM, 11:00 AM, and 1:30 PM, with more tours added seasonally. Closed holidays. Plant shutdowns are unusual and unpredictable.
Plan to Stay: 1 hour for tour, plus time in retail store.
Minimum Age: None
Disabled Access: Yes
Group Requirements: Minimum group size is 15 people; maximum is 45. Reservations needed 2 weeks in advance (4 weeks during holiday seasons).
Special Information: No photography. Best days to see production are before major holidays.
Retail Store: Sells full selection of Malley's chocolates including assorted chocolate creams, molded chocolate dinosaurs, and, of course, Grandpa Malley's Favorite Almond Crunch. Look in rear of store for Sweet Slips, bags of chocolates discounted due to minor flaws. Hand-painted walls and floral prints add to the flavor of a real sweet shop. Open Mon-Sat 10:00 AM-6:00 PM. Catalog available from 800-ASK-MALL.
Directions: From the east, take I-480 West to West 130th St. exit. Turn left onto West 130th. Turn right on Brookpark Rd. Malley's is on the right. From the west, take I-480 East to West 130th St. exit. Turn left at end of exit ramp. Malley's is on the left.
Nearby Attractions: Bonnie Bell tour (call 216-221-0800); Great Lakes Brewing Company tour (call 216-771-4404); NASA-Lewis Research Center (call 216-433-4000); Cleveland's attractions include Cleveland Zoo, Tower City, The Flats, Rock-and-Roll Hall of Fame, and Cleveland Museum of Art.

Mosser Glass ~ *glass*

State Route 22 East
Cambridge, OH 43725
(614) 439-1827

A beautiful country landscape is the backdrop for the little red farm cottage located conveniently just off the road. The front porch framed in white columns beckons you in. As you enter Mosser's "Little Red House" showroom, the sparkle of glass from every corner catches your eye. In this glass menagerie you see glass of all colors and shapes. Walls are decorated with everything from miniature punchbowls to figurines of clowns and frogs—samples of what you will see made in the factory downstairs.

The first part of the tour takes you through the shipping area. After viewing hand-packing, your guide points out a display case of colored particles. These are the various chemicals used in Mosser's recipes for coloring glass. What really catches your eye, however, is stacks of over 200 intricately designed cast-iron molds, used in creating all of the hand-pressed glass shapes.

As you move past the batch room, you see machines that resemble inverted cement mixers forming an initial mixture of silica sand and soda ash. Then large furnaces that heat the mixture to about 2500° come into view as you enter the open, high-ceilinged, cement block factory. From this point on, the pressing of each piece of glass is done by a four-person human assembly line. While you watch glass being made, you are facing a furnace and its four-person team; beyond is an enormous factory window fitted with huge exhaust fans. The window is wide open to a panoramic view of the Ohio countryside.

Watch the glassmaking team in action as the glowing molten mixture is removed from the furnace by the "gatherer." Another person cuts and then presses the hot material into the mold. A third worker removes the hot piece of glass from the mold and puts it onto the fire polisher, which smooths any rough edges or mold marks left from pressing. Finally, the last worker places the glass piece onto a slow conveyor belt for the "lehr," or cooling oven, where it undergoes a gradual, 3½-hour cooling process.

As your tour ends at the lehr, you see the warm finished shapes being removed from the conveyor belt. Along one wall you observe glass figures receiving an acid rinse in a large tub to produce the soft, brushed effect of frosted glassware.

Cost: Free
Freebies: No
Video Shown: No
Reservations Needed: No, except for groups larger than 15 people.
Days and Hours: Mon-Fri 8:00 AM-3:00 PM. Lunch break from 11:00 AM-11:45 AM. Closed holidays, first 2 weeks of July, and last week of December.
Plan to Stay: 15 minutes for tour, plus time to browse Little Red House showroom.
Minimum Age: None
Disabled Access: Yes for factory; 4 steps into showroom.
Group Requirements: Groups larger than 15 should call a few days in advance for reservations. No maximum group size, since large groups will be split into groups of 8.
Special Information: No sandals or open-toed shoes. Factory can get quite warm in the summer.
Gift Shop: Little Red House showroom offers everything from glass candlesticks, paperweights, and miniatures, to antique reproductions. Open Mon-Fri 8:00 AM-4:00 PM. Closed holidays.
Directions: From I-77, take Exit 47. Take SR 22 West. Mosser Glass is ½-mile ahead on the right.
Nearby Attractions: Boyd's Glass tour (call 614-439-2077); Degenhart Paperweight & Glass Museum (call 614-432-2626); Salt Fork State Park and Lodge; Cambridge's antique shops and glass museums.

Navistar International ⟶ *trucks*

6125 Urbana Road
Springfield, OH 45501
(513) 342-5006

This facility is the highest volume producer of medium and heavy trucks and school bus chassis in the world. Navistar vehicles are seen every day on U.S. highways delivering farm produce to market, transporting school children to classes, and moving freight cross-country. A company retiree happily leads your tour through the assembly plant. The nearby body plant produces sheet-metal stamping and subassemblies from the doors to the truck cabs.

At the assembly plant, you'll walk along the two final assembly lines, each a half-mile long and fed by miles of conveyer systems carrying parts to workers stationed along the lines. While many components are received on a "just-in-time" delivery basis, others are stored in the plant's high-rise warehouse. This automatic storage and retrieval complex is bigger than five football fields, with over 40,000 storage cubicles. The computer-controlled stacking elevators are constantly on the move, storing and retrieving parts.

The trucks, each one custom-built for the buyer, begin as two steel frame rails placed on moving conveyors in the "frame room." The frame rails are the part on which the truck body, whether it be school bus or cargo trailer, is installed. After holes are pierced in the frames by computer-controlled presses, steel crossmembers lock the rails squarely together; the front and rear axles are then added. The engine is dropped into place, chassis paint is applied, tires are mounted, and fuel tanks and fuel lines are installed. The cab, which you see painted by robots in the new, state-of-the-art paint facility, arrives through a second-floor hatch and a hoist lowers it into position.

While you observe workers mounting more parts, such as the hood, seats, and bumper, the real thrill is sitting in the completed truck during its "road test" in the dynamometer chamber. The truck moves nowhere at 65 mph (on roll bars), while a worker tests all aspects of its performance. Since workers enjoy talking with visitors, they gladly explain the inspection steps and may even let you try the horn.

Cost: Free

Freebies: Brochures about the plant and International trucks, available upon request.

Video Shown: No

Reservations Needed: Yes. Prefers that individuals and groups of less than 5 people join scheduled group tour.

Days and Hours: Mon-Fri 8:00 AM-3:30 PM. Closed holidays, week between Christmas and New Year's, and first 2 weeks of July. Possible additional summer shutdown.

Plan to Stay: 2 hours (minimum) to tour assembly plant and paint facility; additional hour for body plant.

Minimum Age: 14 or high-school freshman for children with their families.

Disabled Access: Yes

Group Requirements: Groups need reservations at least 1 week in advance. Maximum group size is 65.

Special Information: No photography, shorts, or open-toed shoes. Can be hot in summer and noisy any time. While International likes to give public tours, customer-related tours receive scheduling priority. Body plant tours available upon special request.

Gift Shop: Eagle's Nest sells logoed T-shirts, sweatshirts, pens, and model trucks. Open Mon-Fri at hours based on shift changes (call 513-390-4118).

Directions: Take I-70 to Rt. 68 North; freeway will end. Exit at Rt. 334 East and take second exit to continue on Rt. 68 North, Urbana Rd. Turn left into plant at the big Navistar sign. From the north, take Business Rt. 68 (which becomes Urbana Rd.) and turn right into plant.

Nearby Attractions: Honda Visitors Center, Marysville (see page 184); Dayton's attractions, including Wright Memorial Air Force Museum, are 15 miles away.

Robinson Ransbottom Pottery

Ransbottom Road ⟩ *stoneware pottery*
Roseville, OH 43777
(614) 697-7355

There is something heart-warming, appealing, and even patriotic about being in the deep Midwestern interior of Ohio, winding your way through beautiful expanses of countryside and heavily vegetated landscape, and finally encountering a business that blends so inextricably with its surroundings that you do not realize you've reached a manufacturing facility. The country you have just driven through is the earth from which Robinson Ransbottom mines the clay for its timeless stoneware. The raw materials used in the pottery are all obtained within a 5-to-10-mile radius of this rustic plant.

As you embark on your self-guided tour, you enter one of a series of warehouses and production facilities. A dark earthiness surrounds you, as arrows direct you to various stops. At Stop One you may view any of a variety of glazing and hand-decorating techniques, such as pottery being hand-dipped (the procedure is called "slipping"), rolled, or mechanically spray-glazed.

One of the plant's most interesting areas is the "beehive" kilns. These two kilns were built in the mid-1800s and they literally look like enormous beehives. You may see the kilns being loaded ("set") or unloaded. Each kiln holds about 30 tons or 20,000 pieces of pottery, and reaches a temperature between 2300° and 2400°.

As you exit the plant through the stock area, pass stack upon stack of stoneware bird baths, vases, urns, and crockery. Robinson Ransbottom Pottery is such a "down to earth" operation that it's hard to believe the company processes about 700 tons of clay per month. Since it was founded in 1900, Robinson Ransbottom boasts that its products are "Old as yesterday, modern as tomorrow."

Cost: Free
Freebies: No
Video Shown: 10-minute video on pottery-making process, shown at "Pot Shop."
Reservations Needed: No, except for groups larger than 25 people.

Days and Hours: Mon-Fri 9:00 AM-2:15 PM. Closed holidays and for 2 weeks around the beginning of July.
Plan to Stay: 20 minutes for self-guided tour, plus time for video and Pot Shop.
Minimum Age: None
Disabled Access: Yes
Group Requirements: Groups larger than 25 should call 1 week in advance for guided tour. No maximum group size.
Special Information: No photography. At Stop Two, safety laws prohibit any conversation with employees. You are asked to be silent while watching at this stop so as not to distract the workers.
Gift Shop: Pot Shop offers housewares, gardenware, and novelties at a 15% discount. Seconds shop located at back of store sells items at wholesale prices—about 50% off retail price. Open Mon-Sat 9:00 AM-5:00 PM, Sun 12:00 PM-5:00 PM. May be closed weekends January-March.
Directions: From I-70, take SR. 22 South to Rt. 93 South. After crossing railroad tracks, turn left on Zanesville Rd. Turn left at traffic light onto Elm St. Take Elm St. to end and turn left on Ransbottom Rd. Robinson Ransbottom Pottery is 1 mile ahead on the left.
Nearby Attractions: Roseville-Crooksville pottery-communities attractions include Alpine Pottery tour (call 614-697-0075), Beaumont Bros. Pottery tour (call 614-982-0055), Ohio Ceramic Center (Crooksville), Cope Gallery, and July pottery festival featuring tours of other pottery factories; Zanesville's attractions, including Zane Landing Park, Zanesville Art Center, Historic Freight Station, and Shultz Mansion, are within a 10-mile radius.

Velvet Ice Cream ~ *ice cream*

State Route 13
Utica, OH 43080
(614) 892-3921

A picturesque farm-country landscape welcomes you to Velvet Ice Cream's 20-acre site. The scene is complete with a mill stream, pond, ducks, and an 18-foot antique water-powered grist mill, turning you back in time to another century. Ye Olde Mill, whose original hand-cut stone foundation dates back to 1817, is featured on the company's ice-cream cartons. It's hard to imagine that adjacent to it is Velvet Ice Cream's modern, state-of-the-art ice cream factory capable of producing over 2,000 gallons of ice-cream products each hour!

The company has been owned and run by the Dager family since 1914. A stroll through their ice-cream museum reveals some of the antique ice-cream-making equipment used throughout history—and lots of fun facts about America's favorite dessert. You can just picture the workers slowly and laboriously turning cranks by hand in what must have been a tedious, painstaking process. The museum also tells the history of milling, the world's oldest industry.

After the museum, visit the factory viewing gallery. A sign near the viewing windows proudly boasts: "Welcome to Ohio's Ice Cream Capital." Your attention is drawn to hundreds of feet of stainless-steel tubing, which seems to outline every corner and angle of the factory. You learn that the cold ice-cream mixture of cream, milk, and sugar is being pumped through this elaborate labyrinth of tubing, weaving its way through the processing machinery.

You might see juicy red strawberries being dumped into the mix at the flavor vats. The filling operation follows, as the ice cream is pumped into carton after carton. A maze of conveyor belts transports the filled containers as they are lidded and wrapped in polyethylene for shipping. They finally disappear into freezer storage where, within a few hours, they are frozen. Look for the novelty machines in action, making ice-cream sandwiches, pushups, or the 1817 gourmet ice cream bar—vanilla and peanut-butter ice cream coated in chocolate—yum!

Cost: Free
Freebies: No
Video Shown: 2-minute video shows ice-cream-making process.
Reservations Needed: No, except for groups larger than 5 people that want a guide.
Days and Hours: Mon-Fri 8:00 AM-5:00 PM for the viewing gallery. Lunch break from 11:30 AM-1:00 PM. See Gift Shop section below for museum days and hours. Closed holidays.
Plan to Stay: 1 hour for self-guided viewing gallery and museum, plus time for Ye Olde Ice Cream Parlor and scenic grounds.
Minimum Age: None
Disabled Access: Yes
Group Requirements: Groups larger than 5 people that want a guided tour should call 1 week in advance. School groups receive ice-cream sample.
Special Information: Arrive before 4:00 PM to see production. No photography allowed in viewing gallery. Annual Memorial Day Weekend Ice Cream Festival, Buckeye Tree Festival (second Sunday in September), and other special events throughout the summer.
Gift Shop: Ye Olde Mill contains a replica of an old-fashioned early-1800s ice-cream parlor, restaurant, and gift shop. Restaurant offers homemade food and, of course, ice cream. Gift shop sells nostalgic gifts, Ohio-made handcrafted items, Ohio food products, and Olde Mill souvenir items. Hours for museum, restaurant, ice-cream parlor and gift shop are May 1 through October 31 Mon-Sun 11:00 AM-9:00 PM (after September 1, closing time is 8:00 PM).
Directions: Take SR 62 to Utica. Turn onto Rt. 13 South and go 1 mile. You're there when you see Ye Olde Mill.
Nearby Attractions: Dawes Arboretum; Mound Builders Park (Indian burial grounds).

Frankoma Pottery *pottery*

2400 Frankoma Road
Sapulpa, OK 74067
(918) 224-5511

The name "Frankoma" combines founder John Frank's name with that of Oklahoma, a source of rich clay deposits. In 1927, Frank left Chicago to teach art and pottery at the University of Oklahoma. Five years later, equipped with one small kiln, a butter churn for mixing clay, a fruit jar for grinding glazes, and a few other crude tools, he started his own pottery studio. Several fires, expansions and a generation later, Frankoma Pottery has grown to 70,000 square feet.

As your guide leads you through this facility, you will observe Frankoma's two methods of forming pottery. In the casting department, "slip" (liquid clay) is poured into plaster molds. The molds absorb water from the slip, leaving harder clay against the mold's walls. Excess slip is poured out. After 4 hours of drying, the piece is removed from the mold and allowed to dry overnight. The second, more interesting method is pressing, which is used for plates and flat pieces. A 50-ton hydraulic press slams down on a solid slab of clay to form each object. It smashes the clay around a mold, pushing excess clay out the sides. Regardless of how it is formed, each piece is taken to the trim line where rough edges are hand-trimmed with a paring knife and smoothed with a wet sponge.

After the pottery is fired, it is ready for glazing. A hand-held air gun sprays glaze on flat pieces. Deep pieces are "dipped" in glaze to coat the inside and then sprayed on the outside. The brushing department "dry-foots," or removes the glaze from the pieces' bottoms, so they do not stick to the kiln.

Look through the continuously firing tunnel kiln, which is open on both ends. Long, pottery-filled kiln cars enter one end. Each kiln car reaches a maximum temperature of 2000° at the center, allowing the clay to solidify and the glaze to melt and change color. The car emerges from the other end at 350°. You will leave with a new appreciation for the hands-on nature and collectibility of Frankoma pottery.

Cost: Free
Freebies: No
Video Shown: No
Reservations Needed: No, except for groups larger than 10 people.
Days and Hours: Mon-Fri 9:30 AM-3:00 PM. Lunch break from 12:00 PM-1:00 PM. Call to check for Friday and holiday schedules and for week-long plant vacations around July 4th and Christmas.
Plan to Stay: 30 minutes, plus time in gift shop.
Minimum Age: None
Disabled Access: Yes
Group Requirements: Advance reservations preferred for groups of 10 people or more. Groups larger than 25 will be split into smaller groups. School groups get free clay to take back to their schools.
Special Information: Since kilns fire constantly, it can get hot in the summer.
Gift Shop: Sells full line of microwavable, oven-proof, and dishwasher-safe Frankoma dinnerware and accessories. Look for baking pans, relish dishes, and bean pots shaped like Oklahoma, Texas, Louisiana, and Arkansas. Seconds sold at discount. Open Mon-Sat 9:00 AM-6:00 PM, Sun 1:00 PM-5:00 PM. Closed holidays. Catalog available from above number.
Directions: Take Turner Tpke. to Exit 215 (Sapulpa exit). Turn left on Hwy. 97, then right onto Hwy. 166 East to Old Highway 66 (Frankoma Rd.). Turn left; Frankoma is on your right.
Nearby Attractions: Mr. Indian store; Indian Territory Art Gallery; Tulsa's attractions, including Philbrook and Gilcrease Museums, are about 20 minutes away.

Franz Family Bakery ∼ *breads, buns, and donuts*

340 N.E. Eleventh Avenue
Portland, OR 97232
(503) 232-2191 ext. 365

Since its 1906 beginnings in a simple two-story frame home, Franz Bakery has fed millions of people in the Pacific Northwest. Franz's plant now covers six city blocks and turns out over 85 million pounds of baked goods each year. Your tour guide provides many impressive production statistics, such as the company's daily production of 75,000 loaves, 684,300 buns, and 45,000 donuts from 250,000 pounds of flour. Yet until you see the dough marching in and out of the ovens, it sounds impossible.

To create baked goods in these huge quantities the process is highly automated, with constant movement of dough and bread everywhere you look. Even with machines 100 times bigger than those you use at home, it takes 17 steps to make Franz bread, from the sifting of the flour to the loading it on delivery trucks. You'll stare at dough being kneaded in mixers that work it into 1,200-pound pieces. The divider and rounder machines turn this hunk of dough into softball-size pieces that relax in the overhead proofer before being molded into loaf shapes and dropped into pans.

After the proof box, which allows the dough to rise to its proper size, the pans enter 100-foot-long ovens. Bread stays inside for 19-21 minutes, while buns only need a 7-to-9-minute experience. You'll enjoy the heat from these ovens on chilly, rainy Portland days. Once the pans move out of the oven, vacuum-suction cups gently lift the bread from the pans and place the hot bread onto a 4,000-foot-long cooling rack. After 1 hour and 18 minutes of cooling, the bread moves through machines that slice it, slip it into plastic bags, tie the ends, and code the packages. In the time it takes you to eat one slice of bread, 75 to 100 loaves are packaged.

Cost: Free

Freebies: Donuts, coffee, milk, and take-home Franz sack with bread miniloaf, goodies, and pencil.

Video Shown: 15-minute video on company's history and products.

Reservations Needed: Yes. Individuals and families need to join group tour. Call (503) 232-2191, ext. 365. Company prefers to give tours to people in its distribution area.

Days and Hours: September through June only. Mon-Fri 9:00 AM-4:00 PM. Closed holidays.

Plan to Stay: 1 hour for tour and tasting plus time in thrift store.

Minimum Age: 7

Disabled Access: Yes, for most of tour

Group Requirements: Minimum group size is 5 people; maximum is 60. Tours scheduled 4-6 weeks in advance.

Special Information: No photography. Sneakers or walking shoes required. The intense smells may bother some people. Snyder's Bakery in Spokane, WA, another United States Bakery subsidiary, also gives tours (call 509-535-7726).

Outlet Store: Thrift store sells excess breads, buns, pastry, and muffins at discount. Open Mon-Sat 8:30 AM-5:30 PM. Closed holidays.

Directions: Company requests that you call above number for directions.

Nearby Attractions: Blitz-Weinhard Brewery tour (call 503-222-4351); Oregon Convention Center; Lloyd Center; Holladay Park; Portland's downtown attractions, including Rose Test Gardens and Japanese Gardens, are about 15 minutes away.

House of Myrtlewood

1125 S. 1st Street   *wooden tableware*
Coos Bay, OR 97420   *and golf putters*
(503) 267-7804

The myrtle tree is a broadleaf evergreen found in a small area of the Pacific Coast. The wood looks yellow and brown when finished and its fine grain makes it more durable than well-known redwood. At House of Myrtlewood, videos and guided tours reveal all the mysteries of this beautiful hardwood and how it's turned into everything from salad bowls to patented golf putters.

If you like the smell of freshly cut wood, you'll enjoy walking through the small sawmill area where logs are sliced into 6-to-8-foot sections of varying thicknesses. Watch the workers use disks of various sizes as patterns to draw circles on the wood slabs, trying to avoid knotholes or other flaws. They cut out these circles, called "blanks," and drill holes in the center to prepare them for the initial "rough out" on the lathe. Large, wet wood chips fly off the lathe during the rough-out turning. Next the pieces go to the drying room, where it takes about 9 weeks to dry the wood down from about 50 percent moisture to a 6.5 percent moisture content.

On the main factory floor, watch the "finish turning" of the dried rough-out. Turners do not use a pattern to shape bowls and trays. Instead, each piece is individually turned; no two pieces are exactly alike. Look up at the humming overhead drive line (whose design dates back to the 1850s and the Industrial Revolution), which powers the lathes. The pieces are then sanded and receive either a gloss or oil finish. When workers burn in the company name, you appreciate the effort that went into that finished piece.

Cost: Free
Freebies: Homemade fudge samples in gift shop; coffee or tea.
Video Shown: Three short videos throughout tour describe myrtle tree, sawmill, and processing of myrtlewood products. Videos provide good close-ups of processes you see from behind glass windows.
Reservations Needed: No, except for groups larger than 40 people.

Days and Hours: May through September Mon-Sun 8:00 AM-6:00 PM, October through April Mon-Sun 9:00 AM-5:00 PM. Factory operates Mon-Thur, but tours run every day. Closed Christmas, New Year's, and Thanksgiving.
Plan to Stay: 20 minutes, plus time for gift shop.
Minimum Age: None
Disabled Access: Yes
Group Requirements: Groups larger than 40 people should call one day ahead.
Special Information: Limits on flash photography, for safety reasons. You may not see all 15 steps involved in making products.
Gift Shop: Carries full range of myrtlewood wares, from bowls, trays, cutting boards, and candleholders to Wooden Touch golf putters. (Putting green available for testing the patented, hand-crafted putter.) Also sells other gift items, homemade fudge, Northwest wines, and Oregon gourmet foods. In the hobby room, craftspeople will find myrtlewood for turning and carving. Open same hours as tour. Catalog available from (800) 255-5318.
Directions: From Portland, take I-5 South to Hwy. 38 West. Then go south on Hwy. 101. Company is just off Hwy. 101 in South Coos Bay, in a wood building with large neon myrtle-tree-shaped sign and American flag on top. From California, take I-5 North to Dillard-Winston exit and go west. Follow directions to Hwy. 42 West. Then go north on Hwy. 101. In approximately 5 miles, billboard will direct where to turn.
Nearby Attractions: Tillamook Cheese factory tour (see page 198); The Real Oregon Gift myrtlewood factory tour (call 503-756-2582); Oregon Coast beaches; Shoreacres State Park.

Luhr-Jensen   *fishing lures*

400 Portway Avenue
Hood River, OR 97031
(503) 386-3811

Established in 1932 in an unused chicken coop on a Depression-ridden fruit ranch, Luhr-Jensen has become the largest manufacturer of fishing lures in the United States and possibly the world. The family-owned company manufactures each lure, from raw metal to a jewelry-finished product ready for the dealer's tackle department. The plant is located in one of the country's best fishing areas—about 50 feet away from the Columbia River that separates Oregon from Washington.

A guided tour through the plant reveals all of the steps involved in creating Luhr-Jensen fishing lures, from stamping out the basic metal blade to plating, painting, assembling, and final packaging. Even before entering the punch-press area, you can hear these big machines stamping lure blades from long ribbons of brass. Literally millions of varying sizes, shapes, and thickness are punched out each year. One day you may see the popular Krocodile lures stamped out, while another day it may be spinner blades for the Willy Wobbler. The nearby plating room is a bustle of activity as chromium, nickel, copper, and even 24-karat gold and pure silver are coated onto the brass lure blades.

Nearby, in the paint room, watch workers with airbrushes carefully applying red, chartreuse, green, and other brightly colored fish-attracting patterns to the metal blades. In the main assembly area, hear the sounds of pneumatic wire-twisting machines and the rattle of blades, beads, clevises, and metal bodies. Spinners, lake trolls, and other wire-shafted lures are assembled by hand. In an adjacent area, the steady hum of printing presses signals preparation of the packaging material for the final step in preparing the lures for shipment to dealers throughout the world. You'll want to head directly for the nearby Columbia River and use your free lure to land steelhead and salmon.

Cost: Free
Freebies: Fishing lure
Video Shown: No
Reservations Needed: No, except for groups larger than 15 people.
Days and Hours: Mon-Fri 11:00 AM and 1:30 PM. Closed holidays.
Plan to Stay: 30 minutes for tour
Minimum Age: None
Disabled Access: Yes
Group Requirements: Groups larger than 15 should make reservations at least 1 week ahead. No maximum group size.
Special Information: No photography.
Gift Counter: Lures from catalog can be purchased after tour. Catalog of fishing tackle and accessories available from (800) 535-1711.
Directions: From Portland, take I-84 East to Exit 63. Turn left, back over freeway, and follow frontage road (Portway Ave.) toward river. Luhr-Jensen is on the riverfront, adjacent to a large boardsailing-event parking area. From I-84 West, take Exit 63, turn right and follow frontage road toward river.
Nearby Attractions: Catch The Wind Kites tour (call 503-994-7500); Mt. Hood; river rafting, fishing, boardsailing, mountain biking, hiking, and enjoying Hood River area scenery. Hood River is the "Boardsailing Capital of the World." Companies such as Da Kine Hawaii, makers of windsurfing and other sports accessories, offer tours (call 800-827-7466).

Pendleton Woolen Mills   *men's shirts*

10505 S.E. 17th Street
Milwaukie, OR 97222
(503) 654-0444

A Pendleton virgin wool shirt is more than just a garment—it is an icon of the Northwest lifestyle. Pendleton Woolen Mills started in 1893 as a wool-scouring plant in Pendleton, Oregon. Now in its fifth generation, the company operates on the "vertical" system of manufacturing, which means that it performs all the steps in processing raw wool into finished products. As one of the few brand-name clothing manufacturers which still produces the entire garment in the U.S.A., Pendleton uses its tour to educate the public on how clothing is made.

If all the steps in making their popular woolen shirts were done consecutively, it would take only 19 minutes to complete the finished product. However, in this highly segmented assembly process, it actually takes 3 weeks before all the different shirt parts come together. You'll be surprised at how much of the process relies on hand skills. As you walk on the wooden factory floors, observe workers hand-rolling out and flattening up to 125 layers of plaid fabric onto 20-foot-long tables. Following the top marker sheet, which shows the pattern, they push a band saw through the wool fabric to cut fronts, backs, and sleeves. Rows of seamstresses use sewing machines to stitch together shirt and blouse parts. In another area, manually operated die presses slam 4,000 pounds of pressure down on fabric to punch out pocket pieces.

Some interesting computerized machines make sewing seem easy. Watch a worker slide a shirt-front into a computerized pocket sewing machine that zigzags stitches around the outline of the pocket. A neck size is dialed into the computerized collar-maker and, presto—the collar pieces are sewn into place. Quality control workers inspect finished garments, cut any loose threads, stick an inspection number in the pocket, and then fold shirts at what seems like a fast-forward speed. You leave the tour with a new appreciation of what's involved in making "a damn good wool shirt."

Cost: Free
Freebies: No
Video Shown: No
Reservations Needed: No, except for groups larger than 10 people.
Days and Hours: Mon-Fri 10:00 AM and 2:00 PM. Closed holidays, 2 weeks in summer (usually mid-July), and week between Christmas and New Year's.
Plan to Stay: 45 minutes-1 hour
Minimum Age: None, however children in group tours must be at least 12.
Disabled Access: Yes. Call in advance.
Group Requirements: Arrange group tours for more than 10 people 4-6 weeks in advance by calling (503) 226-4801. Children in group tours must be at least 12. Large bus groups discouraged.
Special Information: Company most interested in giving tours for local community. No photography. About 45 minutes away, Pendleton's Washougal (WA) Weaving Mill gives tours of the fabric and blanket finishing process (call 206-835-1118). Near the Washougal mill is a seconds store open Mon-Sat 8:00 AM-4:00 PM. In Pendleton, OR, watch the weaving of fabric and blankets (call 503-276-6911).
Gift Shop: No
Directions: From Portland, take McLoughlin Blvd. (99E) South. Turn right on either Bybe or Tacoma Rd. Turn left (south) onto 17th Ave. Mill is set back from the road.
Nearby Attractions: Portland's attractions include Washington Park Zoo, Rose Test Gardens, and Japanese Gardens are about 20 minutes away.

Rodgers Instrument ∼ *electronic and pipe organs*

1300 N.E. 25th Avenue
Hillsboro, OR 97124
(503) 648-4181

Next time you're in New York's Carnegie Hall or Philadelphia's Academy of Music, listen for beautiful music from an organ made by this leading builder of classic electronic and pipe organs. Rodgers prides itself on technical innovation in organ-building, whether by making the first transistorized organ amplifier (1958) or by introducing Parallel Digital Imaging technology (1991) to create warmer, more authentic pipe-organ sounds. The technology and craft of organ-building resonate throughout the manufacturing area.

This guided tour shows all the steps involved in organ-making. Regardless of your interests—woodworking, electronics, or music—you'll find the process appealing. Don't expect huge machines or speeding assembly lines here; it takes weeks to make an organ. Instead, you'll see skilled workers painstakingly laboring over each piece. Be sure to look for the Shoda machines in the cabinet shop area, where all the organ's wood parts begin their journey. The Shoda drills, saws, and shapes the wood according to a computerized program, while a vacuum seal holds the wood to the cutting table. This vacuum is so strong that a dollar bill placed on the work table cannot be pulled across the surface!

Once parts are cut from such woods as Sitka spruce, American black walnut, oak, and mahogany, the case is assembled in the case-up area. Here, sides, feet, key deck, back rails, and other support pieces are placed in a clamp, glue is added to the dowel pins, and the clamp squeezes the pieces together, insuring a dimensionally correct case. A "white sanding" process utilizes fine-grit sandpaper to give the wood a white flour-like surface. In the finishing department, instrument cases, benches, and pedalboard frames are stained, lightly sanded, and given a lacquer "top coat." Notice that, despite all the sanding, the area is dust-free: air curtains outside the white-sanding room and finishing area prevent the dust from migrating.

It's often the multiple ranks of 61 pipes each that give organs their powerful presence. Look for pictures of the largest organ Rodgers ever designed and built—the 194-rank (11,000 pipe) organ at Houston's Second Baptist Church, which took 1½ years to build. The designers proudly explain that the Japanese order Rodgers' pipe organs for Western-style weddings. Throughout the tour you'll see and hear the roles that traditional external pipes and internal electronics (now mostly computer circuit boards) play in organ music. This contrast of technology and traditional craftsmanship makes the tour diverse: in one room an artisan hand-sands wood cases, while a computer technician next door tests circuit boards.

Cost: Free
Freebies: Tour guide booklet
Video Shown: No
Reservations Needed: Yes
Days and Hours: Mon-Thur 9:00 AM-4:00 PM, Fri 9:00 AM-12:00 PM. No production Friday afternoons. Closed for 1 week in August.
Plan to Stay: 45 minutes-1 hour
Minimum Age: No, but children must be able to wear safety glasses. Kids will enjoy the tour more if they're interested in music.
Disabled Access: Yes
Group Requirements: Groups must call 10 days in advance to make reservations. Maximum group size is 100 people.
Special Information: No photography. Tours can be customized to your interests.
Gift Shop: No
Directions: From Portland, take I-5 South to Rt. 26 West. Get off at Cornelius Pass Rd. exit and turn right. Turn right onto Cornell Rd. Immediately after Hillsboro airport, turn right onto 25th Ave. Rodgers is on the right.
Nearby Attractions: Shute Park; Fairgrounds' events; Trolley Car Museum in Forest Grove. Portland's attractions, including Washington Park Zoo, Rose Test Gardens, and Japanese Gardens, are about 20 miles away.

See color photos, page 144

Tillamook Cheese ⌒ *cheese*

4175 Highway 101 North
Tillamook, OR 97141
(503) 842-4481

Tillamook may be the largest and most automated cheese-maker in the Northwest, but its tour begins by showing respect for the raw material that underlies its success: a plastic life-size cow with attached milking machine. The 196-member Tillamook County Creamery Association turns one of the finest milk supplies in the U.S. into 40 million pounds of cheese yearly. This self-guided tour and accompanying videos show you what's involved in making and packing its famous Tillamook Cheddars.

On the cheese-making side of the plant, peer through glass windows at the shiny enclosed cooking vats, each the size of an oval swimming pool. Notice the electronic control panels that direct the heating, thickening, and stirring of each vat's 25,000 quarts of milk. When the cooking is complete, the curds and whey are pumped to the cheddar-master machine, which looks like the side of a silver ocean liner with its screen-covered portholes. Inside this machine, the curd is drained of the whey, matted together, turned and tested for proper body, milled by cutting into finger-sized pieces, salted, and stirred.

Then the curd travels to the pressing towers, where pressure and vacuum remove any remaining whey. Watch the 40-pound cheese blocks eject from the tower into clear, vacuum-sealed bags for their stay in the aging room. About 4 months of aging or curing at 40° is required for medium-flavored cheese and 9 months for sharp.

While most of the cheese-making happens inside the machines, on the packaging side of the plant you see more action. The properly aged 40-pound blocks are transformed into 5-pound loaf, 2-pound baby loaf, 9-ounce, random cut, and snack-bar sizes. The spinning assembly-line machines, with help from paper-hatted workers, do all the cutting, weighing, wrapping, sealing, and packaging at a mesmerizing pace. The colorful Tillamook label moves past too quickly for reading, but you know there's tasty cheese inside.

Cost: Free

Freebies: Tillamook Cheese samples. Try the cheese curds that squeak in your mouth!

Video Shown: Throughout self-guided tour, continuously running videos cover Creamery's history, dairy workings, and an inside view of cheese-making machines.

Reservations Needed: No, unless group wants a guide or plans to eat lunch at deli.

Days and Hours: Summer Mon-Sun 8:00 AM-8:00 PM; September through Memorial Day 8:00 AM-6:00 PM. Closed Thanksgiving and Christmas. Not always in full production on weekends and holidays.

Plan to Stay: 30 minutes for self-guided tour and historical and dairy displays, plus time for gift shop.

Minimum Age: None

Disabled Access: Yes

Group Requirements: Bus groups and groups larger than 20 people should call 1 week in advance to reserve a tour guide, who gives brief historical sketch of Tillamook County and explains cheese-making facility and process.

Gift Shop: Sells all varieties of Tillamook Cheese, logoed shirts, hats, other cow-emblazoned items, and Oregon specialty foods. Special sales offer cheeses at 99-cents-per-pound. Open same hours as tour. Call (800) 542-7290 for catalog. Deli and ice-cream counter offer about 30 different flavors of Tillamook Ice Cream.

Directions: From Portland, take Rt. 6 West and go north on Hwy. 101. Factory is on your right about 2 miles north of Tillamook town.

Nearby Attractions: House of Myrtlewood tour (see page 194); Pioneer Museum; Blimp Hanger Museum; Three Capes Scenic Loop; Oregon Coast.

Weyerhaeuser ⟿ *paper*

785 North 42nd Street
Springfield, OR 97478
(503) 741-5478

Weyerhaeuser

We make paper in many forms in the U.S., with much of it coming from the abundant forests of the Pacific Northwest. This Weyerhaeuser mill makes the ubiquitous brown paper that forms the smooth inside and outside layers of cardboard boxes. As in most paper mills, this one bombards you with new sights, sounds, smells, and even touches.

To produce "linerboard," as it's called in the paper industry, Weyerhaeuser starts with wood chips from local sawmills. Before the plant opened in 1949, sawmills incinerated the chips as waste. Now these chips are a precious resource! You'll notice hills of wood chips surrounding the mill buildings, with whole trucks being lifted skyward to unload more chips. The wood chips' density makes them look like a desert of light brown sand.

In the pulp mill, the chips are cooked to separate out the pulp (for safety reasons, you do not see that process). Once cooked, the fibers are washed and refined before entering 500-foot-long machines which turn the pulp into paper at speeds of up to 2,250 feet per minute. Make sure you feel the pulp that the tour guide takes from the front of the machine. To some, it feels like thick apple-sauce.

Follow the pulp's path through the noisy machine, as it is transformed from a slurry (99.5% water) to a finished sheet (8% water). It travels over and under rows of rollers, which press and dry out the water to make the paper that is then wound onto 30-ton reels. A new reel is produced about every 30 minutes. The reels, each holding 15 miles of linerboard, are cut, banded, and shipped to Weyerhaeuser box-manufacturing plants via waiting trucks and boxcars.

Cost: Free
Freebies: No
Video Shown: No
Reservations Needed: No, except for groups.
Days and Hours: Mon and Fri 9:00 AM. Other times may be available. Closed holi-days and week between Christmas and New Year's. Semi-annual closings for maintenance during selected days in April and October.
Plan to Stay: 1 hour
Minimum Age: 5 (children must be able to wear earplugs)
Disabled Access: Stair climbing and extensive walking inside and outside the mill.
Group Requirements: Groups should call 1 week ahead. No maximum group size.
Special Information: As with all paper mills in the Northwest, this one can be hot, humid, and noisy, while outdoor weather is cold and damp. Dress appropriately and wear sturdy shoes. In October 1993, Weyerhaeuser began operating a 450-ton-per-day paper-recycling operation, which may be open for tours beginning Summer 1994.
Gift Shop: Tour guides sell logoed T-shirts, hats, and mugs at end of tour.
Directions: From I-5, take I-105 East to 42nd St. Exit. Go south on 42nd St. Mill complex is about 1 mile ahead. Turn left at second stoplight. Visitors must check in at main gate.
Nearby Attractions: James River paper products tours (call 503-369-2293); Willamalane Park and Swim Center; Lively Park Wave Pool; Springfield Museum; Dorris Ranch; University of Oregon.

Anderson Bakery ⌇ *pretzels*

2060 Old Philadelphia Pike
Lancaster, PA 17602
(717) 299-2321

Although you may not have heard of Anderson pretzels, chances are you've eaten them. Besides their own brand of pretzels, Anderson makes most of the generic and store-brand pretzels in the U.S. For more than 100 years, Anderson has been baking pretzels in almost every flavor, shape and size imaginable, including pizza-flavored, cheese-flavored, unsalted ("baldies"), and their newest recipe, peanut-butter-filled pretzels.

This self-guided tour begins with a walk past a photo display of the company's impressive history, from its beginnings in 1888 in Lancaster to its latest building and warehouse expansion. The pictures also illustrate the history of pretzel-making in the U.S. In 1946, for example, a one-day shift produced 500 pounds of pretzels, compared to the 80,000 pounds each Anderson shift turns out today.

Farther down the observation walkway is a glass-enclosed corridor, where you can watch Anderson's employees and the huge pretzel-making machines. The pretzels' ingredients wait patiently in several huge storage tanks before being piped directly into four large mixers. Batches of pretzel dough are mixed, weighed, and sent to the production line, where machines with small mechanical "fingers" twist slices of dough into thick "Bavarian Dutch" pretzels (at the astonishing rate of 50,000 pretzels an hour) and drop them onto one of the many conveyor belts spanning the factory.

The dough pretzels move to the ovens by way of the "proof belt." Here, intense heat forces the pretzels' yeast to rise, or proof. The longer the proof belt, the thicker the pretzel; thick Bavarian Twists travel up to 140 feet on these belts. The proofed pretzels are sent to the "cooker," which bakes them brown, and then the "salter," where salt rains down on the still-moist dough.

In another area, watch "extruders" force fresh dough slabs through openings in a die plate and slice the strands with moving knife blades. Suddenly, thousands of long, thin pretzel sticks are born. You can see high-

ways of pretzel twists, gems, rods, logs and "minis" travel by conveyor to the cooker and the baking room, where enormous ovens bake them crispy brown. Their final destination is the packaging room where the pretzels, each shape on its own route, dive into boxes, cartons, tins and bags for their journeys to stores all over North America.

Cost: Free
Freebies: Bavarian Dutch pretzel sample
Video Shown: No
Reservations Needed: No, except for groups larger than 40 people.
Days and Hours: Mon-Fri 8:30 AM-4:00 PM. Closed most major holidays.
Plan to Stay: 30 minutes for tour, plus time in factory outlet.
Minimum Age: None
Disabled Access: Yes (there is an elevator to the second floor).
Group Requirements: Groups larger than 40 should call in advance for reservations.
Special Information: Stop by the soft-pretzel shop for a pretzel sample fresh from the oven and a cold drink, April through October.
Factory Outlet: All Anderson products available, plus T-shirts, hats, and other company souvenirs. Special deals on large cartons of broken pretzels. Catalog available from above number. Open year-round Mon-Fri 8:30 AM-5:00 PM, also April through December Sat 8:30 AM-3:00 PM.
Directions: From Pennsylvania Tpke., take Exit 21 (Reading/Lancaster) to Rt. 222 South. When highway ends, take Rt. 30 East to Rt. 340 East exit. Turn right onto Rt. 340 and drive through 1 stop light. Anderson is on the right.
Nearby Attractions: Sturgis Pretzel tour (see page 211); Pennsylvania Amish country; Dutch Wonderland Amusement Park; dozens of factory outlet stores; James Buchanan House.

Benzel's ⟶ *pretzels*
5200 Sixth Avenue
Altoona, PA 16602
(814) 942-5062 / (800) 344-4438

Whether you love trains, pretzels, or big, fast machines, you'll enjoy this factory tour. In 1911, Adolf Benzel stepped off a boxcar at the Altoona, Pennsylvania, train station with his family and all his worldly belongings and started the Benzel tradition. Railroad buffs will enjoy the caboose parked on the grounds and the massive train mural along the Outlet Store's back wall. The mural depicts the railroad's influence on the Altoona area, including an unusual look at the Horseshoe Curve.

Benzel's is one of the few companies in the U.S.A. that still produces pretzels from the flour-malt-yeast-and-salt concoction first used by Catholic monks, except that now machines do it at the rate of 5 million pretzels a day. Through glass partitions you'll see the entire process, from dough being mixed to bags being boxed. Overhead signs on this self-guided tour help you understand what's involved in mixing the dough, shaping it into pretzel form in the extruder, salting the pretzels, then baking and bagging them.

At a rapid rate, pretzels are fed in long rows out of the extruder onto conveyer belts. As they travel down the proofing belt, the pretzels rise, get steamed, and are salted. The belts constantly roll with pretzels marching in and out of the 100-foot oven. Benzel's special slow-bake process bakes out the moisture, producing a lighter, crispier pretzel.

Since you watch the process at ground level, you see what happens inside the machinery. Notice the salt rhythmically falling on each row of pretzels like confetti and the intense flames that bake the pretzels in minutes. While Grandpa Benzel didn't make his "bretzels" the same way in 1911, his grandson's products and factory still continue the family's traditions and basic recipe.

Cost: Free
Freebies: Fresh pretzels hot off the line and 1-ounce sample bag.
Video Shown: Short video explains Benzel family's pretzel-making history and process.

Reservations Needed: No, except for groups larger than 40 people.
Days and Hours: Mon-Fri 9:00 AM-5:00 PM, Sat 9:00 AM-1:00 PM. Usually no production on Saturdays, but you can view video and look at machines. Closed holidays, second full week in August, and Christmas week.
Plan to Stay: 25 minutes for video and self-guided tour, plus time in outlet store.
Minimum Age: None
Disabled Access: Yes
Group Requirements: Groups larger than 40 should call a few days ahead. Guide will be provided upon request. No maximum group size.
Special Information: Benzel's has special seasonal activities and promotional giveaways throughout the year.
Outlet Store: Sells all Benzel's products, including oat bran pretzel nuggets, various decorated tins, logoed T-shirts, bibs, and canvas totes. Also sells other snack foods and candies in bulk. Broken pretzels occasionally sold in 4-pound bags. Open same hours as tour. Catalog available from 800 number above.
Directions: From Pennsylvania Tpke., exit at Rt. 220 North. Follow Rt. 220 North to Altoona, then take Rt. 764 North. Benzel's is ¼-mile past 58th St., on the left across from 52nd St. Look for old train caboose in front. From I-80, exit at Milesburg. Follow Rt. 220 South to Altoona, then to 17th St. bypass in Altoona. Turn right onto 17th St. Turn left onto 7th Ave., which joins 6th Ave. Continue on 6th Ave. Benzel's is on the right across from 52nd St.—1 block past traffic light at the corner of 51st St.
Nearby Attractions: Horseshoe Curve National Historic Landmark; Altoona Railroaders Memorial Museum; Mishler Theatre; Baker Mansion.

Binney & Smith
1100 Church Lane
Easton, PA 18044-0431
(610) 559-2632

Crayola crayons and markers

You can't help feeling like a kid again when you tour Binney & Smith, makers of Crayola products. In fact, don't be surprised if the tour raises many childhood memories. Depending on your age, you may remember when the now-classic 64-crayon box with built-in sharpener was introduced in 1958; or you may remember your 10th birthday, by which time you, like the average American child, had probably worn down 730 crayons.

The minute you enter the factory, you smell crayons. Since this tour is designed for children, the guide combines process explanations with show-and-tell. Look into wooden reusable stock boxes holding 3,000 crayons each, waiting for labeling or packaging. Some crates are filled with naked crayons, some contain one color (like Radical Red), and some hold assorted colors, glitter, or "So Big" crayons. You'll be tempted to grab a handful and get creative.

While it's neat to see markers assembled and the automatic crayon-molding process, the tour's highlight is the flat-bed molder that "grows" a small percentage of their crayons. Watch a worker pour melted paraffin wax and powdered pigment from a double-spouted bucket onto a long table with thousands of small holes. Scented wax colors (like Wild Strawberry, a rich red liquid) seep into the holes. The worker scrapes off excess surface wax for recycling. After 4 to 7 minutes of cooling, 2,400 crayons magically appear as they are pushed up and out of the molds!

Cost: Free
Freebies: Box of 8 crayons, "Welcome to Crayola Product Tours" coloring book, Crayola Color & Activity Book, neon stickers.
Video Shown: 18-minute "Crayola Products' Wonderful World of Color" video narrated by two children and animated characters Tip and Professor Markeroni.
Reservations Needed: Yes. Tours may fill 1 year in advance. Since maximum per tour is 30 people, it's easier for individuals and families to schedule summer tours and not compete with school groups. Tours may be difficult to book since company is planning to replace tours with Visitor Center in Fall 1995.
Days and Hours: Mon-Fri 10:00 AM, 12:15 PM, and 2:00 PM. Closed holidays. No tours in December.
Plan to Stay: 1½ hours for tour and video. Allow time before tour for Crayola Hall of Fame, plus time afterwards for gift area. Crayola Hall of Fame contains 5-foot replicas of the eight colors retired in 1990; Binney & Smith Time Line tracing company history from 1864 to today with photographs, product boxes, and memorabilia; other displays.
Minimum Age: 6
Disabled Access: Yes
Group Requirements: Maximum group is 30 people. Due to tour's popularity, groups should call 1 year in advance.
Special Information: Company plans to build Visitor Center in town to replace tour in future. Photography allowed only in Hall of Fame. Wear close-toed, comfortable walking shoes. Winfield, KS, plant makes crayons, markers, and Liquitex paints (see page 68).
Gift Area: Sells crayon-shaped pins, T-shirts, and watches, the popular "Crayola Baby" stuffed toy, and more.
Directions: From New York/New Jersey, take New Jersey Tpke. South to Exit 14. Follow I-78 West to Phillipsburg, NJ. At Exit 3, take Rt. 22 West across toll bridge into PA. Take Rt. 33 North for about 6 miles to Stockertown exit (Rt. 191). Make right at stop sign and another right at traffic light. In about 1 mile, turn left onto Church Ln. Binney & Smith is ahead on the left. From Philadelphia, take Northeast Extension of Pennsylvania Tpke. to Allentown Exit onto Rt. 22 East. Take Rt. 33 North. Exit at Stockertown (Rt. 191). Turn right off exit ramp. Turn right onto Sullivan Trail (Main St.). Turn left onto Church Ln.
Nearby Attractions: Martin Guitar tour (see page 206); Stroh Brewery tour (call 610-395-7515); Mack Trucks tour (call 610-439-3566); Allen Organ Company tour (call 610-966-2202); Lehigh Valley attractions including Bushkill Falls, Dorney Park & Wildwater Kingdom.

Harley-Davidson ⟳ *motorcycles*
1425 Eden Road
York, PA 17402
(717) 848-1177

The company that Bill Harley and the Davidson brothers started in 1903 when they motorized a bicycle to drive through Milwaukee now produces one of the U.S.A.'s most recognized and respected products. After this museum and factory tour you'll know what it takes to make one of their stylish motorcycles.

Your journey with fellow Harley enthusiasts begins at the Rodney C. Gott Motorcycle Museum for a fascinating look back through the impressive Harley-Davidson annals. Tour guides glory in telling about Harley's resurgence after the management buyout from AMF. The museum displays 90 years of actual Harleys, along with motorcycle club memorabilia and pictures of famous Harley owners with their bikes. Stare at the spectacular examples of sleek limited and commemorative edition cycles, including one of the Harleys donated by Malcolm Forbes' estate from his extensive collection.

The factory tour takes you past many stages of motorcycle assembly. Except for the robots that weld parts of the frame, workers and machines labor together to build the cycles. See how presses transform sheets of metal into fenders, teardrop gas tanks, and tailpipes. Once the frame is assembled, it journeys by conveyor to different assembly stations where workers drill, screw, and attach parts. Notice, however, that three-member work teams follow one ultra-modern XLH Sportster bike through all assembly stages.

When it's almost complete, the cycle cruises into the testing station, where it is placed on rollers and "driven" at speeds up to 75 miles per hour. While the engine rumbles, the stationary rider checks every electrical component, plugging in different devices to test the bike's performance. Although you can't buy one at tour's end, you do get to "test sit" the newest models.

Cost: Free

Freebies: Copy of *The Enthusiast*, Harley owners' and fans' magazine; product catalog.

Video Shown: Continuously running short video in new waiting area shows production steps not on tour, such as paint shop.

Reservations Needed: No, except for groups of 20 or more. Recommend calling, since plant tours may be cancelled without notice.

Days and Hours: Plant and museum tour: Mon-Fri 10:00 AM and 2:00 PM. Museum only tour: Mon-Fri 12:30 PM and Sat 10:00 AM, 11:00 AM, 1:00 PM, and 2:00 PM. Harley-Davidson recommends calling in advance; taped message explains special "no tour" days. Only museum tour (on Saturday schedule) is given in July and when no plant tours.

Plan to Stay: 1½ hours for combined museum and factory tour (30 minutes for museum-only tour), plus time for video and gift shop.

Minimum Age: None for museum, 12 for factory tour.

Disabled Access: Yes

Group Requirements: Groups of 20 or more must call in advance.

Special Information: Photography allowed only in museum. Tours of Wisconsin engine and transmission plant available (call 414-535-3666). Harley Owners' Group (HOG) has annual three-day open house at factory near end of September.

Gift Shop: Small gift shop in plant lobby sells T-shirts, hats, souvenir books, and cigarette lighters. Open around tour hours.

Directions: From I-83, take Exit 9E (Arsenal Rd.-Rt. 30 East). Turn onto Eden Rd. at Harley-Davidson sign. Visitors parking is in first lot on left. From Rt. 30, take Eden Rd., then follow above directions.

Nearby Attractions: Pfaltzgraff Pottery tour (see page 209); Wolfgang Candy Company tour (call 717-843-5536); York County Historical Museum; Gates House and Plough Tavern; many outlet stores and antique shops; Gettysburg, Hershey, and Lancaster nearby.

Herr's ⌒ *snack food*

Visitors Center
Herr Drive
Nottingham, PA 19362
(800) 284-7488

Herr's snack food production has come a long way from when the company used a small, old-fashioned cooker in a barn. It now has an advanced and highly automated plant that makes tens of thousands of potato chips, corn chips, tortilla chips, popcorn, cheese curls, and pretzels every day. The comfortable, specially designed visitors center, creative video, and extensive guided tour provide a tasty education in how Herr's makes its products.

While watching the action through glass walls, you'll "ooh" and "aah" at the panoramic views. In the pretzel area, gaze at a 100-yard stretch of pretzel twists, in rows of 20 to 24 across, marching to massive ovens. In the corn chip, cheese curl, potato chip, and popcorn production sections, your vista overlooks the entire process. Follow the raw ingredients—either corn or potatoes—as they tumble in by the truckload at the beginning of the production line; travel along a conveyor belt through a series of machines that wash, slice, cook, or season them; then head out on bucket lifts to a sorting and bagging area. Other memorable images include machines and workers bagging and boxing together in almost symphonic unison, and the cavernous warehouse filled with snack-food boxes.

Except for boxing of bags, machines do most of the work. Notice how only a few people oversee production in most areas. Smart machines can even sense discolored potato chips and use air shoots to blow these rebels off the line. The guides pepper the tour with interesting facts and figures about the company, including Herr's recycling efforts. But the best thing the guides do is grab samples of warm potato chips directly from the quickly moving conveyer belt. Bagged chips will never again taste the same!

Cost: Free
Freebies: Warm potato chips during the tour; basket of Herr's other products in Visitors Center; small bag of corn or tortilla chips as a souvenir.

Video Shown: 25-minute award-winning video, entitled "The Magical World of Herr's." Chipper the Chipmunk takes two kids on a Herr's factory tour, providing background information on company and close-up views of production through the ChipperCam. Video is very appealing to young children.
Reservations Needed: Yes, but can take walk-ins if space permits.
Days and Hours: Mon-Thur 9:00 AM-3:00 PM on the hour, Fri 9:00 AM, 10:00 AM, and 11:00 AM. Closed holidays.
Plan to Stay: 1½ hours, including video, tour, and gift shop.
Minimum Age: None
Disabled Access: Yes
Group Requirements: With advance notice can handle any size group, which will split into smaller ones for tour. Video shown in 140-seat auditorium.
Special Information: If you are interested in particular products, such as tortilla chips or cheese curls, call ahead for production schedule on day of your visit.
Gift Shop: Sells Herr's food products, logoed clothing items, scale model of Herr's delivery truck, and Chipper the Chipmunk doll. Open Mon-Thur 8:00 AM-5:00 PM, Fri 8:00 AM-4:00 PM. Catalog available from above number.
Directions: From Philadelphia, take I-95 South to Rt. 322 West exit. From Rt. 322, turn left onto Rt. 1 South. Turn left onto Rt. 272 South and right onto Herr Dr. Factory and Visitors Center at end of road. From Baltimore, take I-95 North to Exit 100. Take Rt. 272 North. Turn left onto Herr Dr.
Nearby Attractions: Longwood Gardens; Plumpton Park Zoo; Franklin Mint Museum; Brandywine River Museum; Lancaster County attractions about 30 miles away.

See color photos, page 158

Hershey's Chocolate World

Visitors Center ⟳ *chocolate*
Park Boulevard
Hershey, PA 17033
(717) 534-4900

This visitors center dedicated to chocolate features a wall display of the Hershey's chocolate story and a 12-minute journey through a simulated chocolate factory. The entire chocolate-making process, from harvesting the bean to packaging the bar, will be revealed to you with true-to-life machines, overhead speakers, and videos. You will find new respect for "The Great American Chocolate Bar."

As you stand in line for the ride, take some time to read the company history displayed on the wall; watch the video describing how cocoa beans are cultivated and harvested in South America and Africa before their trek to Hershey, Pennsylvania. Enjoy the indoor tropical garden at the center of Chocolate World. The exotic plants and palm trees displayed here come from regions of the world where cocoa beans are harvested.

Riding inside a cocoa-bean-shaped cart, you pass scenes depicting the chocolate-making process. Glance at the initial process of cleaning and sorting the beans. You'll understand the true cocoa-bean experience as you enter the roaster and feel the air temperature suddenly rise. Ride past the extractor, which removes the center "nibs" from the bean. Smell the luscious aroma of liquid chocolate as it flows by to be mixed with milk and sugar. Toward the end of your ride, an impressive display of Hershey's products will confront you as recorded children sing "It's a Hershey's Chocolate World!" You'll see how Hershey distributes its product worldwide and know why at Chocolate World they say, "Wherever you go, no matter how far, you'll always be near a Hershey bar."

Cost: Free
Freebies: Samples of Hershey's Miniatures, Hershey's Kisses, or other chocolate bars.
Video Shown: Continuously running video in waiting area explains cocoa-bean harvesting and initial processing. Videos throughout ride provide close-up view of the real production process.
Reservations Needed: No

Days and Hours: Mon-Sun 9:00 AM-5:00 PM; some extended hours in summer, so it's best to call in advance. Closed Easter, Thanksgiving, Christmas, and New Year's.
Plan to Stay: 12-minute ride, plus time for displays, gift shops, and restaurants.
Minimum Age: None
Disabled Access: Yes
Group Requirements: None
Special Information: Expect long lines during summertime, although they tend to move quickly. During the 1970s, the company had to close well-known plant tour in Hershey because of overwhelming crowds and safety concerns. Hershey's specially designed factory in Oakdale, CA, is the only U.S. Hershey's plant that gives public tours (see page 16).
Gift Shops: Gift shops and food court sell Hershey's products, ranging from T-shirts and mugs to the more unusual Hershey's Kisses-shaped cap with silver foil and pull string, and a hollow Kisses-shaped piñata that can hold up to 10 pounds of Kisses. Open same hours as ride. Catalog available from (800) 544-1347.
Directions: From the west, take I-83 to Rt. 322 East. Exit at Rt. 39 West to Hersheypark Dr. Chocolate World is the first "Hershey Attraction" on the right. From the east, take Pennsylvania Tpke. to Exit 20 and follow Rt. 72 North to Rt. 322 West, then follow above directions. From Lancaster, take Rt. 283 West to Rt. 743 North and follow signs to Hershey. Call 800-HERSHEY for recorded directions.
Nearby Attractions: Hersheypark entertainment complex (87-acre amusement park); ZooAmerica North American Wildlife Park; Hershey Gardens; Hershey Museum; The Hotel Hershey; Hersheypark Arena, with concerts, sports, and special events year-round.

Martin Guitar ⟋ *guitars*

510 Sycamore Street
Nazareth, PA 18064
(610) 759-2837 / (800) 345-3103

Ever since C.F. Martin, Sr., started making guitars in 1833, Martins have been widely recognized as one of the top U.S.-made products. The company has received highest accolades from the Buy America and Made In The USA foundations. Many popular musicians use Martins, including Paul McCartney, Bonnie Raitt, and Eric Clapton. The craftsmanship you'll see on this tour demonstrates why these famous musicians are among over 500,000 satisfied Martin owners.

The guitar-making area resembles a large woodshop. The Martin family believes that their guitars' rich tone and elegant finish can best be achieved by hand-crafting. Only recently have power tools and machines appeared, although most of the approximately 300 separate steps that go into making a Martin are done by hand. With so many things to see (including string-making), the guided tour moves quickly.

Stand beside workers as they diligently bend, trim, shape, cut, glue, fit, drill, finish, sand, stain, lacquer, buff, and inspect the different woods that will become Martins. Look for the station where a craftsman uses ordinary clothespins as clamps. These distinctly low-tech devices help secure for drying a glued, serrated strip of wood along the interior edge of the guitar's curvaceous sides. This lining provides additional surface area for attaching the front and back of the body.

Craftsmen use a variety of files, carving knives, and rasps to shape, finish, and attach the neck. Notice how the dovetail neck joint is meticulously trimmed and then checked to ensure a proper fit with the body. When you view a historic Martin or play a modern one in the museum after the tour, you'll really appreciate the 3 to 6 months of craftsmanship required to convert rough lumber into a Martin acoustic guitar—a true American classic.

Cost: Free. Group tours, $2 per person.
Freebies: Sound-hole cutouts; product literature.
Video Shown: Optional 17-minute video shows production process, narrated by C.F.

(Chris) Martin IV, the sixth-generation family member who oversees the company. Request showing in Martin Museum.
Reservations Needed: No, except for groups.
Days and Hours: Mon-Fri 1:15 PM. Closed holidays, week between Christmas and New Year's, and week of July 4th. Small lobby-area museum is open Mon-Fri 8:00 AM-5:00 PM.
Plan to Stay: 1½-2 hours, including tour, video, gift shop, and museum.
Minimum Age: None for families, 12 for groups.
Disabled Access: Yes
Group Requirements: Group tours must be arranged in advance. Will split larger groups into groups of 10.
Special Information: Photography permitted without flash.
Gift Shops: 1833 Shop sells Martin guitars, antique and used Martins on consignment, strings, supplies, books, clothing, and other memorabilia. Nearby in the old Martin factory (10 W. North St.) is Guitarmaker's Connection, which sells acoustic guitar tonewoods, kits, parts, instrument-making supplies, strings, and construction/repair books. Both open Mon-Fri 8:30 AM-5:00 PM. Combined catalog available from (800) 247-6931.
Directions: We suggest contacting Martin Guitar for directions from New York City and other points and their detailed map, "Navigating Nazareth." From Northeast Extension of Pennsylvania Tpke., take Exit 33. Take Rt. 22 East to intersection with Rt. 191 North. In Nazareth, Rt. 191 turns left onto Broad St. Stay on Broad St. Pass the Nazareth Boro Park, turn right onto Beil Ave., then right onto Sycamore St.
Nearby Attractions: Old Martin Homestead (call 610-759-9174); Binney & Smith (Crayola crayon) tour (see page 202); Stroh Brewery tour (610-395-7515); Allen Organ Company tour (610-966-2202); Mack Trucks tour (call 610-439-3566). Lehigh Valley's attractions include Bushkill Falls, Dorney Park, and Wildwater Kingdom.

See color photo, page 154

Martin Guitar Company has been producing award-winning guitars since 1833, Nazareth, Pennsylvania

Hand finishing and shaping of guitar neck at Martin Guitar Company

Pennsylvania Dutch Candies *chocolates*

PENNSYLVANIA DUTCH CANDIES

408 North Baltimore Street
Mt. Holly Springs, PA 17065
(800) 233-7082

As the company name suggests, Pennsylvania Dutch Candies specializes in candy with a regional touch. From the Amish horse and buggy parked outside the factory to the small mementos for sale inside the store, some inscribed with Pennsylvania Dutch sayings, you will be surrounded by this uniquely American culture. When in production, the overpowering aroma of chocolate will catch your nose, and entice the rest of you to follow.

Before you enter the factory's production rooms, look at the antique bicycles in the small museum at the rear of the store. Here, bikes date back to the late 1800s, including some that look odd by today's standards. Picture yourself trying to ride the bike with a giant front wheel and tiny back wheel. Displayed on the wall is bicycle race memorabilia, from races all over the East Coast. In the back of the museum, you can see old tools and utensils used by Pennsylvania Dutch cooks who made chocolate and candy years ago.

Once in the production room, you will see how this small factory makes chocolate "the old-fashioned way." Don't expect the huge and intimidating processing machines you may see in larger factories. Here, blocks of milk or dark chocolate become liquid in the melter. The fluid chocolate is poured into molds and formed into one of the many shapes Pennsylvania Dutch sells. Your temptation to grab a piece of chocolate off the conveyor belt will be satisfied when your guide gives you a sample.

In the next room, chocolate is packaged. Piles of boxes patiently wait to be stuffed with chocolate before being loaded onto trucks. This room is also a packing room for candies such as candy corn, gummy worms, mints, and "buttons," which are often brought in from other factories in the area. Measured amounts of hard candies are fed into a machine resembling a giant funnel, which pours the candy into waiting bags. Like the chocolate boxes, these bags are loaded onto trucks and sent to stores across the country.

Cost: Free
Freebies: Chocolate from production line
Video Shown: No
Reservations Needed: Preferred. If guide available, can ask for tour in retail store.
Days and Hours: Mon-Fri 9:00 AM-12:00 PM and 1:30 PM-3:30 PM. Closed holidays and last 2 weeks of December. Museum open same hours as retail store.
Plan to Stay: 30 minutes, plus time for bicycle museum and retail store.
Minimum Age: None
Disabled Access: Yes
Group Requirements: No maximum group size. Will split large groups into smaller groups of 10-15. Should call 1 week in advance.
Special Information: Call to make sure production line is operating.
Retail Store: Sells entire Pennsylvania Dutch Candies line, including chocolate drops, bars, butter mints, peanut brittle, cashew crunch; also other local and imported candy. During holiday seasons, specialty candy is available (candy eggs are an Easter favorite). Don't leave without checking the Pennsylvania Dutch knickknacks and souvenirs—this part of the store is almost a museum itself. Open Mon-Sat 9:00 AM-5:00 PM, Sun 12:00 PM-5:00 PM. Closed holidays. Product list available.
Directions: From Rt. 81, take Exit 14. Follow Rt. 34 South about 5 miles to Mt. Holly Springs. Go through light; factory and store are in big yellow building on left, with Amish horse and buggy parked out front.
Nearby Attractions: Historic Carlisle; Allenburry Playhouse; Gettysburg's attractions about 45 minutes away. Hershey's Chocolate World Visitors Center (see page 205) about 1 hour away.

See color photo, page 152

Pfaltzgraff *pottery*

Bowman Road
Thomasville, PA 17364
(717) 792-3544

PFALTZGRAFF

The Pfaltzgraff family name has been connected to pottery for centuries. George Pfaltzgraff began creating fire-glazed crocks and jugs in rural York County, Pennsylvania, in the early 1800s. Your guided tour takes you through the modern pottery-making process, from the preparation of the clay to the firing, decorating, and glazing of each piece of pottery.

At the cup-forming machines, "pugged" (solid) clay is placed on a pedestal and spun rapidly to form a cup or mug. The new piece journeys through a dryer before being "sponge-bathed" to remove small particles of excess clay. After handles are attached with "slip" (liquid clay), workers methodically and laboriously hand-paint cups or mugs using a sponge-rubber stamp and small brush to create one of Pfaltzgraff's dozens of different designs.

Odd-shaped pottery pieces, squares or ovals, are made in a special station. Instead of molds, ram presses form each piece. Two plaster dies (called male and female) exert 2,200 pounds of pressure on a piece of clay, squeezing out excess water. Suddenly, what was a lump of clay becomes a piece of pottery. The piece joins others like it on shelves waiting for the carousel glaze machines or hand-applied decorations.

As you walk past the enormous kiln, you will feel its heat. The temperature near the entrance is "only" about 500°, rising to 2200° in the center of the kiln! This allows the glaze to achieve its glassy appearance as the clay hardens. Each piece spends about 12 hours in the kiln, until it "cools down" to 400°. Pieces are then shelved, for inspection later.

Since Pfaltzgraff pottery comes in many styles and shapes, including special holiday and seasonal lines, different decorating methods are used. Some pieces are hand decorated with decals which, when soaked in water, come off the paper and stick to the clay. The pieces are glazed and kiln-baked one more time, sometimes for as long as 8 hours, to ensure that the decals adhere firmly.

While a plate made on a plate roller is handled by workers an average of 32 times before completion, only one person handles items made in the dry-press facility from forming through firing and sorting. Even the transporting process, which removes and shelves the plates, is mechanical.

Cost: Free
Freebies: Small pottery piece
Video Shown: No
Reservations Needed: Yes
Days and Hours: Mon-Fri at 10 AM; other times by special arrangement. Closed holidays, week of July 4th, and Christmas week.
Plan to Stay: 1½ hours
Minimum Age: None
Disabled Access: Yes
Group Requirements: Maximum group is 50 people. Reserve group tours 2 weeks in advance.
Special Information: No photography. Floor can be slippery from clay. Machine noise can make it hard to hear the retiree tour guides.
Outlet Store: Pfaltzgraff factory outlet in Village at Meadowbrook (2900 Whiteford Road, York, 717-757-2200) sells all Pfaltzgraff stoneware, including holiday collections, factory seconds, and discontinued lines. Map to outlet store available at factory.
Directions: From York, take Rt. 30 (Lincoln Hwy.) West to Thomasville. Turn right onto Bowman Rd. at Pfaltzgraff sign. Park in visitors lot at left.
Nearby Attractions: Harley-Davidson factory tour and museum (see page 203); Utz Quality Foods potato chip tour (see page 213); Hershey's Chocolate World Visitors Center (see page 205); Wolfgang Candy Company tour (call 717-843-5536); Martin's Potato Chips tour (call 717-792-3565); York County Historical Museum.

Sherm Edwards ⟋⟍ *chocolates*

509 Cavitt Avenue
Trafford, PA 15085-1060
(412) 372-4331 / (800) 436-5424

"Good Chocolate is Not Cheap. Cheap Chocolate is Not Good." The sign greets you as you embark on your tour of this 50-plus-year-old, family-owned candy manufacturer. The inescapable aroma of rich chocolate fills your nostrils as you witness Sherm Edwards' very own special blend of chocolate being mixed in 500-pound melters on the factory floor. Dark, light, and white chocolate blends are then pumped into molds of everything from gourmet chocolate spoons (that really enhance a cup of coffee!) to 3-foot tall Easter bunnies.

As you progress through the 3,600-square-foot plant whose walls are stacked high with huge bars of raw chocolate, you notice workers, hands awash in chocolate, coating the bottoms of fruit-and-nut eggs. Conveyer belts then transport the eggs through enrobers, where chocolate cascades envelop each egg before it travels into the cooling tunnel to solidify the coating.

Another corner of the factory is the candy kitchen, packed with equipment such as 80-quart mixers, enormous copper pots for caramel-making, and marble slabs for cooling fudge and jellies. Sherm Edwards' award-winning Pecan Crisp is created here with lots of real butter and pecans and just enough crunchy-sweet brittle to hold all the pecans together. You'll discover just how they make chocolate-covered cherries and strawberries. The liquid filling around the fruit of these cordials is produced in the panner, a machine resembling a miniature cement-mixer, which spins the fruit to coat it with sugar. The fruit is then dipped in chocolate and the sugar coating liquefies, producing the syrup inside the chocolate cordials.

Cost: Free
Freebies: Various candy samples
Video Shown: No
Reservations Needed: Yes. Prefers to join individuals and families onto group tours.
Days and Hours: Mon-Sat 9:00 AM-3:00 PM. Limited production on Saturdays. Closed major holidays. Easter through mid-September, production slows to 1 or 2 days per week.

Plan to Stay: 30 minutes for tour, plus time for retail outlet store.

Minimum Age: None

Disabled Access: Retail store is accessible. Stairs lead from retail store down to factory floor.

Group Requirements: Can handle groups from 10-45 people with 1 day's advance notice. Local Radisson and Conley Hotels arrange bus tours for groups staying at hotels.

Special Information: Candy production depends on holidays; for example, chocolate hearts produced before Valentine's Day and molded chocolate bunnies and eggs before Easter.

Retail Store: Sells chocolates, fudges, and nut brittles made on the premises, over 300 varieties of molded chocolate novelties, and hard candies and jelly beans. Slightly imperfect factory seconds available. Open Mon-Sat 9:00 AM-5:00 PM. Call about holiday hours. Price list available.

Directions: Take I-376 East to Exit 16A. Take Rt. 48 South to Rt. 130 South to Trafford. Cross over bridge into Trafford. Take first left, then immediate right, then another right onto Cavitt Ave. Sherm Edwards Candies is on the right. From Pennsylvania Tpke., take Exit 6 to Business Rt. 22 West to Rt. 48 South, then follow above directions.

Nearby Atractions: Westinghouse Airbrake Museum (call 412-825-3009); Pittsburgh's attractions about 30 minutes away.

Sturgis Pretzel House ⟿ *pretzels*

219 East Main Street
Lititz, PA 17543
(717) 626-4354

Pennsylvania has many large pretzel manufacturers whose tours will "wow" you with massive machines, fast-moving conveyor belts, and mind-boggling production numbers. At Sturgis Pretzel House, though, pretzel-making is more of a participatory art. The workers, many of whom are fifth- and sixth-generation relatives of the founder, proudly explain that Sturgis is the first commercial pretzel bakery in the U.S.A. (opened in 1861). Housed in a restored 200-year-old building with displays of old pretzel-making equipment as well as modern mixers, extruders, and oven, the company makes the tour an integral part of its business.

Playing pretzel-maker is the most fun on the tour. As you stand in front of a rolling table, your tour guide will give you a small ball of dough. You'll roll the dough into a thin pencil, pick it up from both ends, cross it to form rabbit ears, then twist the ends and pull them back to rest on the loop. As you twist your pretzel, the guide explains that the monk who invented the pretzel in 610 A.D. wanted to make from dough the sign of the prayer, which involved crossing both arms with hands on the opposite shoulders. The three holes in a pretzel represent the Father, Son, and Holy Ghost.

You won't get rich after you receive an "Official Pretzel Twister" certificate. In the days before automation, founder Julius Sturgis paid twisters about 25 cents per thousand pretzels. Now the company manufactures most of its hard pretzels by machine. You can stand near the machine that automatically shapes the dough into pretzels and then bakes and salts them. While contemporary pretzel-making seems so easy, it doesn't compare to the dexterity shown by the Sturgis family member who hand-twists a soft pretzel as the tour ends.

Cost: $1.50. Children under 2, free.
Freebies: Small hard pretzel that doubles as your tour ticket; paper hat that you must wear during tour, and well-earned "Official Pretzel Twister Certificate."
Video Shown: No

Reservations Needed: No, except for groups of 12 or more people.
Days and Hours: Mon-Sat 9:30 AM-4:30 PM, every 15-30 minutes. Closed Thanksgiving, Christmas, and New Year's.
Plan to Stay: 20 minutes for tour, plus time for gift shop.
Minimum Age: None
Disabled Access: Yes
Group Requirements: Groups of 12 or more should call ahead. Groups also receive free soft pretzels.
Special Information: It can be hot standing near the pretzel-baking machine.
Gift Shop: Tour ends at small gift shop area. You enter the pretzel house through larger store which sells gift items and pretzels, including their unique horse-and-buggy-shaped pretzels. Special prices on multiple bags and large bags. Look for book entitled *The Pretzel Story*, which includes photographs, company history, and explanation of evolving pretzel-making process. Open Mon-Sat 9:00 AM-5:00 PM. Catalog available.
Directions: From Lancaster, take Rt. 501 North to Lititz. Turn right on Main St. (Rt. 772). Sturgis Pretzel House is on left with big pretzel in front. From the east, take Pennsylvania Tpke. (I-76) to Exit 21. Go south on Rt. 222 and turn right onto Rt. 772 into Lititz. Follow above directions.
Nearby Attractions: Wilbur Chocolate Candy Americana Museum (interesting exhibits and video on chocolate-making, plus factory candy outlet); Johannes Mueller House; Lititz Springs Park; Pennsylvania Dutch sites and Lancaster attractions all within short drive.

U.S. Mint ⟨⟩ *coins*

5th and Arch Streets
Philadelphia, PA 19106-1886
(215) 597-7350

We all know that money doesn't grow on trees, but do you know where 60 percent of U.S. coins come from? A tour of the Philadelphia U.S. Mint, which currently strikes approximately 2 million quarters, 4.4 million dimes, 2.6 million nickels, and 20 million pennies each weekday, will show you just that. Encompassing an entire city block, the world's largest mint also houses a museum of rare coins, historic medals, and antique mint machinery.

In the lobby area, see all commemorative coin designs issued since 1892 and notice the 1901 Tiffany mosaics on the walls. Press on past the displays to the glass-enclosed observation gallery above the mint factory floor. From this 300-foot-long vantage point, you witness mere strips of metal and blanks being turned into money. An awesome array of machines heats, washes, dries, sorts, edges, stamps, inspects, counts, and bags the coins that are punched out of the metal strips.

You will better understand what you see on this self-guided tour if you refer to the diagram in the free pamphlet distributed at the beginning of the tour and press the buttons to hear the taped explanations. From another area you can see medals and special collectors' coins produced by a process similar to that used for regular coins. The "Hot Off the Press" display shows the latest Mint medals authorized by Congress.

In the mezzanine area, additional displays of coins and artifacts include the original coining press used at the first Mint in 1792. These displays appear more interesting than the earlier ones, probably because you just saw how such coins are made. Then hurry down to the gift shop to purchase your own coins and begin your collection. Or, of course, you can just admire your spare change with your new-found knowledge.

Cost: Free
Freebies: Brochure
Video Shown: No. Developing video on production process.

Reservations Needed: No
Days and Hours: 9:00 AM-4:30 PM. September through April Mon-Fri; May and June Mon-Sat; July and August Mon-Sun. Closed Thanksgiving, Christmas, and New Year's. No production on federal holidays or most weekends. Call above number for recording of schedule.
Plan to Stay: 30 minutes for self-guided tour and coin gallery, plus time for gift shop.
Minimum Age: None, but smaller children may not be able to see or understand displays.
Disabled Access: Yes
Group Requirements: None
Special Information: Read pamphlet before beginning self-guided tour. It also explains the sculptor-engravers' and die-makers' work not seen on public tour. Tours of U.S. Mint in Denver available (see page 31).
Gift Shop: Sells commemorative coins and medals, as well as books on money, American history, and U.S. presidents. Mint your own souvenir medal in gift shop for $2. Open same days and hours as tour. For catalog information, call (301) 436-7400.
Directions: From Pennsylvania, take Schuylkill Expwy. (Rt. 76 East) to Vine St. Expwy., exit right at 6th St. Go south 2 blocks and turn left onto Market St. Go 1 block and turn left onto 5th St. Go 1 block north to Arch St. Mint imposingly occupies entire right side of 5th and Arch Sts. From New Jersey, take Benjamin Franklin Bridge to Philadelphia. Take 6th St./Independence Hall exit on right, follow signs to 6th St. Turn left onto Market St. and follow above directions.
Nearby Attractions: Downtown Philadelphia attractions include Independence Hall, Liberty Bell, Betsy Ross' House, Christ Church, and Benjamin Franklin's grave.

Utz Quality Foods ⌒ *potato chips*

900 High Street
Hanover, PA 17331
(717) 637-6644 / (800) 367-7629

The Hanover Home brand potato chips made by Salie and Bill Utz in 1921 at a rate of 50 pounds of chips per hour has evolved into a large regional snack-food company that produces up to 10,000 pounds of award-winning chips per hour. This self-guided tour allows you to view the entire 30-minute process that transforms a raw spud into a crunchy chip. From an overhead observation gallery equipped with push-button audio and video stations, you'll view the entire factory floor.

Potatoes roll and tumble like marbles past you into the peeling machine, which tosses the potatoes until the skin is removed. Peeled whole potatoes move along to the slicer, which is programmed to chop them into slices $55/1000$ths of an inch thick. The slices are bathed in 340° cooking oil, showered with salt, and dried on long conveyors while being inspected for discoloring. Flavorings (like barbecue or sour cream and onion) are added just before packaging.

Notice the pipes running throughout the factory, along walls and over workers' heads. These pipes carry water and oil to and from the production floor. Utz's innovative in-house recycling program uses water to eliminate most of the discarded product waste, such as unused potatoes, skins, and damaged returns. The "waste" is then sold to local farmers for animal feed, while the oil is used to make soap.

As you walk through the observation gallery, you see several Utz products traveling in different directions until they reach the packaging area. Chips are poured into giant funnels, which dump precisely measured amounts into bags of all sizes. Workers pack the bags into boxes and Utz's almost 300 trucks transport them all over the eastern U.S. Although your potato-chip trip ends above the loading area, don't forget to grab a "souvenir" bag on your way out.

Cost: Free
Freebies: Snack-size bag of potato chips
Video Shown: Two stations on tour show live camera shots.

Reservations Needed: No, except for groups larger than 10 people.
Days and Hours: Mon-Thur 8:00 AM-4:00 PM. If factory is in production on Fridays, tours will be offered. Call above number in advance for Friday schedule. Closed holidays.
Plan to Stay: 30 minutes for self-guided tour, plus time for nearby outlet store.
Minimum Age: None
Disabled Access: Flight of steps to observation gallery; however, all visitors are accommodated, so call ahead for assistance.
Group Requirements: Groups of 10 or more should call 2 days in advance to schedule tour guide.
Special Information: Brochure available on recycling program.
Outlet Store: Located a few blocks east at 861 Carlisle St. (Rt. 94). All Utz products, including chips, pretzels and popcorn, available in several sizes; chips and pretzels in cans up to 96 ounces; also decorator cans with Christmas and other designs. Look for special "Grandma Utz" Pennsylvania Dutch-style hand-cooked chips, and "gourmet" hand-dipped chocolate-covered chips and pretzels. Open Mon-Thur 8:00 AM-5:00 PM, Fri 8:00 AM-6:00 PM, and Sat 8:00 AM-5:00 PM. Catalog available.
Directions: From Harrisburg, take I-15 South to PA 94 South, into Hanover. Turn right onto Clearview Rd. (outlet store is on corner), then left onto High St. Utz is at intersection of Clearview Rd. and High St. From Maryland, take MD 30 North (becomes PA 94) to Hanover. Turn left onto Clearview Rd. and follow directions above.
Nearby Attractions: Synder's of Hanover tour (call 717-632-4477); Martin's Potato Chips tour (call 717-792-3565); Pfaltzgraff pottery tour (see page 209); Gettysburg's attractions about 20 minutes away.

Wendell August Forge ⟋ *metal and crystal giftware*

620 Madison Avenue
Grove City, PA 16127-0109
(800) 923-4438

Wendell August Forge is the oldest and largest hand forge in the country. The company that Mr. Wendell August started in 1923 making hand-forged architectural pieces (such as railings and gates) now makes beautiful metal giftware. This self-guided tour shows you the steps in producing their individually hand-crafted products, from the cutting of sheet metal to the final hammering and polishing of finished pieces.

Die engraving is the most intricate and time-consuming step. Master die engravers use only a hammer, chisels, and their own creative talents to engrave designs into steel slabs. The carved die design, sometimes taking eight weeks to complete, is the reverse of the actual image. Try to find the engraver's initials on the die; they're cleverly hidden in the design.

Your ears alert you to the hammering area. Watch craftsmen carefully clamp a blank piece of aluminum or bronze down over the design. They use specially designed hammers to force the metal into the die's carved-out portions, creating a raised image on the other side. One moment it's a flat piece of metal and the next you see the detailed image of an eagle soaring gracefully over a rocky canyon.

After this initial hammering, the piece moves to an anvil to be flattened, anviled, and edged before the remarkable "coloring" process occurs. Each metal piece is placed face-down onto a specially grated screen and held over an open fire in an early-1930s forge. The fire's black smoke bakes onto the piece. After cooling, special polishing removes 97 percent of the baked-on smoke, leaving just enough color to highlight the design. Although Wendell August craftsmen never produce two identical pieces of giftware, their hallmark and company logo on the back of each item attest to its quality.

Cost: Free
Freebies: Brochure and map; catalog available upon request.

Video Shown: 7-minute video provides close-up view of production steps.
Reservations Needed: No, but recommended for groups of 15 or more.
Days and Hours: Mon-Wed 9:00 AM-6:00 PM, Thur-Fri 9:00 AM-3:00 PM, Sat 9:30 AM-6:00 PM, and Sun 11:00 AM-5:00 PM. Closed holidays. When not in production, see manufacturing process video in gift shop.
Plan to Stay: 20 minutes for self-guided tour, plus time for video and gift shop.
Minimum Age: None for families, above elementary-school age for groups.
Disabled Access: Yes
Group Requirements: Welcomes any size group. Recommends 1 week's advance notice for groups larger than 15. Insurance prohibits tours by groups of elementary-school-age children.
Special Information: You may talk with the craftsmen but, for your safety, do not touch any metal in production. During busy seasons, Wendell Bear may greet you with a hug. New facility in Berlin, OH, heart of Amish Country, opened Summer 1994; features production tours, museum, and theater.
Gift Shop: Store and showroom display all Wendell August handmade items, including intricately designed coasters, plates, serving pieces, trays, and Christmas ornaments. Engraved crystal and glass, other unique gift items also sold. Open Mon-Thur and Sat 9:00 AM-6:00 PM, Fri 9:00 AM-9:00 PM, and Sun 11:00 AM-5:00 PM. Catalog available from (800) 923-4438. Gift shop also has LGB model train suspended overhead on 200 feet of track and authentic nickelodeon.
Directions: From I-79, take Exit 31. Follow blue-and-white signs. From I-80, take Exit 3A. Follow signs.
Nearby Attractions: Daffin's Chocolate Factory tour (call 412-342-2892); Troyer Farms Potato Chips tour (call 800-458-0485); Lake Arthur.

Using hammer and chisel, die-cutters engrave designs at Wendell August Forge, Grove City, Pennsylvania

Showroom displays works made at Wendell August Forge

Vanguard Racing Sailboats ➤ *racing sailboats*

16 Peckham Drive
Bristol, RI 02809
(401) 254-0960

As one of the leading builders of racing boats between 8 and 16 feet, Vanguard prides itself on being the exclusive supplier of Finn-class sailing dinghies for the 1992 Barcelona Olympics. This marked the first time in 25 years that a non-host country won the job of building them. So no sailor will have an advantage, precision manufacturing drives Vanguard's boat-building process to ensure that the boats are identical. If you can tolerate the strong glue smell, you can walk along the plant floor, stand next to the workers, and observe all the stages in making the different Vanguard models.

Fiberglass boats are built from the outside in, starting from separate molds of the hull and deck. The molds are mirror images of these boat-body parts. The precision begins in the room where a bandsaw cuts stacks of fiberglass sheets according to an exacting pattern. In the spray booth, the bright gelcoat that's sprayed into the mold provides the boat's color.

In a process called "laying up fiberglass," workers use paint rollers to glue the strips down into the molds. You'll see them hand-lay the resin-soaked fiberglass sheets, reminding you of making papier-mâché dolls. To ensure that each boat weighs the same, the resin and fiberglass are carefully weighed before being laid into each boat; the hulls are specially measured against a template. The separately made hull and deck are also cored with PVC foam and vacuum-bagged.

In a nearby area, workers add hardware such as the cleats and mast step. Hanging from the ceiling are decks and hulls joined by glue and married together with huge pterodactyl clamps. As these flying dinosaurs are lowered, you realize that hidden inside is a sleek racing boat. Even if you're only an occasional sailor, you'll appreciate what's involved in building a high-performance racing boat.

Cost: Free
Freebies: Stickers
Video Shown: No
Reservations Needed: Yes
Days and Hours: Mon-Fri 9:00 AM-4:00 PM. Closed holidays.
Plan to Stay: 20 minutes for tour
Minimum Age: 10
Disabled Access: Yes
Group Requirements: No maximum group size as long as 5 days' advance notice is given.
Special Information: As with any fiberglass-boat manufacturing plant, there is a strong glue smell.
Gift Counter: Sells logoed T-shirts.
Directions: From Rt. 114, go over Mt. Hope bridge toward Bristol. Bear right on Rt. 136. Turn left at Gooding Ave. Turn right at Broad Common Rd., and left at Peckham Dr. Factory is 200 yards ahead on the right.
Nearby Attractions: Herreshoff Marine Museum in Bristol; Colt State Park; Haffenreffer Museum of Anthropology; Newport's beaches, mansions, Naval War College Museum, Museum of Yachting at Fort Adams, Tennis Hall of Fame, and other attractions are 20 minutes away. (This area of Rhode Island has many sailboat manufacturers, but very few give public tours. However, if you own a boat made by a company in this region, or are considering the purchase of one, a tour probably could be arranged by calling the company directly or your local dealer.)

American Classic Tea   *teas*

Charleston Tea Plantation
6617 Maybank Highway
Wadmalaw Island, SC 29487
(803) 559-0383 / (800) 443-5987

On a small island 25 miles south of Charleston, the last 11 rural miles along a dead-end road, lies the only commercial tea plantation in the U.S.A. Charleston Tea Plantation is a tea farm rather than an Old-South plantation with white columns. Its entrance, however, through a 7-foot high chain-link fence (bearing only the number 6617) and long rows of perfectly manicured 3½-foot-high-by-5-foot-wide tea hedges, is just as enchanting. While factory tours are currently not available, a visit to Charleston Tea Plantation is an experience: part meeting the owners, who explain tea history, harvesting, and production; and part garden party.

Park between the tea hedge rows and check in at the reception area under a live, Spanish-moss-covered oak tree. Under an oak-trees-and-gardenias canopy, watch a video on tea history, harvesting, and processing. Then stroll along the paved walkway to where Mack Fleming, co-owner and president (in alternating years), stands in a tea field next to the 20-foot-long-by-12-foot-high mechanized harvester, a big green monster whose wheelbase straddles a tea row. Mack designed it when he was Director of Horticulture for Lipton (Lipton operated a research facility at this site from 1963-1987, when Mack Fleming and Bill Hall purchased it). The efficiency of this cross between a cotton picker and tobacco harvester allows the plantation to compete with inexpensive Far East manual-harvesting costs.

Farther down the path you'll meet Bill Hall, co-owner and third-generation English tea taster. He earned this honor through an apprenticeship in England, tasting 800-1,000 cups of tea five days a week for four years. Bill explains the processes that harvested tea leaves undergo in the factory. In a 5-foot-high bin, a fan blows air through them to reduce their moisture content. After 18 hours, the flaccid leaves are ground and spread out to oxidize in open air. The green leaves turn coppery orange. Next, in a 250° dryer, the leaves tumble back and forth among seven conveyors and turn from copper to black tea,

which is then tasted, sorted, graded, and packaged. At the end of your tour, enjoy American Classic Iced Tea and Benne sesame wafers while relaxing under a white lattice-work gazebo.

Cost: Free

Freebies: Tea samples with Benne wafers

Video Shown: 8-minute video overviews entire production process, from harvesting to factory.

Reservations Needed: No, except for school groups.

Days and Hours: First Sat of month from May through October only. 10:00 AM-1:30 PM; tours start every 30 minutes. Canceled in case of rain. Tour schedule subject to change. Call (800) 443-5987 for latest information.

Plan to Stay: 45 minutes, plus time for gift tent and relaxing on grounds.

Minimum Age: None

Disabled Access: Yes

Group Requirements: Tours can be arranged for school groups on selected weekdays during May and October by calling 2 months ahead.

Special Information: Wear comfortable shoes and clothing for this half-mile outdoor walking tour.

Gift Shop: Awning-stripe tent offers tea bags, ready-to-drink tea beverages, logoed T-shirts and caps, and Charleston sweetgrass baskets (frequent basket-making demonstrations in tent). Open tour hours. Catalog available from 800 number above.

Directions: From Charleston, take Hwy. 700 (Maybank Hwy.) South directly onto Wadmalaw Island. Plantation entrance is 11 miles from Church Creek Bridge.

Nearby Attractions: Atlantic Littleneck Clam Farm tour (call 803-762-0022), 25 miles away; Angel Oak Park, 11 miles away; Kiawah Island Resort, 22 miles away.

Mt. Rushmore Jewelry ⟿ *jewelry*

2707 Mt. Rushmore Road
Rapid City, SD 57701
(605) 343-2226 / (800) 658-3361

Black Hills Gold jewelry first appeared after the Black Hills Gold Rush of 1876. By law, in order to use the name "Black Hills Gold," companies must manufacture the jewelry in the Black Hills of South Dakota. To produce Black Hills Gold's characteristic green tint, 12-karat gold is alloyed with silver; alloying gold with copper creates a pink tint. This tour shows you the ancient "lost wax" method of casting used to manufacture all Black Hills jewelry.

Imagine a golden leaf, precise in form and detail and smaller than a contact lens. At Mt. Rushmore jewelry such minuscule foliage is commonplace. See workers with soldering needles "tack" tiny leaves and grapes onto the shanks of rings. At the "wriggling" station, watch a craftsperson wiggle a tool back and forth to etch ridges and veins into a leaf one-third the size of a cornflake. Artisans sit at rows of workstations equipped with small drills, jeweler's loupes, and plenty of tweezers.

All jewelry originates in the Design Room. Artists fashion rubber molds into which hot wax is shot. After the wax sets, the mold is pried apart and the wax ring joins others on a wax "tree" about the size of a centerpiece. The tree is then dipped in plaster and this plaster cast slides into a kiln. The wax melts and liquid gold is injected into the resulting hollow cavity. When the metal has set, the hot cast is dunked in cold water. The plaster shatters, revealing an exact duplicate of the original wax model. This gold tree of rings is pruned, and each ring is ground, buffed, frosted, and polished. During busy holiday seasons, Mt. Rushmore Jewelry's 125 employees produce up to 500 pieces of jewelry per day.

Cost: Free
Freebies: No
Video Shown: No
Reservations Needed: No, except for groups larger than 40 people.
Days and Hours: May through September Mon-Fri 8:00 AM-3:00 PM, tours generally on the hour; October through April, tours by walk-in or reservation. Closed holidays and week between Christmas and New Year's.
Plan to Stay: 20 minutes, plus time in Factory Showroom.
Minimum Age: None
Disabled Access: Yes
Group Requirements: No maximum group size. Large groups will be split up. Requests 1 day's advance notice for groups larger than 40 people.
Special Information: This family-run business is one of the few jewelry manufacturers' tours that allows visitors directly onto the production floor.
Factory Showroom: Sells entire 3,600-style line of Black Hills Gold jewelry. Rings are arranged in velvet cases among elegant watches, dishes and crystal bowls. Open May through September Mon-Sat 8:00 AM-8:00 PM, Sun 9:00 AM-5:00 PM; October through April Mon-Sat 9:00 AM-5:00 PM. Closed Christmas, Thanksgiving, and Easter.
Directions: From I-90, take Exit 57. Turn left onto Omaha St. Turn right on Mt. Rushmore Rd. Mt. Rushmore Jewelry is at intersection of Fairmont Blvd. and Mt. Rushmore Rd. From Hwy. 79, travel west on Fairmont Blvd. to Mt. Rushmore Rd.
Nearby Attractions: Sioux Pottery and Crafts tour (see page 219); video and observation booth at Landstrom's Black Hills Gold Creations (call 800-843-0009 or 605-343-0157); Mt. Rushmore; Reptile Gardens; The Ranch Amusement Park; Geology Museum at South Dakota School of Mines.

Sioux Pottery and Crafts   ⟨⟩ *pottery*

2209 Highway 79 South
Rapid City, SD 57701
(605) 341-3657 / (800) 657-4366

The red clay used at Sioux Pottery comes from Paha Sapa, the Black Hills area, and is considered sacred. This clay is carefully fashioned into vases and pots whose exteriors are then graced with Sioux Indian designs symbolizing the Sioux culture, their environment, activities, and dealings. For example, crossed arrows represent Friendship, a zigzag of lightning stands for Swiftness, and a diamond wedged between two backwards Es connotes Horses Killed in Battle.

Along with the red clay, the craftspeople at Sioux Pottery also utilize a more secular variety from Kentucky. This white, elastic clay is used for certain pieces, such as those with handles, which are too delicate to withstand the pronounced shrinkage inherent in firing red clay. About ten artists can be seen working at any one time, each one seated at an old kitchen table. The floors of their workspace are powdered with dust; bootprints lead to a dank back room where the red clay exists as "slip" (earthy red liquid). From outside, the slip is piped into concrete vats where it is mixed and strained, then turned into clay.

The artists employ three methods for turning clay into pots: casting, wheel-throwing, and jiggering. In casting, slip is poured into plaster molds. The plaster absorbs the excess liquid, and the clay takes the shape of the mold. In wheel-throwing, potters bend over spinning pottery wheels, hand-forming original pieces from balls of clay. The third method, jiggering, is used for flat plates and bowls. As the wheel spins, a potter lowers a blade that cuts out the shape. White or red, all unfired pottery is called "greenware." You'll see shelves of greenware, all dull and smooth. The Indian artists paint freehand designs and proudly sign their names on each piece.

Cost: Free
Freebies: No
Video Shown: No

Reservations Needed: No, except for groups larger than 12 people or to arrange tours outside regularly scheduled times.
Days and Hours: Mon, Wed, Fri 11:00 AM for guided tours Memorial Day through Labor Day. Self-guided tours any time during gift-shop hours. Best viewing days are Tue-Fri; not much produced on Mon or Sat. Closed holidays and week after Christmas.
Plan to Stay: 20 minutes, plus time in gift shop.
Cost: Free
Minimum Age: None
Disabled Access: Yes
Group Requirements: Call 2-3 days in advance for groups larger than 12 people. Groups larger than 20 will be split into smaller groups.
Special Information: A lot of clay dust in the back rooms' air.
Gift Shop: Sells hand-made pots, bowls and dishware, as well as mandalas, dance shields, painted cattle skulls, and sacred medicine wheels, all created locally by members of Sioux nation. Factory seconds available at 50% off. Open May through August Mon-Fri 8:00 AM-5:00 PM, Sat 10:00 AM-4:00 PM, Sun 12:00 PM-4:00 PM; September through April Mon-Fri 8:00 AM-5:00 PM, Sat 10:00 AM-2:00 PM except September Sat 10:00 AM-4:00 PM. Catalog available by mail for $2.
Directions: From I-90 bypass, take Exit 59 and go south on LaCrosse St. Turn left (east) on East North St. to Cambell St. Turn right (south) on Cambell to St. Patrick St. Turn right again (west) on St. Patrick to Hwy. 79 South Business Loop. Swing left onto Hwy. 79. Sioux Pottery is 2 blocks ahead on your right.
Nearby Attractions: Mt. Rushmore Jewelry tour (see page 218); The Black Hills National Forest; Mount Rushmore; Geology Museum at South Dakota School of Mines; Reptile Gardens; The Ranch Amusement Park.

American Bread Company   ⌒   *Sunbeam bread*

702 Murfreesboro Road
Nashville, TN 37224
(615) 254-1161

A large Little Miss Sunbeam—the smiling, blue-eyed girl with golden locks—greets you from high over the front entrance of American Bread Company's bakery. She is taking a bite from a slice of white bread—which American Sunbeam Bakery has proudly produced since 1889 under the Evers family's direction. Your guided tour will show you that American now produces a wide variety of breads, rolls, and specialty baked items—everything from hamburger buns to its very own Evers 100 percent stone-ground whole-wheat bread.

The aroma of fresh-baked bread fills your nostrils as you begin your plant tour. You may think you're touring a dairy when you view huge vats and giant mixers (some with up to 2,000 pounds capacity) filled with liquid. A highly automated production system transforms dough into toasty brown loaves of bread in giant ovens. The baked loaves then travel in their own tiny ski-lift-like seats, moving down over your head and winding all around you through the factory. On these steep conveyor belts, the bread continues its journey through the cooling area to packaging.

The packaging of each loaf is fascinating to watch. A machine blows open a Sunbeam bag and in one continuous motion the sliced bread slides into the plastic bag and progresses toward a spool of twist-ties. A length of twist-tie is mechanically fed from the wheel and twisted around the bag's opening to seal in the product's just-baked freshness. One hundred loaves a minute are packaged by this method!

As you pass through the supplies stored on the facility's lower level, you see hundreds of gallons of honey and molasses. Notice stacks of 50-pound bags of flour. Between 130 and 140 of these bags are used every day to produce up to 7,000 loaves of bread an hour! Your tour concludes with a stroll through racks upon racks of packaged, ready-to-ship baked goods—buns of every shape and size (including hamburger buns for Burger King), Roman Meal bread, white bread, wheat bread, and even barbecue bread. This is all in a day's work at the second-largest bakery in the South.

Cost: Free

Freebies: Sunbeam product sample, could be anything from oatmeal cookies or donuts to barbecue bread.

Video Shown: Children up to 3rd grade see "I Am Wheat," 18-minute video about uses of wheat and flour. Older groups see 20-minute slide presentation showing company history and production.

Plan to Stay: About 1 hour

Reservations Needed: Yes. Individuals and families must join scheduled group tour.

Days and Hours: Tours mid-September through mid-May only. Mon, Wed-Fri 10:00 AM and 11:30 AM. Factory is being remodeled; scheduled to open for tours in late 1994.

Minimum Age: 7

Disabled Access: Yes

Group Requirements: Groups larger than 20 people should make reservations 3 days in advance.

Special Information: Factory is very warm and tour involves walking, so dress accordingly.

Thrift Store: Sells cakes, breads, pies, snack foods, and groceries, most items at discount. Offers day-old bread at reduced prices. Open Mon-Sat 9:00 AM-5:00 PM. Closed some holidays.

Directions: From I-65, take Fesseler's Ln. exit. Turn right at end of exit ramp, then turn left onto Murfreesboro Rd. Look for Little Miss Sunbeam sign 4-5 blocks ahead on left. From I-40, take Spence Ln. exit. Turn left onto Spence Ln. Turn right onto Murfreesboro Rd. Bakery is 3 blocks ahead on right.

Nearby Attractions: Nissan tours and Purity Dairies (see pages 222 and 223); Grand Old Opry; Opryland.

Jack Daniel's Distillery   ~~~ *whiskey*

Lynchburg, TN 37352
(615) 759-4221

In the heavily vegetated, woodsy, hilly terrain of south-middle Tennessee, you feel you're visiting a national park rather than the world's oldest registered distillery (1866) when you tour Jack Daniel's. A babbling brook follows you through the entire tour. You learn from the tour guide that the water is no coincidence, that Jasper Newton (Jack) Daniel chose this property because of Cave Spring's iron-free water. This pure limestone water flows at 56° year-round and is one secret of Jack Daniel's fine whiskey.

Your tour begins with a short mini-van ride up the hill to one of 45 aging houses. The large wooden structure's air is thick and musty with the smell of whiskey and wood. Your eyes take in only a small fraction of the 20,164 barrels of aging whiskey lined up seven stories high. Four years of warm days and cool nights inside these white-oak barrels gives Jack Daniel's whiskey its flavor and color.

In the rick yard, landmarked by a black smokestack, Moore County hard sugar-maple wood is burned to make charcoal. The mellowing actually takes place in enormous containers called charcoal mellowing vats. Here the distilled, fermented whiskey seeps through 10 feet of charcoal and a wool blanket at a rate of less than six gallons an hour.

You'll see another interesting whiskey-making step in the hot, noisy mash room. Here, in large tanks called mash tubs, corn, rye, barley malt, water, and yeast ferment for four days. A panel measures the liquid's progress toward becoming 140-proof whiskey.

A wooden structure which resembles an old southern country farmhouse is actually Jack Daniel's original office, which dates back to 1878. Still in its natural setting, it is filled with period furniture, old file cabinets, and ledgers that documented the company's financial transactions.

Cost: Free
Freebies: Ice-cold glass of lemonade in White Rabbit Saloon after tour.

Video Shown: Video at tour's beginning explains Jack Daniel's and whiskey making. Video at end of tour shows bottling process (not on tour).
Reservations Needed: No, except for groups larger than 30 people.
Days and Hours: Mon-Sun 8:00 AM-4:00 PM. Closed Thanksgiving, Christmas, and New Year's. On Saturdays, Sundays, and during 2-week July shutdown, you follow standard tour route, even though distillery isn't in production.
Plan to Stay: 1 hour for videos and tour.
Minimum Age: None
Disabled Access: Yes. Specially designed van tour for people in wheelchairs.
Group Requirements: Groups larger than 30 should call on Thursday of week before visit.
Special Information: Lots of walking, so wear comfortable shoes. Tour booklets available in major foreign languages. Distillery is designated a National Historical Place.
Gift Shop: Sells Jack Daniel's Cave Spring water. Just about every store in Lynchburg, a short walk from the parking lot, sells Jack Daniel's souvenirs but no whiskey. Lynchburg Hardware and General Store has largest selection, including old-time saloon mirror, wooden whiskey chest, stoneware jugs, and playing cards. Open Mon-Sun 9:00 AM-5:00 PM. Catalog available at above number.
Directions: From Nashville, take I-24 South to Exit 111 (Rt. 55 West). As you enter Lynchburg, visitors center parking lot entrance is off Hwy. 55 next to Mulberry Creek Bridge. From Chattanooga, take I-24 North to Exit 111 (Rt. 55 West). Follow above directions.
Nearby Attractions: Lynchburg is filled with southern charm and hospitality. Visit Courthouse; Miss Mary Bobo's Boarding House (southern-style food served); and other local stores.

Nissan ⟨⟩ *cars and pickup trucks*
983 Nissan Drive
Smyrna, TN 37167
(615) 459-1444

Imagine 89 football fields side-by-side and back-to-back, all under one roof! That would be an unfathomable size for a sports complex, but it is the actual size of Nissan's first U.S. manufacturing plant, which employs nearly 6,000 people. Since it began production in 1983, the unemployment rate in Rutherford County has been cut in half. You are shuttled through the enormous production plant on an endless network of concrete polyurethane mini-thruways which covers the entire plant. All around you, everywhere you look, there are light trucks, Sentras, and Altimas being assembled, painted, and inspected.

Zigzagging through the massive welding operation, you feel as if you are on a Stephen Spielberg movie set. Look up at what seems like a conveyor system suspended from the ceiling as sparks fly from tentacle-like robot arms welding together the main body parts of the vehicle shell. This mixture of automation and computerization is called the Intelligent (or "smart") Body Assembly System (IBAS). IBAS robots replace the conventional jigs that hold steel panels together during the initial welding of the vehicle's body. The computerized capabilities of the "smart" system allows for more than one model of vehicle to be manufactured on each line and uses lasers to check accuracy.

As your tour guide maneuvers the shuttle along the 33-mile maze of conveyers, the unmistakable smell of fresh paint begins to fill your nostrils. Gazing through the glass that encloses the conveyer belt, you see employees clothed in what resembles surgical garb. You are now cruising through the paint facility. Here, in a precise and lengthy process, layers of primer and paint are intermittently applied and inspected by robots and humans. Employees carefully check each automobile's finish as part of the quality control system. Heat engulfs you as you pass the enclosed paint-bake oven and air blower zones where the cars are dried.

On yet another line you are reassured of the human touch when you see technicians,

heads bowed in concentration and fingers flying, manually assembling Sentra and mini-van engines. It's fun to witness the finishing touches, in the final production stages, such as workers adding seats and catalytic converters to some of the nearly 400,000 vehicles produced here each year.

Cost: Free
Freebies: No
Video Shown: 10-minute overview of Nissan and manufacturing at Smyrna plant.
Reservations Needed: Yes. Maximum of 55 people per tour, whether individuals, families, or groups. Occasional last-minute cancellations, so it's worth a call to see if you can fit into tour.
Days and Hours: Tue and Thur at 8:30 AM, 10:00 AM and 1:00 PM. Closed holidays, week between Christmas and New Year's, and 2 weeks in July.
Plan to Stay: 1½ hours for video and tour
Minimum Age: 10 (5th grade)
Disabled Access: Yes
Group Requirements: Maximum number of 55 people per time period if no other tours scheduled. Reservations accepted up to 3 months in advance.
Special Information: No photography or shorts.
Gift Shop: No
Directions: From Nashville, take I-24 East toward Chattanooga. Take Exit 70 (Almaville Rd.) and turn left toward Smyrna (Almaville Rd. becomes Nissan Dr.). Nissan is about 3 miles ahead on right. Enter Gate 1.
Nearby Attractions: Sam Davis Home; attractions in Murfreesboro (geographic center of Tennessee) include Stones River Battlefield, Oakland Mansion, and antique stores. Nashville's attractions, including American Bread Company and Purity Dairies tours (see pages 220 and 223) and Grand Old Opry, are 20 miles away.

Purity Dairies   ~~~   *ice cream and dairy products*

360 Murfreesboro Road
Nashville, TN 37210
(615) 244-1900

A cheery ice-cream parlor welcomes you to Purity Dairies' ice-cream plant. In the tour room, the 50-something-year-old company shows a film about milk and the manufacturing of their dairy products. Then the big blue curtain opens, revealing a huge window with a panoramic view of the ice-cream factory.

Seeing the production of ice-cream sandwiches is almost like watching a live theater performance, with each player taking a specific role. The show is a continuous interaction of machinery, humanity, and ice cream. In the foreground, two women handle the sandwich machine. One feeds chocolate wafers into the machine, which squirts out the exact amount of vanilla ice-cream filling for each sandwich. The other worker boxes the sandwiches after they have been automatically wrapped. A complicated labyrinth of overhead piping, frosty and dripping with condensation, runs throughout the plant. A milk-based mixture is pumped to various stainless-steel machines, where it is flavored, transformed into ice cream, and shot into individual cartons. The cartons are automatically shrink-wrapped and sent to the freezer for hardening.

A short walk outside takes you to the milk plant, with more overhead pipes everywhere. The daily production of 10,500 pounds of cottage cheese causes a natural sour odor in the room where Purity makes Little Miss Muffet's curds and whey. An enormous stainless-steel tub filled with the white lumpy stuff comes into view and your guide explains the intricacies of separating curds and whey to produce cottage cheese.

In another part of this facility Purity manufactures its own plastic milk containers. It takes 7,754 plastic beans to make a gallon jug. At the end of the tour, visitors convene at the weigh station and your group is collectively weighed. Here the Purity trucks are also weighed, before heading out to make deliveries. The loud moo you might hear is the horn on one of Purity's special home-delivery trucks, painted white with large black spots that resemble a . . . guess what. (The horn is a hint.)

Cost: Free

Freebies: Children receive ice-cream sandwiches; adults receive frozen yogurt, premium ice cream, sherbet, and gift pack of cottage cheese and other items.

Video Shown: 17-minute movie about Purity's milk and other products.

Reservations Needed: Yes. Individuals and families must join scheduled group tour. Tours may fill years in advance, but individuals or families should ask about available space on existing group tours.

Day and Hours: Tues, Thur, Fri. Children's tours, 9:00 AM, 11:00 AM, and 1:00 PM. Adult tours, 10:00 AM-12:00 PM for tour and 12:00 PM-2:00 PM for complimentary lunch.

Plan to Stay: 2 hours for video and tour, plus time for lunch (adult tour).

Minimum Age: 4

Disabled Access: Yes

Group Requirements: Adult tours need at least 4 months' advance reservations; children's tours, 6 weeks ahead. At press time, company said group tours are booked far in advance. Maximum kids' group size is 50; maximum for adults is 40.

Special Information: Company has expanded marketing territory, so tour is very popular. Book tour as far ahead as possible.

Gift Shop: No

Directions: From the south, take I-65 to Fesseler's Lane exit. Turn right at end of exit, then take first right on Elm Hill Pike. Purity is at intersection with Murfreesboro Rd. From the north, take I-65 to Murfreesboro Rd. exit. Turn left at end of exit. You'll see signs and Purity logo.

Nearby Attractions: American Bread Company and Nissan tours (see pages 220 and 222); Grand Old Opry; Opryland.

Saturn ⟶ *cars*

Visitors Center
100 Saturn Parkway
Spring Hill, TN 37174
(615) 486-5440

To many Americans, GM's Saturn car represents the rebirth of U.S. manufacturing. Since the first Saturn rolled off the line in 1990, these import-fighting little cars have boasted a high quality reputation, a no-haggle sales approach by dealers, and highly satisfied customers. The factory does not offer public tours, however a small visitor center includes a video, displays of two engines, and other exhibits about the company, the plant, and the car.

This highly integrated factory complex, which has power train, general assembly, and body system buildings, sits on 2,400 acres of what was previously farm land. (Saturn employs three local farmers among its 8,000 employees to grow crops on land not used by the factory.) Unlike most mammoth auto plants that you can easily spot from the highway, Saturn built its factory to blend into the landscape. As you enter the Visitors Center, notice how the buildings are slightly sunken into the ground and have a grayish-blue tint that fades into the skyline.

GM started Saturn as a laboratory in which to reinvent the company. The Visitors Center captures some of that spirit. On a wall are the Saturn Philosophy and Saturn Mission Statement—two things that you expect to see at high-profile, progressive companies like Ben & Jerry's (see page 240), Celestial Seasonings (see page 26), and Tom's of Maine (see page 88), but not at a GM subsidiary.

The video provides a quick tour of the car's production. (The Visitors Center plans to install an interactive-video kiosk that lets you select more in-depth videos on different production steps and car features.) The exhibited Standard and Twin Cab engines rotate on pedestals, which makes it easier to study their engineering features. The Visitors Center guides enjoy answering questions ranging from the car's technical features to the factory workers' schedules. While you may be disappointed that you cannot tour the real factory, you get a sense of the company and how it operates.

Cost: Free

Freebies: Product brochures

Video Shown: 10-minute video on Saturn production, with plans to offer more specialized videos.

Reservations Needed: No for Visitors Center. Factory not open to public tours.

Days and Hours: Mon-Sat 5:30 AM-6:00 PM. Closed holidays.

Plan to Stay: 40 minutes

Minimum Age: None

Disabled Access: Yes

Group Requirements: None

Special Information: Visitors Center is currently located in trailers originally used when construction started at the plant in 1985. Saturn plans to improve the center. June 1994 Saturn owners' festival may become an annual event. On a limited basis, Saturn gives tours to corporate and select groups for a fee. For more information, write to Group Coordinator, Corporate Communications, at above address.

Gift Shop: Saturn Breakmart next to Visitor Center sells logoed items including T-shirts, caps, mugs, and hats. Open Mon-Fri 8:00 AM-4:00 PM (Wed until 6:00 PM). Price list available from (615) 486-6066. Closed 2 weeks in July.

Directions: From Nashville, take I-65 South. Exit at Rt. 396 Saturn Pkwy. West. Take Hwy. 31 South to Saturn South Entrance. Visitors Center is on left, outside the gate.

Nearby Attractions: Natchez Park; Nashville's attractions, including American Bread Bakery and Purity Dairies tours (see pages 220 and 223) and Grand Old Opry, are about 40 minutes away.

American Airlines C.R. Smith Museum

4601 Highway 360 at Trinity Blvd.   *air travel*
Fort Worth, TX 76155
(817) 967-1560

You'll recognize the American Airlines C.R. Smith Museum, named after the man who served as company president for most of the years between 1934 and 1973, by the fully restored DC-3 (the *Flagship Knoxville,* which flew for American 1940-1948) in front. The Grey Eagles, a group of mostly retired American pilots, bought the *Knoxville* and a team of active and retired American mechanics restored it to its current glistening condition. One of the newest corporate museums in the U.S.A., this 25,000-square-foot building contains informative interactive displays and video presentations.

The circular glass History Wall in the center of the open floor plan highlights company developments and memorabilia from the first airmail service (1918) to today, including a 767 maintenance manual on CD-ROM. Some of the oldest items, including a letter Charles Lindbergh carried on his first airmail flight from Chicago to St. Louis, bring American's heritage to life. Beyond this section is an "American Family" display with life-size mannequins representing American employees and videos describing their jobs and teamwork.

"Working in the Air," "Working on the Ground," and "Maintaining the Fleet" exhibits detail the equipment and procedures used in airline operations. You can sit in a cabin mockup to feel like a pilot or flight attendant. You'll also get an up-close look at a jet engine, aircraft landing gear, and an air traffic control system. The "Flightlab" has miniature wind tunnels, test equipment, and simulators that teach the basic principles of flight. Near these more-technical displays are brass-plate etchings of four different American Airline planes. Put a piece of paper on your chosen plate and rub it with a crayon to make a souvenir. If only flying a real plane and running an airline were this easy!

Cost: Free
Freebies: Brass rubbings (see above).
Movie Shown: 14-minute film, "Dream of Flight," runs every 20 minutes. Theater's all-around sound system and panoramic screen give you the feeling of flying American Airlines' jets. Also touch-screen videos throughout museum.
Reservations Needed: No, recommended for groups larger than 20 people.
Days and Hours: Wed-Sun 11:00 AM-6:00 PM. Call for holiday hours.
Plan to Stay: 1½-2 hours for displays, videos, and film, plus time in gift shop.
Minimum Age: None
Disabled Access: Yes
Group Requirements: Reservations suggested for groups larger than 20 and for guided tour.
Special Information: Special-event rental of museum available (call 817-967-5910). Summer educational day camp (call 817-967-1560). With the museum's open floor plan, the Map and Guide provide a helpful overview of the numerous displays. Get copy at front desk.
Gift Shop: Unique aviation-related items, such as models, glass and porcelain planes and eagles, clocks, mobiles, toys, and books. Also museum and American Airlines logoed items. Prices range from 35¢ pencils to $750 bronze statues. Open museum hours.
Directions: From Dallas/Fort Worth Int'l Airport (3 miles away), take south exit and follow Hwy. 183 West/360 South curve to the right. Exit at FAA Rd.; turn right at stop sign. Museum is on right. From Hwy. 183 East, take FAA Rd./Hwy. 360 South exit. Follow access road south and turn right at stop sign. Museum is on right.
Nearby Attractions: Mrs. Baird Bread tour (call 817-293-6230); Mary Kay factory tour and company museum (see page 233); Six Flags Over Texas; Fort Worth Zoo and Fort Worth Museum of Science and History about 20 miles away; Downtown Dallas attractions, including JFK Museum, about 20 miles away.

Blue Bell Creameries   *ice cream*

1000 Horton Street
Brenham, TX 77833
(409) 830-2197 / (800) 327-8135

This "Little Creamery in Brenham" maintains its small-town image through its advertising and girl-and-cow logo. At its headquarters, the 19th-century red-brick schoolhouse offices, 1930s-replica refrigerated delivery truck, country store, and ice-cream parlor further that country feel. The visitors center demonstrates the company's pride in its history through rare photos of Blue Bell and Brenham, the company's original wooden time clock, and a film called "Blue Bell Creamery: Then and Now."

In the plant, look down through glass windows at the production floor's maze of stainless-steel pipes and various shaped tanks. Almost everything happens inside the tanks, so your tour guide explains the process. Base-mix ingredients are blended, homogenized, and pasteurized, then cooled and piped into refrigerated holding tanks. The tanks' huge round doors resemble ship portholes. Liquid flavorings are added in the rectangular flavoring tanks.

The mailbox-shaped freezer barrels whip and freeze the mixture to milkshake consistency. The ice cream and "dry" ingredients (fruit, cookie chunks, cookie dough, etc.) meet in the white pipes before traveling into containers. If the flavor of the day is banana split, workers peel and slice bananas in the behind-the-scenes kitchen. In the filler machine, empty, open, half-gallon round cartons spin to mix ice cream and ingredients as they flow into the cartons. Colorful lids slide down to cover the filled cartons.

Another room offers more movement as 3-ounce Dixie cups are filled. Cups resting in a circular disk are filled two at a time; the disk rotates after every two are filled. You will be mesmerized by the repetitive spin-fill, spin-fill process. Nearby, ice-cream sandwiches start as chocolate wafers sliding down a V-shaped holder. Two wafers converge and a hardened ice cream slice drops between them. Paper quickly wraps around the sandwich and helps maintain its shape. The sandwiches travel single-file until they're mechanically pushed into cardboard boxes. All this

whets your appetite for the samples you'll enjoy in the ice-cream parlor.

Cost: Adults, $1.50; seniors and children 6-14, $1.

Freebies: Ice-cream serving in the parlor; logoed paper hat.

Video Shown: 7-minute dramatized film on company's early history. If no plant production, watch 6-minute film of ice-cream-making process.

Reservations Needed: No, except for groups of 15 or more people. Everyone must make 30 days' advance reservations for March and April tours.

Days and Hours: Mon-Fri 10:00 AM-2:30 PM, every 30 minutes in summer. Fall and winter tour schedule varies; call for exact tour times and days. Closed holidays.

Plan to Stay: 40 minutes, plus time in visitors center, ice-cream parlor, and country store.

Minimum Age: No

Disabled Access: Only for films, ice-cream parlor, and country store. Stairs in plant.

Group Requirements: Groups of 15 or more should call at least 2 weeks in advance. Call 1 month ahead for spring and summer tours. Maximum group is 50 people.

Special Information: March and April are busiest tour months because bluebonnets, the Texas State Wildflower, are in bloom. No photography in plant. Since theater holds 50 people, allow some waiting time during summer.

Gift Shop: Country store sells logoed clothing, mugs, scented Frisbees, miniature delivery tractor-trailer, and Texas cookbooks, jellies, and hot sauces. Items gift-wrapped in ice-cream containers. Open Mon-Fri 8:00 AM-5:00 PM, Sat 9:00 AM-3:00 PM. Closed holidays. Catalog available from 800 number.

Directions: Take U.S. 290 to FM 577 North. Blue Bell is 2 miles ahead on right.

Nearby Attractions: Monastery of St. Claire; Rose Emporium; Historic Downtown Brenham; annual Maifest; Washington County Fair.

Collin Street Bakery ~ *fruitcake*

401 West 7th Avenue
Corsicana, TX 75110
(903) 872-8111 / (800) 504-1896

COLLIN STREET BAKERY

Collin Street Bakery is the oldest fruitcake bakery in the U.S.A. (1896). The family-owned company's history is as colorful as the cherries, pineapples, papaya, and pecans on its cakes. The Deluxe Fruitcake has circled the earth aboard an Apollo spacecraft and adorned the tables of royalty, famous entertainers, sports legends, and politicians.

A glass-windowed, metal door opens from the lobby onto a small elevated platform. (Tell someone in the Bake Shop that you want a tour; they'll admit you to the baking area and explain the action. Otherwise, you can watch through the window—minus the aroma and sounds.) From October to mid-December, what you see is one of the most memorable sights of any in this book. A sea of workers, standing in small stalls on both sides of at least three production lines, hand-decorate fruitcakes' tops with pecans and candied fruit. The cakes, at this point only dough in individual round baking pans, flow in from the left. Each worker grabs a cake, decorates it with pecans, then places it back on the line headed for the ovens.

Another worker races about with a big scoop, keeping each decorator's holding bin filled with pecans. During this busy period the staff increases from around 80 employees to over 650 and workers decorate over 30,000 Original Deluxe Fruitcakes each day, with more than 1.5 million made each year. Workers have been known to burst into their own classic holiday song—"I've Been Working on the Fruitcake."

From the platform, look toward the back of the production area at a highly automated bakery operation. To the left, pecan-filled batter is mixed in vats and dough is automatically deposited into baking tins and leveled by hissing machines. To the right, an oven consumes long trays of up to 2,800 cake pans in one swallow. The dough-filled tins travel a precisely timed journey through the long oven and cooling tunnel. As a testament to the fruitcake's quality, hanging from the back of the production area are flags from some of the 200 countries to which

Collin Street ships (Japan is the top fruitcake importer).

Cost: Free
Freebies: Small samples and 10¢ coffee; postcards.
Video Shown: Optional 10-minute video on production process, shown in lobby area.
Reservations Needed: No, except for groups of 8 or more.
Days and Hours: Mon-Fri 8:00 AM-5:00 PM. Closed holidays. October 1 through mid-December, you watch fruitcake production from small landing just inside production area. Other times, take guided tour through baking machinery. Any time of year, need to ask for tour in adjoining Bake Shop.
Plan to Stay: 10 minutes for viewing, plus time for video and Bake Shop.
Minimum Age: None
Disabled Access: Yes
Group Requirements: Requests 1 week's advance notice for groups of 10 or more. No maximum group size, although only 10 people can watch from landing at one time.
Special Information: No photography.
Bakery Shop: Sells over 136 different baked items, including Deluxe Fruitcake, rum cake, pecan pie, and pecan bread. Ask about unboxed factory-second fruitcakes. Also sells logoed T-shirts, caps, and baskets. Open Mon-Thur 7:00 AM-5:30 PM, Fri-Sat 7:00 AM-6:00 PM, and Sun 12:00 PM-6:00 PM. Fruitcake Catalogs and other food items sold under "Cryer Creek Kitchens" name available from (800) 248-3366.
Directions: From I-45, take exit for Hwy. 31 West; becomes 7th Ave. in Corsicana. Bakery is on your left.
Nearby Attractions: Navarro Pecan Co. and Miller Brothers Hat group tours available through Chamber of Commerce (call 903-874-4731); Pioneer Village; Richland-Chambers Lake.

See color photos, page 137

Dr Pepper Bottling ⌒ *soda*

221 South Patrick
Dublin, TX 76446
(817) 445-3466

In 1885, Wade Morrison named his newly developed soft drink after his sweetheart's father, Dr. Charles T. Pepper, hoping to win approval of his marriage proposal. This Dr Pepper plant is the world's oldest (opened in 1891), and still cranks out bottles of D.P. with 1940s machinery. Owner Bill Kloster, a plant employee since 1933, has many stories to tell and proudly displays his extensive collection of Dr Pepper memorabilia. His grandson Mark now helps run the business.

During D.P. bottling, an Amaretto-like aroma fills the air. Reusable glass bottles slowly and noisily shake, rattle, and roll past on old, gray machinery. Gears turn, and bottles rise, drop, and turn like amusement-park carousel horses, then do-si-do and waddle single file down conveyor belts. Since parts are no longer available, many of these vintage machines are held together with ingenuity and baling wire. Compared to the speed of current bottling lines (500 per minute), these machines seem to move in slow motion (32 per minute).

The filling process begins as bottles clatter through the 37-foot-long bottle-washer for sterilization. The bottles pass under the syruper for a squirt of syrup; under 20 valves which fill them with pure carbonated water; and under the crowner for their metal caps. The mixer turns the bottles over in three somersaults, then a worker grabs two bottles in each hand and sets them into bottle-shaped cutouts on a light-board for inspection. After twirling each bottle to ensure consistent color (shows proper mixing) and crack-free bottles, the worker stacks 24 bottles into the slats of each red or yellow wooden crate. People travel great distances to load their cars with these wooden crates of Dr Pepper, made with Imperial Holly pure cane sugar (most bottlers use corn syrup).

In the museum rooms, Bill's artifacts trace Dr Pepper's heritage from its beginnings in an 1885 Waco, Texas, drugstore to the present. His collection includes Dr Pepper signs, billboards, advertisements, every calendar from 1944 to the present, and clocks. His prized possessions are a life-size cardboard cut-out of the red, white, and blue saluting Patriotic Girl, and attention-grabbing motion displays like the carousel with three airplanes bearing the numbers 10, 2, and 4 (representing the times you should drink Dr Pepper for some extra "pep").

Cost: Free. May charge nominal fee in the future.
Freebies: Ice-cold Dr Pepper
Video Shown: No
Reservations Needed: No, except for groups larger than 10 people.
Days and Hours: Mon-Fri 8:00 AM-12:00 PM and 1:00 PM-5:00 PM. Sat 10:00 AM-12:00 PM and 1:00 PM-3:00 PM. Closed Thanksgiving, Christmas, and New Year's. Bottling only on Tuesdays from 9:00 AM-11:30 AM and 1:00 PM-3:30 PM. Other days, they show a bottling simulation.
Plan to Stay: 30 minutes for tour and museum area, plus time in gift shop.
Minimum Age: None
Disabled Access: Yes
Group Requirements: Groups larger than 10 should call 1 week in advance. Groups over 20 people will be split into smaller groups.
Special Information: Dr Pepper Museum, located in a 1906 bottling plant in Waco, TX (90 miles away), chronicles history of soft-drink industry and includes Dr Pepper memorabilia, old television commercials, soda fountain, seasonal exhibits, and classroom. Call (817) 757-1024.
Gift Shop: Sells logoed items including T-shirts, jewelry, towels, and limited-edition watches with old Dr Pepper designs. Can purchase Dr Pepper by case. Working soda fountain next to museum. Open same hours as plant and museum.
Directions: From Fort Worth, take Hwy. 377 South to Dublin. Plant is on left 1 block past center of town.
Nearby Attractions: Just for Dolls Factory (call 817-445-2650); Proctor Dam and Parks.

———— *See color photo, page 138* ————

The Dulcimer Factory ⟋ *dulcimers*

715 S. Washington Street
Fredericksburg, TX 78624
(210) 997-6704

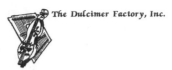

The dulcimer, a stringed folk instrument that originated in West Virginia's Appalachian Mountains in the 1800s, is truly an American instrument. John and Shirley Naylor brought this mountain music to Texas Hill Country in 1986 when they started making dulcimers in their San Antonio garage and selling them at fairs, arts-and-crafts shows, gun shows, rattlesnake roundups, and chili cook-offs. Now their factory and store make and sell eight styles of dulcimers in pecan, walnut, maple, cherry, and cedar. In an industry that's mostly individual artisans, this company is probably the biggest manufacturer.

Your tour begins in the playing room where dulcimers hang from the walls. The tour guide demonstrates how easy it is to play a dulcimer. You learn that the body shape and wood type determine the instrument's sound. Three basic designs evolved: Appalachian hourglass, said to represent a woman's figure (deepest tone, greatest volume); teardrop (bluegrass); and flat, fish-like shape (soft, higher pitch). The number and pattern of holes carved in the body also give each instrument a unique sound. Using a scroll saw with a jeweler's blade, John skillfully carves sound holes in such delicate shapes as hummingbirds, vines, hearts, and flowers, and then wood-burns them.

After admiring the finished dulcimers, you visit the woodshop to see how the process begins. Through windows, you may see 12-foot rough planks being machine-sawed, planed, and sanded into 1/8-inch-thick parts—heads, tails, sides, and bottoms. These thin parts are stacked on shelves, and the potent cedar aroma fills the air. Next is the building room where parts are glued together. You may see a fret board glued to a top, jigs and clamps securing parts, or clothespins holding a thin wooden strip to a dulcimer's inside. This "bracing" provides more surface area for gluing the top and bottom to the sides.

The curvaceous sides are formed when, after the thin wood pieces soak in a water tank, a worker clamps each part around a mold with a heater beneath it. When dry, the wood retains the curves. Peek into the sanding room where workers hand-sand the dulcimers. With your new appreciation for dulcimer-making, try your own hand at playing one in the strumming room at the end of the tour.

Cost: Free

Freebies: Information sheet on mountain dulcimer history.

Video Shown: No

Reservations Needed: Recommended for individuals. Required for groups larger than 8 people.

Days and Hours: Mon-Fri 10:30 AM and 1:30 PM. Closed holidays.

Plan to Stay: 20 minutes, plus time in gift shop.

Minimum Age: None

Disabled Access: Yes

Group Requirements: Groups larger than 8 should call 1 week in advance. Groups larger than 30 will be split into smaller groups. Large-group tours last 40 minutes.

Special Information: Depending on day you visit, you'll see different processes.

Gift Shop: Can purchase dulcimers from factory. Retail store a few blocks away (155 E. Main St.) sells kits as well as finished Broomstick, Hill Country, and Appalachian Mountain dulcimers; books, accessories, and listening tapes. Open Mon-Sat 10:00 AM-5:30 PM, Sun 11:00 AM-5:00 PM. Closed holidays. Catalog available from above number.

Directions: From San Antonio, take Hwy. 87 into Fredericksburg. Factory is on right just before town.

Nearby Attractions: In Kerrville 25 miles away, Mooney Aircraft tour (see page 234) and James Avery Craftsmen (visitors center has jewelry-making video and observation window; call 210-895-1122); Enchanted Rock; Nimitz Museum; Lady Bird Johnson Park; Willow City Driving Loop; Old German stone houses; antique stores.

Imperial Sugar Company   ⟿   *sugar*

198 Kemper Street
Sugar Land, TX 77478
(713) 491-9181

IMPERIAL SUGAR COMPANY
A DIVISION OF IMPERIAL HOLLY CORPORATION

Imperial has refined sugar in Sugar Land (a small town just outside Houston) for over 150 years, making Imperial the oldest continuing commercial enterprise in Texas. On the original site of the 1843 mill and surrounding sugarcane fields now stands a large industrial complex that produces more than 3½ million pounds of refined cane sugar a day. This tour shows you what's involved in making all that sweet stuff.

In the warehouse, which can store 40 million pounds of raw sugar, watch workers use small front-end loaders to remove the raw sugar from open boxcars. A conveyor-belt system carries the raw sugar to the top of the warehouse, where it rains down to form light-brown hills on the floor below.

For safety reasons, the only other refining steps you see are in the Melt House, where centrifugal machines noisily spin and wash the raw sugar to remove molasses and impurities. Overhead pipes then move the washed raw sugar to large, enclosed melt tanks where it is mixed with warm syrup and hot water to form sugar liquor. The guide's explanation at the beginning of the tour helps you better understand what you see, as the hiss and rumble of the machines make it hard to ask questions.

The sugar goes through many more refining steps than you might expect before you see it again in the packaging room. For example, in the Char House (the factory's towering, eight-story red-brick landmark), the sugar liquor is gravity-filtered through long cylinders that contain cattle-bone charcoal. Most of the remaining color and impurities are absorbed by the bone char. In the packing room, you'll stand next to machines that fill, weigh, and package sugar into containers from single-serving packets to 100-pound bags. The sweet-smelling air, the rhythmic machines, and the constant movement of colored bags and boxes have an almost hypnotic effect.

Cost: Free

Freebies: Brochure explains processing of raw sugar into refined cane sugar.

Video Shown: No, however tour guide's detailed explanation of refining process in visitors building starts the tour.

Reservations Needed: No, except for groups of 10 or more.

Days and Hours: Mon-Fri 10:00 AM and 2:00 PM. Closed holidays. Calling first is recommended; refinery occasionally operates on 4-day work schedule.

Plan to Stay: 1 hour for presentation and tour, plus time in gift shop.

Minimum Age: 3rd grade for school groups. No minimum for children with their parents.

Disabled Access: Refinery has old buildings with steps throughout.

Group Requirements: Groups of 10 or more should call 2 weeks in advance. Maximum group is 60 people.

Special Information: No photography. Any jewelry above waist (including watches and rings) must be removed, along with all items from top shirt pocket. Tour involves short bus ride and outdoor walking. On rainy days, tour does not visit raw-sugar warehouse. Commemorative markers on refinery grounds note its unusual history.

Gift Shop: Sells logoed items including caps, T-shirts, mugs, aprons, and golf items. Also sells Imperial Sugar cookbooks, a company tradition since 1915. Open after tours.

Directions: Take I-59 South to Hwy. 6 exit in Sugar Land. Turn right (north) onto Hwy. 6. At Alt. 90, turn right and then left onto Ulrich. Tour building is on right immediately after railroad tracks.

Nearby Attractions: Frito-Lay tour (call 713-342-0951); George Ranch; Confederate Museum; Fort Bend Museum. Houston's attractions 15-30 miles away, including Anheuser-Busch (Budweiser) Brewery tour (call 713-670-1695), Borden Ice Cream factory tour (call 713-744-3700); Space Center Houston tour (call 713-244-2100).

Jardine's Texas Foods

Texas-style foods

Jardine Ranch
Buda, TX 78610
(512) 295-4600

After touring Austin and Texas Hill Country sites, Jardine's authentic Texas-style foods round out a Texas gastronomic experience. The graceful live oak trees, restored chuck wagon, gazebo, and oak rocking chairs on the wide front porch of the company's headquarters all welcome you to the Jardine ranch and invite you to "set a spell."

Head honcho Dan, often clad in cowboy boots and western hat, his wife Lisa, and their grown children make you feel at home at this family-run company. A visit to Jardine's combines ranch relaxation; a warm, homey feeling; and an opportunity to view the bottling and packaging of hot sauce, barbecue sauce, chili, and jalapeño peppers through windows in the limestone ranchhouse "factory."

Legend has it that after many years of cooking for cowboys on trail drives, D. L. Jardine settled in Texas Hill Country. As a chuckwagon "cookie," he added various combinations of chiles, peppers, and spices to beans, meat, and cornbread. Since 1979, D. L.'s nephew Dan and his family have produced foods based on these early recipes—initially packaging them in the family's garage and now on this peaceful 30-acre ranch. To develop new recipes, Dan researches the history and culture of foods that characterize Texas heritage.

As you stroll outdoors under the sloped, ridged-tin roof and awning, look through several windows into a small section of the factory. If they're making Jardine's popular Chisholm Trail Texas Chili Bag O' Fixin's, watch hair-netted workers hand-fill reusable cloth bags with cellophane-wrapped spice packets. Seated at a long table, they grab packets from red plastic bins, insert them into the cloth bags, and pull a string to tighten each bag shut.

In the next area, items are hand-packed. Workers stuff jalapeños, olives, or pickles into glass jars. Through the last window, you'll see the horseshoe-shaped automatic filling line. Sauces, such as barbecue and picante, simmer in the three kettles to the left. The sauce passes through a pipe and a funnel into the bottles, which are capped, suction-sealed, labeled, and sent along a conveyor belt to the shipping warehouse. You leave craving the nearest Texas-style restaurant or your own kitchen so you can whip up some of these specialties.

Cost: Free

Freebies: Bottle of Texas Champagne-brand hot pepper sauce; mail-order catalog.

Video Shown: No

Reservations Needed: Preferred; required for groups larger than 10 people.

Days and Hours: Mon-Fri 9:00 AM-4:00 PM. No production during 12:00 PM-1:00 PM lunch break. Closed holidays.

Plan to Stay: 15 minutes for tour, plus time for grounds, historic graveyard, and gift display case.

Minimum Age: No

Disabled Access: Yes

Group Requirements: Groups larger than 10 should call 2 days in advance. Food tastings are arranged for groups.

Special Information: Picnic tables and open-pit barbecue available on request.

Display Case: Sells Jardine's authentic Texas-style foods, including salsas, condiments, spices, and other ranch-style recipes. Catalog available from (800) 544-1880. Future plans for general store and restaurant on the grounds.

Directions: From I-35, take Exit 221 for Loop 4 toward Buda. Travel 1.1 miles and turn right just past the D. L. Jardine's sign. Turn right onto Chisholm Trail, which leads to the offices. Park on left.

Nearby Attractions: Texas Hatters tour (see page 237); Austin's attractions, including the State Capitol, Lyndon B. Johnson Library & Museum, and 6th Street, are 11 miles away.

J.C. Penney Museum   ⟶   *retail stores and catalog*

6501 Legacy Drive
Plano, TX 75024
(214) 431-TOUR

JCPenney

In 1902, James Cash Penney opened "The Golden Rule" cash-only dry-goods store in the small mining town of Kemmerer, Wyoming. With 36 stores in 1913, the company was renamed J.C. Penney Company and the "Penney Idea," seven mission-statement principles that guide the company today, was formulated. Now, with over 1,300 stores nationwide and a thriving catalog business, the company has a new corporate headquarters to take it into the future. You can take a guided tour of this state-of-the-art home office, and also visit the company's historical museum.

In the central rotunda at the heart of this 125-acre complex is a larger-than-life bronze sculpture of Mr. Penney. A replica of the first Golden Rule store is carved into his desk. A small, open museum area down the hall from the statue displays well-worn, yellowed, early advertisements through recent catalog covers. A replica of the first Kemmerer store—including shopkeeper, dry goods, and original wooden counter—lines one wall. Other displays illustrate company development, including credit cards (1957) and the first electronic point-of-sale system (1960s). Lighted red dots on a map show Penney's growth over the decades.

You will be most impressed with the expansiveness of this three-story glass-atriumed megastructure. With a portion of the profits from selling its 45-story New York City skyscraper (company headquarters 1964-1987), Penney purchased 429 acres in rural Plano, Texas. This 1.9-million-square-foot office unites over 3,300 corporate "associates," Mr. Penney's name for his first employees, who worked "with" rather than "for" him.

The open floor plan and walkway seating areas facilitate communication between associates. Company day-care services and fitness facilities promote employee morale. A robotic mail-delivery system and on-site direct video broadcast system connecting all 1,300 stores enhance productivity. After seeing many of its features, you'll agree that this futuristic home office—located on Legacy Drive—is a legacy to the founder and to the company's associates.

Cost: Free

Freebies: Museum brochures

Video Shown: Small theater shows short nostalgic films, including 1950s interviews with Mr. and Mrs. Penney. Nine-screen video wall flashes commercials and building construction videos.

Reservations Needed: No for museum. Yes for Home Office tour (individuals and groups call 2 weeks in advance, 214-431-TOUR).

Days and Hours: Museum: Mon-Fri 8:00 AM-5:00 PM. Tour: Tue-Thur 10:00 AM and 2:00 PM. Closed holidays.

Plan to Stay: 20 minutes for museum (1 hour for guided tour and museum) plus time for lunch in company cafeteria, where curved glass walls frame a waterpool with fountain.

Minimum Age: None

Disabled Access: Yes

Group Requirements: For Home Office tour, groups should call 2 weeks in advance. Groups over 25 will be split into smaller groups. Other tour times may be requested.

Special Information: Guided tours of museum and company archives can be arranged for individuals and groups 2 weeks in advance; call 214-431-7925.

Gift Shop: JC's, down escalator from museum, sells logoed clothing, pictures of building, and other items. Open Mon-Fri 8:00 AM-3:00 PM.

Directions: From Dallas, take Dallas Tollway North to Legacy Dr. exit. Turn left onto Legacy Dr., then right onto Communications Pkwy. Turn left onto Headquarters Dr. Park in either garage. Tours meet at Mr. Penney's statue in center of building (main rotunda).

Nearby Attractions: Mary Kay factory tour and company museum (see page 233); American Airlines C.R. Smith Museum (see page 225); Dallas' downtown attractions, including Dealey Plaza and JFK Sixth Floor Museum, are 20–30 miles away.

Mary Kay Cosmetics *cosmetics and skin care products*

8787 N. Stemmons Freeway
Dallas, TX 75247
(214) 905-5720

Inscribed at the entrance to the company museum is Mary Kay Ash's motto: "You can do anything in the world that you want to do if you want it badly enough and you are willing to pay the price." This determination and Mary Kay's ability to motivate and reward her (mostly female) sales force has made Mary Kay Cosmetics—founded in 1963 by Mary Kay and her son Richard—into one of America's most admired companies.

A shuttle bus takes you from corporate headquarters to the aromatic manufacturing facility where 38 lines fill and package over 200 Mary Kay products. After viewing the product-manufacturing machines, stroll past the packaging lines. Notice the pink support columns and workers wearing maroon pants and jackets with pink shirts. On the eye shadow line, pink plastic bottoms, clear tops, and eye shadow refills merge on a freeway system that, together with human hands, packages approximately 65,000 per 10-hour shift. Once mascara, concealer, or lip-gloss tubes are filled, workers manually insert applicators with a gentle twist. It's fun to follow a bottle through the fragrance line—filling, manually inserting straws and atomizer tops, stamping down lids, and hand-packing perfume bottles.

The tour highlight, however, is the waxy-smelling lipstick line. Liquid lipstick—wax, emollients, and color—is pumped into oblong metal molds, which are stacked onto an iced cooling table to solidify. Workers manually insert each lipstick bullet into its tube. Upright tubes march into a glass-enclosed oven where flames melt the outer layer to give the lipstick a shine. The next time you apply (or watch someone apply) lipstick, you'll appreciate this labor that enhances women's beauty.

The guided tour's grand finale is the possibility of seeing Mary Kay's personal office at the corporate headquarters, with its pink leather reception-area sofas, porcelain figurines given to Mary Kay by her sales force, and her desk. You can visit "The Mary Kay Museum: Dreams Come True" in the corporate office lobby apart from the tour and without reservations. Its art-deco white, pink, and black granite floors and brass-trimmed dark wood cases artfully display mannequins wearing director's suits since 1963, Mary Kay product lines, and many photographs and awards.

Cost: Free

Freebies: Skin care product sample, pink warm fuzzy, and brochure.

Video Shown: Several videos in museum cover company history, manufacturing process, company career opportunities, and annual seminars.

Reservations Needed: No for museum. Yes for manufacturing facility tours. Individuals, call 214-905-5720 at least 1 day in advance. Groups, see below.

Days and Hours: Museum: Mon-Fri 9:00 AM-5:00 PM. Tours: Mon-Thur 10:30 AM and 2:00 PM. Closed holidays.

Plan to Stay: 20 minutes for museum and videos; 1 hour for guided factory tour, including Mary Kay's office.

Minimum Age: None

Disabled Access: Yes for corporate building and most of factory tour (if one flight of stairs is one too many, call ahead for alternative arrangements). Shuttle buses require wheelchairs folded and carried on board.

Group Requirements: Groups larger than 25 must call at least 1 week in advance for reservations. Groups larger than 15 will be split into smaller groups.

Special Information: Photography allowed in museum and office, but not in plant. Depending on Mary Kay's schedule, tour may not include her office.

Gift Shop: No. (Planned for future.)

Directions: From Stemmons Freeway, take Regal Row exit. Call for change of location fall of 1995.

Nearby Attractions: American Airlines C.R. Smith Museum (see page 225) and J.C. Penney headquarters and museum (see page 232) 20–30 miles away; downtown Dallas attractions, including JFK Museum and West End Marketplace.

Mooney Aircraft *light airplanes*

Louis Schreiner Field
Kerrville, TX 78208
(210) 896-6000

Established in 1948, Mooney is one of the few single-engine, light-airplane manufacturers left in the U.S.A. The high cost of product liability insurance has forced many manufacturers out of the market and cut production to about 10 percent of 1960s output. Mooney prides itself on making planes that rival the speed and performance of larger craft. The walking tour through the plant gives you a close-up view of light-plane construction.

Your tour begins in the preflight building, a modified hangar where the planes receive their instrument panels, seats, and other cabin accessories. Since planes are not painted until they're completely built and tested, most of them still wear their naked aluminum skin. Peek inside a plane—it looks like a mangle of wires and tubes with the "yoke" (steering wheel) sticking out.

Walk along the concrete floor into the appropriately-named "hammer house," where you'll see and hear everything from a basic hand-held hammer to a 2,500-ton press used to shape pieces of metal and aluminum into parts for Mooney and other major commercial aircraft manufacturers. The big green presses are as deep below the surface as they are high above the ground. Workers grind and smooth the edges of the parts on buffers, adding to the industrial cacophony.

The plane is built in the cavernous assembly building. No conveyors or automated assembly lines are used to form the plane or transport parts. Your tour guide takes you through the subassembly stations, where you'll watch a wing constructed in one area and the tail section in another. Jigs (the frames that hold parts together while they are being worked on) are everywhere. Discover how workers stretch the aluminum skin around the steel-tube frame that is the skeleton of all Mooneys. When the wings are married to the fuselage, with workers rolling around underneath the plane to bolt and fasten them together, the silver bird finally looks like it will fly.

Cost: Free
Freebies: Product literature
Video Shown: No
Reservations Needed: No, except for groups larger than 8 people.
Days and Hours: Mon-Fri 10:00 AM. Closed holidays. Usually closed the week between Christmas and New Year's, and 1 week in July or August.
Plan to Stay: 45 minutes for tour, plus time for gift counter.
Minimum Age: No
Disabled Access: Yes
Group Requirements: Groups larger than 8 should make reservations 2 days ahead. No maximum group size.
Special Information: Photography allowed only in final assembly area. Mooney Aircraft Pilots Association Annual Homecoming, second weekend in October. Mooney also subcontracts for several large aerospace companies. Wear comfortable shoes for this indoor and outdoor walking tour.
Gift Counter: Sells logoed items, including hats, T-shirts, mugs, and jackets. Product list available at above number. Open after tour upon request. Information on purchasing planes available from (800) 456-3033.
Directions: From I-10, take Hwy. 27 towards Comfort. Go through towns of Comfort and Centerpoint. Immediately after Kerrville Airport is Al Mooney Rd. Turn right and follow road around to company's offices. Park in lot past security station.
Nearby Attractions: James Avery Craftsmen (visitors center has jewelry-making video and observation window; call 210-895-1122); Sims Spur Company in Bandera (see page 236); The Dulcimer Factory tour (see page 229) about 25 miles away, in Fredericksburg; Texas Hill Country attractions include Cowboy Artist America Museum and Y.O. Ranch tour with exotic and native animals (call 210-640-3222).

Nocona Athletic

208 Walnut Street
Nocona, TX 76255
(817) 825-3326

*baseball gloves
and football equipment*

Nokona

Nocona, Texas, is the leather goods capital of the Southwest. Nocona Athletic Goods Company started making Nokona baseball gloves and other sporting goods during the Depression. While U.S. sporting-goods companies began shifting labor-intensive baseball-glove production overseas in the early 1960s, Nocona proudly stayed at home. (Current imports represent 98% of glove sales nationwide.) The Nokona ball glove is one of three glove lines still made in the U.S.A. and the plant tour gives you the chance to see all of the production steps. While workers have some help from machines, you'll notice that the process is far from automated.

Making baseball and softball gloves begins with selecting the correct leather, which Nocona does "on site," not overseas. The tour guide passes around pieces of cowhide and kangaroo leathers so you can feel the contrasting textures, and explains the differences between leather used in today's gloves compared to that of previous decades. Each glove's 14 to 18 leather pieces are die-cut from big leather sheets. Workers lay a metal frame in the shape of a hand on the correct spot and use a press to cut out a piece. They use experience gained from guiding patterns here for the past 50 years.

After stamping the name and logo on the leather, workers meticulously sew the pieces together. Up to this point the glove has been built inside-out, so it's turned right side out one finger at a time on a hot iron. Workers then weave a long needle in and out of the glove to lace the leather together before stretching it on hot irons and applying leather-conditioning oils. You'll be tempted to pick up a glove and play catch in the middle of the factory.

From the aroma of leather, move to the smell of glue in the department that assembles football equipment, such as shoulder pads and helmets. Workers construct this equipment mostly from pre-molded plastic parts and shock-absorbing pads. Don't forget to visit the company's small collection of old leather baseball mitts and football helmets, conjuring images of Ty Cobb and Knute Rockne in the years of day games, grass gridirons, and all-U.S.A.-made sporting goods.

Cost: Free
Freebies: Product catalogs used for wholesale trade
Video Shown: No
Reservations Needed: Preferred
Days and Hours: Mon-Fri 8:00 AM-12:00 PM and 1:00 PM-4:00 PM. Closed holidays, 2 weeks at Christmas, and 2 weeks around July 4th.
Plan to Stay: 1 hour
Minimum Age: None
Disabled Access: Yes
Group Requirements: No minimum. Maximum group size is 30 people with 1 day's advance notice.
Special Information: Glue smell may initially bother some people.
Gift Shop: Nocona Boot Company Factory Outlet (6 blocks away on Hwy. 82) sells first- and second-quality Nokona gloves.
Directions: From Dallas, take I-35 to Hwy. 82 West exit in Gainesville. Stay on Hwy. 82 West into Nocona, turn right at Clay St., and left on Walnut. Company is in big red-brick building on right.
Nearby Attractions: Nocona Boot Company tour (call 817-825-3321); Nocona Belt Company tour (call 817-825-3271); Justin Park; Lake Nocona.

Sims Spur Co.   *spurs and bits*

1108 Main Street
Bandera, TX 78003
(210) 796-3716

While some people wear Rolexes, cowboys wear boot spurs. As Pax Irvine, the company's owner and a professional rodeo roper, likes to explain, cowboys "spend more money on spurs than on their wives." In Bandera, Texas, the self-proclaimed "Cowboy Capital of the World," Sims Spur Company makes about 200 pairs of spurs and 100 bits per week.

Sims has a "foothold" as one of the largest spur-making companies in the world. You watch the process by going through the glass-windowed door marked "Employees Only," at the back of the retail store (first, ask the store manager). The production area resembles a garage metal-shop with small presses, buffing and grinding machines, metal die molds, and parts for spurs and bits scattered about on racks and tables. As you walk around the production area, the workers will try to show and explain what they do.

Many of the spurs' stainless-steel or blued bands and shanks come from a metal-casting company, although some are shaped right here on the 50-ton punch press. (For you city folk, the band is the U-shaped frame that fits to the boot heel; the shank extends from the back of the band.) Workers weld the shank to the band, then smooth the weld and further contour the spur on grinding machines. Another worker may hammer away on the anvil to add a unique shape to the shank.

At the end of the shank is the "rowel," the round-tipped part that rotates like a wheel. Workers punch out all different sizes of rowels on the press, some looking like round widgets, while others resemble small starfish. The silversmith adds the artistry to the spur, whether it be initials, brands, rubies, turquoise stones, or a twisted wire border. Once the spurs are polished and shiny, they're ready to be worn by Sims customers—working cowboys, or maybe celebrities like Troy Aikman, George Strait, Bum Phillips, or ZZ Top who wear spurs as a fashion statement.

Cost: Free
Freebies: No
Video Shown: No
Reservations Needed: No, except for groups larger than 5 people.
Days and Hours: Mon-Fri 8:00 AM-5:00 PM. No production 12:00 PM-1:00 PM. Closed holidays.
Plan to Stay: 15 minutes for tour, plus time for gift shop and display case of historical spurs.
Minimum Age: None
Disabled Access: Yes
Group Requirements: Groups larger than 5 should call 1 day in advance. No maximum group size.
Special Information: Production area is through the door at the back of the retail store. Hot in the summer. Do not touch or pick up anything in the production area.
Retail Store: Sells all styles of Sims boot spurs and horse bits, spur-shaped novelty items (including ashtrays, bookends, door knockers, and baby teethers), Western-style jewelry and belt buckles, saddles, ropes, cowboy-related books, and logoed clothing. Open Mon-Fri 8:00 AM-5:00 PM, plus May through Labor Day and November and December Sat 9:00 AM-4:00 PM. Catalog available from (800) 441-0804.
Directions: From San Antonio, take Texas Hwy. 16 West to Bandera. Hwy. 16 is Main St. in Bandera. Company is in bright red building at west end of town.
Nearby Attractions: Guest/dude ranches; Hill Country State Natural Area; Medina River; festivals, including Rodeo (Memorial Day-Labor Day), November Hunters weekend, and July Apple festival; Kerrville's attractions, including Mooney Aircraft (see page 234), James Avery Craftsmen jewelry-making observation window (call 210-895-1122), and Cowboy Artist Museum, are about 20 miles away.

Texas Hatters ⟋ *western-style hats*

5003 Overpass
Buda, TX 78610
(512) 295-4287 / (800) 421-4287

By such titles as "Dr. of Mad Hattery," "Wizard of Lids," and "A 'Manny' of Many Hats," you know that Manny Gammage is no ordinary hatmaker. He is one of the few custom western-style U.S. hatmakers left. A character in his own right, he has hatted such personalities as Ronald Reagan, Howard Cosell, Jerry Jeff Walker, Burt Reynolds, and Willie Nelson. Photographs, many autographed by the famous people wearing Manny's hats, form a collage on the shop walls. Baseball caps, each with its own story, hang from the ceiling's wooden beams.

Once inside the small store, make your way over to the wooden counter and take a stool. Amidst all the clutter, you will probably find chain-smoking Manny, often with a measuring tape around his neck, adding the finishing touches to a customer's hat. Ask Manny to guide you through the wooden saloon-door marked "Employees Only," into the small production area. Be careful not to touch anything as you work your way through the cramped quarters to the back.

Hats start as unshaped hat-bodies made of beaver and hare's hair. From cubbyholes lining the walls, a worker selects the correct solid wooden block for the desired hat style and the wearer's head shape. After steam-heating the hat, he uses his muscles to stretch it over the heavy block. With an iron that weighs 15 pounds in the morning but feels like 45 pounds by evening, the worker irons and hand-sands the brim in circular stroking motions. He also irons out the crown as it slowly rotates on a contraption clamped to the wooden work-table. These processes are repeated and fine-tuned to correctly shape each hat.

As you squeeze your way into the next area, Manny explains that there are "too damn many steps" involved in making a hat. Study the well-worn poplar-wood disks or "flanges" stored in slotted shelves. Look for the LBJ flange—you'll recognize it by the letters LBJ on the side. Sandbags are lowered onto a wooden flange to flatten the hat's brim. In the next small area, an old Singer sewing machine puts bindings in the brim; leather sweatbands and satin linings are sewn in by hand. More personality comes from the hatband—elephant hide, snakeskin, lizard, leather, and feathers. But the tour's highlight is Manny himself! Even if you don't buy a hat, you'll leave with some great stories.

Cost: Free
Freebies: A token souvenir
Video Shown: No
Reservations Needed: Recommended; required for groups larger than 10 people.
Days and Hours: Tue-Sat 9:30 AM-5:30 PM. Closed holidays and week of July 4th.
Plan to Stay: 20 minutes
Minimum Age: None. Children require adult supervision.
Disabled Access: Yes, however, difficult maneuvering in tight quarters.
Group Requirements: Groups larger than 10 will be split into smaller groups and need to call at least 1 week in advance.
Special Information: Best time to watch workers is in the morning. Hot in summer. You may miss out on Manny's stories if you visit during deer hunting season, when he's out.
Retail Store: Sells custom-made hats for 1-week delivery. Most popular styles are high-roller and hunter, both in black. Open same hours as above. Catalog available from 800 number.
Directions: Take I-35 to Exit 220. Exit puts you on Overpass Rd. Look for 45-foot-high hat sign.
Nearby Attractions: Jardine's Texas Foods tour (see page 231); Austin's attractions, including 6th Street, Lyndon B. Johnson Library and Museum, and Capitol Building, are 11 miles away.

Kennecott Utah Copper ⟨⟩ *copper mine*
Kennecott's Bingham Canyon Mine Visitors Center
Bingham Canyon, UT 84006
(801) 322-7300

If you moved Chicago's Sears Tower to the bottom of the Bingham Canyon Copper Mine, it wouldn't even reach halfway to the top of the mine. In fact, at over 2½ miles across and a half-mile deep, this mine is the deepest human-made excavation on earth. In 1906, steam shovels began eating away at a mountain that divided Bingham Canyon. Today huge rotary drills and electric shovels have replaced steam shovels, and an open pit has replaced the mountain. Kennecott is still mining copper from Bingham Canyon, which has yielded over 14 million tons of copper—more than any other mine in history.

Your visit begins with an unbelievable view of the mine from an overlook. The view encompasses hundreds of millions of years of the earth's history and lots of brown dirt in a circular pattern. Look down at the workers and machines who remove about 300,000 tons of material daily, knowing that soon you will learn exactly how miners remove the copper ore from this canyon.

Inside the Visitors Center, eight exhibits teach you everything from the mine's history to the daily uses of copper and how Kennecott protects the environment through reclamation and revegetation projects. For those especially interested in history, one exhibit tells how the surrounding area of Utah developed and prospered along with the copper industry. You will also learn about the people of Kennecott and the company's community efforts.

In the center's 80-seat theater, watch a video which provides a condensed explanation of the entire copper-mining process, as well as some of the history behind the mine and its neighboring communities. As you drive away from the Bingham Canyon Mine, be sure to glance back at the mountainside you saw as you drove in; you now have a new appreciation of the mining industry, copper, and Bingham Canyon.

Cost: $2 per vehicle, $1 for motorcycles, with all funds going to local charities.
Freebies: Company brochures
Video Shown: 12-minute video explaining mine history and operation.
Reservations Needed: No, but recommended at beginning and end of season to verify Visitors Center is open.
Days and Hours: Open April through end of October, weather permitting. Mon-Sun 8:00 AM-8:00 PM. Closed holidays.
Plan to Stay: 1 hour
Minimum Age: None
Disabled Access: Yes
Group Requirements: None. $20 entrance fee for tour buses. Booklet available for educators and tour guides.
Special Information: Tour does not permit you to go down into the mine. However, observation deck and exhibits offer views of the mine.
Gift Shop: Sells souvenirs, T-shirts, and postcards, as well as educational books, small rocks, and minerals. Shop is operated by local Lions Club, and is not part of Kennecott. Open same hours as Visitors Center.
Directions: From Salt Lake City, take I-15 South to 7200 South exit, and turn right. Turn right onto 7800 South, which turns into Bingham Hwy. Take Bingham Hwy. toward Copperton. Mine is visible on mountainside ahead. Follow signs to Kennecott's Bingham Canyon Mine.
Nearby Attractions: Salt Lake City's attractions, including Salt Lake Temple, Great Salt Lake, and ski resorts, are about 25 miles away; Mormon Church headquarters.

Basketville 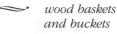   *wood baskets and buckets*
Main Street
Putney, VT 05346
(802) 387-4351

Basket-weaving requires much more skill and hard work than the college gut course with the same name. Basketville employees, most of whom have been making baskets for years, are proud to continue the American tradition of hand-weaving baskets.

Weaving baskets seems to come naturally for the Wilson family, Basketville's owners/operators. Cassius Wilson bought an 1842 basket shop to put his 13 kids to work. His son Frank started Basketville in 1941. Today the company is the world's largest producer of genuine American splint baskets and its seven retail stores offer a large assortment of baskets.

All Basketville baskets begin with wet Vermont ash logs. Basket-makers use draw shavers to slice thin "splints" off 60-to-80-inch planks. The planks move back and forth through a long blade that whittles the splints like meat being sliced at a deli. These knotless splints will be used for the "filling," or horizontal weave, while shorter splints become the basket's "standards," or upright pieces. A worker places standards vertically onto an easel containing a pattern, then interlocks the standards by horizontally alternating them in front of and behind the verticals, thus weaving a flat basket bottom. After the bottom receives a hot water bath for pliability, a hydraulic press bends up the sides. Thin filling is woven between the wide side-slats.

The hooping area greets you with loud banging and hissing noises. Wooden strips ("hoops") are removed from a steambox and attached by hand with a pneumatic nailer to form the basket's rim. A hammer and good old elbow grease do the trick for odd-sized baskets. Once the edges are sawed off, baskets dry in the kiln, shrinking the weave and setting the wood's "memory" to create tightly woven baskets.

In another area, workers make pine buckets. Modeled and sized after those used by Vermont farmers to store maple sugar, the buckets are assembled without nails. A bottom fits into grooves in the bucket's side pieces ("staves"). The staves are drier than the surrounding air and expand to press against the rim, holding everything tightly in place.

Watching the creation of these baskets and buckets you'll be impressed by the New England ethic of hard work and craftsmanship. You'll also be impressed by another traditional New England value, frugality. Not an ounce of wood is wasted—sawdust is used for animal bedding, bark for mulch, and the balance as fuel for Basketville.

Cost: Free
Freebies: Yes, varies.
Video Shown: No
Reservations Needed: No, except for groups larger than 15 people.
Days and Hours: Mon-Fri 9:00 AM-2:00 PM and by advance arrangement.
Plan to Stay: 30 minutes for tour, plus time for store
Minimum Age: No
Disabled Access: Yes
Group Requirements: Large groups split into groups of 15. Please give at least 2 days' advance notice.
Special Information: Company started regular public tours in 1994, so process and route still evolving.
Retail Store: Baskets, buckets, and wooden houseware items (for gardening, picnicking, and carrying hot pies) overflow into aisles and dangle from ceiling. Imported items include Shaker baskets, tough willow pet beds, sturdy wicker furniture, and silk flowers. Look for owner's collection of woven wicker animals hanging from the ceiling. Open summer/fall Mon-Sun 8:00 AM-9:00 PM, Winter Mon-Sun 8:00 AM-5:00 PM.
Directions: Take I-91 to Exit 4. Take Rt. 5 North to Putney. Basketville is in town center. Tour starts in retail store.
Nearby Attractions: Santa's Land; Putney Nursery; Green Mountain Spinnery tour (call 802-387-4528); Catamount Brewing Company tour (call 802-296-2248); Harlow's Sugarhouse.

Ben & Jerry's 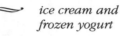 *ice cream and frozen yogurt*
Route 100
Waterbury, VT 05676
(802) 244-TOUR

Given Ben & Jerry's down-home image, you'd expect to see hundreds of workers using individual churns to make its ice creams and yogurts. Instead, from a glass-enclosed, temperature-controlled mezzanine area you look down at a state-of-the-art ice cream factory that can turn out 180,000 pints per day. The grounds are filled with whimsical interactive displays and games, like the "Wheel-O-Flavor," that let you experience ice-cream-making and ease the waiting time for this very popular tour.

Your guide goes down onto the factory floor to identify the different equipment and explain the process, with most of the action happening inside enclosed machines. Ice cream and frozen yogurt begin with an unflavored base mix stored in the 36° tank room. The mix travels to the labeled flavor vat, to the freezer (where it gets the consistency of soft-serve), into the fruit and chunk feeder, to the special automatic pint-filler that handles "chunk intensive" flavors, to the pint bundler, and finally to the spiral hardener. In this last step, the ice cream freezes solid at a temperature of –60°.

On the production area's back wall a giant banner announces an impressive statistic, like the number of pounds of cookie dough used during the past year in making their top-selling flavor. Rock music blares down on the factory floor, courtesy of the Joy Gang. Every half-hour a quality control worker grabs pints from the freezer, slices them open with a machete, and inspects for the proper number of chunks per bite (among other things). On the way out, you may get to watch this inspection. Make sure you peek into the flavor laboratory to see new flavors in development; and look at the Hall of Fame's colorful pictures, posters, and paraphernalia that humorously document the company's proud, offbeat history.

Cost: $1 per person; half the proceeds go to various community and Vermont non-profit groups. Children 12 and under, free.

Freebies: Fresh-made flavor-of-the-day sample hoisted from the production line and Ben & Jerry's button.

Video Shown: Funky 10-minute multi-projector slide show on how two childhood friends turned what they learned from a $5 correspondence course on ice-cream-making into a multi-million-dollar business that shares its success with its employees and the community.

Reservations Needed: No, except for groups of 10 or more.

Days and Hours: Mon-Sun 9:00 AM-5:00 PM (until 8:00 PM in summer). Tours at least every 30 minutes with tickets given out on a first come, first served basis. No production on Sundays, holidays, company celebration days, and Wed and Sat after 3:00 PM, although tours see video of the production line operation. Call tour hotline number for up-to-date schedules.

Plan to Stay: 30 minutes for tour and slide show, plus time for the wait, grounds, displays, and gift shop. Grounds are a low-key family ice-cream park.

Minimum Age: None

Disabled Access: Yes

Group Requirements: Reservations required for groups of 10 or more. Call (802) 244-5641, ext. 2289. No reservations accepted for tours during July and August.

Special Information: Afternoon tours fill up quickly, particularly in summer. Allow for waiting time.

Gift Shop: Scoop Shop features all Ben & Jerry's flavors. Gift shop, with piped-in folk music, offers Vermont gifts, logoed clothes, MeMOOrabilia (like cow socks and floating farm Moobile), and other stuff. Open Mon-Sun 9:00 AM-6:00 PM (9:00 PM in summer). Catalog available from (802) 244-1775.

Directions: Take I-89 to Exit 10. Go north on Rt. 100 toward Stowe. Factory is about 1 mile ahead on left. Look for giant picture of planet Earth outside factory at top of hill.

Nearby Attractions: Cabot Creamery Annex Store; Stowe and Sugarbush ski areas; Cold Hollow Cider Mill; Mt. Mansfield.

Cabot Creamery ⟿ *cheese*

Main Street
Cabot, VT 05647
(802) 563-2231

On a hillside in Vermont, sparkling white 130,000-gallon milk silos emblazoned with the red and green Cabot Creamery logo overlook the entrance to the visitors center and plant where some of the nation's best sharp cheddar cheese is made (winner of U.S. Championship Cheese Contest). This guided tour shows you how the cooperative creamery converts milk from local farms into famous Vermont cheddar cheeses, and also how it packages its yogurts, cottage cheese, and sour cream.

You'll peer through glass windows into the packaging and processing rooms, where workers fill large cooking vats with quality tested, heat-treated milk and a starter culture. The curd that forms is cut with stainless-steel knives which help separate the curd from the whey. Once the whey is separated and drained off, workers vigorously mix the curd on huge metal finishing tables to "cheddar" it until the correct pH level is reached.

In overhead towers, the curd is then pressed into 42-pound blocks or round stainless-steel frames to create cheese wheels. Every 90 seconds another block emerges from a tower and enters an airtight cellophane bag for proper aging (9 months for sharp cheddar, 14 months for extra-sharp). With the cheese-making process in various stages of production, your 10-minute walk captures the 5 hours needed for every vat of milk to become cheese (33,000 pounds of whole milk in each vat yields approximately 3,500 pounds of cheese).

Cost: $1 donation supports various Vermont causes and projects. Children under 12, free.
Freebies: Cabot cheese and dip samples under the "Grazing Encouraged" sign in gift shop.
Video Shown: 10-minute video on history of Vermont farming and dairy industry, development of Cabot Cooperative Creamery in 1919, and highlights of processes used to make different Cabot products.
Reservations Needed: No, except for groups larger than 40 people.

Days and Hours: Mid-June to mid-October Mon-Sat 9:00 AM-5:00 PM and Sun 11:00 AM-4:00 PM; mid-October to mid-June Mon-Sat 9:00 AM-4:00 PM. Tours run every 30 minutes on the hour and half-hour. Last tour is 30 minutes to 1 hour before closing. Call ahead to see if cheese in production during your visit.
Plan to Stay: 20 minutes for tour and video, plus time for gift shop.
Minimum Age: None
Disabled Access: Yes
Group Requirements: Groups larger than 40 should call at least 1 week in advance.
Special Information: Cabot Creamery Annex store (near Ben & Jerry's factory on Rt. 100) shows cheese-making video and sells Cabot products and specialty foods.
Gift Shop: Sells all Cabot products (many not available in local supermarkets), and other Vermont-made food products and gifts. Discount coupon in tour brochure. Look for VCR cheddars, blocks of sharp cheddar cut and packaged with titles like "Chedablanca" in a neon art video box. Open same hours as tour. Catalog available from (800) 639-3198.
Directions: From I-89 take Exit 8 for Montpelier. Head east on Rt. 2 and turn left onto Rt. 215 East in Marshfield Village. Cabot Creamery is 5 miles ahead on right. From I-91, take St. Johnsbury exit. Head west on Rt. 2 and turn right on Rt. 215 to Creamery. Request recording for directions at above number.
Nearby Attractions: Maple Grove Farms and Ben & Jerry's tours (see pages 244 and 240); bird and wood Carvers, family farms (Cabot Visitor's Center has information on carvers and farms); Goodrich's Sugarhouse (call 800-639-1854). For more information on cheese factory tours, call Vermont Department of Agriculture, Food, and Markets (802-828-2416).

Crowley Cheese   ~   *cheese*

Healdville Road
Healdville, VT 05758
(802) 259-2340

When most cheese factories call their cheese "handmade," they usually mean that machines did the processing with a little human involvement. At the U.S.A.'s oldest still-operating cheese factory (established 1882), "handmade" means what it says. Except for modern sanitation and refrigeration techniques, Crowley's cheese-making tools are from the 1800s.

The outside of this three-story brown clapboard building, a National Historic Place, looks more like a house than a cheese "factory." But inside, the solo cheese-maker (formerly a practicing lawyer who took over the business from his father) proudly enjoys showing visitors how to make old-style Colby cheddar using the most modern 19th-century techniques. You can stand near the 1,000-gallon sterile vat that looks like a large bathtub filled with milk. Steam flows through the hollow walls to heat the milk.

The cheese-maker adds the culture and later, rennet (a milk-coagulating enzyme). Once the mixture has a yogurt texture, it is "cut" into small cubes, which separate from the whey and become the curd. Watch how the cheese-maker uses the cheese rake to gently stir the curd. This keeps curd particles separate and helps them cook evenly.

Once the whey is drained, the curds look like mounds of popcorn. The cheese-maker works the curds by hand, rinsing them with fresh spring water before placing them into cheesecloth-lined metal hoops. Overnight, old crank presses remove excess whey. Then the cheese wheels age at least two months for "mild" and over a year for "extra-sharp." After looking at the pictures on the walls, listening to the cheese-maker's explanation, and watching traditional cheese-making techniques, you leave saying the Little Miss Muffet nursery rhyme.

Cost: Free
Freebies: Cheese samples at gift shop and factory.
Video Shown: No, but pictures on factory walls explain process.

Reservations Needed: No, except for groups over 25 people. Since small operation, best to call ahead about cheese production schedule. *Temporarily closed.*
Days and Hours: Mon-Fri 8:00 AM-4:00 PM. Closed holidays. Usually no factory production in November and December.
Plan to Stay: 15 minutes for tour, plus time for gift shop and duck pond.
Minimum Age: None. Tour is very popular with young children; "Sesame Street" filmed feature on traditional cheese-making at Crowley.
Disabled Access: Yes
Group Requirements: Groups larger than 25 should call a few days ahead.
Special Information: Best time to see production and talk to cheese-maker is 11:00 AM to mid-afternoon. When no one is in factory, calls to above number may not always be answered. Don't despair, just call back or try contacting gift shop at (802) 259-2210.
Retail Store: Located 1½ miles away on main Rt. 103; sells mild, medium, and sharp Crowley Cheese in 8 oz. bars, 2.5- and 5-pound wheels, smoked bars, and spiced (caraway, dill, garlic, hot pepper, and sage) bars; Vermont specialty foods and gifts. Open Mon-Sat 10:30 AM-5:30 PM, Sun 11:00 AM-5:30 PM. Closed Christmas and New Year's. Call above number for order form.
Directions: From I-91, take Rt. 103 North. At split with Rt. 100, stay on Rt. 103 for 3 miles. Pass Crowley Cheese Shop, turn left onto Healdville Rd. for factory. From Rutland, take Rt. 7 South to Rt. 103 South. Then go 10¾ miles to flashing yellow light at Belmont Rd. in Mt. Holly. Continue on Rt. 103 South for about 3 miles and turn right onto Healdville Rd.
Nearby Attractions: Cerniglia Winery tour (call 800-654-6382); Vermont Marble Exhibit (call 800-654-6382); Coolidge Family Homestead; Okemo ski area.

Kent Smith, owner and cheesemaker, hand-rakes the curd at Crowley Cheese, Healdville, Vermont (Photo © 1991 Crowley Cheese, Inc.)

The oldest cheese factory in the U.S., Crowley Cheese (Photo © 1991 Crowley Cheese, Inc.)

Maple Grove Farms

167 Portland Street
St. Johnsbury, VT 05819
(802) 748-5141 / (800) 525-2540

maple syrup and
salad dressing

The company that two women started in 1915 is now one of the world's largest packagers of maple syrup and manufacturers of maple products. Maple Grove Farms has also developed a full line of natural fruit syrups and gourmet salad dressings, with its honey-mustard dressing a top-selling New England gourmet dressing.

This guided factory floor tour has a small-town feeling. You'll watch bottles of pure maple syrup or salad dressing filled, labeled, and packed on the assembly line. Downstairs in the "kitchen," workers on one side boil and mix maple syrup for making candy; on the other side, it's salad dressing or fruit syrup. Your nostrils will battle over the conflicting smells, with fruit syrups (especially raspberry) usually the clear winner.

A vintage 1930s candy depositor pours the maple candy mix into rubber sheet molds. The mixture cools for about an hour before the "ladies," as the tour guide calls them, shake the sheets out onto rubber mats. The candies are placed into metal baskets for an overnight bath in a crystallizing mixture of sugar and syrup, a natural preservative. Look through the glass wall at carts filled with candy air-drying on metal trays, and at the quick-moving hands that individually pack the maple candies into boxes (3,000 to 4,000 pieces per day).

Cost: 75¢; children under 12, free.
Freebies: Small sample bag of maple candies. Gift shop offers free tastes of different maple syrups and the salad dressing of the day.
Video Shown: Tour begins with 8-minute video highlighting maple-syrup-making process, company history and manufacturing. When factory tour not operating, this video plays in Cabin Store
Reservations Needed: No, except for groups larger than 40 people.
Days and Hours: Mon-Fri 8:00 AM-11:45 AM and 12:30 PM-4:30 PM, year-round. Tour runs approximately every 12 minutes. Closed holidays.

Plan to Stay: 25 minutes, including tour, video, Maple Museum, and gift shop. Maple Museum is an authentic sugarhouse with all tools and equipment used by Vermont sugarmakers, and complete explanation of evaporation process.
Minimum Age: None
Disabled Access: Only on bottom floor of factory, but company does not encourage it because floor can be slippery.
Group Requirements: Reservations requested for groups, with no maximum group size.
Special Information: Production stops around 3:30 PM. While syrup and dressing are filled and packed daily, candy not made every day during winter.
Gift Shop: Cabin Store sells many maple products, such as maple butter, maple crunch, and maple drops. Also offers company's gourmet dressings and fruit-flavored syrups, along with standard Vermont tourist items. Look for factory seconds at back of store. Cabin Store and Maple Museum open Mon-Sun 8:00 AM-5:00 PM from beginning of May until late October. During winter, store is in factory and open same hours as tour. Catalog available from (802) 748-3136.
Directions: From I-91, take Exit 20 for Rt. 5 North. Take Rt. 2 East (Rt. 2 turns right at Eastern Ave). Factory is about 1 mile from center of town. From I-93, take Exit 1 in Vermont, turn onto Rt. 18 towards St. Johnsbury, then turn left onto Rt. 2 West. Factory is a few miles ahead on left.
Nearby Attractions: Cabot Creamery tour (see page 241); Goodrich's Sugarhouse (call 800-639-1854); American Maple Products tour in Newport (call 802-334-6516); Fairbanks Museum and Planetarium.

Vermont Teddy Bear ~ *teddy bears*

2031 Shelburne Road
Shelburne, VT 05482
(802) 985-1319 / (800) 829-BEAR

A plain little teddy belonging to a boy named Graham was the inspiration for Vermont Teddy Bears. When Graham's father, John Sortino, discovered that none of Graham's stuffed animals—not even that most American of toys, the teddy bear—were made in the U.S.A., he decided to make an American teddy bear. In 1985 John and Susan Sortino developed "Bear-Grams," customized teddy bears delivered for special occasions.

The Bear Lab shows you Vermont Teddy Bear evolution, from the first Bearcho (a Groucho Marx lookalike) to the current line, and teddy-bear lore. After hearing a brief history of the company, you'll don an apron—this is an active tour—and head for the workshop, a magical place that enchants young and old. Moving through the brightly painted, gingerbread-trimmed workshop, you'll expect Santa's elves to appear at any moment. The enthusiastic tour guides ("Bear Ambassadors"), workers, and bears do everything in their power to make sure you have fun.

A yellow brick road leads you to the cutting table. With cookie-cutter dies, a hydraulic press stamps out bear parts from wide rolls of soft fur. Workers at several stations sew together bear limbs, torsos, and heads, inside-out so seams are hidden. Bears are then turned right side out and pumped full of stuffing with 130 pounds of air pressure. Limbs are joined to torsos and eyes are put in. (The plastic eyes are supplied by the last U.S. company that produces them.)

Next you get to fulfill the wish you've had through the whole tour—bond with a cuddly bear. You'll brush a "newborn" bear's fur, then "fluff" it by whacking the teddy against a table a few times. (Be sure to give it a hug afterwards!) Dressed as everything from artists to veterinarians, bears are carefully packed and shipped, complete with a bear-size bouquet of dried flowers, a little box of Vermont chocolates, and a personalized message.

Cost: Free

Freebies: Fuzzy little "Button Bear" that fits over shirt button.

Video Shown: No

Reservations Needed: No, except for groups.

Days and Hours: Mon-Sat 10:00 AM-4:00 PM, Sun 12:00 PM-4:00 PM, every hour on the hour (every 20 minutes during July/August and foliage season). Limited weekend production, however, tours are still fun. Closed holidays.

Plan to Stay: 40 minutes for tour, plus time for gift shop.

Minimum Age: No

Disabled Access: Yes

Groups Requirements: Groups should call 1-2 weeks in advance.

Gift Shop: Bear Shop is stocked with bears waiting to go home with you. Sells four sizes of bears and 120 outfit choices, from hockey player to ballerina. Offers logoed T-shirts. Open summer Mon-Sat 9:00 AM-8:00 PM, Sun 10:00 AM-5:00 PM; winter Mon-Sat 9:00 AM-6:00 PM, Sun 12:00 PM-5:00 PM. For more information on Bear-Grams call (800) 829-BEAR.

Special Information: Company may relocate factory nearby. Call to confirm tour location and schedule. Activity tent available to entertain young children while waiting for summer tours.

Directions: From I-89, take Exit 13 onto I-189 going toward Shelburne (Rt. 7). When I-189 ends, turn left (south) and stay on Rt. 7 for 3 miles. Turn right at green "The Vermont Teddy Bear Common" sign.

Nearby Attractions: Ben & Jerry's Ice Cream factory tour (see page 240); Champlain Chocolate Company viewing windows (call 802-864-1807); Shelburne Museum; Lake Champlain. Company newsletter, *The Vermont Teddy Bear Company Gazette* (free in the gift shop), lists local activities and events.

See color photos, page 147

Simon Pearce ⟶ *glass and pottery*

Route 5
Windsor, VT 05089
(802) 674-6280
The Mill
Quechee, VT 05059
(802) 295-2711

SIMON PEARCE

Simon Pearce, originally trained as a potter, apprenticed in Sweden before opening a glassblowing factory in Ireland in 1971. Because of high energy costs, Simon moved his business to the U.S. in 1981. Simon housed his first U.S. factory in a historic, 200-year-old red-brick woolen mill next to the Ottauquechee River in Quechee, Vermont. In 1993, Simon designed a brand-new manufacturing facility 9 miles away in Windsor, Vermont.

Both facilities offer self-guided tours. From Windsor's raised catwalk viewing gallery, you can observe the entire glassblowing process. The doors of the large furnace in the room's center open automatically, like supermarket doors, when a worker steps on a mat to gather glass from the furnace. Workers may appear to be wandering around, but each has a specific mission as part of a two- or three-person team.

The glassblower chooses a blowpipe from the warmer (glass adheres well to warm blowpipes), gathers the appropriate amount of glass from the center furnace, and blows it into a wooden mold. The apprentice opens the mold and gathers glass onto a pontil iron, which holds the piece during hand-finishing of the rim. The cross underneath each piece, made by this pontil iron, has become the Simon Pearce trademark.

In Quechee, you can watch glass and pottery production. Glassblowing here is much the same as in Windsor; however, you can walk right onto this factory floor (in the Old Mill building basement). The Quechee facility provides a closer view of a smaller, more intimate operation.

In the pottery area, a potter hand-throws pottery on a wheel and a decorator hand-paints a dinner plate, lamp base, or vase. Feel free to ask questions about the processes, from throwing or slipcasting to decorating and firing. Both facilities will impress you with the skill and craftsmanship involved in handmade pottery and glass.

Information below applies to both facilities unless otherwise noted.

Cost: Free
Freebies: No
Video Shown: No
Reservations Needed: No, except for groups.
Days and Hours: Mon-Sun 9:00 AM-5:00 PM. Closed Christmas and Thanksgiving.
Plan to Stay: 30 minutes per facility, plus time in gift shops and Simon Pearce Restaurant in Quechee (802-295-1470 for reservations).
Minimum Age: None
Disabled Access: Yes, at Windsor. No wheelchair access to pottery or glass in Quechee, but gift shop and restaurant are accessible.
Group Requirements: While Quechee discourages bus tours, Windsor easily accommodates buses. Groups larger than 50 should call 1 month in advance.
Special Information: Facilities can get warm because of furnaces.
Retail Shops: Windsor showroom sells first- and second-quality Simon Pearce pottery and crystal glass. Open Mon-Sun 9:00 AM-5:00 PM. Quechee sells Simon Pearce glass and pottery as well as other crafts. Open Mon-Sun 9:00 AM-9:00 PM. Catalog available.
Directions: To Windsor: from western Massachusetts, take I-91 North to Exit 9, bear right onto Rt. 5. Simon Pearce is 1 mile ahead on left. From New Hampshire, take I-89 to I-91 South. Follow above directions.
To Quechee: from western Massachusetts, take I-91 North to I-89 North to Exit 1. Take Rt. 4 West. Turn right at first blinker after Quechee Gorge. Follow signs. From New Hampshire, take I-89 North to Exit 1 in Vermont. Follow above directions.
Nearby Attractions: For Windsor: Vermont State Craft Center; Constitution House. For Quechee: quaint town of Woodstock; Billings Farm; Killington Ski Resort.

See color photo, page 145

Simon Pearce in his studio at The Mill, Simon Pearce Glass, Quechee, Vermont

Historic 200-year-old wool mill converted to pottery and glassmaking factory, Simon Pearce Glass

The Candle Factory ~ *candles and soap*

Williamsburg Soap & Candle Company
7521 Richmond Road
Williamsburg, VA 23185
(804) 564-3354

In 1964, the Barnetts of Williamsburg opened a gift shop along busy Richmond Road. They soon added candle-making as a tourist attraction, and the scent of their 10-inch bayberry tapers lured visitors inside. While The Candle Factory now produces over 13 million candles a year in more than 70 different shapes, colors, and scents, the fragrant aromas of rose, pine, lemon, jasmine, and bayberry still beckon travelers.

The process begins when paraffin is brought to the factory in a specially designed truck. The truck's holding tank is surrounded by steam coils that keep the paraffin hot. Steam coils also keep the paraffin in liquid form in the holding tanks behind the factory and in the pipes that bring it to the production area.

Most of the Candle Factory's production area, where candles are made by dipping, pouring, and molding, is visible through the large observation-booth window. Scents and dyes are stirred into the 180° wax, and parallel rows of hanging wicks are dipped over and over into the bubbling vats. To ensure that the candles are evenly shaped, they are dipped 42 times. Although a machine does the dipping, dexterous workers must then trim the wicks, put the candles in a die-cut mold to shape the bases, and polish and box them. The factory can produce over 1,000 of these tapers in two hours. Each year the factory uses 1 million pounds of wax and 6 million feet of wick.

Poured candles are made by pouring hot wax into a ceramic or glass container with a wick inside. Since the wax shrinks as it cools, a second pouring is needed to fully fill the container. For molded candles, wax is poured twice into a cylindrical mold. Once removed from the mold, the new candles must be trimmed, straightened, polished and boxed. The largest molded candles must be shaped by hand.

Cost: Free
Freebies: No

Video Shown: Pressing a button in observation booth starts informative 9-minute video which describes candle- and soap-making and Candle Factory history. Shows processes not seen from booth.

Reservations Needed: No

Days and Hours: Mon-Fri 9:00 AM-4:00 PM. Candle Factory is in production Mon-Fri but video in observation booth is available same hours and days as gift shop. Closed Thanksgiving, Christmas to New Year's, and July 4th week.

Plan to Stay: 20 minutes for self-guided tour from observation deck, plus time for gift shops.

Minimum Age: None

Disabled Access: Yes

Group Requirements: No advance reservations needed. Tour buses welcome. No maximum group size, however, only 30 people can fit in booth at one time.

Retail Store: Candle Factory sells wide selection of candles and soaps, candle accessories (such as holders and sconces), factory seconds, and market test runs. Open Mon-Sun 9:00 AM-5:00 PM. Call for extended summer and fall hours. Closed Thanksgiving, Christmas, and New Year's. Other shops on premises include Barney's Country Store, Candy Shop, Quilts and Needlework Shop, Emporium, and Christmas House.

Directions: From I-64, take Exit 231A (Norge exit). Take Hwy. 607 in the direction that exit lets you off. Turn right onto Richmond Rd. (Rt. 60). Candle Factory is on right. From I-95, take I-295 South to I-64 East. Follow above directions.

Nearby Attractions: Williamsburg Pottery Factory tour (see page 252); Williamsburg Doll Factory tour (see page 251); Anheuser-Busch (Budweiser) Brewery tour (call 804-253-3039); Colonial Williamsburg; Busch Gardens; James River Plantation; Richmond Road, "the Discount Boulevard of Virginia."

Levi Strauss & Co. ⟶ *jeans*

Highway 3
Warsaw, VA 22572
(804) 333-4007

Following their creation in the California gold fields in the 1850s, jeans' popularity spread in the 1930s as Easterners visited Western dude ranches and saw Levi's jeans in action. In the 1950s, the Levi's craze was reborn after James Dean and Marlon Brando wore jeans in two popular movies. In search of a factory to supply the East Coast, the company operated a small pilot plant in the Telephone Company garage in rural Warsaw, Virginia, for two years before building a permanent, modern facility in 1953. This plant, which has grown from 40 employees to over 300 today, produces children's sizes from Little Levi's up to Student.

The jeans-making process changed in 1991. Before that, it took seven to eight days to make a pair of jeans from start to finish. Cut bundles of fabric had to travel as a group to every department in the plant. On any given day, numerous pairs of jeans were at various stages of production. Under the alternative manufacturing system instituted in 1991, individual teams complete jeans daily. Denim enters as fabric at 8:00 AM and voilà! It comes out as jeans at 4:30 PM the same day. On a tour, you'll watch as seven 33-member teams produce a total of 13,000 jeans per day.

One highlight is the plotter room where stencil designs arrive by computer. The plotter machine seems to just take off and start drawing designs onto long rolls of white paper. These pattern sheets are known as "markers." The denim is spread out onto long tables by an automatic spreader machine or manually by a worker walking back and forth along a table's length to unwind the bolt of fabric. Notice the rows of tables with denim stacked 60 layers high (enough for 60 pairs of jeans). The plotter machine's markers are spread across the fabric and stapled to the top layer. With a hand-held bandsaw, workers follow the markers to cut the denim.

The fabric is cut and ticketed, ensuring that every part of one pair of pants has the same number. Then parts such as loops, flies, and pockets go to the parts department and the balance go to the other teams. After the parts, or "feeder," team is finished, the other teams complete each pair of jeans. These seven teams all do the same tasks, including sewing leg panels together, front pockets on, and front and back rise. Check the next pair of Levi's youth jeans you buy or wear. If the plant number is 581M, you know they were made right here in Warsaw.

Cost: Free
Freebies: No
Video Shown: No
Reservations Needed: Yes
Days and Hours: Tue-Thur 8:00 AM-4:30 PM (winter) and 7:00 AM-3:30 PM (summer). Closed holidays, week of July 4th, week after Easter, and week of Christmas.
Plan to Stay: 45 minutes
Minimum Age: None
Disabled Access: Yes, except steps to plotter room.
Group Requirements: Groups larger than 10 people should call 2 weeks in advance for reservation. No maximum group size.
Special Information: Check photography restrictions at tour time. Flat shoes recommended, since floor tiles can be slippery. Tours also available at Levi's older, less automated San Francisco plant (see page 17).
Gift Shop: No
Directions: From Washington, DC, take I-301 South to Hwy. 3 East toward Warsaw. Factory is on right, before town of Warsaw. From Richmond, take I-360 East to Warsaw. Turn left onto Hwy. 3. Factory is 2 miles ahead on left.
Nearby Attractions: Historic homes such as Stratford (Robert E. Lee's home), and Wakefield (George Washington's home); Westmoreland Park.

Rowena's ⌁ *jams, jellies, and gourmet foods*

758 West 22nd Street
Norfolk, VA 23517
(804) 627-8699 / (800) 296-0022

For a taste of Southern hospitality and mouth-watering pound cake, stop by Rowena's in Norfolk. Rowena's began in 1983 when friends and family urged Rowena Fullinwider to sell her jams and cakes, which were already favorite gifts and charity-bake-sale items. Today, Rowena's is a million-dollar business that ships its foods nationwide and as far away as Guam and Finland.

Your tour begins in Rowena's retail store. Within the maze of their compact operation, you'll see every stage of production. As you enter the kitchen, enjoy the sweet smell of Carrot Jam (a Rowena's specialty) or the zesty scent of barbecue sauce. Watch a cook drain jam from the mixing bowl by turning a faucet at the bottom or stir up a lemon curd sauce with a 3-foot whisk.

Your appetite will be further whetted in the next room, where cakes are made. Most of the equipment will be familiar to anyone who cooks, but on a grander scale. You could curl up in one of the mixing bowls, and make a meal licking one of their huge beaters. A centrifuge separates eggs by cracking them and sorting shells, whites, and yolks. While this is a pretty handy device, Rowena's cooks are especially proud of a huge oven that once belonged to the USS *United States*. Look inside the massive oven's window as 25 large cakes or 250 small loaf cakes take a 4-hour ride on Ferris-wheel racks.

After baking and cooling, the cakes are hand-wrapped and decorated with ribbon. Workers also label all sauce and jam jars with flowery stick-on labels. While this room may be quiet when you visit, it's a scene of round-the-clock action during the busy holiday season. Finally, you'll be able to taste any of Rowena's foods you desire. As you savor pound cake with Raspberry Curd or sample the pepper jelly, you'll appreciate the TLC that goes into Rowena's products.

Cost: Free
Freebies: Paper tour hat; samples of Rowena's products.

Video Shown: No
Reservations Needed: Yes
Days and Hours: January through mid-September Mon-Wed, 9:00 AM-3:00 PM. Closed holidays.
Plan to Stay: 30 minutes, plus time in gift shop.
Minimum Age: Rowena's prefers that children be of school age. For safety reasons, strollers are prohibited and back-carriers discouraged.
Disabled Access: No stairs, however, inquire when making reservations.
Group Requirements: Maximum group size is 15 people. Call 1 week in advance.
Special Information: Photography allowed with special permission. Factory gets hot during warm months.
Retail Store: Sells Rowena's entire line including almond pound cake, lemon-curd jelly, and barbecue and cooking sauce; also foods produced for Colonial Williamsburg. Look for seasonally updated recipe leaflets and *The Adventures of Rowena and the Wonderful Jam and Jelly Factory*, a children's adventure story/cookbook. Open year-round, Mon-Fri 9:00 AM-5:00 PM. Catalog available from 800 number.
Directions: Since street names change frequently, pay close attention to directions. From Virginia Beach Expwy., take I-64 or I-264 to Waterside Dr. (becomes Boush St.). Turn left on 22nd St. Rowena's is on right at end of street. From Richmond, take Hampton Roads Bridge Tunnel to Terminal Blvd. Continue down Hampton under underpass. At first light, turn left onto Azalea Ct., which turns into 21st St. Cross Colley Ave. and turn left through Burger King lot.
Nearby Attractions: Chrysler Museum of Art; Hunter House Victorian Museum; Norfolk Botanical Garden; Virginia Zoological Park; other Norfolk attractions and Virginia beach.

See color photo, page 152

Williamsburg Doll Factory ~ *porcelain dolls*

7441 Richmond Road
Williamsburg, VA 23188
(804) 564-9703

Williamsburg Doll Factory's showroom instantly transports you to a fanciful world of Victorian weddings and Civil War-era southern teas. You'll recognize Bonnie Blue, from *Gone With The Wind*, gaily riding a carousel in her blue velvet dress. This is the world of Margaret Anne Rothwell and her Lady Anne porcelain dolls.

Margaret Anne's mother taught her to make doll clothing as a child in Belfast, Ireland. When she moved to the U.S., she made dolls for her own daughters. Friends and family urged her to go into business and in 1977 she began making dolls in her home. Her first business milestone came when her dolls were accepted by theme parks such as Busch Gardens and Disney World. In 1980, she began making porcelain dolls, which became very popular; to meet the demand, she moved to her present location. A recent deal with the QVC shopping network has led to even more success.

Margaret Anne designs each doll's concept. The dress is most important because it determines the doll's complexion, hair color, and style.   In the porcelain department, Margaret Anne's son David and other artists create molds, mix porcelain slip, paint, and kiln-fire heads and body parts. Through an observation window you'll watch them carefully sculpt delicate hands and paint doll faces. Completed doll parts are strung with elastic to allow joint-like movement.

Craftspeople happily answer your questions and explain doll-making intricacies. Some dolls have porcelain bodies as well as heads and limbs, while others have a "composite" body of latex and clay (a modern version of the glue-and-papier-mâché composite of antique dolls). Every material used in Lady Anne dolls, except some wigs and eyes, is made in the U.S.A.

You can also observe the finishing department operations. Watch a craftperson glue individual eyelashes onto a doll's face, fit a doll's dress, or crown a doll with a wig of golden curls. After being dressed and inspected, these enchanting dolls are matched with a certificate of authenticity and shipped to a collector who will treasure their quality and beauty.

Cost: Free

Freebies: No

Video Shown: No

Reservations Needed: No, unless groups larger than 30 people want guided tour.

Days and Hours: Mon-Fri 9:00 AM-5:30 PM except during 12:00 PM-1:00 PM lunch. Factory does no weekend production, however you can view workstations. Closed Thanksgiving, Christmas, and New Year's.

Plan to Stay: 20 minutes for self-guided tour through observation windows, plus time in retail store.

Minimum Age: None, but children must be kept off doll displays.

Disabled Access: Yes

Group Requirements: Groups larger than 30 should call 1 week in advance to arrange for tour guide, maybe even Margaret Anne herself.

Special Information: No photography.

Retail Store: Sells limited-edition Lady Anne dolls, doll parts for hobbyists, and dollhouse accessories. Open Mon-Fri 9:00 AM-5:30 PM (6:00 PM in Summer), Sat 9:00 AM-6:00 PM, Sun 10:00 AM-5:00 PM. Closed Thanksgiving, Christmas, and New Year's.

Directions: From I-64, take Exit 231A (Norge exit). Take Hwy. 607 in the direction that exit lets you off. Turn left onto Richmond Rd. (Rt. 60). Doll Factory is on right. From I-95, take I-295 South to I-64 East. Follow above directions.

Nearby Attractions: Williamsburg Pottery Factory tour (see page 252); The Candle Factory tour (see page 248); Anheuser-Busch (Budweiser) Brewery tour (call 804-253-3039); Colonial Williamsburg; Busch Gardens; James River Plantations; Richmond Road, "the Discount Boulevard of Virginia."

Williamsburg Pottery Factory

Route 60 — *pottery, wood, floral design, plaster*
Lightfoot, VA 23090
(804) 564-3326

Williamsburg Pottery Factory is a sprawling, 200-acre monument to America's love of discount shopping, annually attracting over 3.5 million visitors—more than Colonial Williamsburg and Busch Gardens combined. Within the 32 buildings and outlet stores you'll find everything and anything: jewelry, gourmet foods, oriental rugs, furniture, shoes, plants, imports from around the world, lawn Madonnas, cookware, and pottery. You can also tour the four main factories—pottery/ceramics, woodworking, floral design, and cement/plaster.

The Pottery's nearly 2 million square feet of factory and retail space took nearly 60 years to complete—and it's still growing. It all began in 1938 when James E. Maloney, still active in the business, bought the first half-acre of land, dug a well, built his kiln and a one-room shack for his young wife and himself, and set up his roadside pottery stand. "Jimmy," as he's always been known in these parts, is first, last, and always a potter. He worked closely with Colonial Williamsburg's archeologists and ceramics experts during that colonial capital's restoration by John D. Rockefeller. In 1952, The Pottery became licensed to make and sell replicas of CW's 18th century salt-glaze and redware. This helped The Pottery grow.

In the pottery/ceramics factory, potters create thousands of pots and decorative home accessories by hand and with molds. Eighteenth-Century-style salt-glaze and slipware is made, glazed and fired here in the giant kiln. Highlights include seeing old-fashioned clay "tavern pipes" and the famous Williamsburg "Bird Bottle" birdhouses being made. Although signs posted in the workshop explain the basics, the craftspeople are happy to explain their work.

While The Pottery was once known mostly for its pottery, many other things are now made here. In floral design production, designers create arrangements of native Williamsburg dried flowers and plants grown right at The Pottery. At the cement/gardenware factory building, you can watch fabri-

cation of lawn and garden benches, birdbaths, and fountains. A tour of the plaster factory takes you from mold-making through the drying and trimming of plaster wall plaques, statues, containers, and other decorative objects. Among the numerous retail stores are greenhouse, potpourri, cactus, silk-flower arranging, and lamp production areas. You leave feeling that you've had a potpourri of experiences.

Cost: Free
Freebies: In pottery factory, mention this book to manager and receive free pot.
Video Shown: At information booth in Solar Building, Section 3. Covers company history.
Reservations Needed: No
Days and Hours: Open Mon-Sun "sunup to sundown." Closed Christmas. Pottery/ceramics factory generally closed Sat-Mon.
Plan to Stay: 1 hour for four self-guided tours, plus hours for shopping.
Minimum Age: None
Disabled Access: Yes
Group Requirements: Group tours available by advance arrangement with Marketing Department.
Special Information: Wear comfortable walking shoes, and watch where you walk.
Outlet Shops: Pottery's shops sell nearly everything. Shops rustic but prices great. Open Sun-Fri 8:00 AM-6:30 PM (opens later on Sundays), Sat 8:00 AM-8:00 PM. Shorter hours January-April. Closed Christmas.
Directions: From I-64, take Exit 55A, then Rt. 646 South to Rt. 60. Follow signs to Pottery. Stores and factories map available from main entrances, gate security guards, and employees. From I-95 South, take I-64 East; follow above directions. Amtrak station on grounds.
Nearby Attractions: The Candle Factory and Williamsburg Doll Factory tours (see pages 248 and 251); Anheuser-Busch (Budweiser) Brewery tour (call 804-253-3039); Colonial Williamsburg; Busch Gardens; James River Plantations.

Boeing ~ *commercial aircraft*
Tour Center
Highway 526
Everett, WA 98206
(206) 342-4801 or 544-1264

Touring Boeing's 747, 767, and 777 aircraft plant is like visiting the Grand Canyon. You oversee the assembly areas from a fourth-story walkway, marveling at the enormity of the facility (world's largest-volume building; 11 stories high, 98 acres) while attempting to grasp the details of the process. As with the Grand Canyon, it's best to just take in the vastness, listen to your tour guide, and be awed by it all.

A short bus ride from this 1,000-acre complex's visitor center, a long brisk walk though an underground tunnel, and an elevator ride take you to the open-air mezzanine observation deck. Gaze out over the subassembly floor as different airplane parts slowly come to life. The loud rivet-guns' spattering fills the air, as earmuffed workers assemble plane wings, passenger bays, and nose cones. Overhead, cranes zigzag back and forth with plane parts.

You may see up to eight 747s, 767s, or 777s on the final assembly floor at any one time. Don't expect to watch an entire plane created before your eyes. A new 747 rolls out about every eight days, helping Boeing capture nearly 60 percent of the global commercial aircraft market. Notice the true colors of the jumbo jet's shiny metals and materials, the miles of wiring, the electronic components, and the other plane innards you take for granted at 20,000 feet. As the bus travels back to the tour center, you'll pass the paint hangar. Sitting nearby on the runway waiting for flight tests are freshly painted jets headed for airlines around the world.

Cost: Free
Freebies: No
Video Shown: 25-minute film on Boeing history from its 1914 start (when lumberman Bill Boeing took his first aircraft ride) to its current projects. One film segment compresses 8-day 747 construction process into 7-minute time-lapse sequence.
Reservations Needed: No, except for groups larger than 15.

Days and Hours: Mon-Fri 9:00 AM and 1:00 PM, but call above number; schedule may change and/or tour times often added during busy fall and summer seasons. Tour center opens at 8:00 AM, and tour capacity is limited, so arrive early. During busy seasons, line may form as early as 6:00 AM. Closed holidays, week between Christmas and New Year's, and for special events.
Plan to Stay: 90 minutes for video and tour, plus time for gift counter and wait.
Minimum Age: 8
Disabled Access: Yes
Group Requirements: Groups of 15 or more need advance reservations—at least 3-6 months in advance for summer tours. Maximum group is 45 people. Group-tour times differ from public tour times. Reservation fee, $2 per person. Call (206) 266-9974 for group reservations.
Special Information: No photography allowed on Boeing property. GrayLine of Seattle also offers tour with guaranteed entrance.
Gift Counter: Boeing Tour Center sells souvenir and gift items with Boeing logo, including clothing, miniature airplanes, postcards, and aviation books and posters. Open Mon-Fri 9:00 AM-4:00 PM. Closed holidays and for special events. Catalog available from (800) 671-6111.
Directions: Located 25 miles north of Seattle. Take I-5 to Exit 189. Go west on State Hwy. 526 and follow signs to Boeing Tour Center turnoff.
Nearby Attractions: Millstone Coffee Roasting factory tour (call 206-290-5232); *Seattle Times* North Creek tour (call 206-489-7015); Everett Center for the Arts; Animal Farm; Firefighters Museum; Kasch Park; Walter E. Hall Park and Golf Course; Silver Lake Park. Museum of Flight at Boeing Field in Seattle (call 206-764-5700). Tour Center desk has Everett Visitor's Guide which includes all local attractions, accommodations, restaurants, and map.

Boehms Chocolates   ∼ *chocolates*

255 NE Gilman Boulevard
Issaquah, WA 98027
(206) 392-6652

A visit to Boehms tells a story, taking you through Julius Boehm's artifact-filled Austrian Alpine home, the candy factory he founded, and the chapel dedicated to mountain-climbers. A climber himself, Boehm was lured to Washington's Cascade Mountains, "America's Alps." Until recently, he was considered the oldest man, at age 81, to climb 14,000-plus-foot Mt. Rainier. A lover of art and music, he filled his home with such items as a marble replica of Michelangelo's *David*, a wind-up music box, a portrait of Mozart, and a potpourri of Bavarian Old World artifacts.

Downstairs from Boehm's home is the candy factory. The pungent chocolate smell fills the air. Depending on the day, different sweets simmer in the kitchen. Mixers' metal blades stir Victorian creams. A worker with a wooden paddle stirs a truffle or peanut-brittle mixture in a copper cauldron before pouring it onto a steel cooling table and spreading it to the thickness of the steel bars at the long table's edges.

Women, trained in the art of hand-dipping chocolate, roll out the day's soft filling into round strips. With one hand they pinch off a portion, gently tossing it to the other hand which continuously swirls the chocolate around on a marble slab to maintain the desired temperature. It coats the filling and decorates the top. Other varieties of centers pass through the enrober's chocolate waterfall to get their chocolate coating. After traveling through a cooling tunnel, all chocolates are hand-packed into gift boxes for distribution to Boehms retail stores.

Next, visit the Luis Trenker Kirch'l, a replica of a 12th-century Swiss chapel near St. Moritz. Boehm built this masculine church with a boulder inside as a dedication to mountain climbers who died attempting to reach their mountains' summits. Current Boehms owner Bernard Garbusjuk, trained as a pastry chef in his German homeland, proudly boasts that your tour isn't too commercialized since it ends in the chapel and not the gift shop.

Cost: Free
Freebies: Chocolate samples
Video Shown: No
Reservations Needed: Yes for guided tour, no for self-guided tour.
Days and Hours: Factory floor guided tours available for individuals and families mid-June to end of September only. Mon-Fri (except Wed) 10:30 AM and 1:00 PM. Guided group tours available year-round. Weekend tours may be available. Self-guided viewing through windows available year-round including weekends. Closed holidays.
Plan to Stay: 45 minutes for factory, home, and chapel tour, plus time for gift shop and grounds.
Minimum Age: None for families. Children in groups must be 5 years or older with one adult for every five children.
Disabled Access: Yes for factory and chapel. Difficult for home.
Group Requirements: Minimum group size is 15, maximum is 50. Groups should call 1 month in advance.
Special Information: Limited production weekends. Foreign language tours arranged with advance notice. Chapel available for rental.
Gift Shop: Sells all 160 luscious Boehms candies including Boehms' specialties, Mozart Kugeln (marzipan and filbert paste center double-dipped in chocolate), and Mount Rainier (caramel fudge and cherry center dipped in chocolate). Open year-round Mon-Sun 9:00 AM-6:00 PM with extended summer weekend hours. Closed Christmas and New Year's. Mail-order brochure available.
Directions: From I-90, take Exit 17. Follow Front St. to Issaquah. Turn left onto Gilman Blvd. Two candy canes mark entrance.
Nearby Attractions: Lake Sammamish State Park; Snoqualmie Falls; Gilman Village; Salmon Days Festival in September. Seattle's downtown attractions, including Pike's Place Market and the Space Needle, 13 miles away.

See color photo, page 138

Hand-dipped nut clusters at Boehms Chocolates, Issaquah, Washington

Austrian Alpine chalet, home of chocolate factory and company founder Julius Boehm, Boehms Chocolates

Boise Cascade ～ *lumber and plywood*
Timber and Wood Products Division
805 North 7th Street
Yakima, WA 98901
(509) 453-3131

This mill began producing lumber in 1904 as the Cascade Lumber Company, which later merged with Boise Payette Lumber Company to become Boise Cascade Corporation. The Yakima facility has two sawmills and a plywood plant. Over 70 million board feet of lumber, 5 million panels of plywood, 2,700 rail cars of wood chips, and 30,000 dry tons of shavings are produced annually. Plant retirees toss off these impressive statistics, along with the mill's history and details of its operation, during your guided tour.

The Douglas fir and ponderosa pine logs arrive at the mill on trucks. Once sorted by size, they go to the large log mill, small log mill, or plywood plants. A world of endlessly moving belts and chains takes the logs through all production stages. No wood is wasted in the production of plywood or lumber, as all trim and bark are used in the powerhouse boiler or shipped to a pulp mill.

In the sawmills, the process starts when logs travel through the debarker. While you may not get a chance to work the huge spinning ring that removes the logs' bark, you can sit in the cage with the person who does the cutting. The whirling saws sing as they seem to gobble up the logs. Every four hours the blades are removed for sharpening.

The logs must then be squared on either two or four sides in what's called the "headrig." Another set of bandsaws reduces the squared logs into boards and lumber. Edger saws complete the squaring of the piece before it is scanned for defects and trimmed to length. Machines automatically sort and stack the lumber by thickness and length before drying in the steam-heated kilns.

Logs at the plywood plant are cut and then peeled down to 2½-inch diameters in the core lathe. This state-of-the-art machine peels up to four logs per minute. The ⅛-inch-thick veneer produced at the lathe travels via belt conveyors to a clipper and is cut into 4-foot widths. On the automatic layup line, sheets of veneer are glued together and placed in the hot press to make plywood. The process produces enough plywood pan-

els to stretch from Seattle to New York and back, with some to spare.

Cost: Free

Freebies: No

Video Shown: No. Video highlighting plywood production and sawmill available for purchase.

Reservations Needed: Yes

Days and Hours: Mon-Fri 9:00 AM; 1:00 PM tour available upon request. Closed holidays.

Plan to Stay: 2 hours

Minimum Age: 8. Tour popular with elementary-school children. All Yakima 4th-graders take this tour.

Disabled Access: Stairs and catwalks throughout facility. Can arrange auto tour of mill with advance notice.

Group Requirements: Can handle groups up to 30 people with 3 weeks' advance notice.

Special Information: Noisy. Must be able to wear provided protective lenses, earplugs, and helmets. Tour of forestry and logging operations available (call 509-925-5341). No video cameras.

Gift Shop: No

Directions: Take I-82 to Yakima Ave. exit. Turn right onto 7th St., which leads to plant.

Nearby Attractions: Yakima Indian Nation Cultural Center; Yakima Historical Museum; Yakima Greenway (4½-mile walk along Yakima River); Toppenish City of Murals (28 murals; longest is 110 feet; call 509-865-6516); Yakima Valley wine tours (call 509-248-2021 for brochure).

Frito-Lay 〰 *snack foods*
4808 NW Fruit Valley Road
Vancouver, WA 98660
(206) 694-8478

In 1932, two entrepreneurs unaware of each other set out on similar paths that would eventually lead to Frito-Lay, Inc. In Texas, Elmer Doolin and his mother Daisy cooked Fritos brand corn chips in her kitchen at night. By day, he sold them from the back of his Model-T Ford. Meanwhile, in Tennessee, Herman W. Lay sold potato chips from the back of his Model A. In 1945, the two companies began selling each other's products; they merged in 1961 and became part of PepsiCo in 1965.

After your guide shows you the color-coded oil- and corn-holding tanks behind the plant, peek through the entranceway into the Fritos, Doritos brand, and Tostitos brand tortilla chips "kitchen" area. Corn is ground between large milling stones to form *masa*, a golden dough. An extruder flattens ribbons of masa, and whirling blades cut them. These raw Fritos fall into a precisely heated blend of oils, where they curl up as they cook. For Doritos and Tostitos, masa is pressed into a thick sheet and fed through rollers. Large cutters then stamp it into triangles or circles. As the shapes flash-bake in large, 700° toaster-ovens, flames create golden flecks and small "bubbles" in them. The proofer equalizes their moisture content, then all three products are salted and seasoned.

At least 7 million pounds of potatoes arrive daily at 40 Frito-Lay plants across the nation. Employees hand-inspect the washed, peeled potatoes, which then drop into a round, spinning tub. Centrifugal force helps straight blades slice Lays brand potato chips; blades shaped like tambourines with rippled edges cut Ruffles brand potato chips. After the slices cook in hot oil, they're salted or seasoned and cooled in a rotating drum. Before packaging they pass through the potato-chip sizer, which sorts out small chips for small bags and large chips for large bags.

Visit the Cheetos brand cheese-flavored snacks area. Stone-ground cornmeal is kneaded into a smooth, hot, elastic dough which is then pressed through an extruder's tiny holes. The change of pressure and temperature when the bits of hot dough leave the extruder causes them to expand and begin to pop and bounce. A sharp blade cuts these nuggets of popped cornmeal before oven-baking or frying. You'll be amazed by the giant, hollow, spinning cylinder in which the pale-yellow Cheetos bounce around to receive a real cheese coating, emerging bright orange.

See the highly automated packaging process before visiting the large warehouse, which can store only 1½-days' output. You'll leave satiated with tastes of all the freshly-made Frito-Lay products—and now you know how Ruffles get their ridges.

Cost: Free
Freebies: Fresh samples during tour
Video Shown: No
Reservations Needed: Yes. Individuals and families must join scheduled group tour.
Days and Hours: Wed 9:30 AM, 10:30 AM, and 11:30 AM. Closed holidays.
Plan to Stay: 45 minutes
Minimum Age: 5
Disabled Access: No, floors can be dangerously slippery.
Group Requirements: Minimum group is 10 people; maximum, 30. Call 2-3 weeks in advance.
Special Information: No photography. No jewelry, shorts, or open-toed shoes. Can be quite warm in summer. Frito-Lay once had national tour program; now only a few factories still give tours, mostly to local groups.
Gift Shop: No
Directions: From I-5, take 4th Plain exit. Go west on 4th Plain Blvd. Turn right onto Fruit Valley Rd. Factory is about 1 mile ahead on left.
Nearby Attractions Fort Vancouver; Officer's Row.

K-2 ⌒ *skis and snowboards*
19215 Vashon Highway S.W.
Vashon, WA 98070
(800) 426-1617

Like a ski run down a mountain, a tour of K-2 traverses you through ski- and snowboard-making from top to bottom. In 1961, using borrowed skis as a pattern, Bill Kirschner made himself a pair of fiberglass skis. These became his prototype for the launch of K-2, named after both the world's second-highest mountain and the two Kirschner brothers.

The ski-making process involves more steps than you might imagine, and this tour shows almost all. Start your trail through the largest U.S. snow-ski manufacturer at "top making." An automated squeegee slides across plastic sheets to silk-screen them with bright graphics. The sheets then slither along the conveyor through the drying oven. Once cooled, they are returned to the screener on a white hospital bed. This process is repeated until 8 to 12 layers of bright graphics decorate each plastic sheet, wide enough for four ski tops. They are baked and cooled, then cut into individual ski-tops by the die-cut (or "Rambo") machine. Look through the glass window at the UV-cured coating area. Here, a clear waterfall of liquid protectant coats the tops. As in a tanning room, UV lights dry and harden the coating.

Several different procedures are used in making ski cores. The "big braider" feeds threads of fiberglass, Kevlar (used in bullet-proof vests), and carbon through 64 frantically do-si-do-ing bobbins. In a braided pattern, these threads wrap around the wooden cores of high-performance skis. Different braiding patterns ("recipes") alter the ski's stiffness. The pressroom makes molded ski cores ("blanks"). Workers wet-wrap a wooden or foam core in colorful epoxy and fiberglass layers. As if making a fajita, a worker places toe and tail protectors, shock-absorber strips, the wooden or foam core and more inside these resin-drenched layers, wraps it all up, and places it into a mold. The worker lowers the 200° press, applying 1,200 pounds-per-square-inch of pressure. In the sanding room, excess resin is sanded off the blanks. The Bostik wheel-topper glues tops

and blanks together. Once sprayed with rubber cement, the Bostik rolls over, or "peels" the top onto the blank.

A special multi-stage process is required for bending, hardening, and sharpening the ski's steel edges. Although the tour doesn't follow the 35 steps in order, by the time you've zigzagged into all the different production rooms you will understand how skis are made. After watching the ski parts finally get sandwiched together (up to 2,400 pairs per day), you'll search for the nearest mountain to try them out.

Cost: Free
Freebies: Ski tops, posters, and stickers
Video Shown: No
Reservations Needed: Yes. K-2 prefers groups. Individuals and families join scheduled group tour.
Days and Hours: Mon-Fri 10:00 AM and 1:00 PM. Closed holidays and 2 weeks starting around Christmas, so employees can go skiing and test out the skis. *At press time we learned that, due to plant remodeling, the tours have been temporarily suspended.*
Plan to Stay: 1 hour
Minimum Age: 3
Disabled Access: Yes
Group Requirements: Maximum group is 50 people. Call 1 day in advance for reservations. Some larger groups can view 10-minute videos on manufacturing process, skis, and skiing, and hear presentations from K-2 employees. Request this when you make reservations.
Special Information: Parts of tour have noise, heat, and strong fumes.
Gift Shop: No
Directions: Take ferry from Seattle or Tacoma to Vashon Island. Vashon Hwy. is main street off ferry. K-2 is in center of town.
Nearby Attractions: Seattle's Best Coffee tour (call 206-463-3932); Vashon Island beaches and peaceful biking roads.

Liberty Orchards *fruit candies*

117 Mission Street
Cashmere, WA 98815
(509) 782-2191 / (800) 231-3242

The story of Liberty Orchards is the story of two Armenian immigrants striving to succeed in the U.S.A. After failed attempts at running a yogurt factory and an Armenian restaurant, in 1918 they purchased an apple orchard, which they called Liberty Orchards to honor their new homeland. Aplets and Cotlets fruit candies, originally known as "Confections of the Fairies," grew out of a use for surplus fruit.

A guided tour of Liberty Orchards, now in its third generation, shows you how they create these natural-fruit-flavored candies. Start your tour in the nut-sorting room where California walnuts and Hawaiian macadamia nuts are sorted. Visit the old-world kitchen where concoctions of fruit juices, fruit purees, pectin, sugar and cornstarch cook at 230° in stainless-steel kettles large enough to produce 256 pounds of candy. As the candy boils, steam emerges from the kettles and a fruity, perfumed aroma fills the air. With long metal paddles, the cook stirs the bubbling concoction and then tastes it for correct consistency—a tough job, but someone has to do it. The cook's helpers pour the hot candy into smaller kettles and add nuts and natural flavoring. Then they pour the candy into long, plastic-lined wooden trays, roll it flat, and cover it for a day's rest in the cooler.

In the factory, workers flip the slabs of cooled candy out of their trays and coat the candy with cornstarch, which acts as a natural preservative to keep moisture inside. Candy-cutters cut the candy into bite-size cubes. Tumblers coat the sides of the cubes with cornstarch and then cover them with powdered sugar. Nimble-fingered packers hand-pack the candies into plastic trays at a rate of 4,000-5,000 per hour per packer. Fortunately the tour guides pass out free samples of these chewy treats, or you would be tempted to reach into the packing bins.

Cost: Free
Freebies: Three different flavors of candies
Video Shown: No, but you can purchase colorfully illustrated 20-page booklet called "The Story of Aplets & Cotlets," which covers family history, product and packaging development, and production process.

Reservations Needed: No, but preferred for groups larger than 12 people.

Days and Hours: May through December Mon-Fri 8:00 AM-5:30 PM, Sat-Sun 10:00 AM-4:00 PM. Occasional weekend production. No production during 11:00 AM-12:00 PM lunch break and after 4:00 PM. January through April Mon-Fri 8:30 AM-4:30 PM. Tours run every 20 minutes starting on the hour. Closed New Year's, Christmas, Thanksgiving, President's Day, and Easter.

Plan to Stay: 15 minutes, plus time for Country Store.

Minimum Age: No. Children under 16 must be accompanied by adults.

Disabled Access: Yes

Group Requirements: Groups larger than 12 people will be split into smaller groups. Call 2 days in advance.

Special Information: Floor can be slippery. Production generally Mon-Fri with occasional weekends. Liberty Orchards is in heart of Washington's apple industry, which produces 5 billion apples per year—half of all the apples eaten in America.

Gift Shop: Country Store sells all Liberty Orchards fruit and nut candies (such as Aplets and Cotlets), apple gifts, and Northwest products. Open same hours as tour. Catalog available from (800) 888-5696.

Directions: From Seattle, take U.S. 2 East. Take Cashmere exit, which puts you on Division St. Follow Aplets & Cotlets signs. Turn left onto Mission St. Liberty Orchards is on left.

Nearby Attractions: Boeing Everett plant tour (see page 253); October Apple Days festival; Nearby Cascade loop attractions include Leavenworth Bavarian Village, Ohme Gardens, and Rocky Reach Dam.

Redhook Ale Brewery ⌒ *beer*

3400 Phinney Avenue North
Seattle, WA 98103
(206) 548-8000

Founded in 1981, Redhook Ale Brewery has become one of the most respected regional breweries in the Northwest, which has the highest per-person beer consumption in the country. Its classic pub-style Ballard Bitter and full, rich Redhook E.S.B. ale have a loyal following in the region.

Both the building that houses the brewery and the technology used in brewing make your visit more memorable than the standard brewery tour. Since 1988, Redhook has occupied the historic home of the Seattle Electric Railway, located in Seattle's Fremont district. The beautifully restored red-brick, green-trimmed trolley-car barn sets it apart from the standard industrial look of most other breweries. It also belies the state-of-the-art technology you'll see inside that produces the company's draft beers.

A century-old German company designed Redhook's brewing equipment, making it one of the most technically advanced breweries. You'll notice computer control panels monitoring the amounts of malted barley, hops, yeast, and water. The rows of polished stainless-steel fermentation tanks, with their maze of pipes and valves, have special automatic mechanisms to regulate temperature and pressure. The equipment even allows brewers to transfer batches from vessel to vessel without manual labor. Although high-tech equipment may play a big role in Redhook's beer-making, one sip and you'll taste the "craft" of beer brewed in the European tradition.

Cost: Free
Freebies: Samples of Redhook ales
Video Shown: No
Reservations Needed: No, except for groups larger than 20 people.
Days and Hours: Mon-Thur 3:00 PM, Fri 3:00 PM and 6:00 PM, Sat and Sun, 1:30 PM, 2:30 PM, 3:30 PM, and 4:30 PM. Closed holidays. Usually no production on weekends. With addition of Woodinville facility, Seattle plant tour times may change. Call ahead.

Plan to Stay: 40 minutes for tour and beer sampling, plus time to drink and eat at Trolleyman Pub.
Minimum Age: None, however minors may need supervision.
Disabled Access: Yes
Group Requirements: Groups larger than 20 should call 1 week in advance.
Special Information: Redhook is building new brewery and tour facility in Woodinville (N.E. 145 Street) to brew and package its bottled beers, modeled after a Bavarian brewery built next to a monastery in Andechs, Germany. Planned 24-acre site includes beer garden and visitor center. Completion of new brewery, scheduled for Summer 1994, will make Redhook North America's largest specialty craft brewer. Call above number for tour information on this new site.
Gift Shop: Trolleyman Pub sells shirts, beer mugs, posters and other accessories with Redhook logo or picture of brewery, along with light, catered menu and full section of Redhook beers. Open Mon-Thur 8:30 AM-11:00 PM, Fri 8:30 AM-midnight, Sat 12:00 PM-midnight, Sun 12:00 PM-7:00 PM. Catalog available from above number.
Directions: From I-5 North, take 45th St. exit. Turn left onto 45th St. and left onto Stoneway. Turn right onto 34th St. and right onto Phinney Ave. From I-5 South, turn right onto 45th St., then follow above.
Nearby Attractions: *Seattle Times* North Creek tour (call 206-489-7015); Rainier Brewing Co. tour (call 206-622-2600); Woodland Park; University of Washington; Lake Washington Ship Canal and Government Locks.

Blenko Glass   ~ *glass*

Fair Grounds Road
Milton, WV 25541
(304) 743-9081

At Blenko Glass, you will see a 3-to-4-inch-diameter "gob" of molten glass transformed into a foot-high water vase or pitcher right before your eyes. This self-guided tour allows you to stand behind a wooden railing and observe glassmaking for as long as you want. Only a few yards away workers hold yard-long blowpipes or "punties" with red-hot glass at the end. You'll feel the heat gushing out of the furnaces. Although there are no signs to explain the glassblowing process, you will quickly figure out the steps by their artful repetition.

It takes six people and about 5 minutes to initially shape each item. A "gatherer" delivers a glass "gob" to a blower seated at a workbench. The blower, who has eight years of experience, rolls the punty along the arms of his workbench with his left hand and cups the glass into a wooden scoop-shaped block held in his right. The blower constantly twirls the punty to keep the glass from sagging. Then he lowers it into a hand-carved cherrywood mold and blows air into the punty's opposite end so the glass fills up the mold. Another craftsman then gently kicks the mold's clamps open and with a two-pronged pitchfork carries the translucent object to the finisher. After several more steps, which require reheating, the finished piece is allowed to cool.

In the second-floor museum, which you walk through on the way to and from the observation area, learn about Blenko's history. The company started in 1933 to manufacture stained glass for windows, but has since diversified. Exhibits include some of Blenko's custom products, such as green and crystal glass buttons made for Miss West Virginia in the 1960s, a paperweight commemorating George Bush's inauguration, and the Country Music Award Trophy. In the Designer's Corner, stained-glass windows made by nine leading American studios glow in the sunlight.

Also in the sunlight, the outdoor "Garden of Glass" affords a relaxing stroll along a gravel walkway lined with stone benches and a menagerie of glass animals. Walk over the wooden footbridge, alongside a fountain, to a peaceful three-acre lake. You'll want to end your tour at the adjacent outlet store which offers great values on Blenko glass.

Cost: Free
Freebies: No
Video Shown: No
Reservations Needed: No, except for groups larger than 50 people.
Days and Hours: Mon-Fri 8:00 AM-12:00 PM; 12:30 PM-3:00 PM to watch craftsmen. Plant is closed for 2 weeks beginning around July 1 and week between Christmas and New Year's.
Plan to Stay: 30 minutes for self-guided tour and museum, plus time for outlet store.
Minimum Age: None, if children are supervised.
Disabled Access: Yes for outlet store and "Garden of Glass." However, flight of stairs leads to museum and observation gallery.
Group Requirements: Groups larger than 50 should call ahead to avoid time conflicts with other groups.
Special Information: Due to furnaces, observation deck is hot in summer.
Factory Outlet/Museum: Store's tables are crammed with various colored vases, seconds, discontinued items, and bargains. Store and museum hours: Mon-Sat 8:00 AM-4:00 PM; Sun 12:00 PM-4:00 PM. Catalog available at above number.
Directions: Take I-64 to Exit 28, then Rt. 60 West. Turn left at traffic light onto Fair Grounds Rd. Follow signs to Blenko Glass Visitor Center.
Nearby Attractions: Gibson Glass, makers of multicolored paperweights, offers self-guided tour (call 304-743-5232); October West Virginia Pumpkin Festival; Camden Park; Berryhill House and Gardens & Craft Center.

Fenton Art Glass ⟞ *glass*

420 Caroline Avenue
Williamstown, WV 26187
(304) 375-7772

In western West Virginia, rich in mountains, sand, and natural gas, the ancient art of glassmaking is kept alive by a handful of artisans and factories. Fenton Glass began in 1905 when two Fenton brothers pooled $284 to build their Williamstown plant. Now in its third generation of family ownership and management, Fenton Glass continues this art in the U.S.A. The tour takes you from the extreme heat and speed of the blow/press shops to the decorating area's exacting calm.

After a brief chemistry lesson (sand is glass' main ingredient), follow your guide onto the blow/press shop floor. Gatherers, handlers, and carriers dodge around you with "gobs" of red-hot glass, handles, and freshly blown or pressed pieces. Each worker, trained by apprenticeship, has a specific function in the team effort of creating each item. To produce a bowl, the "gatherer" rolls the long pole ("punty") inside the 2500° furnace to gather a "gob" of glass, which is put into a bowl-shaped mold. The "presser," one of the most experienced craftsmen in the shop, lowers a lever with exacting pressure, squeezing molten glass into a decorative bowl.

Downstairs, in an enclosed room, fresh-air-masked artisans paint crushed 22-karat gold onto glass eggs. Elsewhere in the decorating area, artists paint designs on glass using crushed-glass pigments. When applying floral designs, an artist first paints flowers on a dozen pieces, returning later to add leaves and stems. You leave appreciating the steps involved in producing tomorrow's heirlooms.

Cost: Free for tour. Museum: adults, $1; under 16, 50¢; under 10, free. No charge when tour not available.
Freebies: Brochure on glassmaking
Video Shown: "The Making of Fenton Glass," 23-minute video in museum theater, covers production, how specific glass items are made, company history, and hand-carving of cast-iron molds.
Reservations Needed: No, except for groups larger than 20.
Days and Hours: Mon-Fri 8:30 AM-10:00 AM and 11:30 AM-2:30 PM. Call for exact tour times, as factory work schedule changes. Closed holidays. No factory tours for 2 weeks starting end of June or beginning of July.
Plan to Stay: 1½ hours, including tour, video, and museum, plus time for gift shop. Museum emphasizes first 75 years of Fenton Glass (1905-1980), and other Ohio Valley companies' glass. Museum has same hours as gift shop.
Minimum Age: 2
Disabled Access: Blowing/pressing area and gift shop are accessible. Stairs to decorating department and museum.
Group Requirements: Groups of 20 or more need advance reservations; receive 20% discount on museum admission.
Special Information: Wear close-toed, thick-soled shoes. Glassblowing area is well ventilated but hot during summer. Watch where you walk.
Gift Shop & Factory Outlet: Sells Fenton's 400-item first-quality line. Only outlet for preferred seconds and first-quality discontinued glass collectibles. Also carries Royal Doulton, Lenox, and other giftware and collectibles. Museum sells glassmaking history books. Annual February Gift Shop Sale and July 4th sale. Year-round, open Mon-Sat 8:00 AM-5:00 PM, Sun 12:00 PM-5:00 PM. Additional hours: April-May and September-December, Tue and Thur open until 8:00 PM; June-August Mon-Fri open until 8:00 PM. Closed New Year's, Easter, Thanksgiving, and Christmas. Catalog available from above number.
Directions: From I-77, take Exit 185; follow blue-and-white signs to gift shop. From Rt. 50, take I-77 North. Follow directions above.
Nearby Attractions: Lee Middleton Doll Factory tour (see page 185); Blennerhassett Island; Historic Marietta, Ohio, across Ohio River.

Array of art glass pieces made at Fenton Art Glass, Williamstown, West Virginia

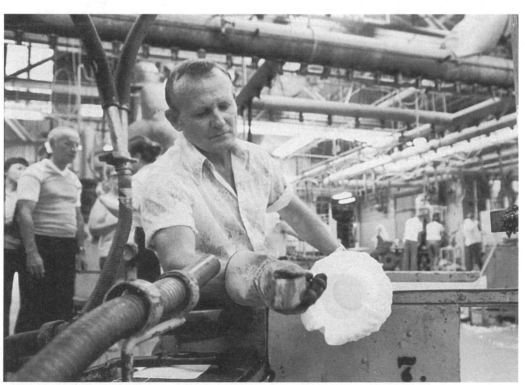

Glassworker shaping molten glass during factory tour at Fenton Art Glass

Homer Laughlin China ~ *china*

6th and Harrison
Newell, WV 26050
(304) 387-1300 / (800) 452-4462

Since its beginnings in 1871, Homer Laughlin has grown into the nation's largest manufacturer of restaurant china. Their bright-colored Fiesta tableware is the most-collected china pattern in the world (first introduced in 1936). On a tour of one of the most automated pottery factories in the U.S., you observe three ways of forming clay, plus the glazing, firing, and decorating processes.

As you walk through this mile-long factory, notice the maze of pipes along the ceiling, the tracks along the floor on which the kiln cars travel, and the row upon row of gray stacked plates, cups, and bowls waiting to enter the kiln. Hear the sounds of dishes rattling together. Watch as automatic jiggers form round plates at a rate of 400-500 dozen per day. Ram presses, used for pieces with such irregular shapes as slanted sides, squared corners, and ovals, squeeze slabs of clay between two plaster dyes. The top die is pressed into the bottom die under 2,200 pounds-per-square-inch of pressure. In the casting process, liquid clay known as "slip" is poured into plaster molds. The slip dries in the shape of the mold.

Regardless of how the china is formed, dry pottery is called "greenware." A spray machine applies liquid glaze to the greenware. Once glazed, each piece is loaded by hand onto the shelves of a kiln car. Robotics are utilized to automatically stack a filled kiln car into the largest fast-fire kiln in the industry.

After the short 11-hour journey (it used to take 48 hours) through this 2400°, 350-foot-long tunnel kiln, the computer directs each kiln car back to its initial workstation. Presses stamp the Homer Laughlin trademark onto the bottom of each piece. In the decorating department, decals are applied and decorative lines are painted on by hand or machine before another firing in the decorating kiln, this time for only 59 minutes. Pieces are shipped out as soon as they're finished, to the tune of 500,000 pieces of china per week.

Cost: Free

Freebies: Souvenir ceramic tray

Video Shown: No

Reservations Needed: No, except for groups larger than 20 people.

Days and Hours: Mon-Fri 10:30 AM and 1:00 PM. Closed holidays.

Plan to Stay: 1 hour, plus time in outlet store.

Minimum Age: None

Disabled Access: Yes, for most of tour.

Group Requirements: Groups larger than 20 should call 1 week in advance. No maximum group size.

Special Information: Photography allowed in most areas. Areas near kilns are quite warm in summer.

Outlet Store: Sells first and second quality of entire product line, including Fiesta dinnerware and flatware and Lyrica dinnerware. Also offers close-out patterns and colors. Open Mon-Sat 9:30 AM-4:50 PM, Sun 12:00 PM-4:50 PM. Closed major holidays.

Directions: From Pittsburgh, take Rt. 30 West to Chester, WV. Take Rt. 2 South for 2 miles and factory is on right. From Youngstown, take Rt. 11 South to East Liverpool. Follow signs to Newell Toll Bridge. Once on bridge, follow signs to Homer Laughlin.

Nearby Attractions: Creegan Animation and Hall China Co. tours (see pages 181 and 183); Mountaineer Park Racetrack and Resort.

Morgan Shirt ⟿ *shirts*

Marilla Park
Morgantown, WV 26507
(304) 292-8451

Tucked away in the hills of West Virginia, Morgan Shirt is one of the few shirt factories left in the U.S.A. In the midst of American service companies expanding, there is a sadness about a small shirt plant struggling to survive. Started in New Jersey in the 1930s, Morgan Shirt made ladies and men's sportswear. Now they mostly produce men's dress and sport shirts on a contract basis for such names as Ralph Lauren and Brooks Brothers.

Enter the old red two-story wood-and-brick factory building. Notice the long tables filled with layers of fabric. A spreader machine unrolls a bolt of fabric along the table. A worker known as a "spreader" flattens the wrinkles by hand with a yardstick. With portable bandsaws, workers follow the lines on a top marker sheet to cut out shirt parts. A die cutter is used for smaller pieces such as pockets, collars and wristbands. Fabric ribbon strips tie together stacks of just-cut fabric pieces.

From the cutting room, walk upstairs to see busy workers feeding shirt pieces into sewing machines. Collars, sewn inside-out, require the most effort. A worker leaning over the Adler machine sews the lining into the collar. As you walk along the old plank wooden floor between the seamstresses, you hear the buzz of the foot-operated sewing machines.

While much of this equipment is not the latest models, these machines serve their purpose. One of the most interesting is the automatic button-hole machine, which automatically lines up a shirt and cuts holes at required intervals. The shirt looks like an inchworm as it moves through the machine. You will be impressed by the rhythm and speed with which a worker operates the button-sewing machine. Watch as six buttons, the standard number for most shirts, are sewn on faster than you could even thread a needle. These skilled workers adapt themselves and the machinery to handle different weight fabrics such as wool, cotton, denim and silk. While it takes only 16 parts to make a shirt, you leave appreciating the many laborious steps required to make the shirt on your back.

Cost: Free

Freebies: Kids receive fabric samples

Video Shown: No

Reservations Needed: Yes

Days and Hours: Mon-Fri 8:00 AM-2:00 PM. Closed holidays. Closed 2 weeks at beginning of July and week between Christmas and New Year's.

Plan to Stay: 1 hour, plus time in factory outlet room.

Minimum Age: None, as long as there is adult supervision.

Disabled Access: Yes, for cutting and finishing parts of tour.

Group Requirements: Maximum group size is 35-40 people. Call at least 2 weeks in advance.

Special Information: Best time to see peak production is mid-morning.

Factory Outlet: Small room with cardboard boxes of shirts marked by neck size. Yellow tags identify seconds. Open right after tour, Fri 4:00 PM-8:00 PM, and Sat 9:30 AM-3:30 PM.

Directions: Directions can be confusing, so ask for them when calling for reservations. Take I-79 to I-68 East. Take Sabraton exit. Turn right and go through two lights. Turn left at first road. Cross railroad crossing, then turn right across small bridge. Follow creek (bear right) through park. Pass tennis courts and swimming pool; factory is ahead on left.

Nearby Attractions: Marilla Park; University of West Virginia.

Pilgrim Glass   *glass*

Airport Road
Ceredo, WV 25507
(304) 453-3553

By experimenting with different products and positioning itself in the upper end of the glass market, Pilgrim Glass has prospered. In addition to being the world's largest producer of cranberry glass (made of 24-karat gold fused with lead crystal), Pilgrim produces a popular 12-animal glass menagerie and a limited-edition sand-carved cameo collection.

From an elevated observation deck you can see the entire glassmaking production area. Even at this height you feel the heat from the furnaces. Watch the creation of glass animals and other Pilgrim art glass. Notice the round assembly line of bowls immediately below you. Workers gather and blow glass while swinging and twirling their punties to prevent the molten glass from sagging. Glass animals, like all art glass, begin as a gob of molten glass. With forceps, workers pull shapes from the center. They stretch, turn, shape, clip, and score the shapeless gob into a glass animal. Only the artisan knows whether it will become a porpoise, cat, or unicorn.

The cameo glassmaking process begins with the blowing of up to 11 layers of molten glass on top of each other. All layers must be the identical temperature to ensure the same rate of expansion and avoid shattering. When the glass has cooled, workers wearing full radiation suits sand-blast away one layer at a time until the initial layer of colored glass is exposed. Each individual pattern is used only once and is destroyed in the carving of a single layer. Many of these multicolored relief designs depict West Virginia's natural beauty, with such names as "Morning Mist," "Clearing in the Forest," and "Silhouetted Trees." Although you cannot see any of the detailed steps in making cameo glass, you will appreciate the skill involved by viewing the cameo collection in the gift gallery.

Cost: Free
Freebies: No
Video Shown: Optional 8-minute video shown in sale room gives close-up view of art-glass production. Recommends watching video before taking tour.
Reservations Needed: No
Days and Hours: Since tour is self-guided, plan to visit during following production times: Mon-Fri 8:00 AM-10:00 AM, 10:30 AM-2:30 PM and 3:00 PM-6:00 PM. May not be in production on Fridays. Closed holidays, 3 weeks from end of June to July, and 2 weeks around Christmas and New Year's.
Plan to Stay: 20 minutes for tour and video, plus time for Glass Gallery.
Minimum Age: None
Disabled Access: Yes, for video and first-floor of gallery. Stairs lead to second floor of gallery and observation deck.
Group Requirements: None
Special Information: Furnaces keep observation deck warm.
Retail Store: Glass Gallery displays Pilgrim's art glass in sunlit sections containing same-color bowls, pitchers and vases. Cameo glass in display cases. Second-floor gallery showcases more intricate and valuable cameo glass. Factory outlet room sells second-quality and first-quality-discontinued glassware at reduced prices. Two cases display historical pieces made at Pilgrim Glass, on loan from master blower Robert McKeand, a Pilgrim Glass employee since 1959. Open Mon-Sat 9:00 AM-5:00 PM and Sun 1:00 PM-5:00 PM. Catalog available from above phone number.
Directions: Take I-64 to Exit 1 in West Virginia. Follow signs to Tri-State Airport. Pilgrim Glass is on left. Signs in parking lot invite you to "See It Made."
Nearby Attractions: Huntington Art Museum.

Allen-Edmonds ⟋ *shoes*

201 East Seven Hills Road
Port Washington, WI 53074
(414) 284-3461

Allen Edmonds

Allen-Edmonds shoes cushion some of the most famous feet that tread the globe. In addition to "shoeing" movie stars, athletes, and U.S. presidents, Allen-Edmonds has some of the most loyal customers of any American company. President John Stollenwerk's company proudly emblazons each black shoe-box with its gold circular logo: "Made In The USA Every Step Of The Way." Each pair of Allen-Edmonds shoes requires 212 production steps, from the cutting of the leather to the final shipping.

From glass windows along the atrium walkway, notice how shoes in progress move down a conveyor belt like ducks waddling along a three-tier shooting gallery. A board describes the shoemaking process. Workers pull unfinished shoes off the conveyor to perform the various procedures. A worker practically hugs a sole as he steers it through the machine that stitches all around the insole. This 360-degree welting process has been a tradition since Allen-Edmonds' founding in 1922.

On specially guided factory-floor tours, walk past hundreds of gray metal bins filled with lasts, the foot-shaped forms used to handcraft shoes to the proper size. You'll wind through racks of soles, uppers, and upside-down shoes in various stages of completion. At one station a worker spreads cork, which resembles chunky peanut-butter, on the insole for additional cushioning. Look for Willie, a 50-plus-year veteran who started at 30¢ per hour. He supposedly can do all 212 steps himself!

In the finishing department, wade through the sea of brown and black shoes and head to the recrafting area where shoes are reborn. Each new pair is blanketed in soft burgundy flannel and tucked into a sturdy black box. They await shipment to a major department store, shoe salon, or the Shoe Bank, a 75,000-pair on-site shoe store which will undoubtedly be your destination at the end of your visit.

Cost: Free

Freebies: Shoehorn on guided tours

Video Shown: Guided tours include "Allen-Edmonds Impressions," 10-minute video shown in sample room, shows uppers-fashioning process in nearby Lake Church facility, and sole production and shoe completion in Port Washington plant.

Reservations Needed: No for self-guided viewing; yes for factory-floor guided tour. Factory-floor tour has become more restricted (insurance reasons).

Days and Hours: Mon-Thur 9:00 AM-3:30 PM. Closed holidays, first 2 weeks of July for tent sale, and week between Christmas and New Year's.

Plan to Stay: For self-guided tour, 10 minutes to observe production through glass atrium windows. For guided tour, 30 minutes for the video and tour. Allow time for Shoe Bank.

Minimum Age: None for self-guided viewing. 12 for factory tour.

Disabled Access: Yes for watching video, observing shoemaking from atrium walkway, and visiting store. No for factory floor.

Group Requirements: Small groups preferred on guided tour. Maximum size is 35 people.

Special Information: No photography.

Outlet Store: The Shoe Bank offers full line of Allen-Edmonds second-quality men's and women's shoes at 25% off standard price. First-quality and other manufacturers' shoes also available. Annual July tent sale sells 13,000-15,000 pairs of shoes. Open Mon-Fri 7:00 AM-9:00 PM, Sat 9:00 AM-9:00 PM, Sun 9:00 AM-6:00 PM. Catalog available from above number.

Directions: From Milwaukee, take I-43 North to Exit 100. Look for big American flag at Allen-Edmonds entrance.

Nearby Attractions: Kohler Design Center and tour (see page 272); Lake Michigan; Cedarburg.

Carr Valley Cheese   *cheese*

S3797 County G
La Valle, WI 53941
(608) 986-2781 / (800) 462-7258

Named after its location, Carr Valley Cheese is one of the few companies that produce cheddar cheese the old-fashioned way. Many Wisconsinites remember the 1930s and 1940s when, as kids, they snacked on fresh curd from cheese factories which dotted Wisconsin's countryside every few miles. You can taste fresh, warm curd which squeaks against your teeth and observe how it is turned into cheese.

In the retail store, a glass wall runs the length of the production area where you may see owner Sid Cook, a fourth-generation cheese-maker, clad in bib overalls. Since each of the four 19-foot-long stainless-steel vats is at a different production stage, it helps to review the picture board and audiotape before taking your self-guided tour. Each day 52,000 pounds of pasteurized milk are filtered from holding tanks into cheese vats, which resemble single-lane lap-swimming pools. A large whisk (an "agitator") twists and turns as it travels the length of a vat and back. A culture (begins ripening process and tastes like sour milk) and rennet (causes milk to solidify) are added, and a wire harp cuts the mixture into small curds. As the whey (liquid) is removed, a separator extracts the cream. The cheese remains in the vat.

Once solid, the cheese is cut into 20-inch-by-2-inch slabs. While they're stacked like slices in a loaf of bread, excess moisture drains from the slabs. The curd mill chops the slabs into small chunks, and workers fill small black metal buckets with 25 pounds of curd. You can see curds weighed, poured into forms, and pressed into wheels.

Walk around to the back of the plant to see wheels waxed and packaged. In the wax room, a rack of cheese wheels is lowered into a 2-foot-deep vat of 200° clear, red, or black wax (color depends on cheese's age). The wax seals out air and protects the cheese from mold as it cures in the warehouse for up to two years (longer aging means sharper cheddar).

Cost: Free

Freebies: Samples of curds and cheeses

Video Shown: No, however picture board and 4-minute audiotape in retail store explain cheese-making.

Reservations Needed: No, except for groups larger than 30 people.

Days and Hours: Mon-Sat 8:00 AM-12:00 PM. Best time is 10:00 AM. Closed Thanksgiving, Christmas, and Easter.

Plan to Stay: 30 minutes for self-guided tour and retail store.

Minimum Age: None

Disabled Access: Yes, however difficult to get into wax room.

Group Requirements: Groups larger than 30 should call 1 day in advance to schedule tour guide; will be split into smaller groups.

Retail Store: Sells full line of Carr Valley cheese. Wheel sizes: 3-pound "gem," 5½-pound "favorite," up to 23-pound "daisy," and 72-pound "cheddar" (once the industry standard). Also sells cut cheese, curds, sausages, and Wisconsin-made jams, jellies, and honey. Open Mon-Sat 8:00 AM-4:00 PM. Catalog available from (800) 462-7258.

Directions: From I-90/94, take Hwy. 12 South. Take Hwy. 33 West through Reedsburg (look for Carr Valley Cheese signs) to La Valle. Go straight onto Hwy. 58 South through Ironton. After 1 mile, turn left onto County G. Brick plant is 2 miles ahead on right.

Nearby Attractions: Wisconsin Dells casinos and boat cruises, about 25 miles away. For complete list of Wisconsin cheese plants, write: Cheese Plants, Wisconsin Milk Marketing Board, 8418 Excelsior Dr., Madison, WI 53717.

J I Case ~ *tractors*
24th and Mead Street
Racine, WI 53403
(414) 636-7818

Jerome Increase Case started his company in 1842 in western Racine County to manufacture threshing machines. He moved the business to Racine in 1844 to take advantage of Racine's proximity to Lake Michigan and its abundance of skilled labor. Case, until recently a 100%-owned Tenneco subsidiary, has become a leading worldwide producer of agricultural and construction equipment (Tenneco also purchased the agricultural asset of International Harvester in 1985.)

The tractor plant is one of three Case plants in Racine and is the only factory worldwide where Case builds the two-wheel-drive Magnum series tractor. Magnum has appeared on *Fortune* magazine's list of 100 products America makes best and has received highest recognition from the Society of Agricultural Engineers. This guided walking tour covers almost half of the 1.5-million-square-foot plant to show tractor-building from start to finish. The plant is huge, which isn't surprising considering the tractor's size—it weighs as much as 8 tons, with tires as tall as people.

When Case launched the Magnum line in 1987, it completely rebuilt the old assembly line and installed the most current manufacturing equipment and procedures. Among the new assembly line's important features are automated handling systems, a robotic wash and paint system, and computerized diagnostic testing. As you move between the subassembly areas, your Case-retiree tour guide points out special production features such as the bar code identification system. Each tractor and cab is identified and tracked with a bar code from the moment the assembly process starts.

After the cab's metal pieces are welded together, it moves down its own line. Workers add components such as glass, fenders, seat, fuel tank, and roof. When cab and body come together it finally looks like the well-known bright red Case International tractor. Just before the tractor receives its tires, a two-member team determines whether the tractor meets Case quality stan-

dards. If it does, the workers place a decal bearing their signatures on the cab threshold. This certifies that the tractor is ready to begin its working life and symbolizes the commitment of the Case/UAW Employee Involvement Program.

Cost: Free

Freebies: No

Video Shown: 18-minute slide show on history of Racine, Case, and the transmission, foundry, and assembly plants.

Reservations Needed: Yes

Days and Hours: Tue and Thur at 9:00 AM and 12:30 PM, Wed at 9:00 AM. Closed holidays, week between Christmas and New Year's, and plant maintenance shutdowns.

Plan to Stay: 1½ hours for slide show and tour, plus time in gift shop.

Minimum Age: 12

Disabled Access: Yes

Group Requirements: Make reservations 2 weeks in advance. Maximum group is 100 people.

Special Information: No photography. Tours also available at Case foundry and transmission plants in Racine (call above number). Other Case tours at combine and cotton picker plant (East Moline, IL; call 309-752-3369) and construction equipment plant (Wichita, KS; call 316-941-2235).

Gift Counter: Sells logoed items, including T-shirts and caps, and scale model Case tractors and construction machines. Open after tours.

Directions: From I-94 exit at Hwy. 11. Follow Hwy. 11 East to the junction with Sheridan Rd. (Hwy. 32). Turn left onto Sheridan Rd., then take the first right. Follow the sign for parking.

Nearby Attractions: SC Johnson Wax Co. Golden Rondelle Theater and Administration Building (both designed by Frank Lloyd Wright) tour (call 414-631-2154); Racine Zoo; Museum of Fine Arts; Racine County Historical Museum; Engine House No. 3.

See color photos, page 155

General Motors 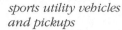 *sports utility vehicles and pickups*

Truck & Bus Group
1000 Industrial Avenue
Janesville, WI 53546
(608) 756-7681

GM has been building vehicles in Janesville since the Samson Tractor in 1919. Through the years this plant has produced a range of vehicles including Chevys, Buick Skyhawks, and now the popular Suburban, Yukon, Blazer, and medium-duty trucks. During WWII the factory made artillery shells. With the factory's long history, it's no surprise that this plant and the retiree who leads your walking floor tour exude a sense of pride. It's also one of the few automotive tours which individuals and families can take without advance reservations.

You'll see plenty of robots assisting the workers. In the Suburban body shop, over 160 robots perform about 70 percent of the welds. These robots, which look more like bird beaks, bend over from their bases to apply spot-welds. The colorful, shooting sparks make you realize how much safer it is for robots to perform this task than workers, who mostly program, monitor, and repair this equipment.

Once the steel body-frame is assembled, it moves through a dimensional vision system that uses laser beams to check the frame parts' sizes against their ideal measurements. In other parts of the factory, robots also apply the base-coat paint in enclosed booths, put the prime and urethane on the window glass before workers pop it into place, and help install the seats. While the body frame is being constructed, other lines build the chassis. Workers assemble the underneath part first and a turnover hoist flips the chassis over like a pancake.

In the final assembly lines, an overhead hoist lowers the vehicle body onto the chassis and workers bolt them together. To the music of electric drills, parts such as fenders and grills seem to arrive from every direction for attachment. You will see the dynamic vehicle-test area, where the vehicles sit on rollers and accelerate to 60 mph so major features can be tested. At this point the assembly process is complete and you're tempted to hop in and hit the road.

Cost: Free
Freebies: Key chain; brochure with pictures of tour highlights; historical timeline that traces plant's lineage.
Video Shown: 15-minute video entitled "We Do It Right" overviews plant history and vehicle production steps.
Reservations Needed: No, except for groups of 10 or more people.
Days and Hours: Mon-Thur 9:30 AM and 1:00 PM. Closed holidays, week between Christmas and New Year's, and 2 weeks in July.
Plan to Stay: 1½ hours for video and tour.
Minimum Age: None, although children under 5 may be frightened by noise and sparks.
Disabled Access: Yes
Group Requirements: Groups of 10 or more should make reservations as early as possible—tours fill quickly, especially in spring and summer. Maximum group is 100 people.
Special Information: No photography. Vehicle-painting by robots is not on tour, but you see plenty of robots perform other tasks.
Gift Shop: No
Directions: From I-90, take Hwy. 351 West. Turn right at stop sign and proceed north on Hwy. G (Beloit Ave). Turn left at Delavan Dr. and left at plant. Enter through doors in center of building, directly under flagpole on roof. From Hwy. 14 West, go straight onto O, which becomes Delavan Dr., then turn left at plant. Call above number for maps to plant from other directions.
Nearby Attractions: Wisconsin Toy Wagon Factory (call 608-754-0026); Rotary Gardens; Palmer Park; Tallman House; Milton House.

Robots weld the body frame at General Motors sports utility and light truck plant in Janesville, Wisconsin (Photo: Jim Furley)

Robots on the production line, General Motors (Photo: Jim Furley)

Kohler   *bathtubs, whirlpools, toilets, sinks*

Design Center
101 Upper Road
Kohler, WI 53044
(414) 457-3699

A visit to Kohler is more than just a tour of the world's largest plumbingware manufacturer. The factory tour begins and ends at the Kohler Design Center, a three-level showcase of products and bathroom layouts that are so attractive you'll want to move in. The Design Center also houses the company museum, which chronicles Kohler history since 1873, and Kohler's own colorful "great wall of china."

Guided by a company retiree, your tour begins in the pottery building's molding area, a humid place where bare-chested men smooth wet clay toilets with large sponges. Next come the kilns: long, brick ovens that bake glazed clay fixtures into "vitreous chinaware." Stroll among glossy stacks of Thunder Grey sinks and Innocent Blush commodes. Watch inspectors "ping" the chinaware with hard rubber balls and listen for cracks.

Next, enter Wisconsin's largest iron foundry—its electric melt system eliminates the smoke and fumes previously associated with foundries. It's still an imposing place, full of molten metal, warning lights, and hissing machinery—a highly memorable industrial experience. Here you'll discover how they make molds to form cast-iron tubs, sinks, and engine blocks. The concrete floor shudders with the heave and thud of massive presses that create sand molds. You'll feel the heat from the "ladles" of glowing molten iron traveling by on forklifts. Deeper inside the building, an automated production line turns out one bathtub casting every 30 seconds.

In the enamel building, workers gingerly remove red-hot bathtubs, lavatories, and kitchen sinks from ovens. Enamel powder that melts into porcelain is quickly sifted onto each fixture. Finally, pass into the whirlpool-bath section, where up to seven tubs bubble serenely. After three hours of touring this enormous plant, you may be more than a little tempted to flop into the water and relax.

Cost: Free

Freebies: Product-line books in Design Center.

Video Shown: 14-minute video in Design Center shows Kohler history and Kohler Village highlights.

Reservations Needed: Yes for plant tour. No for Design Center.

Days and Hours: Factory tour: Mon-Fri 8:30 AM. No tours on holidays, week between Christmas and New Year's, last week of July, or first week of August. Design Center: Mon-Fri 9:00 AM-5:00 PM and Sat, Sun, and holidays 10:00 AM-4:00 PM.

Plan to Stay: 2–3 hours for factory tour, plus time for video, museum, and Design Center.

Minimum Age: 14 for tour; under 18 must be accompanied by adult. None for Design Center.

Disabled Access: Discouraged for tour, because of stairs. Design Center is fully accessible.

Group Requirements: Kohler requests that you call for complete group information. Groups larger than 8–10 people will be split.

Special Information: No photography on tour. Up to 2½ miles of walking, including some outdoors. Be careful where you walk. During tour you'll see examples of works produced by artists in the Arts/Industry Residency program. Ask in Design Center for brochure on program.

Gift Counter: Design Center sells postcards, polo shirts, and Kohler replica trucks.

Directions: From Chicago and Milwaukee, take I-43 North to Kohler exit. Follow signs into Kohler—the company is the town. Stop at Kohler Design Center for orientation information and start of plant tour. From Madison, take I-94 East to Milwaukee, then I-43 North. Follow above directions.

Nearby Attractions: The Shops at Woodlake Kohler; The American Club "five diamond" resort hotel; Waelderhaus, replica Austrian chalet in style of Kohler family's ancestral home; Kohler Village tour (May-October); Old Wade House; John Michael Kohler Arts Center.

Miller Brewing Co. ⟿ *beer*

Visitors Center
4251 West State Street
Milwaukee, WI 53208
(414) 931-BEER

In 1855, Frederick Miller took over the Plank-Road Brewery. Surrounded by woods, the small operation was no bigger than a Victorian house. Today, a replica of the Plank-Road Brewery stands in "Miller Valley," the world of pipes, warehouses and loading docks that comprise the mighty Miller brewery.

After a dazzling video, you walk outdoors and upstairs to the packaging-center balcony. See all the gold-and-red cans roaring along conveyor belts that wind through wet machinery, packing up to 200,000 cases daily. Employees lube the gearworks with soapy water; no oil or grease is allowed. At each viewing station, TV monitors offer tourists inviting close-ups of the scenes before them. The mammoth distribution center covers the equivalent of five football fields. As you look out across its half-million cases of beer, notice the train track that rolls right into the warehouse; a clean boxcar waits, looking like a toy, dwarfed by the high ceiling.

The brewhouse is where Miller Brewing Company makes its beer, up to 8.5 million barrels annually. Climb stairs to look down on a row of towering, shiny brew kettles where "wort," a grain extract, is boiled and combined with hops. Grids of computer lights glow as the age-old aroma of brewing grains sweetens the air. Walk through Miller's historic Caves Museum, a restored portion of the original brewery where beer was stored before the invention of mechanical refrigeration. It features a collection of authentic 1800s brewing equipment. In the Bavarian-style Miller Inn, you and fellow tourists have plenty of time to relax and sample Miller's various beers. Take a few minutes to inspect the impressive collection of antique steins. In the summer, sip your drink in an adjoining beer-garden enlivened by the music of a polka band.

Cost: Free
Freebies: Beer, soda, postcards, and beer-can banks.

Video Shown: 20-minute video shows brewing process and overview of Miller's history.
Reservations Needed: No, except for groups of 15 people or more.
Days and Hours: Summer hours (June through August): Mon-Sat 10:00 AM-3:30 PM, every 30 minutes. Winter hours: Tue-Sat 10:00 AM-3:30 PM, every hour. Closed holidays and week between Christmas and New Year's.
Plan to Stay: 40 minutes for video and tour, plus time for beer tasting and gift shop.
Minimum Age: Under 18 must have adult supervision.
Disabled Access: Tour Center (includes video), Miller Inn, and Caves Museum are fully accessible. Plant not yet accessible.
Group Requirements: Groups of 15 or more, call ahead for reservations (414-931-2467). Maximum of 90 people per group. No reservations for Saturday tours. Non-profit groups can rent Miller Inn.
Special Information: Best time to see production is weekdays.
Gift Shop: Sells full line of clothes, mugs, steins, caps, mirrors, clocks, draft handles, and other beer paraphernalia featuring familiar Miller emblems. Look for popular "Girl-In-The-Moon" jewelry and clothes. Open Mon-Sat 9:00 AM-4:30 PM.
Directions: From Chicago, take I-94 West to 35th St. Turn right (north). Turn left (west) onto State St. Pass through "Miller Valley" (well marked) to last building on left, Miller Tour and Gift Shop. From Madison, take I-94 East to 35th St. Turn left (north) to State St., then follow above directions.
Nearby Attractions: Pabst, Quality Candy/Buddy Squirrel, and Wm. K. Walthers factory tours (see pages 274, 275, and 279); Milwaukee County Zoo; Mitchell Park Horticulture ("The Domes"); Milwaukee County Museum; Milwaukee Art Museum; Boerner Botanical Gardens; Cedar Creek Winery. Miller Tour Center front desk has directions to many local attractions.

Pabst Brewing Co. ⟞ *beer*

915 West Juneau Avenue
Sternewirt Entrance
Milwaukee, WI 53201
(414) 223-3709

You can really feel the 150-year-old heritage of the Pabst Brewing Company on the tour. In 1844, German immigrant brewer Jacob Best and his four sons started what eventually became Pabst Brewing Company with a brew kettle that held just 18 barrels. By 1864, when Captain Frederick Pabst bought half the company, production was 5,000 barrels per year. Today, the heart of Pabst brewery is six 100-year-old hand-wrought copper brew kettles. Each curvaceous kettle, with a capacity of nearly 14,000 gallons, rises two full stories from the ground before tapering gracefully into vents.

As you enter the brewhouse, examine the lighted schematic that explains the entire brewing process. Then climb a flight of stairs to look down on the kettles. As you stare across the open room, your every breath fills with the warm, buoyant fragrance of wet grain. Notice the King Gambrinus (the patron saint of brewing) stained-glass window on the far wall. From the kettles, you're led back outside to another part of the plant. Study the surrounding buildings' curious architecture; how the staid Industrial-Revolution brickwork is ornamented with the quaint crenellation of castles.

In the bottling house, the grain fragrance yields to a kind of chlorinated smell. From a humid observation deck, watch the filling of topless beer cans. Thousands of Pabst labels quickly merge and exit on a sort of beer-can interstate system. Once the lids are on, the cans converge, as if at a vast tollbooth, to enter the pasteurizer at a rate of 120,000 cans per hour. The beer cans are then packaged and shipped by conveyor to the distribution center where, from a catwalk, you'll see cases of beer automatically stacked to the width and height of small mobile homes. Your guided tour ends in Blue Ribbon Hall (with outdoor courtyard in summer), a dark, cozy room fashioned after a Bavarian inn. Visit with fellow guests and sample the various beers you just saw brewed.

Cost: Free

Freebies: Beer samples and soda

Video Shown: No

Reservations Needed: No, except for groups of 10 people or more.

Days and Hours: June through August Mon-Sat 10:00 AM-3:00 PM, every hour. (No 3:00 PM tour on Saturdays.) September through May Mon-Fri 10:00 AM, 11:00 AM, 1:00 PM, 2:00 PM, and 3:00 PM. Closed holidays. Factory closed 1 week in January or February, but tour still runs.

Plan to Stay: 40 minutes for tour, plus beer sampling and gift shop.

Minimum Age: None, but no strollers are permitted.

Disabled Access: No wheelchair access on tour. Stairs lead to brew- and bottling houses.

Group Requirements: Groups of 10 or more should call ahead.

Special Information: Stairs and outside walking along cobblestone streets.

Gift Shop: Sells logoed items featuring different Pabst brands. Open Mon-Fri 9:30 AM-4:30 PM. Also open on Saturdays June through August.

Directions: From Chicago, take I-94 West to I-43 North; exit 4th and Broadway. Go to Civic Center and 4th St. exit. Turn right on Juneau Ave. to Pabst visitors parking lot at intersection of Juneau and 9th St. Tour begins at 915 West Juneau Ave. (look for statue of king saluting you with flask of beer). From Madison, take I-94 East to I-43 North and follow above directions.

Nearby Attractions: Miller, Quality Candy, and Wm. K. Walthers tours (see pages 273, 275, and 279); Milwaukee County Zoo; Mitchell Park Horticulture ("The Domes"); Milwaukee County Museum; Milwaukee Art Museum; Boerner Botanical Gardens; Cedar Creek Winery.

Quality Candy/Buddy Squirrel

1801 East Bolivar Avenue   *chocolates and popcorn*
Milwaukee, WI 53207
(414) 483-4500

This factory tour is actually two tours in one. In 1916, immigrants Joseph and Lottie Helminiak opened Quality Candy Shoppe in Milwaukee's popular Mitchell Street shopping district. In the early 1950s, Buddy Squirrel combined forces with Quality Candy. Today, the two product lines are housed in a 45,000-square-foot factory and warehouse, and the family-owned company operates more than 30 stores in three states. This joint tour allows you to see how Quality Candy makes chocolate candies and how Buddy Squirrel processes flavored popcorn.

Your tour begins in the Quality Candy kitchens. Here, candy-makers prepare and mix the ingredients for the chocolate candies' centers. Centers, made from scratch in these kitchens, include caramel, creams, toffee, cordials, marshmallow, and nougat. From a viewing corridor, you see the centers embark on a short journey to the enrobing room, where they are engulfed in a fountain of either milk or dark chocolate before going through the cooling tunnel. The highlight of the tour is watching a woman in her late 80s, who has been with the company for more than 50 years, molding an assortment of exotic figurines in solid chocolate. All the candies then travel to the packing area to be boxed and sent off to a Quality Candy store or wholesale account.

The Buddy Squirrel segment adds some "pop" to the tour. Tons of corn kernels dive into giant poppers, where they become popcorn. The popcorn is then seasoned with butter, cheese, caramel, and other flavorings. Once again, your taste buds are tempted by the scents in the air. The popcorn meets up with the nuts (also made by Buddy Squirrel, but not seen on tour) in the packing room, and the goodies are prepared for their voyage to candy and nut stores all over the region.

Cost: Free
Freebies: Samples of candy and popcorn
Video Shown: No

Reservations Needed: Yes. Individuals and families need to join scheduled group tour or form group of at least 10 people.
Days and Hours: Tue-Thur 10:30 AM and 1:00 PM. No tours on holidays, November and December, 4 weeks before Easter (except for Annual Open House), and 1 week at the beginning of July and August.
Plan to Stay: 45 minutes, plus time for Kitchen Store.
Minimum Age: 10
Disabled Access: Yes
Group Requirements: Groups of at least 10 people should call 4 weeks ahead. Maximum group size is 50 people.
Special Information: Annual Easter Open House (the two Sundays before Easter from 10:00 AM-4:00 PM) features Mr. & Mrs. Easter Bunny and special factory tours.
Retail Store: Kitchen Store sells all Quality Candy/Buddy Squirrel products, including chocolates, award-winning Butter Almond Toffee, Pecan Caramel Tads, popcorns, and nuts. Open Mon-Sat 9:00 AM-4:30 PM (closes at 2:00 PM on Saturdays in summer). Closed holidays. Catalog available from above number.
Directions: Take I-94 to Layton Ave. exit. Turn left onto Brust, then right on Whitnall. Make a quick left on Kansas St. Quality Candy/Buddy Squirrel factory is on right. Enter under bright red awning on south side of building.
Nearby Attractions: Miller, Pabst, and Wm. K. Walthers factory tours (see pages 273, 274, and 279); Milwaukee County Zoo; Mitchell Park Horticulture ("The Domes"); Milwaukee County Museum; Milwaukee Art Museum; Boerner Botanical Gardens; Cedar Creek Winery.

Trek ⟨⟩ *bicycles*

801 West Madison Street
Waterloo, WI 53594
(414) 478-2197

When does a bike start to look like a bike? At the Trek plant, not until it reaches final assembly. Here the lean frame, little more than a wisp of painted geometry, meets pedals, cables, handlebars, and wheels, which are then boxed together for shipment to bike stores worldwide.

You'll see how Trek, which started in 1975 with four employees building frames for midwestern bicycle dealers, has innovated bike production. Metal frames take their form in the welding area. Thousands of metal pipes and joints, looking like bins of plumbing fixtures, are arranged precisely on steel tables and soldered together. It's a crackly, clattery region made brilliant with spits and stripes of green flame from the welding torch. Trek's frames of carbon fiber, a lightweight, almost ethereal compound, are built in an adjoining area. Workers hustle around the mounted carbon frames, spreading the fast-drying glue before it stiffens and sets. These newly glued frames are baked in an oven, then sanded smooth.

All frames, metal or carbon—about a thousand a day—go to the paint department. They hang like coats on conveyor hooks that trundle toward large sheet-metal closets: the painting booths. While this goes on, robots in a nearby department join rims to hubs, creating the wheels that will eventually meet up with the frames. On the glossy floor heaps of fresh black tires, with the incarnate odor of a bike shop, are stacked hundreds deep. See the spokes bending and weaving into position and the "hop and wobble" process of computer-monitored "rim truing." On your way out, notice the "Employee Parking" area, an indoor rack some fifty yards long that's crowded with colorful bikes. If you drive your car to Trek, the largest manufacturer of quality bicycles in the U.S., you'll find a large gravel lot with plenty of places to park!

Cost: Free
Freebies: Promotional posters and catalogs
Video Shown: No
Reservations Needed: Yes

Days and Hours: Tue-Fri 9:00 AM or 9:30 AM. Closed holidays. Closed for 2 weeks in July.
Plan to Stay: 45 minutes for tour.
Minimum Age: None
Disabled Access: Most of tour is wheelchair accessible.
Group Requirements: Groups larger than 12 people must call 1 week in advance. Maximum group size is 20 people. Does not want traditional bus tours.
Special Information: No video cameras. Photography restricted in some areas.
Gift Shop: No
Directions: From I-94, take Marshall/Deerfield exit. Travel north on Hwy. 73 toward Marshall. Turn right at Hwy. 19 (Main St. in Marshall). Trek plant is 4 miles ahead on right.
Nearby Attractions: In Waterloo, inquire locally about tour of local pickle factory; John Deere lawn tractor plant tour in Horicon (call 414-485-4411); Madison's attractions, including Arboretum, Vilas Park Zoo, and State Capital tours, about 40 minutes away.

Wausau Papers   *paper*

Second Street
Brokaw, WI 54417
(715) 675-3361

Heavily forested North Central Wisconsin is perfect for papermaking. Wausau Papers, established in 1899, is one of the industry's largest independent paper manufacturers. Every day 15,000 eight-foot aspen logs are chopped, washed, chipped, and "delignified," or turned into steamy pulp in the digesters. In the beater room, a humid, wet-towel-smelling place, workers dump clays and fillers into vats loaded with this pulp. See the whole dizzying mass swirl like a tornado 2,000 gallons deep. Your retiree tour guide explains that this mixture, or "furnish," is then dyed by a computerized coloring system and becomes "stock."

In the machine room, the wet stock (99% water) hits the wire section of the paper machine and begins to shed its water, then swiftly coheres as it rockets through the press section and around a series of roaring dryers. At the far end of the papermaking machine, a football field away, a drum reel gathers 10,000 pounds of fresh, warm paper. Over 485 tons of paper spin off the four massive paper machines every day. This new paper is continually tested for quality. In the testing room, you'll see a half dozen curious gadgets, all poking and stretching the newly-made paper. Over fifty samples are scrutinized from each shift.

Hundreds of rolls of paper sit in the cutter room. The rolls are so huge that while passing among them you will glow with the reflection of their many hues. All around the cutter room are machines slicing and stacking, reaming and wrapping. Some machines combine into one smooth operation a cut-sheeter, wrapper, packager, and palletizer. In a 24-hour period these computerized sheet-feeders can transform rolls of paper into 44 million sheets of 8½" x 11" paper.

Your guided tour ends in shipping and receiving, an immense room that reaches four stories to an aluminum ceiling. Each day, 25 trucks leave the docks for all parts of the country. As you stroll the aisles, notice the vast selection of vibrant colors ranging from the typical reds and blues to the amusingly named Fireball Fuchsia, Planetary Purple, or Liftoff Lemon.

Cost: Free
Freebies: Writing pad of colored paper and welcome book.
Video Shown: 10-minute overview of mill's operation.
Reservations Needed: Yes. Prefers that individuals and families join scheduled group tours.
Days and Hours: Mon-Fri 9:00 AM-3:00 PM. Closed holidays.
Plan to Stay: 2 hours for video and tour.
Minimum Age: 12
Disabled Access: Steps throughout plant.
Group Requirements: 5 days' advance notice required. No maximum group size.
Special Information: Best time to see production is before 1:00 PM. Wear comfortable, flat shoes. Loud and quite hot in places. Summer tours available at subsidiary Rhinelander Paper Company (call 715-369-4100), a specialty papermaker and leading manufacturer of release-coated and backing paper for pressure-sensitive label industry.
Gift Shop: No
Directions: From Madison, take I-51 North through Wausau to Brokaw exit. Turn right at stop sign and drive down slope to mill.
Nearby Attractions: Hsu's Ginseng Farm tour (call 715-675-2325); Rib Mountain; Leigh-Yawkey Woodson Art Museum; Marathon County Historical Museum; Andrew Warren Historic District.

Wisconsin Dairy State Cheese ～ *cheese*

Highway 34 & C
Rudolph, WI 54475
(715) 435-3144

The Dairy State Cheese plant, owned for generations by the Moran family, is fronted by a busy little shop. Look through the bank of windows either upstairs or downstairs from the shop and you'll see a vast room filled with stainless-steel pipes, vats, and tables. A few workers move about in hair nets and rubber boots, but much of the "Stirred Curd Cheddar" process you're watching is highly automated. Given the size of the production room, the near absence of people is conspicuous, a testimony to the efficiency of state-of-the-art cheese-making equipment.

Off to your left rise several immense silos filled with thousands of gallons of pasteurized and cultured milk. Ten pounds of milk are used in producing every pound of cheese. A network of pipes carries the treated milk from the silos to four vats, each one longer than a school bus. All day the upright enclosed vats are filled and emptied. The curds and whey are pumped over to long tables. A "forker" swirls as it drifts up and down the length of the long narrow vat beginning the process of separating the liquid (whey) from the milk solids (curd).

When the whey is drained off, what remains is a warm mass of glossy curds. The final step is to salt the curds. The fresh curds are automatically fed into presses, where they are compacted into 700-pound-blocks of brand-new cheese. The massive orange or white blocks are then sealed into wooden boxes for aging. After about one month, the cheese is shipped to Kraft for cutting. When your tour ends, be sure to return to the shop and browse among the coolers stocked with 85 varieties of cheese. Buy yourself a bag of curds so fresh they'll squeak on your teeth.

Cost: Free
Freebies: Cheese samples
Video Shown: Optional 23-minute film promotes Wisconsin cheese and details manufacturing process.
Reservations Needed: No, except for groups larger than 25 people.

Days and Hours: Mon, Tues, Thur, Fri 8:30 AM-5:15 PM, Sat 8:30 AM-5:00 PM. Production ends around 3:00 PM. Sun 9:00 AM-12:00 PM, but no production. Call to confirm holiday hours.
Plan to Stay: 15 minutes for self-guided viewing, plus time for video and cheese shop.
Minimum Age: None
Disabled Access: Yes
Group Requirements: Groups larger than 25 should make reservations 2 days in advance. Ice-cream cones and cheese samples provided for school tours.
Special Information: Guide available by request with 2 days' notice.
Retail Store: Cheese shop sells wide selection of cheeses, sausage, and locally made ice cream. Open Mon-Fri 8:30 AM-5:15 PM, Sat 8:30 AM-5:00 PM. Sun 9:00 AM-12:00 PM. Call about holiday hours. Catalog available from above number.
Directions: Take U.S. 51 North to the Hwy. 73 exit at Plainfield. Turn left (west) on Hwy. 73 to Hwy. 13. Turn right (north) and go through Wisconsin Rapids, following signs for Hwy. 34 North. Enter town of Rudolph, and Dairy State Cheese is on right.
Nearby Attractions: Wisconsin Rapids Paper Mill tour (call 715-422-3789); Stevens Point Brewery tour (call 715-344-9310); Rudolph Grotto Gardens and Wonder Cave. For complete list of Wisconsin cheese plants, write: Cheese Plants, Wisconsin Milk Marketing Board, 8418 Excelsior Drive, Madison, WI 53717.

Wm. K. Walthers ~ *model trains*

5619 West Florist Avenue
Milwaukee, WI 53218
(414) 527-0770

At the Wm. K. Walthers model-railroad manufacturing plant and distribution center you'll observe a huge operation devoted to building and distributing small worlds—worlds about ⅛₇th the size of the real McCoy. Before your tour begins, look at the merchandise in the Terminal Hobby Shop. You'll see tidy bags of oak trees and telephone poles, skyscrapers the size of saltines, and industrial trinkets (like a 55-gallon drum that would stuff nicely into an olive). In one corner of the hobby shop a video shows shots of freight trains, all trundling silently by on the screen.

Your guided tour starts in a one-room museum displaying various model trains, then moves onto the plant floor. Observe the 50-ton presses, each of which can turn a handful of plastic pellets into a boxcar or caboose. Stroll through the decal storage area, a region of file-boxes as vast as any university library's card catalog. In the painting room, you'll find drying racks crowded with green and red boxcars, each one as wet and glossy as a freshly baked pastry. Nearby, in the pad-printing room, workers ink logos onto various cars. One multicolored circus car requires forty different applications.

In the storage and distribution center, which is most of the building, hundreds of shelves border a conveyor belt the length of a food warehouse. Watch workers stuffing boxes with "SKUs" (Stock Keeping Units) for shipments all over the world. In the back of the plant, thousands of these SKUs are brought together into an impressive display: 1,600 square feet of mountains, villages, and, of course, trains—eight scale miles of track displayed on the "HO scale."

Cost: $2; children under 12, free.
Freebies: Train postcard and 10-percent discount coupon for Terminal Hobby Shop.
Video Shown: In Terminal Hobby Shop, continuous video of trains traveling through peaceful surroundings.
Reservations Needed: No, except for groups of 8 or more.

Days and Hours: Mon-Fri 10:00 AM, 11:00 AM, 12:30 PM, 1:30 PM, 2:30 PM. Closed holidays.
Plan to Stay: 40 minutes for museum and tour, plus time for Terminal Hobby Shop.
Minimum Age: None
Disabled Access: Yes
Group Requirements: Groups of 8 or more should call ahead. Discounts for groups of 12 or more.
Special Information: Production varies daily. The privately owned 1,600-square-foot railroad display is displayed behind a bank of windows. To view trains in motion and talk with owners, visit plant Wed or Thurs 7:00 PM-10:00 PM.
Gift Shop: Terminal Hobby Shop sells miniature model trains, tracks, and accessories; also mugs, pins, and caps with railroad company heralds. Open Mon-Fri 9:30 AM-6:30 PM and Sat 9:00 AM-3:00 PM. In summer, closes at 12:00 PM Saturdays. Catalog available from (800) 347-1147.
Directions: From Chicago, take I-94 West to I-43 North. Take Silver Spring Dr. exit west and go 3½ miles. Turn right on 60th St. Walthers is about 4 blocks ahead on right, set back off street. Company's facade resembles a K-Mart (building once housed large discount department store). Park and walk into Terminal Hobby Shop. From Madison, take I-94 East to Hwy. 45 North to Silver Spring Drive exit east. Turn left on 60th St., then follow above.
Nearby Attractions: Miller, Pabst, and Quality Candy/Buddy Squirrel tours (see pages 273, 274, and 275); Train-related attractions are East Troy Electric Railroad and Kettle Moraine Scenic Stream Train; Milwaukee County Zoo; Mitchell Park Horticulture ("The Domes"); Milwaukee County Museum; Milwaukee Art Museum; Boerner Botanical Gardens.

Rocky Mountain Snacks   *potato chips*

1077 Road 161
Pine Bluffs, WY 82082
(307) 245-9287

When Dr. Richard Canfield visited Wyoming, he noticed Pine Bluffs' numerous potato fields. From this observation, Wyoming's only potato-chip manufacturer was born. Having owned a similar business in Pennsylvania, Canfield found a deserted factory and spent months cleaning, moving in, and repairing used equipment. Rocky Mountain Snacks began production in December 1986 with one kettle. Today, with five kettles, Rocky Mountain makes about 50,000 pounds of potato chips each week.

The first thing you encounter when you enter the brick factory building is a 12-foot-tall-by-8-foot-wide stainless-steel storage hopper holding 2,600 pounds of potato chips. In fact, you'll quickly realize that all of the equipment is stainless steel. With the production manager as your tour guide, you'll walk right onto the factory floor—next to the kettles. Notice the clouds of steam which rise into the exhaust fans above each kettle. Smell hot oil and frying potatoes, along with the seasoning of the day.

Native Wyoming potatoes, peeled, washed, and sliced, dive into 220-gallon rectangular stainless-steel cooking kettles filled with 305° oil. In these 8-foot-long-by-4-foot-wide kettles, raw potato slices sizzle in hot oil. Surrounded by steam, "self stirrers" (Teflon-coated metal rakes designed and built by the company's maintenance man) automatically rake the potatoes back and forth. The steam subsides as the cooking cycle ends. After 15 minutes, the rakes raise the chips onto a conveyor. They sit there while another batch cooks, allowing excess oil to drip back into the kettle. Due to the potatoes' water content, each batch of 90 to 100 pounds of raw potatoes yields only 23 pounds of chips.

Workers hand-inspect for dark chips; then the chips travel along a vibrating table underneath a seasoning box, which sprinkles such flavorings as barbecue, jalapeño, or chicken. Each packaging line has a 12-hopper carousel that weighs and releases the correct amount of chips into the bagging machine.

Bags are formed over a tube and heat-sealed shut in this order: bottom, back, and top. Workers then hand-pack the potato-chip bags into cardboard boxes for storage or shipment to nearby states or Canada.

Cost: Free
Freebies: 1-ounce bag of potato chips.
Video Shown: No
Reservations Needed: Preferred for individuals. Required for groups (see below).
Days and Hours: Mon 10:00 AM–3:00 PM. Closed holidays.
Plan to Stay: 45 minutes
Minimum Age: 6, with one adult required for every five children.
Disabled Access: Yes, however floors can be slippery.
Group Requirements: Groups larger than 5 people should call at least 2 days in advance. Groups larger than 15 will be split into smaller groups.
Special Information: Factory is loud and can be quite warm near kettles in summer. Floor gets slippery.
Gift Shop: No
Directions: From I-80, take Pine Bluffs Rest Area exit. Follow signs toward Pine Bluffs. At dead-end, turn left onto Hwy. 30. After ¾-mile, turn right at airport sign. Cross railroad tracks, go 2½ miles, and turn left onto Rd. 161 (if you come to dirt road, you've gone too far). Factory is about 1 mile ahead on left.
Nearby Attractions: Texas Trail Museum; Pine Bluffs Rest Area; Cheyenne's attractions, including Cheyenne Frontier Days Museum, Wyoming State Museum, Wyoming Capitol, and Wyoming Game and Fish Visitors Center, are 40 miles away.

Itinerary Planners and Vacation Ideas

Factory tours and company visitor centers/museums are free or inexpensive high-lights you can add to a family vacation or business trip. This section helps you plan trips based on your favorite products and regions of the U.S.A. Factory tours allow you to watch workers and machines in action, so you will see most production Monday through Friday during normal business hours (some companies' tours are offered only on specified days or times of year). Company visitor centers/museums usually also have weekend and holiday hours. Most of the tours listed in this section are easy to go on. However, they may require advance reservations, so plan accordingly.

Please refer to the full write-ups in the book for more information. Check Nearby Attractions sections to round out these itineraries. Call the destinations to verify times and directions between locations. We also suggest that you use a detailed map of the region you are visiting and plan your trip carefully. AAA offers a route-planning service to its members, highlighting the best roads and highways to your destination.

A. Day Trips

Atlanta's Pride
CNN (television news), page 43.
World of Coca-Cola, page 45 and color photos page 135.

Cajun Country Louisiana
Konriko (rice and Cajun seasonings) in New Iberia, page 84.
McIlhenny Company (Tabasco brand pepper sauce) on Avery Island, page 85.

Chicago Area for Fun
Revell-Monogram (plastic model kits) in Morton Grove, page 56.
Motorola Museum (electronics) in Schaumburg, page 55.
Haeger Potteries (artwork pottery) in East Dundee, page 51.

Traveling to/from O'Hare International Airport:
    McDonald's Museum (fast food) in Des Plaines, page 54.

Chicago on Business (Try to squeeze one in during your next trip)
Chicago Mercantile Exchange (livestock and financial futures and options),
    page 49.
Chicago Board Of Trade (grain and financial futures and options), page 49.
    (See the Nearby Attractions under Chicago Board of Trade for more sites
    related to finance.)
Chicago Tribune (newspaper), page 50.

Traveling to/from O'Hare International Airport:
    McDonald's Museum (fast food) in Des Plaines, page 54, or Motorola
        Museum (electronics) in Schaumburg, page 55.

Dallas/Ft. Worth Area's Corporate Leaders
Traveling to/from Dallas/Ft. Worth Airport:
    American Airlines C.R. Smith Museum, page 225.

Mary Kay Cosmetics in Dallas, page 233.
J.C. Penney Museum and Corporate Headquarters in Plano, page 232.

Fort Wayne Food (David Letterman's home state)
Perfection Bakeries (bread), page 61.
Seyfert's (potato chips and pretzels), page 63.
Sechler's (pickles) in St. Joe, page 62.

Lake Michigan Coast (Western Michigan)
Brooks Beverages (7-Up, Canada Dry, other sodas) in Holland, page 106.
DeKlomp/Veldheer (wooden shoes and delftware) in Holland, page 107.
Original Wooden Shoe Factory in Holland, page 111.

Las Vegas—Beyond the Casinos
Ethel M Chocolates in Henderson, page 128 and color photos page 136.
Kidd's (marshmallows) in Henderson, page 129.
Fisher Space Pen in Boulder City, page 126.

Louisville Area
Hillerich & Bradsby (Louisville Slugger baseball bats and PowerBilt golf clubs) in Jeffersonville, Indiana, page 58.
Louisville Stoneware (pottery), page 77.
Colonel Harland Sanders Museum (KFC fast food), page 74.

New York City on Business (Try to squeeze in at least one during your next trip)
NBC Studios (television programs), page 164.
New York Stock Exchange (stocks and bonds), page 167. (See Nearby Attractions under NYSE for more sites related to finance.)

Traveling to/from LaGuardia Airport:
   Steinway & Sons (pianos) (Friday mornings only), page 172.

Northern Indiana: RV Capital of the World
Holiday Rambler in Wakarusa, page 59 and color photos page 151.
Jayco in Middlebury, page 60.
RV/MH Heritage Foundation Museum and local Convention & Visitors Bureau lists other RV company tours (see Nearby Attractions under Holiday Rambler).

Oregon Coast
House of Myrtlewood (wood products) in Coos Bay, page 194.
Tillamook Cheese in Tillamook, page 198.

Traveling to/from Portland:
   Rodgers Instrument (organs) in Hillsboro, page 197 and color photos page 144.

B. Multiple-Day Trips

Auto Factory Adventure (2-3 Days)
Day 1: Toyota in Georgetown, Kentucky, page 81.
  Ford big truck or Explorer plants in Louisville, Kentucky, page 76.
Day 2: Corvette in Bowling Green, Kentucky, page 75.
Day 3: Nissan in Smyrna, Tennessee, page 222.
  Saturn Visitor Center in Spring Hill, Tennessee, page 224.
OR
Day 2: Navistar International (trucks) in Springfield, Ohio, page 189.
  Honda Visitor Center in Marysville, Ohio, page 184.

Boston and Beyond (2 Days)
Day 1: Boston
  Boston Beer Co. (Samuel Adams beer) (Thur-Sat only), page 92.
  Wm. S. Haynes (flutes), page 102.
  National Braille Press (Braille publications), page 99.
Day 2: Boston to Cape Cod
  Cranberry World Visitors Center (Ocean Spray products) in Plymouth, page 95 and color photos page 153.
  Pairpoint Crystal (glass) in Sagamore, page 100.
  Cape Cod Potato Chips (potato chips) in Hyannis, page 93.
OR
Day 2: New Hampshire's White Mountains
  Stonyfield Farm (yogurt) in Londonderry, page 132 and color photos page 146.
  Anheuser-Busch (Budweiser beer) in Merrimack, page 130 and color photos pages 140 and 141.
  Hampshire Pewter (tableware and giftware) in Wolfeboro, page 131.

Bourbon Bounty in Kentucky (2 Days)
Day 1: Old Kentucky Candies (bourbon candy) in Lexington, page 79.
  Wild Turkey Distillery in Lawrenceburg, page 82 and color photos page 148.
Day 2: Maker's Mark Distillery in Loretto, page 78 and color photos page 143.
  Additional places of interest for bourbon lovers: Rebecca Ruth Candies; Heaven Hill Distillery; Oscar Getz Museum of Whiskey History; Jim Beam's American Outpost; Annual Bardstown September Bourbon Festival. (See Nearby Bourbon-Related Attractions under Maker's Mark.)

Central Colorado (3 Days)
Day 1: Denver
   Stephany's Chocolates, page 30.
   U.S. Mint (coins), page 31.
Day 2: Boulder Area
   Celestial Seasonings (tea), page 26 and color photos page 156.
   Coors (beer) in Golden, page 27.
Day 3: Colorado Springs
   Current (cards, wrapping paper, and catalog), page 28.
   Simpich (dolls), page 29.
   Van Briggle (pottery), page 32.

China, Glass, and Pottery in Eastern Ohio Area (2-3 Days)
Day 1: Homer Laughlin China in Newell, West Virginia, page 264.
   Hall China in East Liverpool, Ohio, page 183.
   Side trip to Creegan Company (animated characters) in Steubenville, Ohio,
      page 181.
Day 2: Mosser Glass in Cambridge, Ohio, page 188.
   Robinson Ransbottom Pottery in Roseville, Ohio, page 190.
   Roseville-Crooksville pottery communities attractions and annual July pottery
      festival featuring tours of other pottery factories. (See Nearby Attractions
      under Robinson Ransbottom.)
   Side trip to Longaberger (baskets) in Dresden, page 186.

Colonial Williamsburg Area (2 Days)
Day 1: Rowena's (jams, jellies, and gourmet foods) in Norfolk, page 250 and
   color photo page 152.
Day 2: Williamsburg Doll Factory (porcelain dolls), page 251.
   The Candle Factory (candles and soap), page 248.
   Williamsburg Pottery Factory (pottery, wood, floral design, plaster), page 252.

Disney World and Beyond (3 Days)
Day 1: Magic of Disney Animation Studios, page 39.
Day 2: Nickelodeon Studios in Orlando, page 40 (part of Universal Studios).
Day 3: Correct Craft (Ski Nautiques water-ski boats) in Orlando, page 35.
   E-One (fire trucks) in Ocala, page 36.

Gastronomic Tours in Texas (4 Days)
Day 1: Collin Street Bakery (fruitcake) in Corsicana, page 227 and color pho-
   tos page 137.
Day 2: Imperial Sugar Company (sugar) near Houston, page 230.
   Blue Bell Creameries (ice cream) in Brenham, page 226.
Day 3: Jardine's Texas Foods (Texas-style foods) near Austin, page 231.
Day 4: Dr Pepper Bottling (soda) (bottling on Tuesdays) in Dublin, page 228
   and color photo page 138.
   Dr Pepper Museum in Waco (see Special Information under Dr Pepper).

Glassblowing in West Virginia (2 Days)
Day 1: Fenton Art Glass in Williamstown, page 262.
   Side trip to Lee Middleton Doll factory in Belpre, Ohio, page 185.
Day 2: Blenko Glass in Milton, page 261.
   Gibson Glass factory (see Nearby Attractions under Blenko Glass).
   Pilgrim Glass in Ceredo, page 266.

Hawaii: Off the Beaches (2 Days)
Day 1: Maui Divers of Hawaii (coral jewelry) in Honolulu, Island of Oahu,
   page 46 and color photos page 142.
   Dole Cannery Square (see Nearby Attractions under Maui Divers).
Day 2: Mauna Loa Macadamia Nut (nuts and chocolates) in Hilo, Island of
   Hawaii, page 47.

Milwaukee—Beer and Beyond (3 Days)
Day 1: Miller Brewing Co., page 273.
   Pabst Brewing Co., page 274.
   Quality Candy/Buddy Squirrel (chocolates and popcorn), page 275.
                                OR
   Wm. K. Walthers (model trains), page 279.
Day 2: Kohler (bathtubs, whirlpools, toilets, sinks) in Kohler, page 272.
   Allen-Edmonds (shoes) in Port Washington, page 267.
Day 3: Choose two of the following:
   General Motors (sport utility vehicles and pickups) in Janesville, page 270.
   J I Case (tractors) in Racine, page 269 and color photos page 155.
   Trek (bicycles) in Waterloo, page 276.

Musical Instrument Mecca (3 Days)
Day 1: Wm. S. Haynes (flutes and piccolos) in Boston, Massachusetts, page 102.
Day 2: Steinway & Sons (pianos) (Friday mornings only) in Long Island City,
   New York, page 172.
Day 3: Martin Guitar in Nazareth, Pennsylvania, page 206 and color photo page
   154 and back cover.

Niagara Falls (2 Days)
Day 1: (depending on your direction of travel to Niagara Falls):
   Corning Glass Center in Corning, page 166 and color photos page 149.
                                OR
   George Eastman House (Kodak and photography) in Rochester, page 162.
Day 2: Choose two of the following:
   The Original American Kazoo Company in Eden, page 168.
   Perry's Ice Cream in Akron, page 170.
   Pepsi-Cola Bottling (soda, ice tea, fruit juice) in Buffalo, page 169.
   QRS Music Rolls (player-piano rolls) in Buffalo, page 171.

Pretzels and Potato Chips in Pennsylvania (2-3 Days)
Day 1: Herr's in Nottingham, page 204 and color photos page 158.
   Anderson Bakery in Lancaster, page 200.
   Sturgis Pretzel House in Lititz, page 211.
Day 2: Utz Quality Foods in Hanover, page 213. (On the way to Utz, visit
   Harley-Davidson in York, page 203, or Pfaltzgraff in Thomasville, page 209.)
                              OR
Day 2: Chocolate Diversion
   Hershey's Chocolate World Visitors Center in Hershey, page 205.
   Pennsylvania Dutch Candies in Mt. Holly Springs, page 208 and color photo
      page 152.
Day 3: Utz Quality Foods in Hanover, page 213.

San Francisco with Kids–Fun for Adults, Too! (3 Days)
Day 1 (May need to choose only two):
   Basic Brown Bear (teddy bears), page 8 and color photos page 157.
   Fortune Cookie Factory in Oakland, page 13.
   Dreyer's and Edy's Grand Ice Cream in Union City, page 10.
   (Consider side trip to Intel Museum in Santa Clara for science-oriented
      children, page 18.)
Day 2: Herman Goelitz (Jelly Belly jelly beans and gummi candies) in Fairfield,
   page 15.
Day 3: Hershey's Visitors Center in Oakdale, page 16 and cover.

St. Louis and Kansas City: Bud and Beyond (3 Days)
Day 1: McDonnell Douglas Museum (airplanes, missiles, and spacecraft) in St.
   Louis, page 124.
   Chrysler (minivans) in Fenton, page 118.
   Anheuser-Busch (Budweiser beer) in St. Louis, page 117 and color photos
      pages 139, 140, and 141.
Day 2: Purina Farms (pets and farm animals) in Gray Summit, page 120.
Day 3: Hallmark Visitor Center (greeting cards) in Kansas City, page 119 and
   color photos page 150.
   McCormick Distilling Co. (bourbon, whiskey, alcoholic beverages) in
      Weston, page 123.

Studios of Southern California (2-3 Days)
Days 1 and 2: Paramount Pictures in Hollywood, page 22.
   Warner Bros. Studios in Burbank, page 25.
   NBC Studios (see Nearby Attractions under Warner Bros. Studios).
Day 3: Universal Studios Hollywood in Universal City, page 24.

Sweet Tooth Tour: East Coast (3 Days)

Day 1: Moore's Candies in Baltimore, Maryland, page 90.

Day 2: Pennsylvania Dutch Candies in Mt. Holly Springs, Pennsylvania, page 208 and color photos page 152.

 Hershey's Chocolate World Visitors Center in Hershey, Pennsylvania, page 205.

Day 3: Sherm Edwards Candies in Trafford, Pennsylvania, page 210.

Sweet Tooth Tour: West Coast (3 Days)

Day 1: Phoenix

 Cerreta's Candy Co. in Glendale, Arizona, page 4.

Day 2: Las Vegas

 Ethel M Chocolates in Henderson, page 128 and color photos page 136.

 Kidd's (marshmallows) in Henderson, page 129.

Day 3: San Francisco Area (fly to San Francisco). Choose one:

 Herman Goelitz (Jelly Belly jelly beans and gummi candies) in Fairfield, page 15.

 Hershey's Visitors Center (chocolate) in Oakdale, page 16 and cover.

OR

Day 3: Seattle Area (Fly to Seattle)

 Boehms Chocolates in Issaquah, page 254 and color photo page 138.

Vermont—Beyond Ben & Jerry's (4 Days)

From the South:

Day 1: Basketville (wood baskets and buckets) in Putney, page 239.

 Crowley Cheese in Healdville, page 242.

 Simon Pearce in Windsor and Quechee (glass and pottery), page 246 and color photo page 145.

Day 2: Maple Grove Farms (maple syrup and salad dressing) in St. Johnsbury, page 244.

 Cabot Creamery (cheese) in Cabot, page 241.

Day 3: Ben & Jerry's (ice cream) in Waterbury, page 240.

 Vermont Teddy Bear in Shelburne, page 245 and color photos page 147.

Washington State (2 Days)

Day 1: Boeing (commercial aircraft) in Everett, page 253. (Get there early in the morning!)

 Boehms Chocolates in Issaquah, page 254 and color photo page 138.

 Redhook Ale Brewery in Seattle, page 260.

Day 2: Liberty Orchards (fruit candies) in Cashmere, page 259.

 Boise Cascade (lumber and plywood) in Yakima, page 256.

Company Index

Product Index

About the Authors

Bruce Brumberg and Karen Axelrod traveled across the U.S.A. to "kick the tires of the American economy." This husband and wife team journeyed from the massive Boeing 747 plant in Everett, Washington, to the ranch-like factory of Jardine's Texas Foods in Buda, Texas (pictured above). During their travels, Bruce earned an "Official Pretzel Twister" certificate, while Karen was awarded an "Honorary Brewmaster" title and "Official Candymaker's Diploma." Fascinated by how things are made and companies grow, they visit factories for fun, business ideas, and free samples. When not traveling, they live near Boston, Massachusetts. Bruce owns a legal and financial publishing company. Before writing this book, Karen was a buyer for 10 years for major retail and catalog companies.

FACTORY TOUR VIDEOS AVAILABLE
From the Authors of *Watch It Made in the U.S.A.*

How To Go On A Factory Tour From Your Living Room

Wouldn't it be great if you could travel across the U.S.A. and visit all the companies featured in *Watch It Made in the U.S.A.*? Since you don't have the time, the authors have gotten permission from some companies to sell the videos that they show on their tours, featuring all the fast-moving machines and cool close-ups.

The videos are almost as good as being there (except for the smells and free samples). Whatever your age, you'll be amazed at watching how your favorite products are made. If you enjoy factory tour segments on *Sesame Street* and *Mister Rogers*, you'll want to see these fun and educational videos!

Videos From:
Dreyer's & Edy's Grand Ice Cream
E-One Fire Trucks and Ambulances
Mauna Loa Macadamia Nuts & Chocolates
Martin Guitar
Herr's Potato Chips and Pretzels (Features "Chipper the Chipmunk")
Fenton Art Glass
Tillamook Cheese
Steinway & Sons Pianos
And More . . .
From $9.95-$19.95 Per Video

Call 617-232-9811 for Complete List of Videos & Prices
Or write to Factory Tour Videos, P.O. Box 486, Brookline, MA 02146-0004

Other Books from John Muir Publications

Travel Books by Rick Steves

Asia Through the Back Door, 4th ed., 400 pp. $16.95

Europe 101: History, Art, and Culture for the Traveler, 4th ed., 372 pp. $15.95

Mona Winks: Self-Guided Tours of Europe's Top Museums, 2nd ed., 456 pp. $16.95

Rick Steves' Best of the Baltics and Russia, 1995 ed. 144 pp. $9.95

Rick Steves' Best of Europe, 1995 ed., 544 pp. $16.95

Rick Steves' Best of France, Belgium, and the Netherlands, 1995 ed., 240 pp. $12.95

Rick Steves' Best of Germany, Austria, and Switzerland, 1995 ed., 240 pp. $12.95

Rick Steves' Best of Great Britain, 1995 ed., 192 pp. $11.95

Rick Steves' Best of Italy, 1995 ed., 208 pp. $11.95

Rick Steves' Best of Scandinavia, 1995 ed., 192 pp. $11.95

Rick Steves' Best of Spain and Portugal, 1995 ed., 192 pp. $11.95

Rick Steves' Europe Through the Back Door, 13th ed., 480 pp. $17.95

Rick Steves' French Phrase Book, 2nd ed., 112 pp. $4.95

Rick Steves' German Phrase Book, 2nd ed., 112 pp. $4.95

Rick Steves' Italian Phrase Book, 2nd ed., 112 pp. $4.95

Rick Steves' Spanish and Portuguese Phrase Book, 2nd ed., 288 pp. $5.95

Rick Steves' French/German/Italian Phrase Book, 288 pp. $6.95

A Natural Destination Series

Belize: A Natural Destination, 2nd ed., 304 pp. $16.95

Costa Rica: A Natural Destination, 3rd ed., 320 pp. $16.95

Guatemala: A Natural Destination, 336 pp. $16.95

Undiscovered Islands Series

Undiscovered Islands of the Caribbean, 3rd ed., 264 pp. $14.95

Undiscovered Islands of the Mediterranean, 2nd ed., 256 pp. $13.95

Undiscovered Islands of the U.S. and Canadian West Coast, 288 pp. $12.95

For Birding Enthusiasts

The Birder's Guide to Bed and Breakfasts: U.S. and Canada, 288 pp. $15.95

The Visitor's Guide to the Birds of the Central National Parks: U.S. and Canada, 400 pp. $15.95

The Visitor's Guide to the Birds of the Eastern National Parks: U.S. and Canada, 400 pp. $15.95

The Visitor's Guide to the Birds of the Rocky Mountain National Parks: U.S. and Canada, 432 pp. $15.95

Unique Travel Series
Each is 112 pages and $10.95 paperback.
Unique Arizona
Unique California
Unique Colorado
Unique Florida
Unique New England
Unique New Mexico
Unique Texas
Unique Washington
(available 2/95)

2 to 22 Days Itinerary Planners

2 to 22 Days in the American Southwest, 1995 ed., 192 pp. $11.95

2 to 22 Days in Asia, 192 pp. $10.95

2 to 22 Days in Australia, 192 pp. $10.95

2 to 22 Days in California, 1995 ed., 192 pp. $11.95

2 to 22 Days in Eastern Canada, 1995 ed., 240 pp $11.95

2 to 22 Days in Florida, 1995 ed., 192 pp. $11.95

2 to 22 Days Around the Great Lakes, 1995 ed., 192 pp. $11.95

2 to 22 Days in Hawaii, 1995 ed., 192 pp. $11.95

2 to 22 Days in New England, 1995 ed., 192 pp. $11.95

2 to 22 Days in New Zealand, 192 pp. $10.95

2 to 22 Days in the Pacific Northwest, 1995 ed., 192 pp. $11.95

2 to 22 Days in the Rockies, 1995 ed., 192 pp. $11.95

2 to 22 Days in Texas, 1995 ed., 192 pp. $11.95

2 to 22 Days in Thailand, 192 pp. $10.95

22 Days Around the World, 264 pp. $13.95

Other Terrific Travel Titles
The 100 Best Small Art Towns in America, 256 pp. $12.95

Elderhostels: The Students' Choice, 2nd ed., 304 pp. $15.95

Environmental Vacations: Volunteer Projects to Save the Planet, 2nd ed., 248 pp. $16.95

A Foreign Visitor's Guide to America, 224 pp. $12.95

Great Cities of Eastern Europe, 256 pp. $16.95

Indian America: A Traveler's Companion, 3rd ed., 432 pp. $18.95

Interior Furnishings Southwest, 256 pp. $19.95

Opera! The Guide to Western Europe's Great Houses, 296 pp. $18.95

Paintbrushes and Pistols: How the Taos Artists Sold the West, 288 pp. $17.95

The People's Guide to Mexico, 9th ed., 608 pp. $18.95

Ranch Vacations: The Complete Guide to Guest and Resort, Fly-Fishing, and Cross-Country Skiing Ranches, 3rd ed., 512 pp. $19.95

The Shopper's Guide to Art and Crafts in the Hawaiian Islands, 272 pp. $13.95

The Shopper's Guide to Mexico, 224 pp. $9.95

Understanding Europeans, 272 pp. $14.95

A Viewer's Guide to Art: A Glossary of Gods, People, and Creatures, 144 pp. $10.95

Watch It Made in the U.S.A.: A Visitor's Guide to the Companies that Make Your Favorite Products, 272 pp. $16.95

Parenting Titles
Being a Father: Family, Work, and Self, 176 pp. $12.95

Preconception: A Woman's Guide to Preparing for Pregnancy and Parenthood, 232 pp. $14.95

Schooling at Home: Parents, Kids, and Learning, 264 pp. $14.95

Teens: A Fresh Look, 240 pp. $14.95

Automotive Titles
The Greaseless Guide to Car Care Confidence, 224 pp. $14.95

How to Keep Your Datsun/Nissan Alive, 544 pp. $21.95

How to Keep Your Subaru Alive, 480 pp. $21.95

How to Keep Your Toyota Pickup Alive, 392 pp. $21.95

How to Keep Your VW Alive, 25th Anniversary ed., 464 pp. spiral bound $25

TITLES FOR YOUNG READERS AGES 8 AND UP

American Origins Series
Each is 48 pages and $12.95 hardcover.

Tracing Our English Roots

Tracing Our French Roots (available 7/95)

Tracing Our German Roots

Tracing Our Irish Roots

Tracing Our Italian Roots

Tracing Our Japanese Roots

Tracing Our Jewish Roots

Tracing Our Polish Roots

Bizarre & Beautiful Series
Each is 48 pages, $9.95 paperback, and $14.95 hardcover.

Bizarre & Beautiful Ears

Bizarre & Beautiful Eyes

Bizarre & Beautiful Feelers

Bizarre & Beautiful Noses

Bizarre & Beautiful Tongues

Environmental Titles
Habitats: Where the Wild Things Live, 48 pp. $9.95

The Indian Way: Learning to Communicate with Mother Earth, 114 pp. $9.95

Rads, Ergs, and Cheeseburgers: The Kids' Guide to Energy and the Environment, 108 pp. $13.95

The Kids' Environment Book: What's Awry and Why, 192 pp. $13.95

Extremely Weird Series
Each is 48 pages and $9.95 paperback, $14.95 hardcover.

Extremely Weird Bats

Extremely Weird Birds

Extremely Weird Endangered Species

Extremely Weird Fishes

Extremely Weird Frogs

Extremely Weird Insects

Extremely Weird Mammals

Extremely Weird Micro Monsters

Extremely Weird Primates

Extremely Weird Reptiles

Extremely Weird Sea Creatures

Extremely Weird Snakes

Extremely Weird Spiders

Kidding Around Travel Series

All are 64 pages and $9.95 paperback, except for *Kidding Around Spain* and *Kidding Around the National Parks of the Southwest*, which are 108 pages and $12.95 paperback.

Kidding Around Atlanta
Kidding Around Boston, 2nd ed.
Kidding Around Chicago, 2nd ed.
Kidding Around the Hawaiian Islands
Kidding Around London
Kidding Around Los Angeles
Kidding Around the National Parks of the Southwest
Kidding Around New York City, 2nd ed.
Kidding Around Paris
Kidding Around Philadelphia
Kidding Around San Diego
Kidding Around San Francisco
Kidding Around Santa Fe
Kidding Around Seattle
Kidding Around Spain
Kidding Around Washington, D.C., 2nd ed.

Kids Explore Series

Written by kids for kids, all are $9.95 paperback.

Kids Explore America's African American Heritage, 128 pp.
Kids Explore the Gifts of Children with Special Needs, 128 pp.
Kids Explore America's Hispanic Heritage, 112 pp.
Kids Explore America's Japanese American Heritage, 144 pp.

Masters of Motion Series

Each is 48 pages and $9.95 paperback.

How to Drive an Indy Race Car
How to Fly a 747
How to Fly the Space Shuttle

Rainbow Warrior Artists Series

Each is 48 pages and $14.95 hardcover. ($9.95 paperback editions available 4/95.)

Native Artists of Africa
Native Artists of Europe
Native Artists of North America

Rough and Ready Series

Each is 48 pages and $12.95 hardcover. ($9.95 paperback editions available 4/95.)

Rough and Ready Cowboys
Rough and Ready Homesteaders
Rough and Ready Loggers
Rough and Ready Outlaws and Lawmen
Rough and Ready Prospectors
Rough and Ready Railroaders

X-ray Vision Series

Each is 48 pages and $9.95 paperback.

Looking Inside the Brain
Looking Inside Cartoon Animation
Looking Inside Caves and Caverns
Looking Inside Sports Aerodynamics
Looking Inside Sunken Treasures
Looking Inside Telescopes and the Night Sky

Ordering Information

Please check your local bookstore for our books, or call **1-800-888-7504** to order direct. All orders are shipped via UPS; see chart below to calculate your shipping charge for U.S. destinations. **No post office boxes please; we must have a street address to ensure delivery.** If the book you request is not available, we will hold your check until we can ship it. Foreign orders will be shipped surface rate unless otherwise requested; please enclose $3 for the first item and $1 for each additional item.

For U.S. Orders

Totaling	Add
Up to $15.00	$4.25
$15.01 to $45.00	$5.25
$45.01 to $75.00	$6.25
$75.01 or more	$7.25

Methods of Payment

Check, money order, American Express, MasterCard, or Visa. We cannot be responsible for cash sent through the mail. For credit card orders, include your card number, expiration date, and your signature, or call **1-800-888-7504**. American Express card orders can only be shipped to billing address of cardholder. Sorry, no C.O.D.'s. Residents of sunny New Mexico, add 6.2% tax to total.

Address all orders and inquiries to:
John Muir Publications
P.O. Box 613
Santa Fe, NM 87504
(505) 982-4078
(800) 888-7504